في ذكرى

مارك لينز

NAGUIB MAHFOUZ

Essays of the Early Mubarak Years

The Non-Fiction Writing of Naguib Mahfouz: Volume III

Introduction by Rasheed El-Enany
Translated by Russell Harris

First published in English in 2020 by
GINGKO
4 Molasses Row
London SW11 3UX

This first paperback edition published in 2026.

Originally published in Arabic.

A CIP catalogue record for this book is available from the British Library.

The authorised representative in the EEA is:
Haus Publishing
Casella Postale 32
50037 San Piero a Sieve (Fi)
Italy
(*gpsr@gingko.org.uk*)

Paperback: ISBN 978-1-914983-43-6
ebook: ISBN 978-1-909942-12-7

Typeset in Optima by MacGuru Ltd

Front Cover: Creswell, K.A.C. Mosque of Khairbay. K.A.C. Creswell Photograph Collection of Islamic Architecture, Photograph Collections, Rare Books and Special Collections Library, The American University in Cairo, Egypt.

Printed in the United Kingdom by CPI Group (UK) Ltd, Croydon CR0 4YY

www.gingko.org.uk

تمت ترجمة هذا الكتاب بمساعدة صندوق منحة الترجمة
المقدمة من معرض الشارقة الدولي للكتاب

This book has been translated with the assistance of the Sharjah International Book Fair Translation Grant Fund

Contents

Naguib Mahfouz (1911–2006) is considered the greatest Arab writer of the twentieth century. Born in the old Islamic Quarter of Cairo in 1911, he began writing when he was seventeen before entering university to study as a student of philosophy in 1930. He is the author of over thirty novels. In 1988, he was awarded the Nobel Prize for Literature.

Rasheed El-Enany is the Dean of the School of Social Sciences and Humanities and Professor of Arabic and Comparative Literature at the Doha Institute for Graduate Studies. He is also Professor Emeritus of Modern Arabic Literature, University of Exeter, where he became Director of the Institute of Arab and Islamic Studies. He has authored several books on Naguib Mahfouz, including *Naguib Mahfouz. His Life and Times*.

Russell Harris holds an MA in Oriental Studies from Balliol College, Oxford, and is an established translator of literary works from French and Arabic. He is a contributor to *The Encyclopaedia Islamica* for the Institute of Ismaili Studies and has written many articles on Middle Eastern art for international journals and magazines.

Introduction

by Rasheed El-Enany

'Politics is in everything I write,' proclaims Naguib Mahfouz. 'You may find a story of mine where love or some other theme is absent, but not politics; it lies at the heart of my thinking.'[1] Mahfouz wrote about politics and a myriad other themes in his voluminous output of fiction, which comprised 33 novels and hundreds of short stories over a writing career that extended from the 1930s until his death in 2006. During this long career of more than seven decades, he dealt with politics and society in Egypt through all kinds of narrative: historical; naturalistic; realistic; allegorical; symbolic; absurdist, etc. He wrote traditional narratives and experimental narratives; extended narratives and short pithy narratives. He visited Ancient Egyptian history to find parallels that can be used to make a statement on the present-day realities of Egypt. He also visited traditional Arabic narratives like *The Thousand and One Nights* in order to recast them into metaphors for contemporary reality. From the bulk of these endless representations of the human condition in the Egyptian context, Mahfouz emerges as a great humanist thinker, an advocate of liberal thought, of freedom of speech, of democracy and human rights, of socialism insofar as it is a means to social justice, of emancipation of women, of religious tolerance and freedom of worship, and of peaceful coexistence in society and the world.

Mahfouz is a great novelist, which means that his attitude towards humanity's big questions must first and foremost be sought in his fiction. This is the only place where his thinking is best expressed and has the most influence, by dint of the living characters and situations that carry that thought unobtrusively in a kind of verisimilitude that talks to us, readers, in a manner outdone only by our own life experiences.

---

1 Gamal al-Ghitani, *Naguib Mahfouz Yatadhakkar*, Beirut, 1980, p. 78. See also Naguib Mahfouz, *Atahaddath Ilaykum*, Beirut, 1977, pp. 92–3, where the author states that politics is the main axis of his work.

However, it so happens that some three years after his retirement from the Egyptian civil service, he was commissioned by the leading newspaper of the country, *Al-Ahram,* where he had hitherto serialised many of his novels before they came out in book form, to write a weekly comment column of around 300 words titled *'wijhat nazar'* or 'a point of view'. And so he did, from 1974 until his death, roughly the last 30 years of his life. Those hundreds of mini-essays were collected in his life in eight volumes and published during the 1990s, and more recently have been reshuffled in three thick tomes published in 2018 by al-Dar al-Misriya al-Lubnaniya in Cairo, who had also published the older set. Because of their thematic classification, the Arabic collections have wreaked havoc with the chronology of the essays, making it near impossible for the reader to trace Mahfouz's thinking from week to week and year to year as he reacted to the events of the day. Thankfully the English translations of the essays rectify this anomaly, doing away with the themes in favour of a strict chronology. Thus, the previous volume in this series of The Non-Fiction Writing of Naguib Mahfouz, titled *Essays of the Sadat Era,* contains the essays of the period from 1974 when he started writing his weekly column to 1981, the year of Sadat's assassination, while the present volume, *The Early Mubarak Years,* includes the essays published between 1982 and 1988.

Now, since the subject matter of these essays is primarily politics and society, and in particular the politics and society of contemporary Egypt, and since Mahfouz is primarily a novelist and not a political columnist, it would serve a good purpose to take an overview of his ideas about politics and society as they evolved over the years in his fiction. This is because the views we encounter in his short essays are but the dry abstractions of views and attitudes he had held and made concrete time and again over decades of fiction writing.

Mahfouz's preoccupation with society and politics goes way back to his early historical romances set in Ancient Egypt, notably, *Thebes at War*[2] (*Kifah Tiba,* 1944) which gives an account of the defeat of the

2 In what follows, I use novel titles as in their published English translations, while giving the original Arabic title between brackets in transliteration ignoring diacritics.

Hyksos by Amasis I in 1550 BC thus liberating Egypt from a foreign rule which had lasted for over a hundred years. In later years, Mahfouz scholars have unanimously, and with the novelist's own blessing,[3] read 'the British' for 'the Hyksos' and interpreted the novel as a wish-fulfilment account of modern Egypt under British rule.

The last of three historical novels, *Thebes at War* was, however, to be the end of Mahfouz's short courtship with historical romance, for the time being at least. His next novel, *Cairo Modern* (*al-Qahira al-Jadida*, 1945) saw him plunge himself into the tumultuous sea of Egyptian politics. In the novels of the realistic phase beginning with *Cairo Modern* and ending with *The Cairo Trilogy*[4] (*Bayn al-Qasrayn, Qasr al-Shawq,* and *al-Sukkariya*, 1956–57) Mahfouz portrays a panorama of Egyptian urban society roughly from the time of the national uprising against British rule in 1919 to the end of World War II. All the main social and political forces active in society during that period are amply and repeatedly represented in the novels of that phase. The Wafdists (members of the nationalist Wafd Party), the Muslim Brotherhood, the socialists as well as the non-committed are all present. In Mahfouz's portrait of the Egyptian socio-political scene, whose neutrality is only surface-deep, it becomes rapidly apparent that of the four categories listed only two command the novelist's respect, namely the Wafdists and the socialists. The non-committed whose only motive in life is self-interest are eternally banished from Mahfouz's social utopia. A classic example of this category is the character of Mahjoub 'Abd al-Da'im in *Cairo Modern*. The Islamist version of social reform is, on the other hand, systematically denounced in Mahfouz's work as anachronistic and obscurantist. Significantly, the denunciation is always effected at the hands of advocates of socialism which, in association with science,

Where I quote from the text of a novel, I provide my own translation direct from the Arabic.

3 *Alahaddath Ilaykum*, pp. 88–9.

4 *The Cairo Trilogy* consists of the three volumes of *Palace Walk, Palace of Desire,* and *Sugar Street*; all of which are place names in Mahfouz's childhood quarter, al-Jamaliya in Old Cairo.

is shown as the only formula for social progress.[5] Mahfouz's rejection of Islamism can be easily construed from works like *Cairo Modern, Khan al-Khalili* and the third volume of *The Cairo Trilogy*.

This leaves us with the Wafdists and socialists. There is no doubt that Mahfouz, like the majority of the nationalists of his generation, had tremendous sympathy for the Wafd as the party that represented the national aspiration for independence, taking on both the British occupation and Kings Fu'ad I and Farouk successively in its fight for independence and a true constitutional life. Mahfouz himself was not a member of the party. In fact he tells us that he did not join 'political organisations', though he always participated in general popular actions such as 'strikes and demonstrations...' as a member of the public.[6] His identification with the Wafd and admiration for its two great leaders, Saad Zaghloul (1859–1927) and Mustafa al-Nahhas (1879–1956) is evident in his work wherever that period of modern Egyptian history is invoked, and especially in *The Cairo Trilogy*.[7] Indeed we need not look further than the volume to hand. See for instance the essay titled, 'Withdrawal Celebrations', dated 22/4/1982, where the two men are described as 'the greatest popular leaders in the life of our nation since its unification under the Pharaoh Menes'.

Elsewhere Mahfouz spells out his personal assessment of the role of the Wafd. He holds that even though the party lived on until abolished by the 1952 Revolution, its mission had in fact ended with the signing of the 1936 treaty with the British, which gave Egypt its formal independence. He goes on to say that with the escalation in the national struggle after the end of World War II which culminated in the unilateral cancellation of the treaty by the Wafd in 1951 and the start of guerrilla warfare against the British forces in the Suez Canal Zone, it

5 For a full discussion of this issue by the present writer, see 'Religion in the Novels of Naguib Mahfouz', in the *British Society for Middle Eastern Studies Bulletin*, vol. 16, nos. 1 and 2, 1988, pp. 21–7.

6 *Atahaddath Ilaykum*, p. 32.

7 See *Palace Walk* (passim) for Zaghloul and *Palace of Desire* (especially chapter four) for al-Nahhas.

would have been natural for such conditions to lead to social change and the emergence of a new socialist party, born out of the left wing of the Wafd. However, before any of this could happen came the revolution of 1952.[8]

With all this in mind, it can be argued that in his fiction written before 1952 – and one must remember here that though published only in 1956–57, the writing of *The Cairo Trilogy* was actually completed in 1952[9] – Mahfouz had already come to believe firmly that Egypt's only hope in a prosperous post-independence future lay in its adoption of a scientific outlook free from the fetters of religion and Islamic revivalist idealism on the one hand, and a just social order founded on the principles of socialism on the other.[10]

Did the 1952 revolution then achieve for Mahfouz his vision which the Wafd, with its constant, energy-sapping battling with the British occupation and the monarchy as well as its restrictive ties with the land-owning class, had fallen short of? It appears that the writer did put his faith in the revolution during its early years and that he had a genuine admiration for its swift and radical reforms in the socio-economic system and its nationalist bent. The fact that, rather mysteriously, he stopped publishing for a period of seven years between 1952 when he completed *The Cairo Trilogy* and 1959 when he serialised *Children of the Alley*[11] (*Awlad Haratina,* serialised, 1959; in book form, 1967) in *Al-Ahram* has been explained enigmatically by himself as a reaction to the revolution. He argued in answer to questions from untiring critics that he felt the world he had been writing about for years had changed overnight and that many of the social ills which moved him to write had been put right by the new regime.[12] There is no reason to doubt the truthfulness of this remark insomuch as it applied to the early years

---

8 *Atahaddath Ilaykum*, pp. 98, 118.

9 See Ghali Shukri, *al-Muntami*, Cairo, 1969, p. 452.

10 See the present writer's full discussion of this issue in the article referred to in footnote 5 above.

11 An earlier translation was titled *Children of Gebelawi.*

12 G. Shukri, p. 239.

of the revolution. But as the years went by and the shortcomings of the Nasser (Gamal Abdul-Nasser, 1918–70) era began to make themselves felt, one critic's remark that Mahfouz 'rather than finding nothing to say… was unable to say what he wanted to…', rings true.[13] This seems so much more the case when we look at the content of what Mahfouz began to say when he had regained his balance and summoned to his assistance the tools of his art. His first novel after the silent period, viz. *Children of the Alley*, was an allegorical lamentation of the failure of mankind to achieve social justice and to harness the potential of science in the service of humanity, rather than its destruction. Masked in allegory though it was, the novel could hardly be seen as the offspring of an intellect basking in a sense of revolutionary fulfilment.

His next novel, *The Thief and the Dogs* (*al-Liss wa al-Kilab*, 1961) dispenses with the camouflage of allegory, showing his disillusionment with the revolution in stark terms. All the novels of the 1960s can in fact be seen as a barrage of bitter criticism aimed at a revolution that has abjectly failed to deliver the promised goods.[14] *The Thief and the Dogs* is about betrayal, and mainly the betrayal of revolutionary ideals once power, with the privileges that come with it, is achieved. Thus the relationship between Said Mahran, 'the thief' betrayed and seeking revenge, and Raouf Alwan, his fallen idol, is Mahfouz's metaphor of the rapid dissipation of revolutionary ideal and purity, and his indictment of the newly-emerged establishment which inherited all too soon the privileges and complacency of the *ancien regime*.

Autumn Quail (*al-Summan wa al-Kharif*, 1962) which, taken at its face value, appears to be an account of the mental agony of an old Wafdist displaced by the new regime is, on closer inspection, a rebuke of the revolution for its contemptuous alienation and total banishment from political life of a vastly popular political force and the only one with a creditable national record in the generation preceding the revolution.

Adrift on the Nile (*Tharthara fawqa al-Nil*, 1966) is another powerful

---

13 Ibid.

14 The only exception perhaps is *The Search* (1964) which poses a metaphysical question within a symbolic framework and is without a direct political message.

impeachment of the revolution. The apathy and corruption of the privileged middle class is vividly illustrated. In the words of one of the characters: 'Everyone is writing about socialism, while most of them dream of wealth.'[15] Their apathy, from which they are shaken by a disaster towards the end of the novel, is shown to be partly generated by their frustration at their inability to play a genuine role in the affairs of their country in the absence of basic freedoms. *Adrift on the Nile* was in a sense prophetic of the inevitable disaster of the 1967 defeat in the war with Israel.

Mahfouz's next novel, *Miramar* (1967), was to be his last *cri de coeur* against the aberrations of the revolution before the 1967 catastrophe. In a sense, it is a recapitulation in concentrated form of some of the themes of his earlier novels of the 1960s. Each of the lodgers of the hotel Miramar represents a section of the then contemporary society with the peasant maidservant standing for Egypt. Significantly, the most sympathetically portrayed male character is that of the old Wafdist journalist who, in a manner reminiscent of the hero of *Autumn Quails*, is shown to have been mercilessly swept aside by the new regime despite his old nationalist role. The most abhorrently depicted, on the other hand, is Sarhan al-Buhayri, the representative of the lower-middle class, the class empowered by the revolution to inherit the office and authority of the ousted aristocracy and upper-middle classes. Torn between the trappings of his political office and his modest means, Sarhan betrays, like his predecessor Raouf Alwan in *The Thief and the Dogs*, the principles of the revolution to which he never ceases to pay lip service. His moral bankruptcy and eventual suicide are Mahfouz's condemnation of the revolution's failure to lead by example. Most interesting perhaps of his creations in this novel is the character of Mansour Bahi, the socialist advocate. He is unlike any of Mahfouz's socialists in the pre-revolutionary novels. In those novels, the socialist/communist types figured as strong young men full of vigour, zeal, belief in their ideals and boundless hope in the future; they were, as the novelist portrayed them, Egypt's promise of the future. But none of this in *Miramar*; the socialist character here is distorted out of recognition.

15 Naguib Mahfouz, *Tharthara fawq al-Nil*, Cairo, 1973, p. 55.

Mansour Bahi is a weakling who betrays the socialist cause rather than resist pressure or go to prison. He hates himself for it and is rendered unable to enjoy life or love. He is the novelist's elegy of the emasculation through persecution by the revolution of the socialist intellectuals who ironically might have expected to be the revolution's favourites, itself having undertaken policies of a strong leftist inclination. Amidst all this, the maidservant (who, as mentioned earlier, stands for Egypt) has to fend for herself all the time against the sexual advances of all lodgers with the exception of the old Wafdist and the psychologically unbalanced socialist. The girl however proves more than a match for her harassers put together. Thus 'Egypt' emerges as strong and self-reliant; as poor, but dignified, with none of her 'sons' sufficiently free from self-interest to do something for her.

Such then was the extent of Mahfouz's disillusionment with the 1952 revolution during its heyday in the 1960s, even before its crowning failure in 1967. His criticisms were mostly direct and unsweetened and it is common knowledge now that some of his novels during that period would not have seen the light of day if it were not for the influence of Muhammad Hasanayn Haykal (1923–2016), then confidant of Nasser and editor of *Al-Ahram*, where the novels were first serialised in weekly instalments. The publication of his work may indeed have been a calculated attempt to use it as a safety valve to let off some popular steam and to give a semblance, however faint, of tolerating criticism. It must be stressed however that Mahfouz's quarrel with the revolution has never been over principles; it was rather over practices which failed to live up to principles. He asserts in an interview in the relatively freer climate of 1973 under Sadat:

> There is no doubt that the declared aims of the 23 July Revolution would have been to me and to my entire generation very satisfactory only if they had been carried out in the spirit in which they were declared... I wanted nothing more than true socialism and true democracy. This has not been achieved.[16]

16 *Atahaddath Ilaykum*, pp. 98–9.

Despite his belief in socialism as the way forward for his society, Mahfouz asserts that he does not consider himself a Marxist regardless of his immense sympathy for Marxism. He admits that he has his doubts about the Marxist theory as a philosophic system, but confesses to his faith in its application in spite of the faults and tragedies of experimentation.[17] He goes on to spell out what amounts to a political credo and merits to be quoted in full.

Mahfouz believed:

1. That man should be freed from the class system and what it entails of privileges such as inheritance... etc;
2. That man should be freed from all forms of exploitation;
3. That an individual's position [in society] should be determined according to both his natural and acquired qualifications;
4. That recompense should be equal to need;
5. That the individual should enjoy freedom of thought and belief under protection of law to which both governor and governed should be subject;
6. In the realisation of democracy in the fullest sense;
7. In the reduction of the power of central government so that it should be restricted to [internal] security and defence.

He rounds off by stressing the all-importance of the other integral component of his formula for social progress, namely 'science'.[18] Interestingly, Mahfouz's belief in socialism and science is not without its metaphysical dimension; for he has repeatedly expressed the opinion, both in his fiction (esp. *Children of the Alley*) and direct statements, that a socially harmonious humanity where science reigns supreme may eventually be able to discover the ultimate truth and conquer death.[19]

This credo is obviously the yardstick by which Mahfouz judged

17 Ibid., pp. 16–17.

18 Ibid., p. 17.

19 Ibid., pp. 17, 74, 150.

the revolution as a failure, and it must serve as the background for understanding the novelist's deep sense of frustration at the collapse of national aspirations yet again at the hands of the very regime which initially seemed capable of achieving what earlier generations had failed in. After the 1967 defeat and the death of Nasser in 1970, encouraged by the relatively more liberal political climate which then prevailed as well as the secret glee of the new establishment under Sadat at any publication undermining the Nasser era, Mahfouz began to write a series of novels (not to mention short stories and playlets) in which he continued his evaluation of Nasserist Egypt. The picture emerging from these novels, published intermittently in the 1970s and early 1980s, is stiflingly depressing in its evocation of the national sense of loss and humiliation at the defeat; the irreparable damage to the dignity of the individual following years of government repression of opponents; and the public apathy to events engendered by the people's lack of trust in the regime and the habits of long years of being led from above without any measure of democratic participation in the government of their country. Inevitably these novels are more candid in their criticisms, often dealing directly with issues which would have been too dangerous to address in the 1960s. These novels are in chronological order: *Love in the Rain* (1973); *Karnak Café* (1974); *The Final Hour* (1982); *Before the Throne* (1983); and *The Day the Leader Was Killed* (1985). All these novels are of a documentary nature, dealing with issues topical at the time of their authorship and some of them are already dated; they are therefore the most akin to the essays of this book, though they continue to make much more entertaining reading than the dry essays, which are only of historical value today. The novels are artistically negligible in themselves, though immensely useful for understanding Naguib Mahfouz's thought and elucidating his more important works. Posterity shall treasure them as a priceless source for the social and political history of the Egypt of their day. Mahfouz himself seems aware of this fact when he argues in the course of commenting on *Karnak Café*:

> I am prepared to write a novel … to support a view which I respect,

> or in order to make a personal comment on certain political circumstances, even if such a novel was destined to die as soon as the occasion for which it was written had elapsed.[20]

Love in the Rain (*al-Hubb tahta al-Matar*, 1973) was the first of those novels. It is set in Cairo during the period 1967–70 which has come to be known as 'the war of attrition' referring to the continued warlike action between Egyptian and Israeli forces across the Suez Canal until Nasser accepted a temporary cease-fire shortly before his death in 1970. The novel depicts a demoralised society, with city people sunk in apathy, hardly aware of the war going on at the front, with young people seeking refuge from the harsh reality by thinking of emigration and indulgence in sex and empty pastimes. The fact dawns on people that they had been living in 'a myth',[21] from which the military defeat shocked them into reality. The gap between myth and reality is sardonically summarised by a nameless character in these words: 'We used to be concerned with pan-Arabism and pan-Africanism and now we are concerned with the elimination of the effects of the aggression,'[22] quoting a euphemism for the Israeli occupation of Arab lands, much used in the state media at the time.

Published a year after *Love in the Rain*, *Karnak Café* (*al-Karnak*, 1974) is set two years earlier, namely in 1965–67,[23] i.e. in the two years or so leading up to the 1967 defeat. *Karnak Café* concentrates on an issue lightly touched upon in the previous novel, namely that of the repressive methods of the police state and their destructive effect on the dignity of the individual and the nation. The novel is written in the first person and the narrator, who puts the pieces of the action together from encounters with other characters over a period of two years in the eponymous café, is himself a writer from an older generation.[24]

---

20 Ibid., p. 111.

21 Naguib Mahfouz, *Hubb tahta al-Matar*, Cairo, 1973, pp. 10, 15.

22 Ibid., p. 36.

23 Naguib Mahfouz, *al-Karnak*, Cairo, 1974, pp. 19, 37.

24 Ibid., p. 32.

Thus it is not difficult to see him as a mouthpiece for the novelist. *Karnak Café* is essentially a refutation of the classic argument often used by repressive regimes to justify their excesses, namely sacrificing the individual for the collective good of the nation. Commenting on the repeated arrests, torture and lengthy detainment without charges or trial of some of the student customers of the café, the old narrator's thoughts run like this:

> I wondered at the condition of my country. Despite its deviations, it is turning into a mighty giant. It has strength and influence. It manufactures everything from sewing needles to rockets and sponsors the great causes of humanity. Why is it then that the human being in my country has become so small and trivial like a mosquito? Why is he without rights, dignity or protection?[25]

The anguished narrator tries to provide the answer to his own question:

> Does not the creation of our scientific, socialist, industrial state – the most powerful in the Middle East – does it not deserve that we bear for its sake all those pains?[26]

The narrator knows all the time in his heart of hearts that nothing can justify the sacrifice of man's humanity; 'all the time,' He argues, 'I felt that with this kind of logic I could persuade myself of the necessity, nay, the benefit of death itself!'[27] The novel exposes a boastful, totalitarian and hollow regime that collapses in the aftermath of the first real test.

Though published in 1982, *The Final Hour* (*al-Baqi min al-Zaman Sa'a*) was almost certainly written before the assassination of Sadat. For one thing, Mahfouz was known to be usually some two years ahead of his publishers with two or more novels in his drawer at any time

25 Ibid., p. 28.
26 Ibid., p. 20.
27 Ibid.

awaiting publication.[28] Furthermore the novel is advertised as forthcoming at the back of *Layali Alf Layla wa Layla* (translated as *Arabian Nights and Days*), an earlier novel by Mahfouz, published in 1981. *The Final Hour* documents the political history of twentieth-century Egypt from the time of the nationalist uprising against the British in 1919 down to the Camp David Accords and the Peace Treaty with Israel in 1979. It stops just short of the assassination of Sadat in 1981, which is dealt with in a later novel, viz. *The Day the Leader Was Killed* (1985). Thus it can be argued that the novel is in a sense both a condensation and an updating of the political narrative of *The Cairo Trilogy* which stops at the end of World War II, a few years before the 1952 revolution. Like *The Cairo Trilogy,* it portrays a family saga (though without the extended narrative associated with this type of novel), with the youngest generation reaching maturity during the Nasser era. The novel is written in simplistic symbolism with each of the characters standing for one or other of the political ideas or forces rife in the Egyptian scene during the 20th century up to the time of writing. Most important is the character of Saniya, the grandmother who represents the spirit of Egypt herself. She is shown within the symbolism of the book as impervious to the ageing process. Although by the end of the book she is well into her eighties, she continues to be energetic with no sign of mental or physical deterioration unlike her own children who seem older than her. She lives in a house with a garden in a suburb of Cairo, of which we are told that it had seen a few good days and suffered ages of decay. Within a few pages of the start of the novel, it becomes obvious that the house and the garden stand for Egypt as a country in need of material development and social welfare, but constantly being deprived of the chance to achieve that goal. The house is shown to be in a rundown state from the outset, since Saniya's early married years. Her thoughts run like this:

> Food and clothing eat up all our earnings. What will become of this large house? It needs repairs and redecoration. And the garden!

28 From a personal communication with the novelist.

> The trees no longer bear fruit; the shrubs are withered and sand has covered most of the soil. It badly needs to be revived.[29]

Throughout her life, from her youth to her old age, Saniya has only had one recurring dream: to renovate the house and the garden. But generation after generation and one political era after another, her dream is shattered, and her waiting is indefinitely prolonged. One regime after another fails to deliver the promise of prosperity and Egypt, like the house, remains poor and dilapidated. Her final hope is centred on Sadat's peace initiative which, he promised the nation, would bring prosperity with it. But this hope too is dashed, on the symbolic level in the novel as in reality. Rather than having been rejuvenated, the garden Saniya is left with in the end looks like 'a target in the aftermath of an air raid'.[30] The novel is written in one long piece of continuous narrative: a hundred and ninety pages without chapter divisions. It is as if the novelist wanted to delineate the history of modern Egypt as a flux of suffering and frustration, a homogeneous continuum of lost opportunities. The book bleakly ends with a family gathering in the old derelict house under a thunderstorm which underlines the tumultuous time Egypt is struggling through. As one turns the last leaf of the book, suddenly the sense of prophetic doom implicit in the title dawns on the mind: 'the final hour', or more precisely as the Arabic title says, 'only one hour left'. Mahfouz obviously believes that modern Egypt has wasted enough opportunities; that history's generosity is not boundless and unless something is done and done quickly, Egypt may be eternally doomed to a fate of poverty, backwardness and dependency.

Still preoccupied with the predicament of his country, Mahfouz decides to write yet another book in which he again addresses himself to a consideration of Egypt's political history. This time he does not however limit himself to the present century but goes back some 5000 years and starts at the beginning with Menes, the great king of the first dynasty who united Upper and Lower Egypt into one kingdom,

---

29 Naguib Mahfouz, *Al-Baqi min al-Zaman Sa'a*, Cairo, 1982, p. 20.

30 Ibid., p. 187.

and thence works his way up to the assassination of Sadat. The book is called *Before the Throne* (*Amam al-'Arsh*, 1983); the throne being that of Osiris, god of the underworld, before whom are brought all past rulers of Egypt for judgement according to their achievements for Egypt. It is a difficult book to classify, being unlike anything written by Mahfouz. It certainly is not a historical novel, nor is it a scholarly book of history despite its strict adherence to historical facts. Based mainly on dialogue rather than narration, it uses a fictitious dramatic situation (i.e. the underworld trial) to bring into focus a certain vision of Egyptian history in its entirety. This however does not make the book a play as it consists of independent scenes held together only by the unities of space, action and theme without either plot or character development.

Regardless of the form of the book, its content is invaluable as a writer's pronouncement on his age placed in historic perspective. Mahfouz's division of eternity takes after Dante's paradigm of hell, purgatory and heaven. Viewing the book in its totality, it is not difficult to determine the author's yardstick (for he is the real judge here rather than Osiris) in judging Egypt's rulers throughout history. Those who go to heaven are the strong rulers who preserved the country's independence and national unity; their personal shortcomings are forgiven in return. Those who go to hell are selfish and weak rulers who favoured their personal interests over their country's and put at risk its unity and security through poor policy and neglect. As for those who go to purgatory, they are rulers who were well-meaning but were faced with adverse circumstances beyond their control. The spectrum of the book is as vast as the period it purports to cover, but throughout, the past is continuously interpreted in terms of the present and vice versa, with the result being that what emerges in the end is a sense of the unity of history and a unique failure to learn from it.

I will limit myself here to outlining a summary of the trial of Nasser, for whom Mahfouz has more rebuke than praise. According to the regulations of Osiris's court, rulers accorded a place in heaven automatically occupy a seat as members of the jury, as it were, and are involved in trying subsequent rulers. Thus we have the great Pharaoh Tuthmosis III railing at Nasser: 'Despite your military training, you have shown no military prowess at all; indeed, you were a general of no consequence whatsoever!'[31] This reproach sounds natural, coming from a great ancient military victor. Equally natural is an accusation of despotism from a modern democratic leader, Saad Zaghloul.[32] The most bitter attack on Nasser, however, is reserved for Mustafa al-Nahhas, the great leader of the Wafd Party and erstwhile prime minister in the pre-1952 era, who was thrown into oblivion by Nasser after a quarter of a century of heading the Egyptian national struggle. Al-Nahhas's impassioned tirade deserves to be quoted at length:

> You suppressed freedom and human rights. I do not deny that you brought security for the poor, but you were the destruction of the intellectuals who are the vanguard of the nation. They were detained, imprisoned and killed indiscriminately until they lost their sense of human dignity and initiative... If only you were more moderate in your ambitions! Developing the Egyptian village was more important than sponsoring the revolutions of the world; supporting scientific research was more important than the Yemeni campaign, and fighting illiteracy was more important than fighting international imperialism. Alas! You lost the country an opportunity which it had never had before...[33]

This outburst is evidently Mahfouz's final dictum on the Nasser era; it is the culmination of all the hints and lesser pronouncements he has been making since the early 1960s and, as such, it comes as no surprise. It is the pained lamentation of a liberal, socially committed writer who witnessed the demise of freedom and hopes of progress at the very hands of the regime that initially promised to achieve them.

Let us pause here and have a look at what Mahfouz the opinion page columnist was writing around the same time. In an essay, dated 25 February 1982, 'Lessons from Deceased Leaders', he rails at the

31 Naguib Mahfouz, *Amam al-'Arsh*, Cairo, 1983, p. 194.

32 Ibid., pp. 195–6.

33 Ibid., pp. 197, 198.

Nasser era, almost in the same words as al-Nahhas does in the above extract, lamenting policies which left the country defeated and impoverished, 'because we did not cut our coat according to our cloth… we were so obsessed with leading revolutions and liberating other nations that we abandoned our own people to wallow in illiteracy, nakedness, hunger and disease.' Again, on 22 July 1982, the eve of the anniversary of the 1952 revolution, he writes enumerating some of the reforms of the revolution before going on to accuse it of having 'produced an authoritarian and repressive state that has experienced bitter defeats, … squandered funds, destroyed human dignity…' Again, on 30 June 1983, in an essay titled, '5 June', the date of the start of the 1967 war with Israel, he reduces Egypt's ignominious defeat in the war to one underlying cause: 'the disease of authoritarianism which had turned the state into a grand inquisition emitting terror and dread, and which turned the people into victims deprived of their security and sapped of their will. No nation ruled by fear … can effect a real victory in war or peace.' Never tiring of the point, he repeats soon after on 21 July 1983, anticipating the anniversary of the 1952 revolution, that 'autocratic rule may well have led to the founding of great institutions, but it has also destroyed the most important of institutions: the human character…'

Returning to *Before the Throne,* Nasser is eventually admitted to heaven but, significantly, not before some hesitation on the part of Osiris who tells him: 'Few people have served their country as you have and fewer still have damaged it as you have…'[34] In contrast, Sadat sails through his trial. He is quickly acquitted and recommended to be sent to heaven on the basis that his reign was mainly devoted to the task of trying to put right the mess he had inherited from Nasser. It was in a later book that Mahfouz was to give his more studied evaluation of the Sadat period.

The Day the Leader Was Killed (*Yawma Qutila al-Za'im,* 1985) is a novella of ninety odd pages. The 'day' of the title is 6 October 1981, and the leader is Anwar Sadat. The story deals with the predicament of Egyptian youth during the Sadat era, and is told, in the fashion of

34 Ibid., p. 198.

Miramar, from several points of view; namely those of Muhtashimi (the grandfather), Alwan (his grandson) and Randa (the latter's fiancée). The grandfather is a kindly octogenarian who has lived a long life during which he witnessed the political life of the nation from the times of Saad Zaghloul to those of Sadat – much like Mahfouz himself and a familiar archetype in his work, normally standing for the atemporal, all-encompassing character of Egypt, having survived many leaders and conflicting policies without ever being engulfed by any one current.

The grandson and his fiancée are introduced as two young people in love. They belong to the lower-middle class and live with their respective families in the same block of flats. They are both graduates working in the same government office, both honest and morally upright, both religious without being fanatics, and full of the love of life. In short, together they represent what Mahfouz believes to be the positive and generally moderate characteristics of the Egyptian personality, and it is interesting to note here the element of continuity between the grandfather's character and that of the new generation. In their late twenties and having been engaged for many years, Alwan and Randa are still unable to fulfil their dream of marriage. There is no way, we are shown, that they can afford to rent and furnish a flat under Sadat's consumer-oriented *infitah* or open-door economy, wild inflation and soaring prices. Their dilemma is even more poignant because their moral rectitude holds them from seeking a way out through devious means. Thus the engagement is broken under pressure from the girl's family and the high ideal of love is shown to be futile in a society where all values have become relative. Randa is married off to her wealthy boss – a sacrifice raised at the altar of economic necessity. Soon after, it transpires that the man only wanted her in order to use her beauty in his business-brokering. The old spark of dignity flares up again and she obtains a divorce. The young man, on the other hand, is nearly tempted to marry a much older, rich widow, but he withdraws at the last minute. Amid all this despair in the life of individuals, Sadat is killed and, in a parallel action of rebellion, Alwan attacks the corrupt executive who robbed him of his love and, though he does not kill him, he causes his death. Thus the simplistic parallelism of the plot shows the fall of the supreme head of a corrupt regime and one of its distant satellites at the same time. However, as pointed out earlier, the purpose of the novelist here is not so much to write good fiction as to record critically the features of an age.

Against the backdrop of this story, Sadat's Egypt is described in scathing terms. To give a few examples, the *infitah* economic policy has resulted in the Egyptians becoming 'a deprived community amidst a circus of thieves',[35] and 'many nations living in one country'.[36] The individual, furthermore, is repressed: 'The Nile itself is no longer able to show anger,'[37] while the time is one of 'nauseating catchphrases... that swamped us,'[38] and 'lies fly in the air like dust' when a presidential speech is broadcast.[39] Sadat himself is 'an actor manqué... dressed up like Hitler, while his actions resemble Charlie Chaplin's'.[40] On the other hand, a sense of nostalgia for Nasser's days seems the only comfort in an age without heroes or ideals; a nostalgia so strong, it almost serves as a substitute for looking forward to the future.[41] The nation's initial sense of shock at the news of the assassination is shown to have soon given way to a sense of relief, almost glee. Comments among customers at a coffee house run like this: 'Serves him right for thinking the country is dead... In a moment the thieves' empire has collapsed...'[42] Indeed, while the novella ends with the death of Sadat, this is not at all shown as cause for gloom or despair. On the contrary, the final thoughts of the young protagonist are very positive: 'I was filled with a mysterious sense of anticipation; with unknown probabilities which promised to crush the fixity and monotony of things and advance towards a horizon without boundaries...'[43]

---

35 Naguib Mahfouz, *Yawma Qutila al-Za'im*, Cairo, 1985, p. 21.

36 Ibid., p. 46.

37 Ibid., p. 9.

38 Ibid., p. 17.

39 Ibid., p. 47.

40 Ibid., p. 47.

41 Ibid., pp. 22, 43.

42 Ibid., p. 82.

43 Ibid., p. 82.

It is remarkable that in this novella about the Sadat era, no accolade is accorded Sadat for leading Egypt into the 6 October War (also known as the Ramadan War and the Yom Kippur War) for the liberation of Sinai in 1973, nor of his daring peace initiative in 1977 culminating in the peace treaty with Israel in 1979; both of which acts were publicly supported by Mahfouz in his non-fiction writing, particularly the peace initiative which scandalised most Egyptians at the time. In fact, his wholehearted embracing of the peace initiative exposed him to accusations of betrayal from leftist intellectuals in Egypt and elsewhere in the Arab world. Against this stark blanking in Mahfouz's fiction, compare the adulation in his newspaper column, 'In What State Has the Festival Returned', dated 21/4/1983, where he calls on his readers on the anniversary of the liberation of Sinai to remember 'with honour and respect the person who managed to achieve this, the late president Anwar Sadat … [who] waged the first noble and successful war since Muhammad Ali [founder of modern Egypt and the Muhammad Ali dynasty (1805–1953)] … [and who] embarked on a bold and pioneering policy which shattered the stasis in which the Arabs were mired, and created a new perspective for those who wished to move forward.' While the reason why nothing from these repeated public avowals of appreciation has filtered into his fiction remains an open question, there is no cause to doubt the genuineness of Mahfouz's support for Sadat's rapprochement with Israel. It may be that Sadat's continuation with autocratic rule, his creation through *infitah* of a quasi-capitalist, consumer-oriented economy in a very poor country, and the genuine unpopularity of his policy of naturalisation of relations with Israel – it may be that these were what Mahfouz wanted to portray in a realistic, semi-documentary novel, rather than his own views which understood the realism and long-term potential of Sadat's rapprochement with Israel. Be that as it may, his apparent condemnation of Sadat's era in *The Day the Leader Was Killed* should not however be understood as an acquittal by implication of Nasser's reign. If anything, his criticisms of both periods are links in the same chain. The root of all the works briefly discussed here is a long-standing sense of disillusionment with the 1952 revolution in both eras of Nasser and Sadat.

Mahfouz never forgave the 1952 revolution for its role in abolishing democracy and political pluralism, and for its consecration of autocracy and the creation of a police state. For him the 1919 uprising against the British remained the ideal, because it was truly a 'popular' revolution, while 1952 was a military coup in origin regardless of the 'revolutionary' changes it introduced in society after usurping and monopolising power. For Mahfouz all the later grievous mistakes of 1952 were corollaries of the original sin of autocracy. Over the years he never tired of celebrating in his weekly column the anniversary of the death of the leaders of 1919 and the Wafd, Saad Zaghloul and Mustafa al-Nahhas, both of whom died on 23 August, in 1927 and 1965 respectively. Consider by way of example his essay '23 August', dated 23/8/1984, where these two leaders whose memory was all but consigned to oblivion post-1952, are described as 'the greatest popular leaders whose names are linked with the greatest popular revolution in our history: the 1919 Revolution'.

In an interview given in 1973 Mahfouz listed some subjects which were abandoned when he decided to switch from history to the modern social scene. One of these subjects which he considered to be 'very important' was Akhenaten, the Eighteenth Dynasty monarch who ruled Egypt some fourteen centuries before Christ and preached a new religious cult based on the worship of the one god, Aten, symbolised by the sun disc. Little did Mahfouz know then that some twenty years later this subject was to reach out from the dark recesses of the past and claim its primary right to be written and its secondary right to be useful in elucidating the present.

The novel, whose title evokes the king-prophet, is *Akhenaten, Dweller in Truth* (*al-'A'ish fi al-Haqiqa*, 1985). It takes the form of a quest for the truth about Akhenaten. The narrator is a young historian from the generation born after the fall of Akhenaten. In his boyhood he was taught that the king had been an 'infidel' (*mariq*), whose policies had brought division and destruction on the country. Now he wants to discover the truth for himself and thus he embarks on a series of interviews with important men and women who were contemporaries of Akhenaten and who either supported or opposed him at the time. Through these interviews a picture emerges of Akhenaten whose shades are conflicted between holiness and madness, wilfulness and effeminacy, tolerance and fanaticism according to the point of view. The High Priest of Amun, the god ousted by Akhenaten, accuses him of having been weak 'to the point of hating the strong. He invented a god in his own image, weak and effeminate with only one function – love... He sank in the marshes of folly neglecting his royal duties ... until the empire was lost and Egypt laid waste.'[44] On the other hand, we see Queen Nefertiti, Akhenaten's wife, question the integrity of the High Priest who, according to her, pretended to worry about the empire whereas all he cared for was the clergy's share of the wealth.[45]

Mahfouz portrays Akhenaten in idealistic terms – he is at once a sensitive poet, a mystic who experienced a moment of divine revelation, and a prophet who calls his people to a faith based on love and peace. On the other hand, he is also pictured as a ruler guilty of neglecting the affairs of the state and striking division among his people through his fanaticism and persecution of religious non-conformists. Faced with a deteriorating situation, Akhenaten asks the advice of his chief general, who recommends the 'declaration of freedom of worship'.[46] This liberal call falls on deaf ears, however, and the king persists in imposing his religious dogma on the affairs of the state until the sad end.

Written in the 1980s, at a time of worldwide Islamic resurgence when the influence of the Islamic Republic in Iran was at its highest, and when religious fundamentalism in Egypt was calling for *jihad* (holy war) against the 'infidel' state and the adoption of *sharia* (religious law) in a society which, on the one hand, was largely secularised, and which, on the other, had a sizeable Christian minority, the ancient message of the tragedy of Akhenaten could not have sounded more contemporary. Once more Mahfouz harnessed history in the service of the present, as he had done more than 40 years earlier in *Thebes at War*.

---

44 Naguib Mahfouz, *Al-'A'ish fi al-Haqiqa*, Cairo, 1985, pp. 11–12.

45 Ibid., pp. 35–6.

46 Ibid., p. 58.

Morning and Evening Talk (*Hadith al-Sabah wa al-Masa'*, 1987), Mahfouz's penultimate novel, contains sixty-seven sketches of characters, arranged alphabetically by name and drawn mainly from three families whose members are all related either through blood or intermarriage. Though of moderate length (217 pages), it is Mahfouz's most ambitious *roman fleuve*, tracing the lives of three whole families across five generations and a period of nearly 200 years. In earlier works, he limited himself to three generations while containing the events within his own lifetime, i.e. beginning at about the year 1919 with its dramatic events of the popular revolution against the British and continuing to the time of writing – the mid-1940s, as in *The Cairo Trilogy*, or the 1980s, as in works discussed above. It appears, however, that as he grew older and the perspective viewed from his year of birth extended, he felt an urge to extend it at the other end too, perhaps the better to understand his own life and times in a wider temporal context. Thus *Morning and Evening Talk* has its beginning in the late-eighteenth century, namely with the arrival of Napoleon in Egypt in 1798 and concludes with occurrences from the post-Sadat era. The French campaign in Egypt (1798–1801) and the rule of Muhammad Ali (1769–1849), shortly established in 1805 after its departure, represent together the beginning of modern times in Egypt. The novel, concerned as ever in Mahfouz with the interplay of public time and personal time, is thus a panoramic view of post-medieval Egypt to the time of its writing, i.e. the early Mubarak years.

The three main families of the novel represent together all sections of Egyptian urban society. Significantly, the author shows all the families to have originated at the bottom of society for changes of time, personal or public, then to have raised some of them into a higher class and a different style of life. As generations pass, old links are severed and the elevated forget their former humble station.

Morning and Evening Talk is a sad novel. On the public level, it amounts to an elegy of the failure of the experiment of modernisation in Egypt. On the individual level, it is a bizarre celebration of death, of the incessant massacre by time of people's hopes and lives. Each of the sixty-seven sketches contains in a very condensed manner a whole lifetime, always beginning with birth and ending with death. Considering the lexicographical arrangement of the sketches, we are made to feel that individuals are no more than short, insignificant entries in the huge, ongoing lexicon of time.

The Coffeehouse (*Qushtumur*, 1988) is Mahfouz's last novel, written when he was in his late seventies. Like much else in his work, the novel is concerned with public events in Egyptian society and their effects on individuals over a considerable stretch of time. But rather than approach his subject through the generations of one family, as he did for instance in *The Cairo Trilogy*, Mahfouz chooses to do it here through a quick review of the lifetimes of a group of friends, representing among them a cross-section of Egyptian urban society.

The Coffeehouse is the story of four inhabitants of Abbasiya, brought together by friendship from their primary school days, a friendship which transcends differences of temperament and class. Two of them come from the lower-middle class, while the other two belong to the aristocratic class. Their inclinations, on the other hand, vary between the binaries of religiosity and doubt, capitalism and socialism, or complete nihilism. Their friendship, however, withstands all these differences and withstands too the test of time with all the changes that it brings about on both the public and private levels. The action extends over the familiar Mahfouzian period: 1915 to the present day. All four characters enjoy equal attention from the novelist and there is no pivotal protagonist. We follow their growth from childhood games and the discoveries of puberty to the formation of religious consciousness and political affiliations. Later we follow their different fortunes in the arena of life; some succeed and some fail; some make families and some stay single; some get involved in political life and some stay aloof, and so on. Since the interaction of public and private is essential in Mahfouz's world-picture for producing personal tragedy, he chooses here, as he often does, to reveal to us the fortunes of his four characters against the backdrop of Egypt's contemporary history from 1919 to the time of writing.

There is nothing substantially new in Mahfouz's last novel. It does not amount to much more than a variation on *The Final Hour*, discussed above and published seven years earlier. All its characters are borrowed with only cosmetic changes from previous works and so are the public and private events. There is nothing new either in its view of man and society, or in the author's reading of his country's socio-political history in the present century. Its value lies in none of these, but in the gush of nostalgia which impelled Mahfouz to write it, in his desperate grip on time in the memory and in his attempt to take refuge from the inexorable flux of time in the permanence of place and human sympathy as represented by the coffeehouse and the friendship that has held its four patrons together for so long and against many odds.

In addition to the novels of the 1980s cited above, Mahfouz published a collection of short stories titled *I Saw in a Dream* (*Ra'aytu fi ma yara al-Na'im*, 1982), followed two years later by another, *The Secret Organisation (al-Tanzim al-Sirri*, 1984). The stories of these two collections represent yet further variations on the author's familiar repertoire of themes, his inventive powers apparently never failing to find fresh and memorable metaphors for old concerns.

The period covered by the essays of this volume, 1982–88, coincides with the end of Mahfouz's creative career. With the fanatic attempt on his life in 1994 and the usual frailties of old age, not least dwindling eyesight and hearing, what little he published in the 1990s and early years of the 21st century was mostly of a pensive nature, often preoccupied with thoughts of death and the dead, written in lyrical language and consisting often of short parabolic narratives and aphorisms, or in the retelling of dreams where the surreal and the fantastic mingle seamlessly with the real.[47]

Looking back at the survey of works above written during the early Mubarak years, the fact will stand out that nothing can be found there that can be construed as constituting criticism of Mubarak's rule, in contrast with what we have witnessed in relation to both the eras of Nasser and Sadat. Nor indeed can we find any direct criticism of Mubarak in the scores of essays contained in this volume, again unlike

---

47 Examples of these works include *Echoes of an Autobiography* (1994); *The Dreams* (2004); and *Dreams of Departure* (2007).

the case in relation to both Nasser and Sadat. A few observations may be of help in explaining this. We must recall that all criticism of Nasser's regime during his lifetime, as in the novels of the 1960s, was indirect, using allegory, metaphor, symbol and various objective correlatives to convey the critical message, which was always directed at the regime but never at its head. Criticism of Nasser's person was simply beyond the pale: loss of freedom and livelihood was the starting price to pay. We must also recall that as a writer of *Al-Ahram*, Mahfouz enjoyed the protection of its editor at the time, Muhammad Hasanayn Haykal, a close friend of Nasser's. Explicit criticism of Nasser and his dictatorial rule, whether in Mahfouz's fiction or his newspaper column, was to happen only after his demise, when undermining the Nasser era became a gleefully tolerated exercise under Sadat. Again during Sadat's decade in power (1970–81), Mahfouz seemed more preoccupied with a reassessment of the Nasser period and its aftereffects in Egypt, than with Sadat's shortcomings especially in light of his burdensome legacy from Nasser. Although Sadat was hardly any less autocratic than Nasser, his undertaking of the 6 October War to liberate Sinai and his later courage in recognising the necessity of achieving peace with Israel may have somewhat improved his standing with the author. It was again after his assassination and during the Mubarak era, as can be seen in the essays of this volume as well as in a work like *The Day the Leader Was Killed*, that direct criticism of Sadat's authoritarian regime and damaging economic policies can be found.

Nasser's rule ended in disaster and so did Sadat's, whose policies were instrumental in giving rise to violent political Islam, whose first victim he ironically became. When Sadat was killed, hundreds of his opponents of all political hues were in prison at his behest, including many prominent political and religious figures and leading intellectuals and writers. This left Mubarak with a heavy legacy. He began his rule with conciliatory gestures and Mahfouz gave him the benefit of the doubt as can be seen in the essays of this volume. His was seen in the early years as 'A New Age', as in the title of an essay, dated 31/5/1984, where Mahfouz expresses the hope that the new era 'will be able to restore a healthy and natural balance to society, to offer a sound and untrammelled democratic way of life, which will bring about solid development and will stimulate a conscious march towards the implementation of full human rights.'

Perhaps one good way to end this account is to quote another of Mahfouz's essays in this volume which epitomises the three regimes of Nasser, Sadat and Mubarak as he saw them. He writes on 9/5/1985, reminding the reader of Egypt's tribulations since 23 July 1952, 'You can recall the attempts at governance that moved from authoritarianism to authoritarianism tinged with democracy to unhurried democracy.' 'Authoritarianism', as any contemporary reader would have readily deciphered is a reference to Nasser's rule, while that 'tinged with democracy' is an assertion of Sadat's essential authoritarianism despite gestures such as allowing the formation of political parties. As for the 'unhurried' or slow-moving democracy, the reference is to Mubarak's early rule in 1985. Mahfouz goes on, 'You can remember the hardship of isolationism, economic liberalisation and its catastrophes, the middle way and its pitfalls.' Here the author's typification turns to the economic policies that accompanied those political regimes. Authoritarianism went hand in hand with 'isolationism' with restrictions on imports, travel, hard currency, and private enterprise and the hardship of occasional food shortages. Democracy-tinged authoritarianism brought about Sadat's *infitah* (open door) economic liberalisation, removing the previous restrictions overnight with dire results for the poor majority and a quick accumulation of wealth by a few opportunists. As for the unhurried democracy, its economic companion had as yet not taken shape at the time: 'the middle way' beset with 'pitfalls'.

Egypt's political history in the second half of the twentieth century was not a happy time for Naguib Mahfouz nor for his fellow Egyptians. Reading the essays in this volume and his parallel fiction presents us with vivid evidence. By the time of his death in 2006, the authoritarianism and flagrant corruption of Mubarak's regime was paramount, but he still had four years in power before he was toppled by a popular revolution in 2011. I have no doubt that Mahfouz, who all his life never ceased to sing the praises of the popular revolution of 1919, would have welcomed this second one of 2011 and would then have had his heart broken at its subsequent failure to achieve for Egypt the dream of democracy and prosperity that continues to elude her.[48]

January 2020
Rasheed El-Enany
Professor Emeritus of Modern Arabic Literature
University of Exeter

48 In writing this introduction, I have made recourse to previous work by me on Naguib Mahfouz, including the following: 'The Novelist as Political Eyewitness: a View of Najib Mahfuz's Evaluation of the Nasser and Sadat Eras', in *Journal of Arabic Literature*, vol. 21, no. 1, 1990, pp. 72-86; *Naguib Mahfouz: the Pursuit of Meaning*, London, 1993; and *Naguib Mahfouz: His Life and Times*, London, 2007.

Substandard Food in an Age of Discipline

And now substandard food has become one of our pressing concerns. That means that greed and neglect know no limits and that the inebriation of sloth and indifference have not refrained from destroying our lives. It is even more catastrophic that the criminal incident of the rotten cheese distribution has taken place in the aftermath of a campaign for discipline which set throats, pens and laws a-quivering. There was then revealed to have been wholesale negligence in the distribution and storage of foodstuffs for schoolchildren, but the whole issue did not receive any attention until the catastrophe happened and some children fell victim. It may be some form of defence that officials did not think that the new laws applied to the storage of foodstuffs in schools – as if they should only follow the procedures dictated by the law. In fact, good working procedures should stem from common sense rather than having to be stipulated by law and that we should only introduce new laws in any regard as an unavoidable step in our current campaign against sloth, and that the final aim of good working procedures should be that they become a mode of behaviour and a value which pulsates through our living conscience. The officials responsible for school food should have stirred themselves from their daily routine, cast an analytical eye over their own management systems and set their procedures regarding the delivery, storage and distribution of food as tight as possible without having to be told, in response to the general call for better working procedures, without waiting for a catastrophe to take place or new legislation to be enacted. This is what every civil servant should be doing, and this is what everyone who called for an improvement in working procedures meant as part of their efforts to prevent outbreaks like this. I will never tire of republicising my previous suggestions that a general monitoring organisation or complaints procedure should be set up, and that a special official should be appointed both to supervise and to investigate the operating procedures of every ministry. I would also state that good working procedures are something that should attract the most interest and attention. They are not an issue like the economic situation, the youth question, subsidies or housing and so on. They are the most important issue of all, as they are the basis upon which the success of any initiative can be predicated on any issue at all. I ask God to convince you of this or to provide you with a better solution.

7 January 1982

Defamation of the Country

Sometimes voices are raised accusing some of the artistic establishments of defaming the country. This accusation could only become just and logical if the country actually had a good reputation which was then whittled down by the arts establishment who twist and distort it for some purpose or other. As for art echoing the negative aspects of society, drawing back the curtains on falsehoods and hypocrisy in order to stir people's consciences and rouse public concern in an effort to bring about change and reform, this should not be the grounds for accusations of defamation or iconoclasm. For there is no defamation taking place, and moreover there is no good reputation to be defamed. What damages the reputation of the country, of any country, is its very own backwardness, its lack of the building blocks of civilisation, its rampant ignorance, disease, poverty, tyranny, lack of consideration for human rights as well as its underdevelopment in thought, science and art. The country's reputation is even more harmed by its own disdain for reform and the eradication of the plague of passivity. The country's reputation is harmed even more by the accusations levelled against anything that reminds Egypt of its duty which only leads it to redouble its efforts to ruin its own reputation. It is impossible to try and hide what is going on in one country in the world now that it has become one large global village thanks to the new means of communication and tourist activity. The arts establishment is not divulging secrets or publishing hearsay, but is carrying out one of its core jobs, which is to criticise society, life and mankind, and to play a role in constructing a good and fair society. If the artistic establishment ignores this truth or presents a mendacious and false depiction, it betrays itself, it betrays Egypt's citizens and its own mission, and thereby becomes no more than a commercial public relations establishment or simply yet more opium for the masses. We should state here that the country is not completely devoid of positive aspects, so why should art not concentrate on those? The truth is that only rarely is a critical artistic work devoid of any allusion to positive things, and even if it is, the media trumpet these achievements morning, noon and evening, and the issue is not whether we should keep publicising our achievements as much as it is the media's resistance to criticism and reticence to reveal painful truths – along with the media's displeasure at being reminded of its duty. Let us remember that, and let us also remember the daringly critical artistic works created abroad which are not considered defamatory by those countries, and which are published worldwide without engendering a crisis of confidence. And it is precisely for that reason that those countries deserve the same respect and admiration as the works themselves.

14 January 1982

Indifference and Education

Education is a highly efficient force which leaves a deep imprint on us. It is responsible for shaping the citizen from his formative years. You might not have forgotten the fuss which has lately been pervading the educational establishment and the national councils around the issue of 'the Egyptian human-being' and the reforming of his personality, but has this been translated into educational action in our schools? In our heritage we have the healthy seeds which can help provide a decent form of education and which can be used to mould a youngster into the model demanded by our times, and for that we need to inculcate in our youth a love of the homeland, the veneration of work, a love of science and knowledge, a passion for discovery and invention and an openness toward other beliefs and religions. It is fortuitous that we can use our fount of religion and enlightened religious thought with its sounds, texts and faithful historical reports to help and motivate this shaping of our youth. How wonderful when the requirements of the religious and the mundane come together, when thought, science, the work ethos and the other foundations of modern civilisation become religious duties and steer people towards guidance and piety, when the believer can be a symbol of the renewal of civilisation with his religion neither holding him back nor causing him to deviate from his lofty humanistic aims. Religion can be the symbol of the decent working man with an honest conscience who writes what he wants to write, who loves those who agree and collaborate with him just as he should love and collaborate with those who disagree with him provided this is based on mutual respect and within the framework of human rights. We can state that the effects of education are not seen overnight, but they stay implanted and become passed on to the next generations.

21 January 1982

The Forbidden Opposition

In this new era the opposition is entering a period of political life from which, we hope, there will emerge some real support for democracy and human rights, as well as serious participation in reinforcing political education, as befits a state seeking peace and prosperity, good governance, social justice and unity. And talk of legitimate opposition leads me to talk of the unconstitutional opposition, that is those political movements whose right to exist on the political map has not been recognised and who, as a result, can neither form themselves into a party nor carry out any political activity. I am not going to discuss their unconstitutionality, but I would like to state that this situation will not change the reality by an iota. Ignoring the current circumstances will not make it go away and these political movements exist whether we like it nor not. However, would it not be useful for us, at this stage of our democratic experiment, to differentiate between practice and theory? Practice can be prevented, but theory cannot, and should not, be prevented. Theory should not be subjected to positive law but should be discussed and corroborated by the laws of philosophy itself to stop it from sliding unnoticed into practice. More than that, we are liable to reject any theory, even if some of its details do not seem devoid of merit – an example of this being how we might reject Marxism, but this does not mean that we should not give any thought to it as we review how the public sector operates. We might reject the notion of a religious party being formed, but that should not prevent us from finding some merit in the religious way of thinking when it comes to solving problems facing education and the economy. For that reason, I would suggest co-opting the best thinkers of the extra-constitutional movements onto some of our national councils, since these councils are think-tanks whose modus operandi is far removed from propaganda, rabble-rousing or any sort of influence by the masses. Ideas will converge from various sources reflecting all angles and perspectives, deriving strength and enthusiasm from opposing points of view, and enabling any given topic to be subjected to scrutiny. We should become accustomed to holding discussions under the banner of the intellect and logic, and become used to some give and take, to agreement and disagreement, in a nationalist atmosphere and in the full light of day.

21 January 1982

Behaviour Appropriate for Our Lives

During this period of our life, and this is a harsh period of transition, every active domain is subject to being re-created. We are building up our essential industries and overhauling our traditional industries, we are marching into the desert to conquer it with water and cover it with green, we are renewing the old infrastructure, and even more than that our ambition is to reconstruct the national character on new foundations and to anchor our institutions on real democratic and socialist supports. Last but not least, we are endeavouring to cleanse the principles of our religion from distorting accretions. It is a life characterised by the serious and requiring effort and care. Consequently, this requires us to behave accordingly, on the one hand falling in with the seriousness of modern life, and on the other according respect to national inclusion. From time to time the matter requires us to look again at fixed wages and prices, just as those with large incomes need to channel their excess funds into productivity rather than consumerism, and we must give our support to the public sector and free it of any impediments which hold it back. It also requires us to stop dealing in unethical and extravagantly expensive super-luxury items and holding ostentatious parties[1] which are out of kilter with people's needs and conditions. In a nutshell we need to show restraint in the way we act and think, in order to dedicate ourselves to work, to moderation in our entertainments and to frugality in our life needs. That is how we will prove that we have reached a level of responsibility and awareness regarding the demands of this era, that this is something inspired by our conscience, and that we have no further need for government oversight or further legislation.

27 January 1982

---

1 This is a reference to wedding parties held in luxury hotels amid great displays of wealth and ostentation.

The Debt Fund

Our debts have piled up so much that they have now peaked at eight billion Egyptian pounds according to the latest newspaper reports. Indebtedness has almost become such a general phenomenon that our age is one of space travel and debt. All the developing countries take out loans and amass debts and Europe only recovered from its post-war slump with the help of loans and subventions and it has continued borrowing until today, with some countries borrowing from the Arab oil-producing states. There is nothing wrong with taking out a loan when the need arises, providing that it is spent on real aspects of development, that it is translated into permanent productive capacity and that the resultant profits are spent on services and on servicing the loans themselves. Now as we are trying to reform our economy, the nation's parliamentarians must provide accurate figures about our indebtedness and the aid we receive so that they can come up with a method of investing the funds and sensibly applying the results of this form of investment, so that they can, with some sense of confidence reassure the people that there is an urgent need for us to shoulder this burden of servicing the debts, and that this should be done with all due diligence, without any creeping apathy, neglect or bending of the rules. Perhaps we should establish a special national debt fund to supervise all this, to check what the funds are being spent on, to make sure debt repayments are hedged from the general budget in order to avoid any obfuscation of loans and income so as to avoid any discrepancy between the deficit and savings and so that the man in street will know where he stands and consequently what is demanded of him. Then we can all safely emerge from this bottleneck and kick-start our development.

28 January 1982

The Return of Administrative Control

Administrative control will come back one day soon. I will never forget what I wrote one day suggesting the broadening of accountability specialisations as an efficient tool for bringing about efficiency, and then that very same week I was surprised to see administrative control and other similar accountability tools in the field being held up as an example of how to oversee, detect and rationalise an administration, and as a tool for uncovering the extent of apathy, neglect, mistakes and bad practices. The need for administrative control grows especially great during times of crises during which values are brittle, during which people are tested by temptations of one kind or another, and consequently the general good is subjected to many trials. The return of administrative control could be a sign of a revival of interest in efficiency long after the very concept appears to have almost vanished into such oblivion that I can only detect its traces in the operations of the one ministry, the Ministry of the Interior, in its daily assiduity to control the traffic and to establish a public relations centre in every police station, thereby giving the Ministry some new character and publicising the creation of some sort of civil relationship between the security forces and citizens. After the return of administrative control, the best thing would be for a station to be established in every ministry, to monitor discipline from close up, to take on the complaints of the public, to lighten the burden of the ordinary man or woman whom circumstances ineluctably drive to having dealings with government offices and who has to negotiate their way through enormous bureaucratic hurdles for no practical reason whatsoever. For this reason, those who carry out administrative control must be granted immunity, authority and the powers to carry out their duty in a manner which is satisfying to both God and man.

10 February 1982

The Democracy of Labour

Today the public sector is taking on appropriate powers within the framework of the economic question. Not being a specialist, I am not going to embark on a diagnosis of the causes or come up with high-falutin economic methods of treatment. I would prefer to speak about the philosophy of labour in the sector, for that is what will hold true for all the political, social and cultural sectors which are drawing up plans and aiming to achieve success. I would say that labour in these sectors needs to progress as one robust front. It is not enough for the leadership to set out a plan. It must not meet only with the executive, administrative or clerical workers, but also with those in menial jobs. The leadership must present each plan, with all its political aspects and targets, for general discussion and listen to all and every, and opposing, opinion. It must be ready to take on board various amendments so that everyone feels that this is their plan and that they are responsible for carrying it out whatever their position. The sector must designate a location for the receipt of proposals. It must study every proposal and recompense the person who has made it if it leads towards greater discipline in work, a reduction in costs or an increase in output.

The sector must also designate some of its staff to study the activity of similar sectors abroad in order to discover leading-edge technology, work out how to integrate this into the appropriate sector, and study useful methods for mastering the domestic market and penetrating new markets.

This is how labour will be able to have a firm democratic and cooperative basis – by inviting workers to think continuously about creative innovation and by inspiring feelings of brotherhood, respect and motivation.

11 February 1982

Opposition Newspapers

These are heady days for those who wish to follow the various examples of opinions which are flooding our society. Alongside the daily newspapers, and *May*, the organ of the National Democratic Party, opposition voices are enthusiastically, diligently and subjectively reported in *al-Ahrar, al-Shaab* and *al-Ahali* newspapers. Moreover the nationalist press and *May* are not devoid of opposing views, which points to a general desire to investigate truths and discover paths to doing the right thing. Perhaps one day we will triumph over all other opinions and emerge from our state of duality and confusion and finally become a society in which things can be freely debated. On this occasion I should like to state how I have noticed that the press refrains from presenting articles by the opposition except in the culture page in *al-Ahali*, and I really fear that over time we will become sick of articles that generally deal with the same old, or almost the same old, topics. Hence it occurs to me to suggest that the press should devote some pages every week to literature, theatre, the cinema, radio, television and the short story, not just so that they can cover new artistic and cultural fields, but also because the party, or any party, is no more than a singular and integrated vision that encompasses politics, the economy, religion, women, literature and art. For that reason, the pages I have suggested should not just reprint what appears in other newspapers, but provide sounding boards for different and perhaps contradictory opinions which can add richness and variety to the opposition. These can both illustrate their approaches to matters with various examples on the one hand, and on the other they can imbue our culture with a new spirit.

17 February 1992

Lessons from Deceased Leaders

Thinking about the future starts in the present and extends into the past. The past, present and future are a continuous and indivisible trajectory. For that reason, we cannot avoid speaking about our leaders of yore as their positive and negative effects on our lives are long-lasting and we have to deal with this in one way or another. This naturally leads us to assessing their imprint on us and as objective or high-minded as we might be, we cannot be devoid of the confessional or party overtones which assail our thinking.

That is why a complete and just assessment of any leader can only come about after his era has passed. At that time, the whirlwinds will have calmed down, the dust will have settled on their image, and it will have become easier for us to see them for what they were and how history has depicted them. We, people in the contemporary world, have to make as much effort as we can in an endeavour to head towards what is good for us and for our nation, and if we are successful in this we might come up with lessons which are of use to our present and our future. I am not free from the blurring of history which I have just referred to, but I believe that many people agree with me when it comes to an appreciation of what we have inherited from the past in terms of values such as freedom and social justice, and in terms of achievements such as the Egyptianisation of the economy and the means of production as well as reforms to the class structure. In order to benefit from a re-examination of the past, we need to remember how we stumbled towards defeats which were then officially denied,[1] how we suffered from financial, human and territorial losses, and how we saw our beautiful country deteriorate into a pile of ruins with overflowing sewers. We teetered towards these defeats because we did not cut our coat according to our cloth, we were so intoxicated with the image of our own greatness, we were so obsessed with leading revolutions and liberating other nations that we abandoned our own people

1 This would appear to be a reference to the 1967 war with Israel when the Egyptian state media proclaimed success after success.

to wallow in illiteracy, nakedness, hunger and disease. We started our blessed revolution at almost the same time as the Chinese revolution but the Chinese concentrated on domestic matters whereas we took on the problems of the whole world, and just look at where China is today and where we are. That is what I hope we can benefit from when we look at the past and remember our leaders. The final assessment of any individual figure will take place at the right time and not before.

25 February 1982

How Should We Deal with Deviation?

Since time immemorial the world has overflowed with a myriad ways of thinking. These include reactionary thoughts, which concern a paradise lost in the past. There are also the futurists who concentrate on the near and distant future. There are the moderates who take something from all eras. We have the wise people who base their thinking on development and personal opinion, and the extremists who believe in guns and firepower. These are all such common or garden ways of thinking that even children learn about them at school.

Some people may think that believing in one of these ideas comes as a result of careful study or academic comparison, and I cannot deny that that is sometimes the case with some students. However, in my opinion, we generally incline towards one type of thought or another according to our psychological and emotional state, which itself is the result of an accumulation of social, economic, cultural and political factors.

When we incline towards balance, harmony and psychological and social well-being, our choices also lean towards constructive and humanistic thoughts. When we lean, or when the circumstances make us lean, towards fear, oppression and hatred, our choices incline towards deviant thoughts and brutal visions. For that reason, many of those who follow trends of thought have little faith in them and lack the patience to discuss them, so why do they keep opting for one of the two extremes?

This should be taken into consideration by those who attempt to treat political deviation through debate. I do not intend to diminish the value of debate and education; I am trying to say that a patient should be treated with medicine, and holistically through fighting the infection, and not just with the medical theory of an illness.

18 March 1982

The People of the Cave Wake Up

One day western civilisation took us by surprise as we were sleeping in the cave and we fell into a state of confusion from which we have not yet woken up. In response reactions sprang up which crystallised over time and which are still being fought over: one reaction, blinded by the daylight which showed up just how backward we had become, fundamentally rejected our present and our past and called for the setting up of a new edifice based on the science, endeavour and the values of the West. A branch of that trend eventually embraced Marxist thought and believed in its revolutionary creative destruction.

A second reaction was to bolt when confronted by the daylight, and, out of a visceral fear for traditions and heritage, was to turn in on oneself, clinging on to a glorious past and virtuous ancestors and fighting everything that was new. A branch of that trend eventually went on to become a form of extremism which deemed all those who opposed it infidels and engaged in a violent and bloody struggle against them.

There was a middle reaction which took the most enduring and useful from their own history and from modern civilisation it took those things which it could plant in its own soil. Incredibly, years passed but the three forms of reaction continue to be discussed and the same questions continue being posed, as if we are stuck in a vicious circle. We continue to anguish over rebirth or being stuck in a rut, and whenever we take a step forwards we take a step backwards, mind – I do not say two steps. I lay the responsibility for all our hesitancy and the resultant catastrophes at the feet of this middle reaction and that is because this middle approach, which has taken over the governance of the country since our cultural rebirth came about, and had the opportunity to push the nation onto the path of progress and the power to include extremists of both sides and thereby mitigate their attraction. However it[1] did not prove itself fit for purpose and despite its undeni-

1 Mahfouz appears reticent here to use the word 'government' and although he hedges his criticism in terms of 'the middle way', it is clear that he is launching a stinging attack on the ineffectiveness of the government to deal with social issues.

able reforms it became unavoidably taken up with side issues, with overweening ambition, and has so crumbled in the face of corruption and injustice that it has almost come to an impasse. We can only hope today that it has become aware of its historic role and can recognise its mistakes and rash decisions and determines to adhere to what is right and proper. Is that how it will be able to bring about the legitimate right of the nation to a dignified life and to avoid the woes of extremism?

1 April 1982

A Small Nation in a World of Giants

In this world where great giants clash against each other, what is left for the small nations to ensure themselves a decent life worthy of humanity? The giants monopolise power, authority, resources, weapons and numbers, while the small nations have to fumble their way along with caution and trepidation. They cannot experience any form of cultural rebirth if they do not have good relations with this or that superpower – for they are the ones lending the funds for developments which include food as well as the armaments a small nation needs to defend itself. They lend the funds for the technology needed for development and progress, as the small nations go on dreaming of unadulterated and meaningful independence and of some of the human rights which stability brings for its people. The small nations cannot suddenly become large, or suddenly find untold treasures within their land. The small nations cannot also put up a barrier to the stream of thought, beliefs or innovation which flow in and have the potential to harm the heritage, traditions and will of the small nations. What can they do to make the most of themselves, to keep their distinctive character and aim for the freedom which allows them to determine their own future in a sentient and enlightened manner? The truth is that the small nations can control two important elements of development, those of their own character and education. By their own character I mean the type of education which focuses on the best contemporary and historical principles and values of a country which have made that country a model for humanity characterised by decency and forgiveness, a country loved by its people who love it in return, a country in which people respect each other and co-exist peaceably. By education I mean the scholarship and research that helps transform a country from the receptive to the participatory and giving stage. That is how a small nation can build up a cultural and material leadership disproportionate to its size and declare its indispensability to the world and vice versa. The small nation has a role, just as the superpowers do, for it is made up of individuals who can act and think and is not just a marketplace for commodities.

8 April 1982

The Task of the Centre

I have previously blamed the centre for the obstacles and prevarication in our national rebirth while recognising the progress it has brought to the country. I also demanded that the centre should take a more alert stance with regard to labour, and I now return to the subject in order to throw some light on the role required for wide-ranging plans. This is a difficult task given the diametrically opposed visions that are set to become a tradition in our firmly grounded culture. In order for the centre's leadership to succeed, it must reconcile these opposing visions – an attempt condemned in stinging terms by the extremists. The centre must reconcile Egyptian patriotism with Arab nationalism. It must reconcile individual and social freedom. It must reconcile Islam with the age we live in. In all circumstances it must preserve our national unity as the foundation of our existence and the benchmark for reconciliation. It is a difficult task, as I have said, but it is an inescapable fate. It is only with the help of the centre that we will achieve political stability and dissuade people from violence and bloodshed. Our patriotism has been the very essence of our character over the course of history. Arabism has been our heritage, calling and destiny. Freedom is the greatest thing a person can possess, and social justice is the basis of property. Islam is the religion of people and our national heritage. As for the age we live in, it is one of unbridled science and civilisation. For all the difficulties inherent in realising our task, its fulfilment is possible if we evince sufficient resolve and dedication, if we think more about the long term, and if we can bring ourselves to be less negative. It is also possible to succeed if we take the masses as our inspiration and if we understand our rightful role as a small nation in the new world of giants.

15 April 1982

Withdrawal Celebrations

I have been fated to celebrate the withdrawal of occupying troops four times in my life: the first time was on the occasion of the Anglo-Egyptian treaty of 1936, and despite this taking place twenty years too late I was more delighted that I had ever been at anything else, because this came about after years of suffering and struggle, after the sacrifice of thousands of people, and after we had almost become convinced of the impossibility of getting Britain to withdraw from the land of Egypt. Hence we should revive the memory of the greatest popular leaders in the life of our nation since its unification under the Pharaoh Mina, Saad Zaghloul[1] and Mustafa el-Nahhas.[2]

The second time was the day that the English[3] actually withdrew from the Canal Zone as a result of the struggle of the revolutionaries of July 1952, and was one of the miracles of the early years of their revolution. Hence we should keep alive the memory of Gamal Abd al-Nasser, may he rest in peace and may God forgive him any sins he may have committed.

The third time was when the three armies evacuated our territory in the aftermath of the tri-partite aggression[4] thanks to the position taken by the United States and the Soviet Union, the steadfastness of the people and the tenacity of its leader.

Then we come to the fourth and latest withdrawal which I hope will take place on time and which will remove the last political traces of that black day, 5 June 1967.[5] We should be reminded to set up an academy in memory of the hero of the withdrawal, Anwar Sadat, who thought, planned and set out using all the strength, bravery and faith he

---

1 (1859–1927), revolutionary and statesman.

2 (1879–1965), five times prime minister and one of the founders of the Arab League.

3 Although he says the English, it is clear that he means 'the British'.

4 The 1956 invasion by the forces of Israel, Britain and France, an incident known in the West as the Suez Crisis.

5 The date of Israel's surprise attack on Egypt and the beginning of what is known in the West as the 6-Day War.

possessed, and created the propitious atmosphere for his army to fulfil the heroic role it has been known for in all periods of our history,[6] and our prayers for his soul[7] should unite those who loved and hated him, and those who supported and opposed him. There is no Egyptian with any other opinion regarding the day of the withdrawal and I imagine Sadat now in the proximity of his God, still preaching to his opponents and repeating the words of the poet:[8]

'I do not bear any ancient hatred towards them,
for the president of the nation is not one to bear hatred.
Although they ate my flesh, I saved theirs,
And though they destroyed my glory, I built glory for them.'

22 April 1982

---

6 Here Mahfouz is speaking about Sadat's success in the October War of 1973 which put an end to the much-vaunted notion of Israeli invincibility.

7 He was assassinated on 6 October 1981.

8 The poet is Abu Yusuf Ya'qub ibn Ishaq al-Sabbah al-Kindi (801–73), known as the father of Arabic philosophy. Mahfouz has changed a few of the words, such as the substitution of the phrase 'the most noble of the nation' by 'the president of the nation'.

After the Withdrawal

The evacuation of Israeli occupying forces from Sinai has taken place on time. Some opponents of Camp David[1] insisted that this would not take place, just as they insist on every occasion that Israel is a warmongering and expansionist state and that it only speaks of peace as a form of manoeuvring. However facts on the ground have proved that Israel has stuck by its obligations and that despite its sacred and historical memories it has evacuated Sinai out of a desire to achieve some peaceful coexistence with one of its neighbours. Perhaps the Arab trend which has recently become convinced of the inevitability of a peaceful solution to the Palestinian problem will become stronger and more motivated, and perhaps the other side will review their position, so that both sides of the dispute might be able to meet at the negotiating table and come to some agreement over a reasonable solution which will restore their usurped rights to the Palestinians and provide the Israelis with security. This will staunch the squandering of Arab capability on rearming and will enable economic and cultural integration before too long. Egypt and Israel must move forward with their economic and cultural cooperation at full throttle, and without any attempt to exploit or control, so that their cooperation can become a good example of human cooperation and an encouraging paradigm for the Arab nations to imitate. They will then realise that the Israelis are also flesh and blood and they have their component elements of good and bad, and that they are not, as some prejudiced people constantly trumpet, the root of all evil, greed and bad intentions – as if they were created from a different clay from the rest of mankind. Indeed, peace is just as much a burden as war, and needs just as much wisdom, courage, faith and insightful politics.

29 April 1982

---

1 The Camp David Accords signed by Anwar Sadat and Israeli Prime Minister Menachem Begin on 17 September 1978.

The Army of War and Peace

Field Marshall Muhammad Abd al-Halim Abu Ghazala,[1] the minister of defence, announced that the ministry has completed the preparation of an integrated plan to exploit the period of mobilisation to train new generations of workers and technicians, and that it is within the capability of the armed forces to provide around 100,000 workers annually to various fields while at the same time eradicating the illiteracy of these workers. This is a praiseworthy and highly beneficial initiative, full of perceptiveness and wise vision which is being carried out for the purpose of mobilisation in the prevailing conditions during which the country is struggling for its existence and progress. Thanks to this, mobilisation has become an act of service for the citizen and not just something for the defence of the homeland. It has also become something which can be used during peacetime in our effort to develop and build up the country.

The announcement of this plan is the embodiment of the new spirit we hoped for which not only combines words and deeds but which has been preceded by action and words, and we learn from this announcement that the Ministry has indeed finished its studies and that the plan will be carried out this year starting from 1 July and will then continue without having any adverse effects on the armed forces' intake of new recruits. We should not be beset by any doubt regarding the success of the plan; based on what we know about the army's ability to show discipline, preparedness and execution, on what unites reality and dream, planning and execution both today and tomorrow, I can only hope that this will be followed by an amendment to the mobilisation law, whereby those suitable for service and training will be accepted alongside those deemed fit for fighting so that this new sort of mobilisation becomes a one-year national duty for war and for peace with exemptions only for those unfit to serve. It is truly a praiseworthy and highly beneficial initiative.

2 May 1982

---

1 Minister of defence, 1981–9.

On the Issue of Change

A half-hearted debate is going on around the issue of change. Among the things the supporters of change are saying is that it is unfeasible for us to wait for any substantive improvement in the quality of those officials who have put up with corruption and who consequently bear its stamp. In truth, I am one of the first to have called for change, by which I mean a change in the law, in our methods and in the way we treat things as well as a review of the constitution itself. I continue to be aware that the prevailing spirit of political behaviour has gone beyond the constitution and the law and has already reached a higher level of democracy inasmuch as the change I am calling for is for legislation to be updated in order to accord with a realistic way of handling issues. We should endeavour to remove from their posts all those of ill repute, and when it comes to those who have put up with corruption, not a single one should be exculpated – right down to the ordinary citizen, unless he has openly expressed his opposition and people like that are few and far between. In addition, attempting to change people is something which usually undermines the stability required for commercial continuity and for attracting capital both at home and abroad. Perhaps it would be better from the point of view of democratic culture if we postpone change until the people have had their decisive say in the forthcoming general election. What will be, will be according to the will of the people alone, and it will be so out of respect for the will of the people as the source of authority. This will also establish in the conscience of officials that they are answerable, first and foremost, to the people, that public opinion will be their judge and that they will be rewarded according to their work. We should also perhaps demand that the opposition parties, in addition to their recognised efforts in opposing the government, should also concentrate on a plan. That is our supreme aim at this time. By setting out and critiquing a plan of action, by carrying out field research and coming up with suggestions to improve it, such a plan will be the central pivot for opposition activity as a form of working responsibly within the state.

5 May 1982

On the Egypt of Tomorrow Conference

This conference is taking place in order for us to come up with an image of tomorrow's Egypt and to examine the main issues the country will face, such as the housing crisis, democracy and social justice. It has become clear to us that these are the questions of the hour, of the day and of the near future as an extension of today, as opposed to the title of the conference which refers to the Egypt of tomorrow, to that Egypt which has been the remote aim of successive generations. All of these and similar issues are topics of never-ending study in many countries who all agree about the problems but whose solutions differ according to the basic philosophy underpinning each society. In the West, democracy means something different from the East, and the same applies to social justice. Hence it is clear to us that philosophies differ from problems, and that solutions differ according to varying philosophies. If we simply adhere to the vision and principles contained in the constitution, we would first have to amend the title of the conference in order to avoid ambiguity, so that the new conference can be more than a run-of-the-mill economics conference that has been convened, this time, to deal with any and all of our current problems.

If what is really intended is to discuss the Egypt of tomorrow, the conference will need to restrict its deliberations to general principles which can serve as a basis of discussion for a whole variety of issues. Perhaps the best opportunity the Egypt of Tomorrow conference can offer is a discussion of the constitution itself and the laws derived from it in recent years, such as the Party and Media Law amongst other things.

Some people may be of the opinion that it is not the right time for such a discussion, but we ought to remember that the Egypt of Tomorrow conference is an unavoidably late opportunity for us to set the system on *terra firma* after it has been through so many vicissitudes.

6 May 1982

When Will Change Begin?

During a meeting the president held with members of the National Democratic Party, an important discussion took place regarding our problems and their solutions. I am saying nothing new if I point out that we heard some fine words – for we have become accustomed to hearing fine words, but this time they were uttered by a man wary of unguarded speech and of words disconnected from fact. This allowed him a welcome opportunity to underline the sort of hopes held by people and included, in the meeting of 23 March, some words spoken about the constitution and the need to put off amending it until such time as we can agree on a foundation for our economic structure, when we can stand on our own two feet. I cannot deny that putting off such amendments represents a form of prudence, provided the purpose is to be able to garner the mobilised strength to establish an economic foundation. However, I believe that we can start preparing a new constitutional format, or at least review the laws which have caused so many differences of opinion, without touching upon the energy that has been wasted on the economy, and I also believe that we can form a committee of experts who can undertake a calm and considered study, and who can finish their work at the appropriate time without detracting from the importance of any other reforms. Moreover, these reforms should generally come about as an acknowledgment of the reality we live in, for it is of note that our lives ought to progress in the spirit hoped for by the constitution and the laws derived from it. Change is necessary in order to make legislation conform with its application and so that new modes of behaviour find their roots within the constitution and legislation. It is incontrovertible that change will provide support for some aspects of democracy, social justice and spiritual values which will provide new reasons for us to encourage the forces of creativity, innovation and self-discipline, and to come up with a new force to push forward the raft of comprehensive development in all its economic, social and cultural aspects.

13 May 1982

Political Activity as the Harbinger of Good

It has been reported in some newspapers that the National Democratic Party is preparing a simplified summary of its programme to be distributed as widely as possible among citizens. The Party would also do well to prepare a simplified summary of its principles – not only so that it can be grasped by the public, but also so that it will stick in their memory. Among the things which may hit the mark and help the public to realise the Party's message is that it should allow these two summaries to be discussed in as broad a manner as possible, particularly in its youth associations so that they can get a feel for them and have them anchored in their consciousness as a vivid experience of positivity and participation in political activity and as an experience which obviates their sense of negativity and emptiness. It is of great importance for us to concentrate particularly on the youth, because a party which has no youth has no future, notwithstanding any broad popular base it may have. A feeling of emptiness is the most dangerous disease to have afflicted a significant number of our youth and this has resulted in a section of them falling into the grip of apathy and another group being attracted to murky political trends with all the concomitant educational and material losses from which society suffers in terms of its spirit, cohesion and development. It is unarguable that a party that enjoys a majority and thereby wields power must be held responsible for this sense of emptiness whenever and wherever it is to be found. This points to shortcomings in its methods of providing public information and its systems of mass education, as well as to a deficiency in the way it connects with the man in the street, deals with his issues, pays attention to his hopes and carries out a conversation with him about things that concern him and the state. The role of the majority party in political life is a risky one. It should represent a basic popular fundament and it should be a beacon of guidance and awareness and a locus of social inclusivity and not restrict its activity to state institutions or election campaigns. Hence, perhaps the preparation of a simplified summary can provide a fillip to ongoing and socially-conscious party activity.

27 May 1982

The Bitter Truth

The bitter truth is that the responsibility for what has befallen the Palestinians and their cause is due to what happens to the Arabs themselves, and that any issue is solved to the benefit of one of the disputing parties by force or to the benefit of both the parties by negotiation. The Arabs have plunged into wars which have brought upon them enormous losses and proved – due to international and local circumstances – to any rational person the ineffectiveness of war. But the Arabs have persisted, in the name of solidarity and resistance, in a state of no war no peace which is a permanent drain on their forces and funds. Thanks to Sadat, Egypt has exited from that predicament, offering an example to others of a strong awareness of reality while being subjected to a stream of accusations without any other way forwards being offered. The Arabs have not stopped at that but have included side disputes in their ineffective political discussions which have torn them limb from limb, such as the tension between Morocco and Algeria, between Tunisia and Libya and between Syria and Iraq. To top it off, war has recently flared up between Iraq and Iran, and all of this has turned Arabism, once a hope for unification and unity, into a symbol of disintegration and loss. In so doing the Arabs have given their enemy the opportunity to solve the Palestinian issue in their own manner and according to their own vision, while the Arab states outdo each other in trying to uncover Israeli-American conspiracies, with many of them forgetting that the states who profess solidarity and resistance have dropped their support for the Palestinian cause. The bitter truth is that the only conspiracy is an Arab conspiracy which the Arabs have cooked up against themselves. There only remains one hope, and that is that they are capable of coping with the consequences.

24 June 1982

Towards a New Five-Year Plan

This month we will see the launch of a new budget which will open the new season of the five-year plan in which we will place our hopes and upon which its success is based. It is perhaps the first budget to have been preceded by wide-ranging feasibility studies which have taken in a wide range of opinions and views and which has been set in motion by a new philosophy for a new era the essence of which is reform, self-criticism and the avoidance of past errors. The budget's recommendations and guidelines will be sent out to the specialised government agencies to be translated into legislation and numbers. It will then need to be put into action on a day to day basis, with the responsibility for distancing us from the things we have been complaining about and bringing us closer to what we have hoped for. At that time, we will have some idea of what the increase in productivity will be, what support will be given to the public and private production sectors, how it will guide consumerism and increase investment and savings, how it will strengthen nationalism and the country's development, how it will support our personal values and character, and how it will make legislation conform with the interests of the masses. All of this, I hope, will be accompanied by activity from the political parties in their interaction with the grassroots, by attracting our youth to the essential pivots of a sense of belonging and commitment and through a campaign in all forms of mass media in support of spiritual, nationalist and cultural values. All those with something to offer should be invited to have a free and democratic debate. So let us take a firm first step on the long path which demands of us to give the best that we have and which will reward those who make the most effort.

1 July 1982

An Ongoing Period of Trial... and a New Dawn

This is a period of trial of far-reaching harshness which causes the greatest sorrow and grief, but the lesson we should learn is not to discard our experience and not to hold the outcome of discussions to ransom. This period of trial has not only uncovered many defects in the infrastructure of the Arabs which were actually almost impossible to discern, but it has also uncovered the steadfastness of the Palestinian guerrilla, his noble spirit and his perseverance in holding onto his rights until death. It has also highlighted Egyptian political wisdom in terms of the country's pragmatic approach and Egypt's laying down of the first foundation for a just peace in the Sadat era. We do not wish to see this era of trial pass by without it having produced some positive results from which we can profit in a future beset with risks. We may be able to turn defeat into a form of victory.

1. The Arabs who are still hesitant to declare their faith in Egyptian policy should establish, along with Egypt, a unitary and fraternal approach which would be the basis of a new Arab association, even if it does not include every Arab state.
2. This new Arab association should agree with the Palestinians upon an approach to a realistic and feasible vision for the solution of their problem.
3. The way Arab funds are invested should be revisited with a focus on the Arab states and Arab economic integration, as this has the potential to reimburse the Arabs for what they have lost politically and militarily.
4. The Arab peoples should be liberated from lies and authoritarianism so that they can control their own fates in such a way as they choose.

If we could bring about these results, in the near future when we recall today's Arab predicament, we will say:

'It was a bloody trial which caused sorrow and grief, but from its dark places a new dawn emerged.'

8 July 1982

The July Revolution

The July Revolution was a political experience brim-full of deeds and lessons. It comprised unforgettable positive as well as negative elements which should also not be forgotten. It brought about independence. It pioneered the republican system, brought an end to the unjust and unethical class system so beloved by the oppressors. It brought about further industrialisation, enshrined the right to education and work, stoked the fire of Arabism, struggled against global colonialism, among other factors which can only be seen by examining the statistics. The Revolution has also produced an authoritarian and oppressive state that has experienced bitter failures. It has squandered funds, destroyed human dignity and has witnessed corruption, dissolution, destruction, ruination and debt. History has not yet had the final word. That moment is yet to come. However, what should concern us as people who have lived through these times is that we draw upon our experience of the Revolution and come up with lessons for both today and the future. Thus, for example, we can say that we see no benefit or security in a form of governance in which the people do not take pride of place. It follows that building up the interior of the country should take up most of our efforts, so that it can sit on a firm foundation of civilisation and progress, and that our external policy should be shaped in such a manner that it affords opportunities for more jobs at home even at the cost of some people's aspirations for ever greater power and our determination to achieve the desired superiority in culture and science. It follows that we should believe that what we are doing is not for the sake of the system or development, but that the system and development are there for sake of humanity. It also follows that human rights should not be restricted to food, clothing and shelter, but should also include freedom, dignity, justice, equality and all the other declared rights. Finally it is better for the people to fight their own struggle against backwardness, even if they falter over the long term, than to remain on the side-line as onlookers even if they are showered with countless benefits. Whatever the case may be, a mistake will not remain a mistake if we are aware of what caused it and if we can learn from that. I send greetings to the heroes of revolutions – to those who have passed away and to those who are carrying on the struggle!

22 July 1982

Ramadan – Should It Be Serious or Fun?

It has been said of the Ramadan programmes[1] that they are over-serious. Perhaps some people's expectations have been disappointed with regard to how they felt in years gone by. I do not believe that blame should be levelled against those responsible for the programming. They actually deserve our support and encouragement so that they can create new tastes in viewing and respond to the public's openness to a higher level of scheduling. It is unarguable that satisfying all of the people all of the time is an impossibility. There are some people who vociferously demand that the broadcast media should be completely devoted to edifying programming and then there are others who think that the output should be entirely light entertainment. It would help if media executives could try and stop keyholing every programme as 'serious' or 'light entertainment'. This categorisation encourages the presentation of serious matters in a dry and alienating manner, and has led to light entertainment programmes being generally rather trite. Actually any topic can be made into a programme, and its contents might be deeply serious, but that should not stop the programme being made in a manner attractive to the eye and interesting to the ear. In the normal course of events, the media offer much of this type of programming, and I am not exaggerating when I say that I find some serious programmes to be no less entertaining than the best drama series. If we can try and avoid categorising programmes as serious viewing or light entertainment this will lead to an increase in programmes on serious subjects but will have no repercussions on the light entertainment side of things. While acknowledging that there are indeed cases in which the two cannot be combined, I should like to conclude here by congratulating the media executives for their ongoing and sincere efforts in the service of our noble people.

29 July 1982

---

1 The month of Ramadan in the Muslim world sees a plethora of specially made television programmes and serials.

Who Are We?

Who are we? This is a question we should often ask ourselves in a year whose culmination will see a general election. The answer will reveal the ambiguities and the confusion our political lives suffer from in confronting the truth, two factors which expose us to repression and its psychological consequences. A glance at the current situation shows that the following trends pulse through the heart of our nation:

1. A democratic-socialist trend. The forerunner of this trend appeared in a section of the Wafd Party just before the July Revolution. It then crystallised and expanded in successive phases along with the Revolution. Today its supporters are spread among the National Democratic Party, the Labour Party, the Nasserites and the Wafd.
2. A religious trend which emerged at the end of the 1920s. Today it is divided into extremist, moderate and modernising factions.
3. A liberal trend which believes in traditional democracy and economic freedom.
4. A Marxist trend whose roots go back to the 1919 revolution and is characterised by its clear aims and means and has a small number of supporters.

Our political map needs to be reshaped to conform with observed reality and its principles, paying no heed to personal differences or historic circumstances, thereby allowing us to breathe healthy air from both sides – the personal and the social. It might not be the right moment to revisit the constitution to make sure that it can confront current challenges, and perhaps those who feel deprived of constitutional legitimacy can do nothing other than dissimulate and join other parties.

In saying all this, I only wish to remind people of the reality of things, for 'the reminder benefits the believers'.[1]

4 August 1982

---

1 Qur'an, 51:55.

Ten People Who Have Not Received Any Good News

Whenever the honours season comes around there are many names I do not find among the nominees. The many nominating institutions operate on a high level of knowledge and expertise, but they ignore those names year after year, even though they are really big names whose achievements constitute national treasures, people who have been accorded every recognition throughout the Arab world and beyond, but for some strange reason their names are obstinately never proposed here.

It is as if educated public opinion is no longer astonished or dismayed by anything, as if they have been overcome with idleness and inertia, or resigned themselves philosophically to the dreary routine of their lives, no longer willing to fight for their values as these fade away and become no more than a will-o'-wisp.

We can do no more than wait patiently until the murk clears and the sun shines through again.

Should you not wonder, along with me, about the absence of those names? Should you not share my grief and sorrow? There are only ten or so of them, but my arithmetic is not always the most accurate. Let me just mention the great thinkers Abdel Rahman Badawi and Louis Awad, and the great literary innovators Yusuf Idris and Fathy Ghanem. What particular obscure secret of existence has prevented them from being nominated until this day?

I understand that many irritations bedevil our cultural life, and it takes time to treat and heal them all, but honouring those who deserve to be honoured for their academic achievements is not a problem and should not be one either.

6 August 1982

The Youth Also Have a Literary Problem

While the youth have their problems which are being discussed today in all the state institutions, young writers have their own particular problems which should not be overlooked or ignored. Perhaps the core problem is: how do we discover the talent? How do we get them the appropriate recognition? And how do we assure them their rightful place?

It has been said that a young writer must wend his own way along the stony path using the power of his faith and will, and that the hardships along the way are part of his or her necessary education and natural selection. However, we have to remember that the world of art is today overflowing with thousands of people working away on short stories, novels, plays and poetry in contrast to the scores of people who were doing that at the turn of the century. We have to bear in mind the difficulties of getting published which have been exacerbated by the economic crisis.

I have a suggestion in this regard, which I put forward years ago and which I am not ashamed to raise again – that it may be of some use to form a national committee made up of specialist university teachers with the co-opting of two representatives from the ministries of culture and education, whose aim should be to examine and assess the literary output submitted to them by as yet undiscovered literary talents, or by writers who have not managed to get their works published systematically. The committee should select those works worth publishing and the two ministries should use the manpower at their disposal in the various forms of the print media to have these works published, i.e. in a magazine if it is a short story, or in book form if it is a novel, to get it into in a theatre's repertoire if it is a play, or prepare it for broadcast on the radio or television. The committee members should take on the task of promoting these works by preparing introductions to printed books, by writing articles in magazines, or speaking about them on panel shows in cultural programmes.

I believe that this proposal would save many talents from getting lost and would create a level playing field for artists in the capital and from the provinces.

12 August 1982

The Role of Culture in Our Rebirth

We have recently witnessed a general mobilisation for a green revolution with the aim of increasing foodstuffs for the people, and we have been and still are subjected to another mobilisation in order to confront our economic problems and find solutions for them. We also notice comprehensive and profound interest in our external policy and defence matters, and we praise those who have brought this about and we hope for the best in preparing for a better tomorrow. However, when I compare that groundswell of interest with the passing interest which culture garners, I feel that it, i.e culture, has not been given its due rights in terms of vital support or been accorded its active role in society. People generally think that we are doing the right thing in strengthening the foundations of our cultural infrastructure, that the issue is one of priorities, that culture has not been put on the back burner and that its time will come sooner or later.

However, culture is not a spiritual luxury to be put off, nor does culture signify that period of putting your feet up after a hard day's work to spoil the senses and refresh oneself. In reality culture has within it inherent meanings and implications, information, colours and melodies whose varied elements create our human spirit, intelligence and insight as well as affecting what we think and our attitude towards the world. In other words, culture is at the forefront of those components which build up the human personality with all its peculiarities and attributes. In the final analysis a citizen is nothing more than a combination of instinct and acculturation.

In researching our economic and political problems, we may arrive at fair solutions, but what is the value of these solutions if carrying them out and working with them does not lead to improving the lot of the citizen. In our recent past great institutions have been set up and have then fallen prey to negativity, indifference, neglect and sloth. Therefore, we should pay attention to human endeavour and to the fruits of human spirit and character, along with, or before, directing our attention to buildings and institutions. By this, I do not mean just hearing fancy words about culture, but I want these words to be translated into action and verbal promises into funding so that we can celebrate the efforts expended in these fields of endeavour and be sure that any edifice will be constructed on a really firm foundation – which is that of the engaged and cultured citizen.

19 August 1982

The Egyptian Path and the Age of Productivity

Were we to search for an appropriate name for this age, it would be the age of productivity as it is the pillar of our existence, our hope of salvation, and the object of both our dreams and reality. It is no surprise that the National Democratic Party has prioritised productivity and marshalled its forces to that end in this delicate stage of our development in order to bring about the greatest service it can perform for our country in this peace-time battle. Consequently, I have thought about those factors which motivate a person to give all he can to his work. This vital question arises as a result of what we hear about all the inaction and apathy that have affected our resolve and tarnished our traditional reputation for patience, perseverance and fine workmanship. So what are the factors that drive a person to work hard?

1. He is motivated by receiving increased wages for increased productivity and this is generally referred to as the wage-productivity quotient.
2. He is spurred on by his individual conscience, if his education has taught him to do his duty and see it as a moral and religious value that can be applied to all stages of his education as well as to all stages of his life.
3. Work may be sacrosanct in his conscience and his commitment to others, but this conscientiousness does not stem from education alone. It comes from a feeling of responsibility towards others, but this feeling in turn comes about by participating positively in the sort of life which can only come about in a true, democratic environment.
4. Work may also be sacrosanct by dint of its consecration of values, and this flourishes in an atmosphere dominated by seriousness and sincerity which offers a good example for every situation.

26 August 1982

The Egyptian Way… and National Mobilisation?

Let us go back to the question of productivity as a matter of life and dignity, a principle that should be instilled in every citizen – particularly following the president's latest speech. The matter is one of extreme seriousness and requires all the effort, faith and devotion we have and more! To that end, there should be a call for comprehensive national mobilisation in which every individual does his duty whether his politics are pro-, anti- or neutral. To that end, we should also reconsider organising classes to ensure this is done properly while conforming to social and psychological well-being. I do not believe I am overstepping the mark if I articulate my following requests:

Firstly: we need to eradicate the scourge of corruption and those who participate in it. We have been closely following the news of laudable action in this area in the hope that this will reach the point where the air becomes cleansed of its impurities and people will regain confidence in themselves, in others, and in our values. Work will again be set on a noble pedestal as a cherished and holy value and as the only method for gaining respect and promotion.

Secondly: the great National Democratic Party should open its arms to incorporate the Labour, Liberal, and Wafd parties, and overcome any obstacles throughout the path, since those parties represent the middle line, the line of socialist democracy, which was founded in the spirit of religion and tolerance, and of national unity. The resulting critique will be a form of self-criticism, and not intellectual casuistry. Such inclusivity will presage a broad popular base willing to make even greater efforts at home and abroad.

Thirdly: we should recognise that there is a real opposition, whether it is represented by the religious or Marxists trends, in order to gain a true picture of things as they are. We should pass legislation so that these movements can come out into the open and take part in the political debate, and to use their education, knowledge and expertise as part of the national effort.

These wishes of mine can be carried out even without the need to effect any precipitous change in our institutions or civil servants. I believe that hearts and minds are more important than positions or authority.

2 September 1982

The Arab Way

The Arabs are going through a period of trial and are facing a destructive challenge. This is an uncomfortable and painful state, but it is not the worst when set against the trials the Arabs have undergone in both their distant and recent past. We can recall the trial we faced from the Mongols in the distant past or the trial we faced from imperialism in the recent past. We can also recall how the Arabs pulled together in face of these two trials and overcame them, springing back to life in both cases with a new flourishing of their culture. But these cases called for a reworking of how the Arabs saw themselves and their vision of life in order to carry themselves forward and achieve self-determination. They concluded on:

1. The need to free themselves from their local overlords just as they freed themselves from foreign overlords, and to bear responsibility for their own fate. You might call this a return to the principle of consultative rule or the adoption of the principle of democracy, but what concerns me is the content and not what it is called.
2. The belief that the assets of their country are a common right, for each according to his need and for each according to his effort with compassion for those incapable of working. You might call this Islamic inclusivity, social justice or socialism, but what concerns me is the content and not what it is called.
3. The need to revive the memory of a past glory when their domains were the abode of the intellect and knowledge, of the opening of new vistas and human rights which protected members of various religions with the minority communities enjoying a feeling of security. You might call this Islamic tolerance or a new spirit of civilisation, but what concerns me is the content and not what it is called.
4. The need to invest their excess funds in their own countries and turn their disjointedness into an integrated cross-cultural economic union capable of participating in the modern age.

> You might call that Arab-Islamic brotherhood, or politico-economic sagacity, but what concerns me is the content and not what it is called.

The Arabs should do that, and they should do it without hesitation or prevarication, or they can carry on without peace and God will appoint better people than them to look after the earth.

9 September 1982

How Can We Confront Life?

It is self-evident that life goes on changing continuously, and every day brings something new to the way we think, live and conduct our social relationships. The very first stages of our education prepare us to face life, but this is often based on a changing perception of reality and this consideration may make us lose sight of some beneficial elements and may overlook some factors which are still in a developmental stage and in need of some imaginative thinking to publicise them. Hence the way we adapt to our lives is constantly subject to a stream of difficulties accompanied by anxiety and obstacles. For that reason, education must equip us, in a stable and reassuring manner, with the capability to face new problems and to find solutions for them, or in other words, education must be like a friendly guardian challenging the unknown in order to develop within us the capacity to create and innovate.

This power is the real basis for development and progress, and for that reason we must encourage it in any way and endeavour to create the right climate for freedom to thrive.

This creative force has to cope with two negative factors which can be clearly seen throughout the course of history. The first includes revanchism which sometimes takes the form of laws which hamper freedom of thought as well blind tradition which threatens those who attempt to think freely with oppression or ridicule. The second negative factor is the belief of some nations who, as a reaction to an emergency, think that they possess within their culture all the solutions to the problems of today and tomorrow, and hence rely upon their memory rather than on their creative and innovative strengths, and end up slumped in stasis and inertia. Let us be aware of both of these negative points. Let us open our hearts to everything new, not because everything new is better, but as starting points for debate with the possibility that they may be worth putting into action based on rational, scientific and experiential evidence. In saying this it is evident that I am not calling for our heritage to be thrown into the dustbin, for that is as naïve as imparting divine infallibility to it, but I am calling for us to be able to think freely about how we face life and how we can overcome our intellectual and emotional laziness, for in the end only the right solution will work.

16 September 1982

The Value of an Individual and Civilisation

The value of an individual is represented by the human rights he enjoys – a benchmark which can be used to judge a civilisation. Even totalitarian systems, which are based upon unlimited power – which claim to be exerting their unlimited power in order to achieve more and overcome entrenched obstacles more quickly – claim that their final aim is the dignity and welfare of the individual. The history of civilisation is a continuous chain whose every link should protect the rights of the individual and give some recognition to his value. The rights of the individual are many and include, by way of example, equality in the face of the law, safety and security, freedom of belief, thought and work, education and culture, self-fulfilment, the election and accountability of leaders, and the citizen's right to health services, communications and public hygiene. Last but not least is the citizen's right to fair treatment by the authorities. The salient point here is not that the general laws should include this or that right but that they should be applied both in the private and the public domains. The real point is that the wording of the law in this regard should go beyond wishful thinking and become the *sine qua non* of our inherited customs and traditions and the law should be carried out with good faith and without undue delay. What could be better than taking a good look at our circumstances from time to time in order to see what progress our civilisation is making? What needs reforming? What needs renewing? What needs reshaping? We need to do all of this in order to make sure that we can make serious and calm progress and avoid unwelcome surprises.

30 September 1982

Democracy and the Ethics of Leadership

It is a generally accepted truth that every individual has ineradicable points of weakness. There is also some truth behind the words 'pride goes before a fall'. However, people view the high and mighty in a special way, demanding perfection from them and holding them accountable in matters for which they would forgive the man in the street. That is because the high and mighty of the land are supposed to provide an example for others, on the one hand, and on the other hand we generally recognise them for the great feats they have accomplished and we never imagine that they might behave in a way that jars with their wonderful accomplishments. Reality can disturb that image and engender a violent emotional reaction.

We can allow people to have a weak point, if its consequences play out on them, but how can we cope with a weak point that affects the message of the leader himself, that underplays it and even deviates from its purposes? In a case like that it is no consolation for us to dwell on the truths about the weakness of human nature when the matter concerns the fate of everyone and may have ramifications that last for generations. It is for this reason that the democratic method of governance shows that it provides protection from innumerable evils that arise when a dictator, even a just dictator as some people dream about, applies his talents to the benefit to his people, developing, changing and building, while at the same time torturing them. A dictator is given to making countless mistakes out of anger or when in the throes of a tantrum, destroying what he has spent a lifetime building up and hence bringing everything toppling down around him. A democratic leader places his talents in the service of his nation where freedom, the opposition and public opinion are all safe from his evil inclinations or other undemocratic scourges. The situations and conditions we have lived through have taught us valuable lessons. We have been sorely tested but perhaps this has all convinced us, on all levels, of the wisdom of democracy as the ultimate means of salvation.

7 October 1982

Indifference... and Performance

By 'performance' I mean the development projects which have been translated into reality and which are the tangible results so long hoped for by conscientious nationalists and people of forbearance and insight and which remain the foremost dream of Egypt for the year 2000. No doubt there are some projects which have been completed here and there, but these are only given scant mention in the media or are conflated with promises and they become lost in the plethora of political and security events due to the fact that they only have some effect on those who benefit from them directly. In addition to that, our economic crisis will not be overcome in a day and it will require a comprehensive awareness of its dimensions and no small amount of patience in order for dawn to appear on our horizon. For that reason, regular updates must be issued regarding projects completed in the various fields. These should be honest and forthright so that we can know with ringing clarity what has actually taken place with regard to reforming agriculture and irrigation, food security and bringing our industry up to date, as well as any steps taken toward turning consumerism and the import of consumer goods around into productivity and export, what steps have been taken to fix prices and battle inflation, how educational reform can be brought about, what is being done to save culture and spiritual values and whether we have started dealing with the negative impact of the Aswan High Dam. We need to monitor these issues regularly. Four months of this year of stabilisation have already passed and the sort of information suggested above should be published so that the citizen can feel that the caravan is actually lurching forward, that the darkness is being dissipated, and that a new step has been taken along the path of peace. At that point our national conscience will be salved, people of patience will find that they are capable of being a little more patient, and a fresh wind of hope will drive away the clouds of indifference.

11 November 1982

Indifference... and the Army

All the suggested solutions for curing the plague of indifference need time for discussion to convince people. They then will need extra time to carry them out, so how can we face this reality and the work necessary in terms of manpower, motivation and continuity which cannot stop for a moment under any circumstances? It is certain that we need a quick stop-gap fix so that we can gain control of the situation in all its dimensions. That is where the army comes in, and fortunately the army became aware of the need for it to take on this task before anyone had to call on it. It has participated in industrial output and the management of the workforce, its working practices are a by-word for self-discipline, precision and integrity as its own operations are based on discipline, good management and seriousness and its intolerance of apathy and slackness. What we require of the army in these times is only an expansion of its activities into the general work sector, to keep us to the national development plan and to make sure that it is carried out within the allotted period as a support to the nation in its difficult times and in order to lighten the burden on the masses. I feel here that I should restate a suggestion I made in these pages a few months ago, which is that mobilisation should be a general duty with exemptions only for those totally incapacitated, so that an excellent division can receive the appropriate training for battle while the rest are made fit for life in terms of their health, education and literacy so that they undertake a specific period of public service in fields which have a lack of manpower or which have been struck by apathy and are then returned to civilian life to continue their work in the private or the public sector as need dictates. In this manner we will have two armies: an army of defence whose aim is well known, and an army of commitment for the purpose of strengthening our infrastructure during this rough period of our lives.

25 November 1982

Social Justice

Social justice is a process society is committed to providing for its people regardless of their colour, belief or rank. Its ultimate aim is to offer people their rights, without which their humanity cannot be realised. It includes things such as shelter, health, education, culture, labour, safety and security, freedom of opinion and belief, and other human freedoms, in an atmosphere of equality and equal opportunity. Even if society in any of its developmental stages is unable to guarantee one right or another, or to provide them all to the same degree, the basis of this process must be untrammelled justice in all cases. Perhaps the greatest enemy of this form of justice is nepotism, whether tribal, familial, class-based, financial or religious. In a just society there must be equality of opportunity and the arena should be open to those with talent and appropriate education, so that every individual can occupy a position for which his capabilities and mental and moral faculties qualify him – without bias or discrimination. Good, hard work may make some people legitimately wealthy and they may enjoy a lifestyle that is beyond the reach of others, but they should not use their money as a means of exploiting others, of doing harm to them, or withholding any of their rights. Because of this, social justice can only come about under the following conditions:

Firstly: in a democracy, as the guarantor of legal, political and personal rights.

Secondly: the state must protect the have-nots from the haves. It must guarantee the provision of vital services and foster an atmosphere conducive to creativity and innovation.

Thirdly: there must be sound planning for the use of labour and productivity so that society enjoys equality of satisfaction and not equality of need.

These conditions represent the minimum necessary for a society to be described as a humane society and one with human values.

2 December 1982

The Real Criminal

Corruption is a social phenomenon which does not spring out of nowhere and which is committed behind the scenes. As soon as the law becomes aware of it, it determines its hiding place and metes out punishment. However, if the law itself is flawed, if it is weak or ineffective, or if it falls from its natural place which is above everyone, corruption breaks out of its constrains like a beast that cannot be held back or deterred, and nothing makes the law more ineffective than having to operate in the penumbra of unchecked individual rule or dictatorship. The moment an individual takes on unlimited authority, he himself becomes the sole law and there is no law other than his name. Thereafter there is no value to the ruler's good intentions or to his declared respect for the law or his obligation toward justice, and the reality of the situation confirms that in the end the law is hostage to his behaviour. It is respected when he is satisfied with it and violated when it goes against him. Citizens live in reality subject to his mercy and not in the shadow of sanctified law which spreads its wings over everyone, including the ruler himself. As a result of that, those who deem themselves above the law find unlimited temptation stretching out in front of them and they are so sorely tested that rarely does anyone escape the perils. If they respond to the temptation they fall hook, line and sinker, and corruption in their hands becomes a state within a state even if the ruler is innocent of what they do. Perhaps they are victims just as much as they are criminals. In a nutshell they are the poisonous and bitter fruit of the ruler's monstrous regime which we call individual rule or dictatorship. And today the law has got hold of a number of these accused victims – even though the regime itself should have been put on trial before its victims. I hope that we can draw a lesson from our tragedies and that we can convince ourselves that the time has now come to take another look at our laws; that we can find a way to plug the loopholes which provide an opening for rigging the will of the nation or for appropriating the nation's legitimate right to be the source of all authority and the guardian thereof.

9 December 1982

Your Voting Slip

This month every year every citizen over the age of eighteen may place his name in the electoral register as the preliminary step in practising one of his important political rights, which is the right to vote. Voting is a right but at the same time it is a national duty by which citizens choose their representatives and leaders, and complacency in doing so is a slight on the whole nation's commitment and represents a deficiency in our political education and a disregard for the will of the people when necessity calls upon it to make its choice. What we hope for, from the authorities, is to make it easier for students to register and to simplify the complicated and exhausting paperwork necessary. We should also keep registration open throughout the year so that any student, who for one reason or another, has missed the appointed month, can still register. I would demand that the authorities institute a public relations campaign urging citizens to register, explaining out the procedures they need to complete, and informing them where they can do so. I do not think that I have to advise the political parties on their duty in this regard, or tell them what persuasive measures they ought to take to get their youth members to register. Without this crucial first step there is really no point to the practice of politics.

My proposal is that a voting slip should be like a tax receipt for companies and it should be distributed to everyone who sits their final school examination or is accepted for a job, among other options. It may be a form of justice for society to ignore those who ignore it, and to shun those who shun it.

12 December 1982

The Giza Drain Told Me…

The Giza drain burst[1] says many things that I hope will be heard.

1. This reminds me of the stupidity which transpired in the past when we intervened in some weighty matters and which made us ignore the simplest and foremost of the duties which represent the very fundamentals of any civilisation, when we beat the drums of hollow glory and forgot about the sewers, the electricity, telephones and illiteracy, and so, from today, we should no longer concentrate on the living room and ignore the staircase which is about to give way, for a house cannot be a house without a staircase, but it can still be a house without a living room.
2. This reminds us of the streets which are flooded with drain-water from time to time and incessantly, and of the people who live in the mosques, in the cemeteries and in tents now that accommodation is so unaffordable, so how is it that we have become so accepting and even blasé about this? Would we also accept the situation if the same things happened to society's elite as happened with the Giza drain?
3. This reminds us how capable we are of achieving things if we are well-intentioned and determined. The truth is that all the concern of officials, the work organisation, the sheer dedication to carrying out their duty night and day, exposing themselves to mortal risk in the process – all of this represents an enormous and unbelievable amount of effort, and this has us unfortunately asking ourselves: Where has all this steel been hiding in the public sector? Why have we seen so little of them and ourselves become mired down in apathy, listlessness and sloth? Why have the people responsible for such a man-power

1 *New Scientist*, 15 April 1989, 38: 'In December 1982, a steel main… burst in Giza on the west bank [of the Nile], flooding housing and making residents furious. Only 17 days of concerted efforts quelled the chaos.'

treasure been so reticent to reveal their existence or set them to good use for the country and the people? Should we not remove any obstacle that obstructs their path or demeans their wonderful value?

4. Finally, I congratulate the governor of Giza for his uprightness, dedication and concern. Actually I already wanted to congratulate him, as a resident of his governorate, as it is only in his era that there is no part of Giza through which I travel that does not make me realise that cleanliness is not just a word in the dictionary.

23 December 1982

The Other Side of the Moon

There are some positive aspects of our lives which I would like to point out, not because they need to be recalled amid the flood of negative criticism, but because these positive aspects are deserving of attention and should be highlighted whenever we take a look at a proposal or new policy:

1. First and foremost of these positive aspects is our move towards social justice, which is the best opportunity provided for the grassroots by the July Revolution and whose beneficial outcomes include the public sector, free education and a welfare system.
2. Movement towards democracy. At the start this met with some delay, and we have paid an extortionate price for that. This factor was picked up again by the Corrective Revolution of 15 May 1971, went through a crisis, and was subsequently restarted. I would declare here that the country will not benefit from the respect it has enjoyed until recently unless it can be said that we are a nation in which democracy as practised is perceived to be based on laws, and we must revisit our laws so that legislation is in conformity with things as they actually are.
3. The peace, which we have snatched from under the cover of hardened political complications and which has allowed us to expend our greatest efforts in improving our situation and driving our fate forward, is something we must look after and turn into the basis for a policy from which we should not diverge unless the disadvantages of following it outweigh the benefits.
4. The uncontrolled opening up of the economy which almost destroyed us before it was directed towards productivity, as it should have been. It is perhaps a laughing and a crying matter at one and the same time that any nation should suffer as we have from a deficiency in our budget and in state services, and not a penny should be spent on matters for which there is no convincing need.

5. Union with Sudan. This is the start of a new life which promises better and stronger progress for the valley of the Nile. Not one day should pass without this alliance being supported.
6. Last but not least, the tangible desire to found our cultural rebirth on a basis that takes an ethical pride in technology, and which makes visible efforts to rid us of corruption.

These are just some of the issues and I would like us to keep them in mind and not stray from them.

30 December 1982

Signs of a New Age

What was published some time ago about the development of arms and armaments is worth noting, not just because of the arms trade's value in defence, but because these developments were described as great scientific achievements in this era when we are trying as much as possible to absorb modern science and transform it from the purely theoretical to a stage of innovation and implementation. Previously we had also read in the press about the peak in rice and corn production and the role played by Egyptian expertise in bringing this about. Amongst other things we also read about the adoption of a plan by the Academy of Scientific Research to prioritise its scientific research activities with the aim of eventually increasing and developing national production. Hence, we are entering a new era – the era of reliance upon science and its local, comprehensive and systematic application to the challenges of life. This is a new era of self-reliance in scientific activity at a time when the humanity is being ranked according to his scientific superiority and achievements. In this field of endeavour, a nation does not gain status through its size, nor is its importance adversely affected by its small size. A nation does not progress by dint of its financial reserves and nor is it held back by its lack of them, but it occupies that stage of existence which matches its scientific superiority and achievement. Science is progress, leadership and strength, and a wise nation is one which knows and works with this truth and which grants its scientists the requisite funding, services and appreciation. That is the magic of the modern age which brings time and place together to create wealth and affluence, which brings about leadership in its most noble manifestation and which values scientific methods as the most successful means of discovering the truths of the world in which we live. So why should a nation with an eternal heritage not put this into practice and build a towering edifice supported by its immutable human values?

2 January 1983

Good Tidings

The spirit of democracy can be discerned in our behaviour and general manners. Not only can it be realised in laws, institutions and the practice of political rights but it is also underscored by laws and institutions. It stays above the surface for a while, while it is whittled away at by the traditions of a dying age which are as remote as possible from real democracy. Those who follow the course of life these days cannot help but notice signs of real democracy characterised by spontaneity and sincerity which deserve to be mentioned as good tidings of a better future. Top of the list is freeing ourselves from politicians and their meetings with the president with all the ensuing high and mighty noble sentiment, and instead recognising the small group of men, deserving of recognition and admiration, in these modern times of our history – people who have done their best through self-sacrifice and hard work. This should be accompanied by what the president said in his speech about reinstating those journalists who had been dismissed. This would go beyond simply setting things aright. It would represent the declaration of a new approach to thinking and would enshrine this approach with respect in the life of the nation, no matter what the political trend or current. We might hear something like this from the university professors who were dismissed in order to calm opinion-makers, and that could represent an opening into a new cultural life and a home-grown intellectual rebirth. I would like to see repeated something similar to what the Governor of Giza has done in setting aside one day a week to hold a surgery where he can hear his constituents' problems in person and find solutions within the dictates of justice, thereby setting a good example of devotion, self-discipline and democracy. These are signs of a new life which we hope will grow and take firm root in order to open up new horizons towards a better future.

6 January 1983

Studies of the National Councils

I was happy to read a notice in a newspaper about some newly published works which include studies by the specialist national councils. I hope other works will follow and that all the studies will be published, covering a multitude of aspects of activity in our lives, such as national production and agriculture, manufacturing, teaching, education, culture, youth and manpower. In order for these to create a strategy for dealing with the future they must be based on the needs, study and criticism of our current situation, must offer a comprehensive vision of the present and the future and should be written by expert members of the academic community backed up with experience, knowledge and science. As such these publications can serve as a resource and guide for the researcher and the good citizen who is working for the betterment of his country in general. They are lamps lighting the way for the youth, calling upon them to study the concerns of their country, to take on their national duty and preparing them to take on this responsibility at the start of their working life. I would call upon the official in charge of nurturing our youth to distribute these publications as part of his job, allowing the material to be duly examined and debated so that it can play the appropriate role in the formation of our youth's character. I would also suggest that the Ministry of Education should commission a book including selections of these studies and publish it at no cost to the reader so that it can be one of the resources used when deciding which development activities to establish. No book in the national curriculum will be better than this book in terms of its influence on education and character building. We hope that all the proposals covered by these focused studies will be put into action in order to build up a national and humanistic culture founded on a firm base and combining material and modern elements with refined spiritual values.

13 January 1983

Welcoming the New Masses

These days a general complaint has been voiced about the failure of the stage and the cinema. If you were to ask the people who work in these two areas of the media for the reason, they would tell you at great length about the fickleness of the public now that their material conditions, having passed through a long historical period of poverty, have improved in leaps and bounds thanks to the present economic conditions. The truth is that there have always been bifurcations in every art form. For example, there is art theatre and popular theatre, so along with the Ramsis and Fatma Rushdi theatres there are the popular theatres of Rawd al-Farag.[1] The same is true when it comes to singing which can be either of a classical or popular style. There are also good films and bad films. The new element here is the retrenchment of serious art which has suffered greatly from the economic crisis. The sense of equilibrium has been so disturbed that some people believe that this new phenomenon has taken over the entire artistic world.

The matter seen as a whole does not call for unbridled pessimism, for it is not completely lacking in positive aspects. We must again improve the conditions of those who strive to present good performances and we must thank the beneficial prevailing circumstances for that – for those people actually represent the multitude of our people for whom we have been trying to achieve a better life. Their connection with the theatre and the cinema – no matter how slow artistic improvement is in manifesting itself – is another positive phenomenon as they do display some artistic sensitivity, and it is thanks to them that plays run for years at a time, and films for months. The improvement in their material circumstances will bring with it an education and cultural improvement in the next generation of our children. They will grow up with the theatre and cinema as part of their family traditions and will hence support a more refined form of artistic endeavour in the near

1 This area [of Cairo] had its own collection of music halls and theatres. Danielson, *'The Voice of Egypt': Umm Kulthum, the Arabic Song, and Egyptian Society in the Twentieth Century*, p. 43

future. We must not therefore criticise them too heavily for their artistic endeavour is still in the developmental stage and is bound to improve.

The first responsibility of those angry playwrights is to study the taste of the masses – not so that they can pander to them unconditionally but in order to create a new style which can reconcile a playwright's serious thought with the innate tastes of the masses and perhaps that is the desired form of art at this stage of our social development.

20 January 1983

Making Donations to Pay Off Our Debts

I started a campaign to urge citizens to make a donation toward paying off our debts. This obviously came about as a result of some pertinent national reflection on the current thinking regarding the serious challenges which require us all to pull together and do our very best. However, this may seem like a call to the people to participate in an unprecedented type of duty, whereas it is the people themselves who undertake every great and small achievements in the public domain. It is the people who are the producers, it is they who do the work, it is they who provide the funding by dint of their labour, and it is also they who hand over their money in the form various taxes. Donations are things given willingly as opposed to a non-negotiable demand imposed on people.

Before we start to think about donations, we must be absolutely sure that the workforce is not being wasted, that their time is being correctly used, and that sloth is being fought against.

Before we start to think about contributions, we must make certain that everyone who is eligible is brought under the jurisdiction of the tax authority, so that no one can evade it or claim ignorance of its regulations. We need to do this comprehensively. Thereafter, we will be able to call for people to make donations as an extra charitable action, and as a real response to a call for the sort of mass action which has characterised us for centuries.

This is a praiseworthy call for action, but we demand that it should be preceded by a programme to establish proper working practices and to oblige those under-performers to do their duty on the one hand, but on the other hand no matter how much is donated it will only be a drop in the ocean of debt. Thus, it would perhaps be better for the call to action to be directed to industry which is dedicated to supporting economic development, and they could set aside some of their profits to pay off the national debts as one of the essential services they provide to the individual and to society.

Perhaps the best area in which these funds could be exploited is that of Egyptian-Sudanese integration.[1]

27 January 1983

1 *New York Times*, 12 October 1982: President Hosni Mubarak of Egypt and President Gaafar al-Nimeiry of the Sudan signed an accord today aimed at consolidating economic, foreign and military policies.

The Minister and the Opposition

Before the revolution, a minister was first and foremost a man of politics who could spend his time devoted to general politics, parliamentary activity and confronting the opposition in parliament, in the press and on the street. He could limit his ministerial duties to shaping policy along party lines. When it came to creative work within the ministry, that was the speciality of the civil servant, the person who studied the regulations, carried them out, followed them up and supervised their implementation. The situation changed completely after the revolution when a minister became the foremost creative worker in his ministry and any new plan was subject to his interest or capabilities. He had to spend all his time doing this at the expense of undertaking new initiatives. If he did have some time left over, he would have to draw on the remnants of his nervous energy, and this may be one of the reasons for the limited capacity of the opposition and their tendency to help, rather than undermine, the minister in his work, even though the opposition's aims went beyond that in many cases. This method of working describes the nature of the first stage of the July Revolution, the inclusive phase. However, the means changed and a new democratic direction was established. This has been restated to the current president and we must take another look at how a minister deals with things in accordance with a democratic spirit and how he fulfils this spirit's new demands without driving himself to a state of nervous exhaustion and debilitation. Perhaps, and I am making this suggestion for the third time, we should designate a creative civil servant to oversee the five-year plan and associated matters, someone who can share the workload with the minister and take on the weighty tasks of implementation and follow-up, someone upon whom we can rely continually to further the plan notwithstanding all the extra focus and hard work our general lives are subjected to. That way we will be able to preserve freedom of political practice, continuity in productivity and steady progress.

9 February 1983

When Will We Learn the Value of Time?

It seems that the Arabs do not wish to take any new step before the Israeli withdrawal from Lebanon is completed, or at least before there is an agreement for the Israelis to withdraw. There is some justification for this policy, and it is characterised by wisdom and logic, as withdrawing from Lebanon would be some sort of sign on the part of Israel that it wishes to find a solution for the problem and put the lie to suspicions of its expansionist greed, to say nothing of the fact that for us it would pave a serious path towards stability in a brotherly country[1] which would reflect the positive and the negative that takes place there in the whole Arab region. However just doing nothing and paying no attention to the time element could mean the loss of an opportunity which will not return any time soon but will expose the region to tension which can only make matters worse.

Total reliance on the United States may have negative and disappointing effects, and I think that even the most optimistic moderates are feeling some disappointment in this field. We must be self-reliant while waiting for some American movement as well as using this as a means for urging America into action. If it is the intention of the Arabs to enter into negotiations with Israel, they should at least pave the way for that by acknowledging as much, and perhaps that could be not only the positive grounds for the success of the current negotiations in Lebanon to bring about the desired withdrawal, but entering into the long-awaited negotiations also has in front of it obstacles in the path of the current negotiations, and those obstacles, such as normalisation and security, stem essentially from the status quo of no war and no peace between the Arabs and Israel. There is a great need for some resolute movement to deal with this situation, and we have lost so many lives and so much money due to unrealistic sloganeering that

---

1 In the language of pan-Arabism, other Arab countries are often referred to as *'shaqīq'*, or half-brothers, indicating their shared culture and heritage.

the bitter truth has been revealed about the shameful stance of the extremists on the war between the massively strong Israeli army and a handful of heroic *fedayeen*. It is not enough for us to learn from events, or just to discover the right path eventually. We have to follow it without hesitation.

10 February 1983

A Relative, Not an Absolute, Majority

Ibrahim Shoukry[1] has put forward a proposal to parliament for a law concerning elections for the Consultative Council based on a relative, and not an absolute, majority. I hope that parliament will study the proposal as something demanded by every citizen who believes in democracy and in the right of the people to elect its members of parliament and rulers. I hope that it will become the source of de facto and de jure authority, and I believe that there is no space here for the sort of horse-trading which may induce some parliamentarians to reject the proposal as the brainchild of the opposition. The conditions of our lives have already brought about a climate of debate between the government and the opposition on many matters, such as the fight against corruption, a focus on productivity, and a not insignificant aspect of foreign policy. This latest proposal is a rational and just demand which we hope will not divide opinion but will ensure that every citizen's vote is respected and effective. It will make parliamentary representation just in a way that cannot be realised under any other system of election, in addition to giving the minority parties of any size their rightful weight, particularly because the minorities can easily be overlooked in Egypt by virtue of the homogeneity of the populace, their cultural identity and unending participation in things both good and bad. I sincerely hope that the suggestion will be crowned with the approval of the parliament and that it will be a first step in breaking down restrictions, abolishing emergency laws, bringing the leadership out of seclusion and ushering in a new era of complete freedom.

24 February 1983

---

1 In 1978, Ibrahim Shoukry resigned as minister of agriculture to found the Socialist Labour Party. He was elected to parliament in 1978, 1984 and 1987.

Signs of the Value of the Individual

The way an individual is treated in a nation is a good benchmark for measuring the quotient of its democracy, or, if you prefer, of its humanity, or even its ethics and religiosity. A country may lag behind in the right of an individual in one stage or other of its development, not because it wishes to ignore this but because of a budgetary shortfall with the result that it cannot find a way to offer education and culture to all its citizens, provide sufficient means of transport, housing for every family or establish the necessary number of parks and museums. But what is the excuse for neglecting the way a citizen is treated, whether out on the street or in one of the ministries, or for not protecting the welfare of pedestrians, for not dealing with the potholes which endanger the safety of drivers, for leaving electricity junction boxes wide open with the risk of electrocuting anyone who might touch them, for the endless bureaucracy that plagues business owners, and so on and so forth with all the things that we witness or hear about, and from which we, from time to time, have the bad luck to suffer.

Of course we should not imagine that the state apparatus enjoys torturing, grinding down or attempting to ruin the populace. The only way to explain what is going on is that the value of the individual is considered negligible. He cannot receive the respect, consideration and kind treatment he deserves, whether as a citizen or as a human being honoured by God. Perhaps what has led to complacency in this matter is that the privileges of the 'elite' mean that they enjoy a certain level of protection from harm, which, were this to change, would subject them overnight to the same sort of treatment as meted out to the ordinary citizen. We, in the complaints department of the ministry had a hope of putting an end to this outrageous situation, but where did this get us? This hope seems to have started out with a burst of enthusiasm only to fade away again in its infancy. However, we consider elevating the value of the individual both a necessary and indispensable endeavour, and something that should not get lost among the daily routine of paper shuffling, but should rather lead to immediate action and the requisite investigation should punish those who deserve to be punished. In a situation like this we only need one achievement, particularly if it is publicised in all the necessary public relations machinery. In doing so, we will no longer have to stand with our arms folded in the face of ignorance, apathy or mistreatment.

30 February 1983

What Does Israel Mean?

Many Arabs believe that Israel is made up of a gang of extremist, racist colonialists, that there is no hope of ever achieving peaceful coexistence with them, and that if they are forced into peace at some time they will use it as a transient or subjective plan which they can carry out by various means in order to realise their dream of exploiting and subjugating the whole area, forcing it to remain in the abyss of backwardness for ever and a day. They also believe that if there arises inside Israel some opposition to the policy of violence and if members of this opposition call for peace, this is no more than some form of cheap theatricals or deal and that in the final analysis they have the same aim as the others. Even the investigations carried out by the Kahan Commission of Enquiry[1] and its damning conclusions are not actually proof of any real democracy, they are not part of any ethnical or moral conscience, and are just another act of the play, or another round of the game. They believe that the report's conclusions are a comment on current Arab policy and on Arab political analysts. It should be added that this opinion is not accepted by everyone, and at the very least those who strive to establish a just peace in the region, and those who are prepared to join in with the peace-makers at the right moment, do not believe this. Moreover, the leader of the Palestinian militants has not accepted this as far as I can see, all the while he has agreed to hold discussions with some leaders of the Israeli opposition whom he has found to be acceptable partners for discussion. Perhaps this is the peaceful vision required by human cohesion as evidenced by history. The least that can be said about the Palestinian militant leader is that he should be allowed to give it a try, even if just one time, after the repeated bitter experience of war. In this situation we must encourage opposition groups and give them credibility rather than trying to

1 Kahan Commission, formally known as the Commission of Inquiry into the Events at the Refugee Camps in Beirut, was established by the Israeli government on 28 September 1982, to investigate the Sabra and Shatila massacre (16–18 September 1982).

show them up as tricksters and plotters. Perhaps the experiment will eventually bring about a comprehensive and just peace. We, who have embarked so ill-equipped on a series of wars, we should not fear the burden of peace, its ramifications or challenges.

3 March 1983

The Message of the Conference

Today let us take a serious look at the conference of the Non-Aligned Movement.[1] They are discussing some subjects of interest to us as citizens of this problem-ridden East, and some which interest us as people who are part of a world beset with problems that are no less serious or significant. The conference might agree with us on a point of view, and might issue helpful recommendations, but what is the practical value of these recommendations if resolutions from the summit hall vanish into the thin air?

There is however at least one area in which the conference, if they can agree upon it, can change the state of the world and open up a route towards a better future, and that is if it manages to find solutions to the disputes which are tearing apart many third world countries, and if it manages to convince them that in trying to resolve their multilayered problems they should not resort to war. Nothing is as destructive for the poor world as war. It is war that destroys the souls of its young men, it depletes much of its financial resources and plunges it into debt. We should remember that the two superpowers who avoid confrontation with each other out of fear for the gravity of the consequences actually push others towards 'traditional' warfare by which they both attempt to carry out their policies in the knowledge that they are safe from the consequences of direct warfare. They wage a series of proxy wars among the poor and the weak of this world which drain their population, hamper their development and rebirth, and push them towards spheres of influence in terms of money and security. This is no more than a dirty game into whose snares we fall. We die out of fear of death, and we fall into poverty out of fear of poverty. And out of fear of military defeat we fall into a permanent moral defeat of our own choosing. If the conference succeeds in saving the poor from the spectre of war, it will save them from the knot of evil, and will push the two superpowers to take on the direct responsibility of confronting their own fate without an intermediary. Incessant war damages

1 Held in New Delhi, 7–12 March 1983.

the people who wage it, but comprehensive peace is of benefit to the whole world.

10 March 1983

A Return to the Discussion of Debts

This is a sad topic. Debts themselves are a predicament from which third world nations, and many developed nations, are not safe. We accept that they are an inescapable necessity and that wise policy must invest these loans in projects which are of benefit to the people. It has often been said that our debts piled up during the era of economic liberalisation and that the war in Yemen, the 5 June[1] war or other wars had nothing to do with this. Among those who hold this opinion is the great Ahmad Baha' al-Din,[2] as he wrote in one of his diaries. I find him to be of sound and trustworthy opinion, but I would ask him how much of our money have the Yemen war, the 5 June war and other wars, eaten up? And did the five-year development plan not come to a standstill after 1967 when we were in credit and England was in debt to us? Had the era of economic liberalisation started, and had we found our treasury brimming, would it not have been the case that we would not need loans, or at least only reasonable amounts of borrowing? The truth is that the economic liberalisation came about in the aftermath of bankruptcy, or semi-bankruptcy, and the state relied upon loans to cover its own needs, from bread to missiles. These two eras are like a father and son, when the father finds a large amount of money and invests some of it but then gives in to unprecedented financial recklessness which eats away his funds and increases his debts. When his son takes over from his father he finds the only way for him to survive is by taking on more debt, either for his necessities or for things which are unnecessary particularly considering the state in which he finds himself, and at first glance he may appear to be an example of impetuosity and extravagance in comparison to his father. However, this comparison ignores the fact that the father was the one who originally invested the funds and entangled himself in debt. Furthermore, my aim is to draw a comparison between two eras and not between two men. However, I would like us to remember always that straying from the

1 The Six-Day War of 1967.

2 (1927–96), journalist, author and editor.

aim is what eats away at funds in an uncontrollable manner and spends it imprudently leaving us to inherit troubles and grief.

17 March 1983

A Stand on Corruption

We should praise the current era for its activity in fighting malfeasance and corruption, and for tracking down wrongdoers whatever their position in the state or their previous experience in public service. This is a deterrent policy regarding evil in its hiding places and wrongdoers cannot stay protected forever or delude themselves into thinking that they are above the law. A glance at the dishonesty with which our society is afflicted shows that over the various eras people have been able to depend upon authority in their attempts to infringe the law, to eat away at values, to cluster around people in power, and to rely upon their help in realising their own interests and privileges. All of this is an old plague in our lives and a standing tradition which is practised the way religious rituals are performed. This causes unbridled danger under authoritarian rule when the ruler and those in the circles of power seek his protection to remain above the law, and this allows the forces of evil to run amok in a frightening race which sweeps away anyone who objects and can commit unimaginable crimes. Only one of two types of people are exempt from this: either a man who has no power or any connection with the centres of power, or a man who has been granted enough power of personality to place him within the ranks of the heroes of history. At the forefront of the victims of a system like this are the civil servants, from ministers down to caretakers, and which of them do you think would say no, and refuse to benefit from nepotism when he knows that this could help him along to a better life and income? Did the sacred juridical system not become over-sanctimonious when it dismissed some bribe-takers in what has been termed a juridical massacre? But what can the minister or the caretaker do? Thus I would hope that we do not think that judging some or firing others is a salutary cure for this chronic plague. The cure can only come about when the law runs its right course in the protective shadow of real democracy, and then only by respecting equality in word and deed and by deeming nepotism one of the greatest social crimes. Sending people for trial or dismissing them from their jobs is tantamount to treating the symptoms and not the cause and just allows the real disease to inflict our bodies with yet more of its poison.

24 March 1983

The Lesson of Oil

The oil crisis has come along to remind the Arabs that the era of oil will have an end just like all other eras, and that perhaps it is an opportunity to look at again at their whole position during a happy and comfortable period that will not come back again, to see it as a test for humanity from which they will either come out safely and successfully or which will end badly. It has long been known that the wealth from oil will not be everlasting, but that if exploited with vision, insight and foresight, the Arabs might be able to come out from the darkness of backwardness into the light of civilisation. Common sense would demand that they use the funds to solve their problems and create an infrastructure within the framework of cultural and economic integration, but unfortunately they fell into the dreadful and shallow international trap of spending their billions on weapons which will not be used, and on importing unnecessary luxury goods. They have been riven by lateral conflicts, spent billions on stupid wars and global conspiracies with the whole region having become a byword for divisiveness, chaos and defeatism even though by dint of history, culture, language and contiguity they should be one large family. Is there thus any hope that we can take a new look, with a clear vision that goes beyond selfishness and hatreds? Is there thus any hope of saving anything by self-reliance, of having a good aim ahead of us and of robustly steering ourselves towards a policy of cultural and economic integration as the only way towards achieving civilisation, progress, power and dignity? Will the Arabs forget the disputes which split them asunder when the Mongols came to batter their doors down? Today the Arabs are divided by even more calamitous and bitter quarrels while an enemy who is stronger and more arrogant than the Mongols threatens them and their state of backwardness in an era when progress advances at lightning speed. There is no point putting our hope in God if we do not change ourselves.

31 March 1983

In What State Has the Festival Returned?

We are now celebrating the liberation of Sinai for the second time. This is an event which deserves to be celebrated and which we should be happy to commemorate, and we should recall with honour and respect the person who managed to achieve this, the late president Anwar Sadat. He waged the first noble and successful war since the time of Muhammad Ali.[1] Sadat embarked upon a bold and pioneering policy which shattered the stasis in which the Arabs were mired, and which created a new perspective for those who wished to move forward. In truth the celebrations are taking place in new circumstances beset with evil, blood, tears, disappointment and hope, and they come after a brutal invasion and a shocking and vicious massacre[2] which, for all that, has brought about a new Arab position which is realistic and prudent, and which in spirit is a return in some way or another to the plan of Sadat and which recognises his vision. This transformation could have come about without any bitter or harsh reactions, but in his wisdom the late president, in his foreign policy, had to overcome obstacles and sniping from both sides, from the Israelis and the Arabs alike. The rulers in Israel went beyond the state's aims and resorted yet again to war as a means of solving their problems, thereby besmirching themselves indelibly forever. The Arabs misunderstood and took a position of rejectionism and contempt, and their stance was one of the reasons which led to the frequent invasions of Lebanon along with all the destruction caused to the Palestinians and the Lebanese. The truth is that Sadat did not just solve a problem but set a successful example which was ahead of its time. I think that the time has now come for us

---

1 r. 1805–48.

2 After the September 1982 assassination of Bachir Gemayel, the president-elect, Israel invaded Lebanon. Between 16 and 18 September, the Phalangists, Israel's allies, carried out a massacre of up to 3,500 Palestinians in the refugee camps of Sabra and Shatila.

to move on and face the challenges with all the requisite determination, courage and flexibility and perhaps next year we will celebrate the liberation of Sinai along with the liberation of all the occupied Arab territories, the Palestinians will be re-settled in their longed-for state, and we will be able to hold celebrations unsullied by bloody memories.

21 April 1983

On the Opposition

I should like to talk about the opposition in response to a call from the president over what I noted in his last statement regarding his sincere desire for democracy and his far-reaching concern for its progress. I do not think I am overstepping the mark by making the following observations:

1. Every country has its own national character. One nation is characterised as cool and clear thinking, and another as excitable and imaginative. Accordingly, their respective reactions comprise varying degrees of enthusiasm and vigour in all aspects of life, including the political opposition in its very nature. The worst thing that could happen in the British parliament is for someone to shout out 'shame on you!', whereas parliamentarians in Turkey and Italy have been known to throw chairs and even fire guns.
2. The opposition in our country is fulfilling its duty not only after a long period of deprivation, bitter experience and painful ordeal, but in the wake of dreadful events which have shaken the dignity, security, economy and ethics of the country. The opposition is angry with due cause.
3. Even in its worst form, the opposition is better than the most benign dictatorship, for even if it oversteps the mark, there is a just method of reining it in. On the other hand, the errors of dictators, such as defeats, accumulated debts, corruption and terrorism, can only be fixed over a long period of time, with painstaking care and through people making sacrifices generation after generation.
4. In what I have said here, I do not mean to defend the opposition unconditionally, show favour to any form of rabble-rousing, downplay the objectivity of approach, the value of debate, constructive criticism or claim any responsibility for the usefulness of public opinion and proposals. In addition, I really do hope in all these things that the opposition can set a fine

example and gain control of itself before beating its opponents. However, I hope that those in charge will be open-minded enough to accept harsh criticism, for that is an inseparable part of the trust they have been given and the inescapable price they have to pay for living in a state governed by the intellect, by freedom and human values.

12 May 1983

Wielding Some Legal Clout

We have passed through circumstances which can be considered a trial for our ethics and values, and of all those who have lived through this only those few with a rare and superior form of immunity have managed to escape. These were circumstances in which the power of the law waned and became a tool for the powerful, during which the opportunists became active and multiplied like never before, when the economy was turned upside down and some people became wildly rich while others could hardly make ends meet. Corruption was so rampant that it became a general phenomenon, it became the rule and not the exception. There were constant reports of the sale of unfit foodstuffs, land became infertile, new buildings collapsed, etc. We made an effort to resist all this with a clear determination to do something about reforming matters and purifying the atmosphere, and a good example was established by which the crooked could easily be made straight. We engaged in constructive work and our sincere resolution augured well as long as the tools we were using were intended to bring society back to a sense of equilibrium, to a capacity for satisfying its own needs and for bringing about social justice for individuals. However, the law has a role to play in reform and it must be applied with great care. We need to take another look at the sanctions possible under the law and the extent of its applicability for emergency situations, how it can be used to attack the new social diseases, at its suitability for our desire to do away with sloth and apathy and how it can be applied to the reckless use of manpower and public funds. Then comes the role of the oversight organisations in carrying out the laws and pursuing those who break the law. This should be carried out comprehensively rather than waiting until we are laid low by catastrophes or spurred into action by disasters. Matters will not be set right during this period by lectures and pontificating, as these only bear fruit in the long term. We need some real clout to be wielded against all sorts of lawbreakers in order to defend our manpower, funds, development and other values, as well as to defend the fate of the nation and its citizens.

19 May 1983

About a Higher Aim

Every age has a higher aim which so polarises minds and wills that other aims rotate around it like the planets rotate around the sun. Examples of that are the call for political awareness that was the aim during the period of the British occupation before the 1919 Revolution, and that complete independence and democracy which were the aim after that revolution. If we were to ask ourselves today about the higher aim, we would agree that it is the comprehensive development whose initial steps materialised in the first five-year plan. It is our hope of to exit from the crisis we are in, regain some equilibrium, and then move steadily forward toward liberty. This is a test for the ruling party in terms of its capabilities, will and political awareness. It is the benchmark by which we should choose which people to elect or reject. It should also be what summons the youth to participate in both thought and action. It should also be broadcast in the mass media so that every citizen can know what he should and should not do wherever he is.

Indeed the state is qualified to undertake the great work of drawing up just such a plan, carrying it out, following it up and making sure it runs properly, but the people also have a role and that is to take on the general ethics which should prevail during a time of construction and development. These are ethics based on discipline and economy, on an avoidance of extravagance, and on directing any excess funds towards channels of investment. It is evident that by this I mean the capable citizens and not the downtrodden, and not those who set out full of good intention but increase the grief of the downtrodden unintentionally by giving in to frivolity, selfishness and apathy. In this regard the media must publicise these ethics and define the role of each community in the great work so that development becomes the duty of the state and the people alike. On this occasion I should like to demand the printing of the five-year plan with all its details, in simple language which the ordinary reader can understand, and it should be distributed as widely as possible so that the citizen can read all about the constructive steps being taken and be able to discern the shape of the future.

26 May 1983

The Desired Wisdom

Our Arab world along with most developing countries fumble their way around a maze from which they do not know how, or do not wish, to exit. They are all striving to conquer backwardness by means of comprehensive development, and on the road to that they incur loans from the developed nations under whose tutelage and under the consequences of whose exploitation they have lived. At the same time, they spend money they cannot afford on armaments and consumerism, the latter of which includes luxury items and entertainment. The result is that they are drowning in debts without being able to realise the desired development, or without being able to realise it appropriately. They are thus in need of discipline and wisdom, and they will not acquire those unless they take a new look at their position in life in general, which means taking a resolute and sincere decision to resolve their external problems even if this demands some form of austerity and approaching the needs of life with a determination that concentrates their populations upon the necessities of life and weans them off idle extravagance. Then they will gain some relief from the burden of the mad and revolting race for armaments, thereby saving the funds which are haemorrhaging into thin air, saving their future from deterioration and breakdown, and bringing about the necessary civilisational capacity so indispensable in this world which is rushing forwards at breakneck speed in the fields of progress and innovation hour after hour. And now the global arms statistics organisations announce from time to time that the Middle East region is the highest spender on arms purchases and have published utterly unbelievable numbers to prove this. If the Arabs spent the same amount on economic and cultural integration, they would become developed agricultural and industrial nations, be able to support themselves and apply themselves to being one of the world's food sources.

All of this can be set out clearly in figures. It is not just the stuff of dreams or legends. If we were to make a simple comparison between what can be and what actually is, you would see the difference between wisdom and folly. We told the Arabs as much one day in one of their leading newspapers and our reward was that we were put on the black list, the list of traitors to the Arab cause – and how many crimes have been carried out in the name of the Arab cause!

4 June 1983

The Privilege Disease

We are in need of new traditions in order to turn our society into an ethical one. There are indigenous diseases which bring our lives down from the level we desire to enjoy – diseases which cause the most awful harm to justice, to the will to work and to dignity. I will start by talking about one of them which is the privilege disease. We put an end to the Capitulations in 1938, but the indigenous privileges remained, the privileges of the various centres of power whether administrative, class-based, capital-based or family-based. These privileges continued to corrupt our lives, making our youth exasperated and rebellious. Had these privileges been a way of getting things done which were only rarely used, the matter would not be so serious, but they are the essential foundation, a *sine qua non* that has never disappeared. Nepotism is the way of getting anything done when you have to go to a government authority, it is the way that an individual has to deal with the ministries and other institutions, of getting what you deserve or what you do not deserve. It works unashamedly at dividing the citizens among themselves. It invalidates efficiency and values, it arouses rancour and discord, insisting on depriving us of a pure life based on justice, virtue, intelligence and the law. Ten per cent of the population enjoy security, dignity and good treatment, while the rest suffer from dreadful bureaucracy and the impertinence of injustice or – in the best cases – the evil of apathy and sloth. The only cure for this disease is to close the loopholes through which it can infiltrate, and that will only come about through vigilant oversight of the demands of the public and the treatment that they receive and by according all complaints the due care they deserve. Nepotism must be considered a form of corruption subject to the sanction of the law, and the sanction must be a deterrent for those who grant privilege, demand it, or enjoy it. All force must be used to uproot this disease from its hiding places, so that over time people will be able to operate justly without the need for oversight or the sanction of the law.

16 June 1983

5 June

You carry with you a bad memory just as you do a good memory or even more so. We do not go back to the past just to cry over it, or to relive happy moments, but to try and learn some lessons from it which can enlighten us and direct our footsteps in the present time and the future. If we could not do that, then 6 October, for all its dazzling achievements, would not be able to make us forget the day of the defeat or uproot it from the depths of our memory. We did not take the defeat of 5 June[1] as one of history's defeats, meaning that our army did not wage a war in which we suffered many casualties, but that the army received the order to be defeated, and it was defeated. The defeat came from behind, not from in front. The shambles of the army's leadership was the last manifestation of a long chain of ineffectiveness sapping away so much at the infrastructure of the state and the people that there was nothing they could do. Let us not broaden the discussion now to a diagnosis of the diseases inflicting us as a whole or individually, as fortunately there are decent historians beavering away at that with great gusto. It is enough for me to mention one disease that could be behind all the other diseases and which worked its way ever more strongly into the system, and that is the disease of authoritarianism which has turned the state into an inquisition which emits terror and dread, and which has turned the people into victims deprived of their security and sapped of their will. No nation ruled by fear, which forces its sons into exile or negativity, can effect a real victory in war or peace. Let us remember that so that we remember each other, for it is apparent that some people forget, and in their oblivion they secretly join together in blaming our democratic journey for some of the passing errors, and incite people to try and abort democracy or shackle it even more. I am not absolving democracy of all mistakes or errors, but give us the hell of democracy, as the popular proverb goes, and not the paradise of authoritarianism, as yearning for authoritarianism is simply

1 The disastrous first day of the 'Six-Day War' of 1967 when Israel launched a pre-emptive strike on the Egyptian air force.

a wild yearning for selfishness, injustice, corruption and defeat. That is what 5 June tells us, so let's learn it by heart.

30 June 1983

A New Year of Development

One year goes, another year arrives. Published figures show that last year was a productive and successful one, and no doubt the civil servants will start giving these figures due attention and will pursue any discrepancy in the figures to ensure greater implementation in the new year, and we hope that the year of hardship has passed and that a year of ease has now begun. Indeed, the effects of this success have not yet started to appear in our daily lives, for we are like a man submerged in water, and although the water level has gone down, we are still not safe. However, success, seriousness and devotion require patience and bring their own reward. In truth, in a darkening cloud of neglect and recklessness the five-year plan provides a glint of light which will grow in size and intensity until it outshines the clouds of misery. A glance at the new budget confirms that productivity is growing steadily and that much effort has gone into encouraging exports. This has been accompanied by a wise programme of increasing taxes on those with high incomes and by the expenditure of a great amount of effort to apprehend those who have evaded tax. There have also been serious ramifications for inflation by the reduction of the amount of money in circulation and the rationalisation of expenditure. All in all this does not just mean reforming our economic life, but it also at the same time aims at the social welfare aspect and will create a capacity for social justice, just as it will narrow the gap between the classes and provide urgent help for the civil servants whom the economic liberalisation managed to plunge into the deepest penury. Comprehensive development is a battle for today and tomorrow, one we should fight for passionately and with all our will.

7 July 1983

Our Scientific Expertise and Development

Until today the Academy of Scientific Research has never been allowed to participate fully in the five-year development plan. If that points to anything it is that the state has decreed for science the role it should play in welfare and development, for ever since our first rebirth[1] in modern times the state has been aware of the positive role to be played by science and expertise. Of course science is global by its very nature, having no homeland of its own so to speak, but every environment has its own circumstances and its potential can only be discovered by its own experts and scientists and dealing with these local issues is generally their first step towards global achievement. For this reason, our own odyssey through world history may well have achieved an outstanding depth of culture and have left behind an enormous heritage to be studied, but our present-day achievements remain unknown or semi-unknown, under-examined and under-studied. We are like a sick man whose illness defies treatment – whenever the pain gets too much for him, people suggest giving him tried and tested medicine while others suggest giving him medicine whose efficacy has been vouched for in Europe or America, whereas the real cure may only be found when we examine his illness. The right medicine may lie in the desert or the mountains, or it may lie in the hands of his children who know him more than anyone else and can diagnose his illness and cure him. The time has come for us to depend upon ourselves, to exploit the creativity and expertise we already have, to turn from being people who adapt things from history or from the West into innovative creators. In a nutshell, the time has come for us to examine the sick man in person and prescribe the right medicine for him. In a time of need, there is nothing wrong in going around to other people for help, and scientific activity in the East or West does not delegitimise that. But let us always remember that we live in an age when independence only

1 The period following the Napoleonic invasion of Egypt in 1798.

has value when it is based on a modicum of scientific independence and when we are not in a state of enforced subordination despite our strength in numbers and the length and depth of our history.

14 July 1983

The July Revolution

It is natural that anyone who has lived through a revolution such as the July Revolution will have an opinion about it. It is also natural that this opinion will differ slightly, or greatly, from the historical account which only expresses its vision at an appropriate time, when it has gained a complete image and can avoid reflecting any personal or conflicting influences. From the standpoint of a contemporary view, on the occasion of its anniversary, I should like to state what the Revolution told me:

1. It told me that it is not enough for the leadership of a national rebirth to love the people, but they should also respect the people. Love drives people to realise their own interests inasmuch as possible. Respect, on the other hand, calls upon you, first and foremost, to hold sacred those human rights for which you bear complete responsibility. A dictator might love his nation, but he does not respect them, no matter how much he may say to the contrary, or he would not hold the country in his thrall and infantilise the people.
2. It told me that rule by an individual may well have led to the founding of a great number of institutions, but it also destroys that most important of institutions which is the human character, which an individual's patronage may turn into no more than a locus of negativity, hypocrisy and indifference.
3. It told me that when the law is in a state of inaction with no popular oversight, centres of power start to appear, situations deteriorate, greed becomes rampant, values crumble, corruption spreads and evil has its day.
4. It told me that no matter how much a dictatorship may flaunt its progressive thinking, it disallows any other form of thinking and creates a form of intellectual patronage in whose shade any original and innovative thinking withers.
5. It also told me that every action has a generic reaction, that dictatorship begets secret activity, and oppression begets violence.

Let us gratefully remember the most recent revolutionary reform that is taking place today and let it be based on supporting freedom, the rule of law, productivity and eradication of corruption.

21 July 1983

We Are Not Unaware of Our Faults... But!

There is a disease of which no one is ignorant, and our general lives remind us of it on a daily basis due to its unfortunate everlasting reappearance. It is best described by the old Arabic proverb which states: 'warm in the evening and cold in the morning.' And when a plan is rejected or when people make an enormous effort, an outpouring of enthusiasm comes to the tongues of the officials, is repeated by the state information bureaus and is then passed on by people at home and in the street. This all translates into resolute action in which everyone touched by a new development plan participates to such an extent that the citizen thinks that we have eradicated our sense of negativity once and for all. Days pass and the heat gradually starts to disappear, the hue and cry dies down, worries dissipate and work on the plan stops. Then everything goes back to its original course and the curtain comes down on this act. That means that we do not ignore our faults, and we are not devoid of the wish to treat them, but we do not gird ourselves with the strength of will vital for performing our duty. That also means that the relevant institutions become lax in carrying out the duties they are entrusted with, not due to the lack of an alternative for proving their efficiency during the period of hue and cry, but out of laziness and apathy. The only cure for that is to have some watchful oversight and permanent follow-up which can extend into every situation to defend the masses from being afflicted by any form of hardship and to prevent any evil affecting the general welfare. And I should like to remind you that we do not lack the laws or the manpower, but we do lack the interest, the will, and the active sense of duty. Anyone not moved by his own conscience can be motivated by monitoring and sanction. That is how we can move from problem to problem in an unwavering straight line rather than fruitlessly going around in circles.

23 July 1983

More Cars

I find it difficult to understand the wisdom behind some aspects of our grand development plan, and it seems as if they not only have to do with a reality which is not our reality but are intended to increase our woes.

I read in the newspapers that 'it has been decided to increase the manufacture of passenger vehicles to 45,000 cars within two years. This year 22,000 cars have been produced, an increase of 6,000 over last year.'

Anyone who looks at the streets of Cairo at any time of the night or day will be shocked by the frightful sight of the streams of cars covering every inch of the ground and the queues of cars lined up at traffic lights is one of the most awful sights witnessed by our revolutionary era. We are all disheartened at the way cars have to crawl around the city in huge jams. All of this should stir those responsible for the traffic to move heaven and earth in order to come up with various suggestions for easing the crisis.

With all that in mind, how can we announce an increase in car production. Should our development plan not be based in our reality and aim to develop it for the better? Why are the car factories not turning out vehicles for public transport? Why do we not put off the manufacture or import of private vehicles for an unspecified period?

The truth is that I do not understand the sense behind this. Perhaps the wisdom of the matter is only apparent to some specialists, or maybe there is some unavoidable economic necessity. However, it would be better if we were to know that and become convinced of it, especially since Cairo has a pressing need for someone to lighten its pains and ease its agony.

27 July 1983

The Unreasonable War

Whatever the outcome of the Iran-Iraq war, the squalid ramifications will be no less serious. Iraq will continue to suffer a loss of manpower and capital; its development and culture will continue to be adversely affected and it will be an earth-shattering cause of convulsion in the general Arab infrastructure which will take hits from all directions. You can look for the reason for all of that, but you will not come up with any logic to explain this adventurism or to justify the bad decisions. It only needs a thought to occur to the ruler which then carries him away as he thinks he has received divine inspiration and off he rushes to carry it out, with fresh wind blowing in his sails and covering the land with their shadow. The consequences then swoop down on him like a savage animal, destroying men, dispersing the country's wealth, and the leadership disintegrates dragging along with it honour and hope. This is a two-headed plague: one head is called greedy leadership, and the other is called blind tyranny. If an individual has to pay the price for a slip of the tongue that is no great thing, but when he makes a mistake and continues on his path he leaves his people a heavy legacy of defeat and destruction which will last for generations. The people may appear to be the innocent victims, but an observer should take a deeper look and perhaps he will see, along with me, that the people's responsibility is no less than that of the executioner, and they have had some share in creating their rulers, submitting to their whims and fearing their anger. Perhaps the observer will also see along with me that forbearance is not the right thing, and apathy and self-interest at any price will only leave a long legacy of regret during the long night of grief.

5 August 1983

Conflict and Civilisation

Conflict over power is a natural social movement in whose clashing waves you will find the indicator pointing to the type of civilisation that social dynamics wishes to see prevailing in any era.

It is not impossible for someone who follows events closely to discern the direction the indicator is pointing at. In a situation where democracy has a firm anchor, all you have to do is weigh up the various political parties, or take the pulse of public opinion through recognised methods of data collection. If a particular form of democracy suffers from restrictions, or has been partly or completely abolished, you must take a comprehensive look at the society, examining its institutions, governing bodies, prisons and detention centres, for clues which may shed some light on the near or distant future.

It is intellectually and historically naïve for us to think that ignoring one's opponents will simply make them vanish from existence like a puff of smoke. Ignoring them will not put off their victory over the long term if they have a programme to fill a previously unfilled void or achieve a vital and otherwise unachieved goal.

Perhaps the best and wisest method in a civilisational conflict of this type is for you to be guided towards an active centre of power which, by dint of its own strength, can fill a void and achieve a goal, and can bring people together in the shade of complete freedom and the requisite respect for human rights. That will be a form of guarantee as you wage the battle with the aim of winning it, not just by taking part in debate, propaganda or good administration, but by setting a good example, through righteous labour and fruitful giving. In doing this, you will not just win the battle, but you will also benefit from having civilisation and history as your witness.

11 August 1983

The Benchmark of Civilisation

Where can we find a benchmark like this so that we can affirm the wisdom of the ruler? Can we find it in the average individual income? In industrial progress and agricultural self-reliance? In scientific and cultural activity? In the system of governance and the relationship between the ruler and the ruled? Each one of these elements is highly significant and is individually of benefit for governing. Each element it incorporates makes the system of government stronger and wider reaching, but the foremost benchmark in my opinion, the unmistakable benchmark, is to be found within the individual himself, within the citizen of one civilisation or another, within one's character as a whole and the concomitant dimensions of values, vision, stances, deeds and reactions, and through his vision of himself, of other people and of life, and the way he deals with himself, with other people and with life.

This last element is the sum total of all the educational, scientific, social, economic, psychological and religious forces. It is the human as he can be, and in accordance with all the facets with which his culture has empowered him.

It is also my opinion that it is a person's acculturalisation which is the strongest element in the way he treats the minorities who share his culture and homeland, the minorities who by the very nature of being a minority are less in number than he is and who follow a different denomination, whose politics are different or who are of a different ethnic group. Look at these minorities wherever they are and look at the respect for human rights that they enjoy as well as the feeling of safety and security they have for the future. Look at that minority person and his community and you will see the best type of benchmark for judging the level of civilisation of that society, its spiritual progress, its ethical loftiness and social equality. If all of that does not come about, then believe me in that science, industry, agriculture and wealth, inter alia, have no value.

There is no value to a people who are successful in all areas of civilisation if they fail in that essential area which is to uncover the real element of humanity which is the individual himself.

25 August 1983

The Ministry of Wealth

That is, the Ministry of Education. There are ministries of agriculture, industry, energy and so on, and they are unarguably all great treasures, but our primary wealth is our population, both men and women along with their intellects, hearts and wills. If the population is properly employed they can be an unassailable force, and what do we hope for from a ministry which specialises in investing in our citizens? We hope:

1. That it will eradicate illiteracy by broadening general education to take in every child, and to make sure that he or she does not fall by the wayside or be overlooked. That is the shortest route to eradicating illiteracy.
2. That it will eradicate intellectual illiteracy by providing a cultural education and training children to love and savour knowledge from their early years and through all stages of their education.
3. That it turns them into human resources through liberal and national education anchored in the values of religion.
4. That it can change the method of education from one of learning by rote to one of practising innovative thinking and thereby create new generations of thinkers and innovators.
5. That it prepares young people for work in contemporary life and equips them for the most delicate as well as the most difficult jobs starting from manual work to the most complex technological operations.

This is an enormous, complicated and risky task which to the utmost degree is part of the development of the nation and its preparation for being re-formed and equipped for the complications of modern life. The ministry which bears this responsibility is a ministry of hope. It bears responsibility for the past, the present and the future, and fortunately the ministry is overflowing with efficient, devoted and hard-working staff. What has it achieved so for? And what is yet to be achieved?

1 September 1983

Looking for the Missing Money

Last year revealed a deficit in tax revenues which reached more than 750 million pounds and a large number of wealthy people still avoid paying the rightful amount of tax as stipulated by the authorities. We should have done everything within our power to enable the state to collect the full amount of tax, and that should have been done before we start thinking about austerity or increasing taxes, in the knowledge that we are the ones who take on the burden of austerity and tax increases in order to achieve social justice. However, at the same time we see that any move towards austerity or tax increases before the complete amount has been collected as a fair method of handling and managing matters is not devoid of patent injustice as long as many people still manage to avoid paying their tax and enjoy unfair privileges at the expense of their fellow citizens as those tax avoiders pile up their money, undermine our values and still manage to live in safety. The government must concentrate its attention on the tax authority and provide it with the requisite amount of manpower. It must reform the tax authority drawing on the experience of other states for whenever a tax authority becomes stronger and more meticulous, you will end up with more money and power. The matter cannot be subject to a policy of patience or delay, or what is known as a softly-softly approach, and the situation is one in which any extra spending will result in a massive increase in return. How much have we heard about new processes being instituted, and the constant daily and monthly deadlines for clearing the backlog, and then days pass and all the promises vanish into thin air and dreams become as nothing. Then, when we examine the matter, we find, to our great sorrow, that nothing at all has been achieved in this grinding crisis.

8 September 1983

Censorship

The job of the censor is to protect society from moral, political and religious aberrations within the framework of the law. He does so in the texts and books which he monitors. However, by the very nature of his work and the dictates of logic his influence spreads further afield than that. The censor also protects art from the creeping banality of commercial influences – for most of the aberrations which harm society come from crass commercialisation – hence protecting art means protecting society. I just wrote 'most of the aberrations' rather than 'all of them', because I know that censorship also silences some serious subjects despite the legislated freedom to criticise in the political and social arenas. Censorship is a medicine with risks and must only be prescribed for the benefit of art and society within our new democracy. Censorship has a third role which is to protect the capital investment in the field of art and not to leave the producers to their own devices so that they produce works which are then subjected to censorship, leaving the investors with serious and unforeseen losses. The censor should monitor these works as they are in progress, starting from the concept, the treatment and the final shape of the artwork, and then it should grant a performance licence as a sort of final stamp of approval.

Thus censorship is in fact responsible for society, art and capital, and it must bear its full responsibility with honesty, transparency and courage. The censor may make mistakes, for who does not? In that case he has to do what he feels is right but without doing any injustice to the artistic community or going against other officials in the censorship department. There should be some form of reimbursement for losses incurred on the one hand, and we should see whether the censorship administration can be reformed in order to put in place extra checks and balances. Carrying out investigations and applying sanctions should not be part of the work of the censor. That is really the job of a judge and might drive the censor to a state of paralysis or cause him to play it safe and attempt to avoid responsibility. I hope that censorship will pass through its crisis safely and not create obstacles in the path of true art, freedom of opinion or divinely-sanctioned values.

15 September 1983

A New Censorship Law

I do not think that censorship needs a new law as promised by the minister of education. Criticism has been levelled against the censor himself, not against the law and we should bear in mind that the work the censor does is delicate and sensitive and that not everyone will be happy with it. It needs fine tuning for the ever-changing circumstances which means that it cannot just stand still for a long period. Perhaps the shot it needs is for the minister, in his role as the representative of the state and of the majority of the population, to set up regular meetings, preferably with the cinema industry and the art and literature unions where they can have an exchange of opinions and discuss public opinion in order to be of more service to art and society. That would be sufficient for their ongoing development and to establish bonds of cooperation between them, art and the artistic community without the need for some new law to interfere. This also applies to the popular art forms whose special conditions call for an enlightened form of censorship. When it comes to including the printed book among these art forms subjected to censorship, the suggestion leaves us in a state of astonishment and disbelief, because the book has its own special sanctity and readers and authors are an elite group in the cultural establishment. They are unfortunately a small minority with such a sense of social responsibility that we do not have to worry about them going off-track or leading us astray in their works and it would be unthinkable to place them under supervision. For various reasons, the book has been freed from censorship in a period which from the democratic point of view has arrived rather late and so how could we even consider turning the clock back when we are building a democratic edifice, opening the doors and windows to the air of free thinking and making advances every day? Democracy is not just a monolithic concept, but first and foremost it is a way of behaving, a system of ethics and traditions which reaches its apogee in freedom of thought. The book is the palpable symbol of this free thought and hence its freedom from censorship is the real benchmark of true democracy. What I know of the minister of culture's great interest in serving culture, of his zeal for democracy and freedom, his patriotism and love of progress, gives me hope that his approach to this issue will silence any expressions of pessimism or despair.

22 September 1983

Thought and Freedom

Whenever there is public mention of freedom of thought, voices arise all around calling for controls and caveats, as if for all the murderous subjugation we have endured for any intellectual adventure we have become so familiar with oppression that we accept it with no further ado. We have gone on fearing freedom, fearing thought, or fearing both of them together. I might be aware of the significance of a law against murder, theft or aggression, or traffic offenses, but I am not aware of the significance of a law against thinking about the practice of the law's natural role, which is to seek for the truth in any way possible, for there is no place for a law which by its nature is subject to laws of another type. These are the laws of thinking itself in whose light we can find the way out of error. Is it not enough that public opinion, as prim and backward as it might be, for all its power of censure and deterrence, might during periods of decadence turn into a beast of prey whose influence surpasses that of conventional law? In defence of that it might be said that thoughts do not do any harm the way that murder or worse crimes do. The truth is that correct thinking can in no way do any harm. It might well take us by surprise before we are ready to cope with it, and it might appear worrying or painful or harsh, but we must always train ourselves to confront truths, adapt to them and be convinced of them no matter how much effort or sacrifice that takes, so that life can continue along its straight path which is based on nothing other than the truth. It might also be said in defence of that, that thinking is capable of error, and that is the truth, but can that be corrected by the sanction of the law, the terror of the masses or a law against thinking itself? As much as correct thinking draws us to a new life, it also requires us to hold discussions and conversations and to create intellectual wealth, for in the end only what is correct will hold water. However, we will not be able to have freedom of thought or to work to defend it with the necessary enthusiasm unless our consciousness really sets to work sanctifying intelligence as a gift of God Almighty.

29 September 1983

6 October

The days pass, the months follow each other, and the words flow, the analyses keep on coming, and dust is thrown on intentions and aims, but the mordant truths stand firm in face of violent storms, and 6 October remains an eternal symbol of rebirth and victory, a devoted nationalist voice for peace, an admonition for us to think back over events and a memorial for a rightly-based peace. On the historical level the positives and negatives of an era become crystallised, and by an accident of fate they can either become a textbook for negativity or a new field for positivity. No sooner has an event disappeared in the sands of time than we start to look at everything anew, examine again its legacy in all its dimensions, and study the steps ahead of us. Then we move with determination towards renewing the spirit of democracy, trying to establish it firmly, reforming the route of the economic liberalisation, rationalising it and purifying the air of miasma and dishonesty. Then we set off trying to put the development plan on a comprehensive scientific footing, to carry it out with strength and devotion, and the first year brings about notable success which augurs well for further success and we concentrate our thoughts on our worries and woes. The year continues wisely and prudently extricating the region from divisiveness and defeat. I am not denying the depth of suffering or the extent of the effort or sacrifice that we still need to make, but the heat of hard work is not affected by pain, for hard work flourishes with patience and renews one's soul with hope. So on this day let us remember the hero and martyr, the late President Anwar Sadat, and let us think about his heroism and martyrdom so that our honouring his memory can be a stubborn continuation of the programme of eradicating negativity and of a redoubling of effort to achieve the many positive things made possible by peace and progress.

6 October 1983

The Police in the Service of Democracy

I read in the opposition *Ahrar* newspaper that some chairmen of the election committees believed that the instructions issued to ensure neutrality and integrity in the elections for the Consultative Council were simply declarations made for local consumption and so the chairmen went along their usual path of forging ballot papers with the result that the police have arrested them and have submitted their cases to the prosecutor general.

My eyes lingered on the article in a state of amazement, not out of any ill-feeling towards the police, but because I was overwhelmed by a flood of sad memories of the recent and not-so-recent past, when officials made use of the police to falsify the will of the people and create a parliament that acted as a rubber stamp for unbridled royal rule. At that time, we viewed the police as the enemy of the people, of human rights, and as a tool for oppression and tyranny.

The truth to tell, the police were the first victims of the tyrant. He was the one who forced them to set aside their duty towards the nation and to serve his own whims and ambitions. Today the police have returned to their natural status as the guardians of the law, of values, and of the rights of the people, and as watchful guardians of the constitution of democracy. In the past, a dictator would hand the Ministry of the Interior over to a bold, wily man with an indifference to values, something tantamount to handing it over to a highwayman rather than to a minister of state in a civilised country. Today the ministry is headed by a man[1] of great intelligence, a man of noble intent, whose heart beats with love for a democratic homeland and human rights. He has made promises and pledges and has fulfilled. Rain falls lightly before turning into a downpour.

13 October 1983

---

1 Hassan Abu Basha.

Television and the Cinema

I am not a great fan of showing made-for-television films in the cinema. The television format frees films from direct public pressure and from what is termed the constraints of capital and the film-star system and in so doing creates a good opportunity for the clever use of language, for creativity and seriousness, for experimentation and for encouraging budding talents within a format appropriate for the thousands of households where the television is on more or less all the time. For this reason, the television film is a model which we hope will set a standard for an improvement in the cinematic film in terms of art, content and quality. The fact that the film is shown on the small screen in no way detracts from its power or influence. On the contrary, by television's very nature it gives a film a greater chance to be part of people's everyday reality than the large screen would. However, I worry about the direct influence of the made-for-television film on the audience – for the audience is the partner of the author when it comes to mass entertainment. I also worry that financial success might become the primary benchmark of a film's success and the primary motivation of those involved in making it, for there is no way on earth that anyone can get away with paying no attention to the audience reaction, or resist attempting to satisfy the audience. Hence there is a fear that over time the made-for-television film might become just another commercial offering rather than providing an ideal model for refined art and the ability to tell complete stories. It would perhaps be a good thing for television, the cinema and the audience, if this notion could be given some consideration.

20 October 1983

The Etiquette and Conventions of Catastrophes

Yes, catastrophes have an etiquette and conventions which are observed, or that is what should happen in refined human societies or those that aspire to refinement. We follow some of this etiquette and these conventions and we ignore the rest which are perhaps more crucial. Whenever a catastrophe takes place, and when we are furnished with evidence that this catastrophe has been caused by neglect, we send those directly responsible for trial to receive a deterrent sentence, and sometimes we take another look at the laws governing the whole situation. That is fine, but it is less than required. There are civil servants who, by dint of their positions, are absent from the picture and who benefit from their distance from the location of the incident, but refined etiquette and conventions make it incumbent on them to place their independence of activity at the disposal of the supreme leader so that he can decide whether they should be fired or kept on. There is no injustice, or even semi-injustice, in that for behind every negligent civil servant is a negligent supervisor, behind him is a negligent departmental manager, behind him is a negligent sector manager, behind him is a slack representative of a ministry, and behind him is a minister. I really do believe that work is an indivisible unit under whose aegis all the ascending stages of a job should be joined together. If a minister were to feel that he is shouldering a responsibility on behalf of all his support staff right down to the simplest worker, he would rethink his duties and follow them up with a very careful and alert reporting system and the whole workplace would buzz with never-ending activity. This would lessen the trials and tribulations of the ordinary man which bring about so many disasters and losses for him and which threaten his security, safety and health, and which have brought about his loss of self-confidence and his confidence in the state. This would also restore his value and dignity as a human being. Yes – just as catastrophes have their victims among the people, they also have their own etiquette and conventions.

27 October 1983

On the Emergency Law

I read what the opposition have to say about the emergency law and I was convinced. Then I read how the minister of the interior responded and he appears to be sincere, particularly since current events appear to show that this law is not being applied inappropriately and also because the minister's character seems to be inspired by integrity and a sense of democracy.

But there is a sign, that cannot be hidden while this law continues to be enforced, that our country is not without the necessary resolve to resort to exceptional means to defend itself, its security, its values and its integrity.

For that reason, we should not be persuaded to take shelter behind the emergency law, but we should try to work out what the underlying problem is, what methods we should use to treat it, and how we can eradicate the causes, first and foremost. That is how we will be able to overcome terrorism and not just defend ourselves from it – a move which history has proved ineffective, just as it has shown us how it may be an exacerbating factor if carried out by people who have the misfortune to lack insight and wisdom. The matter calls for a great deal of careful study in order to uncover the causes, in all their aspects, for there may well be apparent causes upon which we can all agree. The solutions may include:

1. Encouraging people to work to strengthen democracy and remove the obstacles that lie in the way.
2. Redoubling our efforts to carry out the development plan in order to exit from the ordeal of suffering that creates the climate for the emergence of aberrant ideas and actions.
3. Continuing the serious pursuit of delinquency and delinquents, and the collection of funds withheld from the nation by tax avoiders.
4. Spreading a spirit of respect, enshrining human rights and considering any violent attacks against them a grave crime for which there should be the greatest moral and financial sanction.

In order for us to fulfil our wish, we might think about issuing a special emergency law that we can use for instances of terrorism when the situation requires it. For God is the final judge of what is right.

3 November 1983

What Does Experience Tell Us?

Something that has been repeated so often that it has started to take on the force of truth is the impression that we experimented with democracy before the July Revolution and that the experiment ended in failure and breakdown, and that we experimented with socialism after the July Revolution and that likewise ended in failure and destruction. Hence we might be able to state that repeating the experiment would be a reckless waste of time and energy.

When it comes to our experiment with democracy, we did not really trial democracy in that we did not give it a chance to see whether it worked, and the pre-revolutionary era ended with an admixture of royal dictatorial rule with a false parliamentary veneer which lasted for twenty years, and popular rule which continued in fits and starts for less than nine years and which was beset by domestic and foreign crises with the Palace or the British or both of them at the same time. Despite that, the reign of hopeless anxiety gave Egypt some reforms during that period and if there was a failure, it was the failure of royal dictatorial rule.

Throughout the second experiment, nationalisation decrees were issued and socialists were arrested. The public sector was dragged down by stultifying bureaucracy and could only operate within the shade of terrible, dictatorial rule that gave protection to tyrants and fostered fetid corruption. If there was a failure, it was the failure of dictatorship and bureaucracy.

Neither democracy nor socialism were instituted in their true forms, but their enemies seized the opportunity offered by mistakes and catastrophes to lay the responsibility blame on them.

In truth the thing which had an unparalleled opportunity, but whose failure has been proven beyond any doubt – confirmed by grave consequences – is first and foremost dictatorship, with bureaucracy in a close second place.

All the negativity, neglect and apathy we are suffering from to this day are the product and result of those two things. We need to know who our real enemy is so that we can weed it out and move forward on a straight and level path.

10 November 1983

Arab Considerations

Every nation has its own spiritual and material concerns, but what arouses consideration and sorrow is that the gap between some nations should become so large that one group can be obsessed with the modalities of setting up a permanent space station whereas another group is still marshalling its forces to try and provide its people with the bare necessities of life and civilisation such as the provision of foodstuffs, the eradication of illiteracy and the reform of essential infrastructure.

Every party has its own circumstances and conditions which may explain their progress or stasis, but how can those who lag behind find a taste for leisure and sleep easy at night when they are aware of this terrible gap which threatens their very existence, their long-term existence, and the meaning of their humanity? What could the solution be when they not only suffer from age-old backwardness and self-created obstacles, but also fight each other over thousand-year old issues, argue over things not worth arguing about, or compete to see who can best ignore reality and escape from the truth. Days pass and the situation continues aimlessly with no real plan to confront the backwardness which threatens everyone with annihilation.

We have been granted not inconsiderable capabilities such as are rarely given to a nation. We have been granted justice and huge amounts of capital, a unique homogeneity of language and culture, identity of history and aim, and we have a long heritage of honourable historical experience, so what do we still need in order to get going? Moreover, what are we waiting for in order to put an end to our side squabbles and to flock together like birds of a feather? Is it that we have lost our sense of awareness or our will, or do we have a secret death wish? When will a miracle come about? For which man or nation will fate decree a miracle in the coming days?

17 November 1983

The Minister of Culture Said…

In an article written by the minister of culture, in which he responded to criticism directed against him the *al-Ahali* newspaper with regard to censorship, he wrote some things which are worth restating. Among other things he stated that 'I do not agree with the imposition of any censorship on the freedom of thought or of creativity', and 'it may well be my own personal position but I can also confirm that this is the official government position and also mine as a member of that government'. He added: 'There have been many important topics on which the censors had a different opinion but when these were passed on to me I decided to certify them for public distribution' (here he is referring to the film *The Ghoul*).[1]

He further wrote that 'the Ministry of Culture, as it thinks of reforming the censorship law, did not think for a second that any reform might bring about even heavier censorship, but rather organise the remit of the censor to look more deeply into matters laid in front of them and to take more responsible decisions'. Elsewhere in his article he stated that 'finally any reform of the law that targets a specific social group must take into account the opinion of that group as regards the reform'.

As far as I can see, these are enlightened views, worthy of a man who bears great responsibility for thought and creativity in this early period in the democratic rebirth of our country. I have already stated my opinion about the censorship law which is that the present law is sufficient, but that the impetus should be on supporting it with various steps intended to rationalise it and bring it into accord with ever-changing realities. If a reform to the censorship law is based on these

1 IMDB: 'Ali Abd-El-Zaher is a member of an Islamic radical group which has been launching attacks against the government and society under the orders of the spiritual leader Brother Saif. Ali manages to assassinate an officer but as he escapes from the authorities he gets hit by a car driven by Sawsan, the daughter of a respected Muslim family living in the Maadi district. Sawsan's father who is a surgeon and his family take care of the injured terrorist who then tries to conceal the truth about his personality, such as his dislike of music, unveiled women and western life styles.'

principles this may have a positive effort on the way censorship operates on the one hand, and on thought and creativity on the other hand and with that in mind I send my greetings to the minister of culture.

24 November 1983

The Hope That Remains

What is the opinion of the Arab peoples regarding the bloody and alarming farces taking place in the Arab region? This may be a question for which there is no decisive answer at all.

The voices of leaders ring out loud from all directions with statements and directives, with decisions being made both secretly and in public. There may rage rivers of blood and chaos, and you can listen as carefully as you wish but you will not hear people in authority coming out with the reason for that, as if there is a rule of silence and we must remain the permanent victims of authoritarianism. There are many interpretations for that: there are those who say that it is the policy of this or that ruler, or that it is an American, Soviet or international plot, but you will never hear anyone say that it is an Arab plan – as they are in permanent disarray and have little opportunity to speak up, much less to take any action. How long will we have to wait as the train of life rushes on at top speed and stops neither for prevaricators nor for those waiting at the station? Our only hope today is with the rich Arab countries who have performed memorable duties in supporting Arab defence and who have made various investments in the Arab and African countries, but they should remember that it was fate which put into their hands the capability of saving the Arab countries from the pit of backwardness and of propelling them on to confront the modern age. Yes, their permanent duty is to put in place a comprehensive plan for economic integration and to carry this out without prevarication or hesitation. This will only cost us half of what has been spent on suicidal Arab arms purchases, and any amount invested in development will not disappear down the drain but will bring us benefits, civilisation and security. The Arab states must follow this path and turn the page on political squabbles. Not only that, but they must start, if you wish, with the countries with which they agree, and who knows – the announcement of such a plan and its execution may have an effect greater than can be appreciated by those who work on settling conflicts, and who knows, the intellectuals who work on the philosophy of progress and reform may end up occupying the place of those whose philosophy leads to madness and mass suicide. That is our remaining hope in this time of darkness which is so stained with the blood of the innocent.

15 December 1983

A Golden Age of Culture

Much has been said about cultural decline, and we are not the only ones to discuss this matter. However, after reflection I believe that the crisis needs a new diagnosis in order to get to the bottom of it with more clarity and this may enable us to arrive at a more precise treatment. How could that not be the case when everything around us indicates that we are living in the greatest cultural period in all our history! The present time is the golden age of culture in the full sense of the word. Just compare it with any other period of our ancient and modern history and you will find that culture was the remit of only a small proportion of the population whereas the great majority wallowed in illiteracy and were deprived of any real culture. Even in the period of the giant cultural figures at the turn of the twentieth century 90 per cent of the population were illiterate. We just need to take a look at what is happening nowadays in the various fields of culture. Thanks to the state radio and television, the doors of culture have been flung wide open to millions of men, women and children, throughout the countryside, the cities and the remote districts, unconditionally, available equally to the educated, the cultured and the illiterate who can now watch or listen, night and day, to all manner of useful information, public information, and news about our Egypt and the Arab world in general, about the sky at night, or a huge variety of dramatic and artistic output. What institution in days of yore could fathom that culture might be spread across such a fantastically broad area have dreamt that in a few hundred years' time or that the state would end up spending millions on culture? Would it be an exaggeration to say that we are now living in the greatest period of culture in our entire history in the full sense of the word? However, it is incontrovertible to say that a decline has befallen literature and the art of the word. These form the very basis of culture and it is on them that the cure must be focused in order to effect a real cultural revival.

22 December 1983

The Crisis of Literature

The crisis of culture is almost restricted to the domain of literature and it has both global and local causes. On the global level, television and other new means of expression have had a negative effect on the pastime of reading and television's ever-increasing influence has made it almost irresistible. This has been furthermore exacerbated by regional reasons, first and foremost being the state of teaching over the last quarter century and our ill-preparedness for the consequences of the disappearance of that refined cultural education in schools previously taught by competent and qualified teachers, and provided by libraries, magazines and dramatic and musical activities. And we should not neglect to mention the sorry state of Arabic teaching. This has produced generations of children who have not been raised with a love of books or fine culture. Then there were all those wars, our loss of freedom and that bout of heavy inflation which left everyone eking out a living with no time left for spiritual needs. That is how the crisis has gripped the public despite our human resources and national productivity which was good both in terms of quality and quantity. It is the public, the victim, which is responsible for the slump in literary works, the diminution of serious theatrical output and the scarcity of good films – it is not the fault of the authors or critics. Hence we know that long-term corrective action has to start in the Ministry of Education and the ministries responsible for the success of our general development.

In the short term we have to remove the obstacles in the way of book export and make books available for free in branches of Dar al-Kutub,[1] in cultural and youth centres. I should like to take this opportunity to convey my gratitude for the wonderful initiatives being taken by employees in the cultural sector such as preparing a low price *Library of Culture* series, setting up permanent book displays, providing a mobile library service and publishing the *Fusul* and *Ibda'* magazines with a third one on books coming out soon. However essential corrective action is needed for us to remould the public and to prepare the right cultural climate.

29 December 1983

1 State publishing house with many bookshops.

The State Media and Culture

My words today are directed towards both forms of the media and I wish to clarify their role in the service of literature because of its essential influence on high culture and thought. We also need to take a look at how the media have instilled such a sense of indolence into our cultural life that we now have to marshal all our good intentions and willpower in order to shake it off. I have previously acknowledged the ability of the media to broadcast popular culture to the millions and I have lauded it for its service to fine culture in presenting discussions, masterpieces of world theatre, excellent films and other artistic programming but I wish there were more of these. Therefore, I have come up with the following suggestions:

1. We should strengthen the broadcast power of Channel 2 so that it can reach all the Arab countries, starting naturally with nationwide coverage here in Egypt.
2. We should have a television channel just for Arabic which will cover good pronunciation and offer readings from the most beautiful Arabic poems and texts, as the radio already does.
3. There should be an hour-long weekly programme which will present newly published works with some readings as well as some critical analysis of the contents.
4. There should be regular competitions. Members of the book-reading public would be asked questions about an important book with the winners receiving a selection of books.
5. Books should be included among the prizes handed out by television and radio programmed on various occasions and books should make up at least a quarter of all prizes.

These types of free public relations will convey the idea that books are a cultural duty, that they are tempting to read, that they present valuable ideas and encourage critical thinking among the young. If the state media were to institute these suggestions, they would be providing a yet greater service to the public.

5 January 1984

Martyrs of the Pen

The press has reported that the number of journalists killed while carrying out their professional duty has reached more than 254 over the last thirty-two years, most of them having lost their lives to random shelling in war zones, and the others having fallen victim to the blind bigotry which leads to assassination. The number of victims in the two categories testifies to the danger of the role which the profession carries out, as well as to the spirit of self-sacrifice evinced by the intellectual and moral preparedness of journalists. Those reporters who were murdered are not the only victims in the field of journalism for the profession has a long history of towering figures who spoke their minds and were forced into exile or imprisoned for having dared to write in defence of higher human values. This includes journalists who emigrated to the West when the windows of self-expression were closed to them in their homelands, as well as writers who have not emigrated but have been forcibly discouraged from providing news reports and made to write about subjects they are not interested in, made to keep their thoughts to themselves, painfully deprived of their human right and made to express their duty towards their homeland. All these people should also be counted as victims, and although they have not been floored by bullets they have in fact been defeated by bigotry and selfishness. What a great profession journalism is but how numerous are its victims.

12 January 1984

The Crisis of Thought

Is there a crisis of thought? Some great thinkers deny the existence of this crisis, considering it a groundless charge and stating in defence of their claim that it is not a topic of any importance and that democracy, artistic authenticity, modernity or economic affairs have been given full coverage in the various organs and mouthpieces of the press. In so saying they have forgotten that we have only been allowed to do this in recent years due to the fact that a crisis of thought does not mean no opinions whatsoever have been allowed to appear in print. So who has the power to stop people thinking?

The situation becomes clear when this notion and the reactions to it are made public, just as it becomes clear from the extent and the types of response received from the educated public. I think it is unarguable that any type of thinking which deviates from what the establishment or the general public have found traditionally acceptable comes up against accusations, control and suppression, with most of the educated class turning a blind eye or showing indifference to this, as if this has little or nothing to do with them. So if this is not a crisis of thought, what is? It is the fruit of the years of terrorism and authoritarianism which have diverted intellectual output from thinking to justifying, from criticism to obsequiousness, from leading to following and from being adventurous to seeking peace and quiet at any price. This has been carried out to such an extent that people hold thought and thinkers in little regard, paying no attention to intellectual debates and despising what they write, with the result being that the great thinkers have fallen prey to the trend of indifference. Consequently, whenever these thinkers wage an intellectual battle over some topic or other or are subjected to vicious criticism, they find themselves alone and hung out to dry. We are undergoing a real crisis and democracy alone is not sufficient to cure it. The matter needs courage and tenacity.

19 January 1984

Between the Cause and the Aim

In the prevailing Arab situation, everything that can be said has been said, and every day that passes counts against us, not for us. However, we must remember some things before we lose our memory even though we have almost lost our perception and insight. We must remember that we have an aim and are not just people with a cause and nothing more. Wisdom dictates that we should not forget the aim in the turmoil of trying to find a solution to the cause.[1] As for the cause itself, we are all perfectly aware of it. For its sake Egypt has plunged itself into consecutive wars, and for its sake Egypt has moved towards peace as a first step in anchoring the foundations of comprehensive justice in the region. As for the aim, that is civilisation itself, progress or complete integration, or if you prefer: that we should just exist after we almost stopped existing. It is natural that the Palestinian cause should take priority, and their leader should pursue the desires of his people in all his political positions regarding their legitimate requirements and the means he suggests for realising them. All the Arab states which agree with his vision should offer help and strive to achieve some action without paying attention to their opponents, and without putting off their efforts until there is some sort of begrudged consensus. It is also natural that there should be no argument about the aim[2] and even those with various opinions about the Palestinian cause should agree on it as a general principle for the matter cannot be subject to further delay. We must also carry out this vision with no further ado and on a sound basis as part of a well-thought-out plan. Even if one nation rejects this as inconsistent with their stance on the Palestinian cause, the others should carry on without hesitation and the recalcitrant state will catch up with them sooner or later. Perhaps it is the role of Egypt at this time to redress the cause and the aim along the lines suggested above, or in some better manner. This may entail even more risks than when Egypt faced off the Mongols and their wave of destruction which

1 Here 'cause' refers to the 'Arab cause', i.e. the ideals of pan-Arabism.

2 i.e. gaining justice for the dispossessed Palestinian people and nation.

almost put an end to the whole world. For God rewards those who do a good deed.

26 January 1984

What a Neutral Ministry Cannot Do

The opposition is demanding that a neutral ministry should guarantee the impartiality of the elections. It is the right of the opposition to demand the integrity of the elections, and to demand robust guarantees such as the elections being placed under the total supervision of the judiciary with the help of the populace, a sense of ethics and our hopes which are pinned on the establishment of popular rule expected to foster freedom, dignity and social justice. However, the opposition does not have the right to demand an independent ministry.

Firstly: because such a demand implies an unfair accusation against the existing ministry who has proven its complete neutrality more than once.

Secondly: because this demand shows an ignorance of the forthright declarations made many times by the president of the republic, the prime minister and the minister of the interior, in addition to the general approach of the state in respecting the law and declaring its supremacy.

We do not aspire just to elections with impartiality but we want to see a general principle firmly anchored in the government's dealings with the people and in respecting the will of the people – a principle that will open a new page in our democratic life and work its way to becoming one of our most revered traditions for generation after generation. All we want is that this aim should be realised by a neutral ministry which has no interest in the campaign. Impartiality is what is needed to produce the best result. This goal will only be achieved, goodwill will only be built up, and this principle will only be established if the elections are run by a ministry that is participating in the campaign and whose neutrality and impartiality can be guaranteed. Only then will we be reassured enough to embrace a new and noble tradition in our political life; a new trust will come about between the government and the people and a new foundation will be created for political behaviour in our country. We will be able to say that we have uprooted a dark legacy from our history which has polluted our lives in both the distant and near past and turned it into a lie or a tragi-comedy.

2 February 1984

A Campaign Guide for the Citizen

We are in the midst of the election campaign and everywhere around us is buzzing with party activity. The people, now and forever, are the pitch, the referee and the goal. They will have their say and place men in positions of responsibility in a democratic spirit that brings the rulers and the opposition together. It might be of some use if each party was to print its manifesto in a small booklet so that we can discern the conflicting voices since it has been so difficult to make out the differences between the many parties. When it comes to the people as a whole, they should be addressed in a clear language that deals with their everyday issues, with a commitment to keeping promises, and using objective criticism and integrity in their argument. It is my belief that every citizen should wish to know clearly the opinion of every party on the following:

1. The five-year plan. Does he agree to its shape and how it is being carried out, or does he have some other vision?
2. Democracy. Does he agree with its slow and steady progress? Or does he have some other plan?
3. Social justice. What does he think about its current state, and does he have something new to add?
4. Religion and its relationship with the state, with everyday life, and with national unity.
5. The treatment the people receive when carrying out their normal business, and what sort of red-tape and unhelpfulness they come up against.
6. Overarching issues such as inflation, housing, transport, education and health. Do you have any better or quicker solutions?
7. Foreign policy, such as our relations with the two blocs, with the Arabs, the Palestinian issue and the Lebanese issue.

These are the things about which we would like to know their opinion, and we would like to hear them speak it calmly and in a manner far removed from histrionics, amateur dramatics or point-scoring. May

God inspire our parties with a sense of rectitude, and may God guide us to the best election for our nation.

9 February 1984

In Defence of the Five-Year Plan and the General Public

In our present circumstances we should have two senior civil servants in every ministry, one of whom should be in charge of the supervision and follow-up of the five-year plan, working on overcoming any obstacles it may face and presenting a regular report to the cabinet. The other should be responsible for looking after the interests of the general public, responding to their demands and dealing with their complaints.

I am making the first suggestion due to the fact that party political life demands that a minister changes from being a dilettante to a politician and because of the noticeable preoccupation of the ministers in political activity and communicating with the masses, whether in the media, in ministerial visits or by publishing reports, in addition to their regular activity in parliament, which doubles their workload. We welcome all this extra activity and would hope to see more of it with the proviso that it is not at the expense of the energy being directed towards the five-year plan upon which we have pinned our hopes as we emerge from our crisis and move along the path towards better economic times and progress.

I am making the second proposal since I have seen how people who are trying to get things done fall into a vicious cycle of fatigue, disrespect and time wasting. They are met with ignorance regarding the right place to go to within the bureaucracy, the required paperwork, and a lack of cooperation from officials, and they have to try and function under conditions which would be considered improper for a regular citizen in a country decent enough to recognise the rights of its citizens and the dignity of its people. Any high official must support the interests of the public, treat them with dignity and help them to work their way through the red tape.

What I have suggested is for the sake of the five-year plan and the general public. Today there is nothing more important than the five-year plan, other than the general public for whom it has been drawn up.

12 February 1984

For an Honest Battle

Long years of oppression have left us with a particularly bad habit – that we have two ways of speaking about every issue: the guarded way we speak in public, and the actual thoughts and feelings that we whisper to each other in private. We deal with our daily affairs, including the riskiest matters concerning our fate as a whole, in this meandering double-edged manner. This includes issues of war and peace, of socialism, the role of religion in our life, Arabism, education, and so on. Finally, our lives have seen some change with the law becoming paramount, conflicting voices being heard, and the establishment of welfare and security, but the bad habit has not yet been eradicated. Then comes along the atmosphere of the election campaign, sowing competitiveness and a desire to win, and the old habit returns to the fore and the masks reappear. How much longer can our vital affairs be subjected to whims with no clarity or resolve? I would implore our politicians, from whichever party, to forget that they are trying to win an election campaign and to use their energies for the benefit of the homeland. They should make this a campaign carried out with truth and clarity, whatever the results may be. Every party should declare what they truly and sincerely stand for, and not just make promises about how everything will be fine, without taking the consequences into consideration. Some of us may believe in one-man rule and should simply declare as much, for a person who honestly supports one-man rule is better than a fake democrat. Some of us may believe in an open capitalist system and should say as much. A devoted capitalist is better than a mendacious socialist. If someone believes that there should be separation of religion and state, let him say so loud and clear. An avowed secularist is better than a devout person who just repeats what others tell him. This is all to say that we should prefer honesty and clarity. There is no point in winning the campaign but losing yourself. Using lies to win can only result in the eventual downfall of a politician. Praise should go to those who make the election campaign one of honour and not one of political opportunism.

22 February 1984

Catastrophes and Us!

Over the course of their long history the Arabs have been subjected to various catastrophes some of which almost sent them into the abyss of non-existence or the void of oblivion. Dredging up this fact is not without benefit in this day and age when the Arabs find themselves torn between all sorts of stances and opinions, with dangers staring them in the eye, when they are threatened by ferocious hostility, and when they have been ground down by bitter defeats. Generally these disasters have either been caused by internal disagreements among the Arabs, or by external enemies who wish to kill or annihilate them or to control their destiny. At the height of their glory and the apogee of their victories, the first dispute arose among the Arabs over who was to be the third caliph. They disintegrated into factions and reverted to something akin to the gangs of pre-Islamic times or worse, with internecine squabbles and bloodshed diverting them from their real mission, and the grounds of these disputes have extended their tentacles down to this day. This was debilitating but it did not immobilise them and they succeeded in establishing an empire and a civilisation.

At another time the West marshalled its forces in an attempt to overpower the Arabs in a series of imperialist wars which took place behind the mask of religion and which lasted for years and years and, when crowned with victory, they established hereditary kingdoms[1] in our east which they took as a broad base for further adventurism in the years ahead. With a sense of pessimism people thought that the matter was settled, but the enemy's good fortune came to an end and the pessimists were proved wrong as kingdom after kingdom crumbled, the land was cleansed of its invaders and soon there flew over every fortress the flags of the patient and valiant fighters.

In a subsequent era the earth was occupied by a black destructive horde called the Mongols, who attacked fortresses, subjugated cities, killed people and crushed underfoot the elements of civilisation, until they became a byword for fear in everyone's hearts. However at our

1 i.e. the Crusader kingdoms in the Levant.

borders they found someone[2] to stand up to them and challenge them, to put an end to their energetic expansionism, to smash their blood-stained swords, to turn their victory into defeat, to restrain their shadow and to save the earth from their destructive evil.

For a fourth time a victorious sultan[3] invaded the Arab world, subjugating it to his will for around four centuries, during which lights were extinguished everywhere, the people were humiliated, their money confiscated, and their good deeds and intellectual output suppressed. The Arab world was plunged into total darkness until the sleepers of the cave woke up to find prophets of the new age and then the Arab world woke up, in a state of great confusion, and started building bridges to the world around it and stretched out its neck to try and absorb everything that had passed it by during its long slumber and brought about a blessed renaissance to a world considered long dead.

In our modern period, in the aftermath of the First World War to be precise, the Arab world by international agreement fell into the grip of European colonialism which had already taken over much of it for various reasons. Darkness fell on people's hearts and the future seemed full of gloom and despair. The victorious leader[4] stood on the grave of Saladin and challenged him to arise and save his people. Then [in 1919] the first anti-colonialist revolution broke out in Egypt, followed by a series of other revolutions. This led to row after row of martyrs and within less than half a century all the Arab countries had gained their independence, exercised suzerainty over their own lands and continued on their everlasting mission to develop themselves and their civilisation.

I direct this narrative to those who regard the situation of the Arabs today with dejection and despondency, not in order to make light of the situation for it is a really tough one, and not to console them over

2 Sayf al-Din Qutuz (r. 1259–60) who defeated the Mongols at the Battle of Ayn Jalut in 1260.

3 Here Mahfouz is referring to the Ottomans who added Egypt to their empire in 1517 and who ruled most of the current Arab world.

4 This must be a reference to Allenby's 1918 capture of Damascus.

past glories which can do nothing to change the present, but to say to them that catastrophes are nothing new for us. How often we have had to deal with them, and how often have we contained them and gone beyond them towards the good and the proper. So there is no real reason for despondency or pessimism, or to imagine that anything can last, for neither evil nor good last forever. There is no reason for us to fear war when necessary, nor to fear peace when necessary, nor to shy away from experience, or worry about vying with an adversary. We should always prepare ourselves with the conviction of our unblemished civilisation to face life with all its vicissitudes.

24 February 1984

Towering Intellects

We must count the month of February 1984 as one of the most auspicious months in our long history and no less splendid than February 1919,[1] July 1952[2] or October 1973,[3] for during this month we saw the first exhibition of thirty crucial Egyptian inventions and the announcement was made that Dr Muhammad al-Far had made a discovery for the treatment of that most threatening illness which is cancer.

That leads us to recall our towering scientists, such as Dr Ali Mushrifa and others who work in eminent international scientific research centres such as Drs al-Wakeel, al-Baz, Magdi Yaqoub and others whose names escape me for the moment. Today we can state proudly that we have in Dr al-Far a man who has made great scientific discoveries, with all the glory and greatness that term inspires and with all that it implies in terms of effort and service to humanity. No honour we could give him would be as much as he deserves and no praise could match his work, for only those who love truth and those who suffer from that awful illness of cancer can appreciate how great his achievements are. It may be that science has only come into its own after two hundred years[4] during which we applied ourselves to studying, acquiring and absorbing knowledge. We should not be ashamed of our past for education represents the first steps towards enlightenment, and acquiring knowledge is the correct way to go about that. Education has woken us up from our long slumber and made us start thinking about ourselves and the world around us. It has brought about a rebirth in agriculture,

1 The Revolution of 1919 was a countrywide revolution against the British occupation of Egypt and Sudan and helped move Egypt towards Britain's recognition of Egypt's independence in 1922.

2 The Revolution of 1952 saw the overthrow of the monarchy and the installation of a republican government.

3 The October War, also known as the Yom Kippur War, when the Egyptian army succeeded in crossing the Suez Canal into the Sinai Peninsula which had been occupied by Israel since 1967.

4 Mahfouz implies here that Egypt's modern scientific, or rational, educational system began after the Napoleonic invasion of 1798.

industry and management. However, the foundations have remained unstable, the edifice reliant upon others, and our feelings of inferiority have not diminished.

We will not regain our equilibrium or guarantee our future until we can think for ourselves, rather than allowing others to think for us, and until we move forward with our own creativity and innovation.

At that time, and only then, will we achieve self-confidence, will the edifice become stable and will we achieve progress. At that time, we will be able to overcome our intractable problems and ensure ourselves a place among the leading creative nations with whom we will be able to have a profitable exchange of information.

We must honour our scientists, create a favourable climate for thought and work and accord them a status appropriate to their ability to innovate. They are lamps in the dark, the banners of truth and our hope for tomorrow.

8 March 1984

An Era of Rationalism

The most important duty of the press, radio and television is to provide the public with facts, whether regarding their homeland or the world at large. To achieve this, the best thing the media can do is to gain the audience's trust, by which I mean that they should broadcast information that accords with reality and logic and is a faithful reflection of events as they take place as well as giving some mention to the future repercussions of these events. If a citizen thinks that the media is being complacent or biased, he will believe that he is hearing just one side of a news item and that the media are befuddling rather than informing him. His trust in that organ of the media will be shattered and he will seek the truth in other, rarely neutral, foreign sources and will end up with a welter of contradictory reports. We live in an age which is sometimes called the age of explosive information where living in ignorance is an unforgivable sin. All countries have their own policies, their own way of viewing events and they have the right to shape the way they present them. However that does not mean having to plunge the news consumer into a state of ignorance, much less anaesthetising or drugging him, with the implied undervaluing of his intellect and his person and attempted control of his mind, and it makes no difference if we state that access to a variety of news sources is one of the elements of democracy and freedom. Moreover, facts cannot be kept hidden for ever in this era of data and instant communications. The best way to present news is to have it broadcast as seen by the reporters but then to have journalists here provide localised comment. Nothing should be kept from the public and reporting should neither attempt to downplay events nor spread false hope. We should surely be educating people to face facts and learn how to deal with them. For a long time now, all we have known about people who think differently to us is that they are blood-shedders, agents and terrorists. They might well also have their own politics and way of seeing events. What is more, they might not differ from us in some of their aims, even we believe that different means of achieving them should be used. I do not think it will be long until we witness some drama being played out on our national stage without no accompanying commentary. Some characters will enter stage left and others will exit stage right as if we have nothing to do with them and they have nothing to do with us. I pray that real democracy can be kept away from having to decide what is 'right' or 'true'.

14 March 1984

A Multi-Party System

The logical and social justification for the existence of separate political parties is their difference of vision and principles as well as their inevitable difference in political platform; however, party politics should not descend to the level of personal animosity or act as a cover for a vision or principles that have not been publicly declared. Within the purview of our current laws, the choices available to politicians and the various existing political trends are rather narrow as a result of our having been deprived of the right to form new parties which can express their higher aims.

What I truly fear is that we will be presented with similar and convergent visions, principles and platforms, where every party calls for democracy, social justice and Arabism, and so on, and that the voters will allow themselves to be swayed by personality rather than principle, and will vote in accordance with their own personal interests or be dictated to by their feelings of satisfaction or discontent. I also fear that public opinion can be affected in some instances by those political currents which have been deprived of legitimacy and that the result will be unjust or unfair for those taking part. The only way we have of dealing with this deficiency is for every party's public communications to concentrate on what sets them apart from other parties inasmuch as possible, and to suggest new solutions for old problems in order to show its distinctive character within the prescribed limits.

A party that cannot do this should merge with a party of a similar ilk, or invite that other party to merge with it. A quick glance at the political arena confirms that it can support only two large parties under the conditions currently prevailing: one democratic-socialist and the other liberal.

This system may not please some, but it is better than superficial pluralism and saves the voter from confusion.

15 March 1984

The Trust of the People

It would appear that our government is marshalling all its strength to ensure the availability of foodstuff and weapons as two of the most pressing of its domestic targets. This is no surprise, for the clouds of a hitherto unwitnessed global food crisis are looming on the horizon. At that point the world will be divided into foodstuff-rich countries and countries begging for the same commodity from the rich countries and having to be subservient to them in a way that brooks no rebellion. Food self-sufficiency means the possibility to live and be able to practise freedom and dignity. When it comes to the question of weapons, they are indispensable even to a peace-loving country that has placed peace at the top of its list of deeply held aspirations – for every last value is worthless in this world unless it is held in place by some form of force. On the other hand, there is an important target which is never mentioned in any list. It is like the spirit, invisible and impalpable, but without it any body will become no more than a mass of discarded and immobile limbs. It is the trust of the people. The government should work to gain the trust of the people before anything else. That is the unshakeable foundation of respect, the incentive for a sense of belonging, and it is what drives people to work and to make sacrifices. It is the spirit of the people and their unwritten covenant, their family consciousness that brims with love and warmth. It can only be gained through courage, integrity and altruism, by a dedication to the public interest. It can only be gained through complete sincerity when it comes to making promises and public statements, by people who act and speak transparently, through the just and equitable treatment of citizens with no differentiation based on class, party affiliation or religion, by serving the masses with honesty, straightforwardness and respect, by including both opponents and supporters in our national endeavour, by taking pride in useful work and by acknowledging our mistakes. The trust of the people is born from the guarantee of continued good governance and lies behind every step, every war and every outbreak of peace.

22 March 1984

On the Generation Argument

It is the right of every new generation to criticise the preceding generations, to view their values in the light of their current reality and to prepare the ground for a new way of seeing. Many well-intentioned people have been angered by this criticism, considering it an act of ingratitude, national iconoclasm and intellectual subversion. They mistrust the intentions behind this criticism and accuse the younger generation of having bad intentions. This type of defensiveness turns the argument from a literary struggle which has the capacity to enrich thought and uncover new truths into a spurious nationalist battle which can only lead to bickering and the outburst of hatred. I would say again that every generation has the right to re-evaluate its predecessors, to pave the way for the dissemination of new views and the progress of thought on its never-ending path. This re-evaluation, however harsh it may be, cannot floor a tiger unless it is made of paper, nor eradicate a truth unless it is made of thin air. We all remember the way the Diwan school criticised Ahmed Shawqi heavily but how this criticism was based on a new poetic sensitivity which did not undermine Shawqi or his unique position within Arabic poetry. Before him, al-Mutanabbi had to face much worse attacks than Shawqi did but al-Mutanabbi has retained his fame as a great Arab poet down the centuries. Thus, a re-evaluation paves the way for new visions without undermining values whose validity is long-lasting. If we were to discuss what is being said with objectivity and rationality, we would be supporting the discovery of new truths and we would be participating in an intellectual battle which has the potential to enrich thought and art. This would be much more beneficial than throwing out accusations which, in the final analysis, can only create a sort of intellectual terrorism which is one of the worst forms of censorship and oppression.

29 March 1984

A Serious Campaign in a Serious Period

The election campaign reaches its peak in April and May, which is roughly the end of the second year of the five-year plan and almost the start of the third year, thus offering a unique opportunity to showcase last year's achievements and the productivity and services that are slated to be achieved during the third year. This latter is what interests us more in this current period of our lives than past achievements and failures and is therefore more suitable as a topic for the election campaign during which the views, aspects of the vision and practical positions of the parties will be reflected without us needing to delve more deeply into the candidate's own views and opinions. If everyone is committed to objectivity and sincerity and puts forward their opinions and criticism, this will have a good effect in terms of being a means of examining and evaluating the five-year plan. At the same time, the voters will able to differentiate between the various views that reflect the natural ideological differences between the parties without the need to scrutinise their opinions and theories. We will find no topic for an objective and balanced campaign like the comprehensive Five Year Development Plan, and perhaps it is the most important thing occupying our hearts and minds in this critical era of our lives by virtue of the Plan encompassing all aspects of activity in our society, including agriculture, manufacturing, science, education, culture, foodstuff, clothing, health, construction and the bases of governance and legislation. In addition, this focus stops us being bogged down in worthless side campaigns and conflicts over the past which, for all its good and bad aspects, is over and done with and about which everything that can be said has been said. Going on and on about the past will only lead to argument, violence and a lot of hand-wringing in a sensitive time of problems, risks and seriousness which demands from all of us to pull together and work hard.

5 April 1984

The Cause of Art

We do not permit ourselves to comment about a legal ruling or to discuss a case which is sub judice but that does not mean that we can absolve ourselves from showing any ongoing interest in the freedom of innovation or in the role which art has to play in society and life. That is perhaps what has moved the Artists' Union headed by Saad al-Din Wahba to hold consultations with regard to the enormous responsibility of art, artists and the way art can develop or modify society. The Union issued a statement which contains two pertinent truths for us: the first asserts full respect for the Egyptian judiciary and complete faith in its rulings, and the second deals with the thinking necessary for artistic creativity and innovation to be co-opted in order to change the world permanently for the better. Then we read a report in the *Ahrar* newspaper that the Union decided to send an aide-memoire to the prime minister with certain suggestions regarding the freedom of thought within the artistic domain.

In so doing, the Union was carrying out its appropriate duty, and I cannot say how much I would like to see not only the Writers' Union and the Supreme Council for Culture, but also anyone involved with creativity and innovation, undertake a similar course of action in attempting to guarantee the freedoms necessary. We would hope to see this bring about a clear constitutional understanding of the freedom of art and the permissibility of criticising life and society, which distinguishes between the libellous and scurrilous on the one hand, and constructive criticism of the sub-standard whatever or whoever its source is on the other hand. We would hope to see freedom and security guaranteed for the artistic and intellectual community for there can be no constructive movement without criticism, there can be no criticism without freedom, there can be no freedom without guarantees. Freedom can have no value if there are class or sectarian privileges standing in the way of criticism.

Let us remember that we are embarking on a democratic journey and that democracy does not merely consist of councils and institutions but, first and foremost, democracy represents a method of discussion, thinking and working together as well as a general acceptance that no individual or group should be free from the constructive criticism which aims at the general good. This might direct our interest to some core axes, including:

Firstly, censorship: it would appear that censorship is carried out in the manner required by the performing arts and does not live up to the values which it has been entrusted with preserving. Censorship must be rational, constructive and must protect freedom and values at the same time. It should not trickle down into routine matters. Censorship should not be applied without any cultural or social awareness, without a sense of taste or ethics and it should not be a hindrance to, or whittle away at, our freedom of expression. At the same time, it should attempt to prevent baseless and degrading attacks on our values and humanity.

For a long time now I have been calling for regular meetings to be held between the censorship apparatus on the one side and artists, intellectuals and critics on the other, under the aegis and supervision of the minister, to discuss and exchange views in order to arrive at a mutually-agreed formula for a way forward that will allow art to spread its positive and uplifting message and to support the values of a constructive society in its struggle for a better life.

Secondly: the leaders of the art and literary trade unions and some of its members who represent the various artistic trends who must hold meetings with a select group of lawyers and arbitrators to read over the legal material which deals with creativity in order to gain a better and clearer understanding and to delineate the dividing line between fair criticism and that form of criticism which can be considered libellous or defamatory. The general aim will be the welfare and development of society, and the elevation of art to a position where it is guaranteed freedom and security.

Thirdly: the Artists' Union should restrict itself to dealing with the conditions prevailing in the state of emergency, but it must develop a permanent policy for general positive artistic endeavour and to that end it must have the participation of the Writers' Union and the Supreme Council for Culture in meetings to be held from time to time in the Chamber of the Cinema Industry along with the leading directors, screen-writers and actors, with the aim of finding a rational way forward during this crucial period of our social development and of reconciling the needs of the new public inasmuch as possible with the principles without which art would not be art. The best way would be for the Artists' Union to establish a permanent committee to monitor artistic output and to enable an exchange of views or to read some texts and after due consultation to provide advice in a collegiate spirit, without arbitrariness or slight to artistic freedom. This might be able to offer art, in our current circumstances, what all the constant harping and carping have not been able to do, and it might be able to mitigate the campaigns against art which we read about these days in the press and hear about from the government.

Indeed, the time may well have come for the artistic community to rise up and defend the quality of their output which is struggling to establish itself for the long term.

12 April 1984

A Renewal of Interest

There is a new phenomenon making the rounds of the circles I move in – people are talking more and more about the election campaign, equality of access for the parties, and the way the campaign is being run, and you may see this reflected in some opinions expressed by the readership of the newspapers and magazines, which only leads us to conclude something about the generality of this phenomenon and the fact that it presages a return to our showing some interest in public life and participating in it after a period when the concerns of daily life seemed to have taken over the conscience of Egyptians. In its essence this is a healthy phenomenon and has perhaps been translated into an increase in the number of people entering their names on the electoral register. It is true that the chance to register is now over, but this new interest has effected a significant change even if there has not been a noticeable increase in numbers. This interest augurs a new life for the nation, a decisive change in the future of our political lives, and progress towards positivity, participation and a sense of belonging. Perhaps the reason for this interest can be traced back to two important factors:

First, the clear statements from officials regarding the integrity of the elections which we must ascribe to the practical steps taken by the minister of the interior, the atmosphere of freedom of speech and activity in which the election campaign is taking place, and the ruling party's insistence that those entering the election campaign should campaign based on their achievements and promises and not on the strength of others.

Second, the return of the Wafd Party to political life as an expression of the grassroots and not the Socialist Union from which the other parties have emerged, something which has created new openings in the field as well as real arguments and unavoidable challenges. This is something that could inject new vigour into the campaign. Notwithstanding, if I am right about the phenomenon of renewed interest in the election campaign, this will represent a victory for the nation even before it takes part in the campaign, regardless of the outcome. In my opinion this is more important than the election itself or its results.

10 May 1984

The Election Campaign and the Revolution

Whichever you read of our parties' programmes, you come across the image of the July Revolution in all its distinctive sections – and this applies to all the parties, whether the Wafd, the National Democratic, Tajammu' or Labour parties. Terms such as the public sector, achievements made for workers and peasants, free education, agricultural reform, industrialisation and Arab solidarity are bandied about everywhere, along with a plethora of opinions ranging from moderation to extremism, as well as proposals for reform and renewal. This is one of the positive achievements that the Revolution has brought for everyone, the proof being that it has become an inseparable part of the spirit of Egypt and of its development and future. This all goes to prove that this has been the most real of our constant revolutions, a natural link in the chain of our ongoing and continuing struggle, and the great feats it has achieved can neither be overlooked nor lost. The Revolution has been confronted by enemies wishing to erase it from the pages of history, using its negative aspects as an argument to undermine it. They also attempt to undermine its positive achievements. They persistently and stubbornly attempt to show up the Revolution's shortcomings, something we ourselves cannot deny, but let us not forget that despite dictatorship, terrorism, corruption and defeats, all the Revolution's achievements stand tall and the force of truth obliges us to acknowledge and accept that. The election campaign has made all those taking part stop and take stock and rise to the historic responsibility facing the masses. And good, sincere nationalists as we all are, everyone is convinced that the appropriate language to use in addressing people is one which includes the achievements of the Revolution which has freed them from many shackles and opened up new gates of hope, extending the hand of brotherhood to all those who work hard. It has spurred the nation on to new degrees of justice, education and progress. In truth, democracy has come about not to sidestep the Revolution, but to afford it recognition and to include it on the roll call of honour and eternity.

17 May 1984

The Parliament We Are Waiting For

The parliament we are waiting for will be the fruit of a decisive transitional period between a past laden with contradictions and a future which we hope will be based on firm foundations of government by the people for the people. The five-year plan, which is the pivot of our lives, will benefit from a whole range of opinions and points of view, guaranteeing increased power and success, and our external policy will be backed by nationwide support, helping the policy to avoid the errors of the past while keeping it on the straight and narrow. It is indisputable that there will be an opportunity to review the constitution, the emergency laws and the election law in their day-to-day practices – which will afford our daily lives more balance, stability and trust. It will become clear how the parties radically differ from each other and in what areas they have a similar and fundamental approach, and this will clear the way for a shake-up of the parties along sound social bases rather than personal leanings. I am perhaps not mistaken in my conviction that we may be able to create a middle party out of the Wafd, the National Democratic, the Labour and Liberal parties, alongside the Marxist and Nasserist parties, and a third party representing the religious faction. Each of these parties will have its own constituents and vision, and will be able to deliver its national message in parliament by creating a climate that is conducive for firm and continual progress. A middle party, for all its strength and popularity, will need the experience of others, particularly as it will have to deal with the Marxists in its quest for justice, with the Nasserites in order to preserve the achievements of the July Revolution, and with the religious faction in respecting spiritual values and a life free of corruption. We are waiting for the election results in order to see the first popular democratic coming together since the 1950s, and thereafter we would hope to see the birth of a new humane life operating under the aegis of complete respect for human rights.

24 May 1984

A New Age

We have now seen the end of the election campaign for better or for worse. It has yielded its legitimate result, notwithstanding what has been said about its shortcomings. The police have been obliged to take a neutral and just stance, which we hope will lead to a new and sanctified era in which the police will be more aware of the way it treats people in Egypt. Indeed, the opposition did not gain the guarantees they demanded, but the success of the majority can be traced back, first and foremost, to the merit of its leadership, its purely constructive behaviour and the achievements it has made in the exercise of governance. All of these are legitimate marks of honour that deserve support and encouragement. We welcome the person who has won the majority of the votes and is now in power as someone who has managed to win great trust in a critical period encumbered with problems at home and abroad. We hope, now that the people have blessed his work and accorded him their trust, that he will continue to function ever more forcefully and with even greater enthusiasm. We do not doubt for a second that the opposition is a vital part of the apparatus of governance and will offer its constructive criticism and sound advice, directing his steps towards the greater aim desired by the whole nation, whatever their party affiliation or dreams. We particularly hope that they will be able to restore a healthy and natural balance to society, to offer a sound and untrammelled democratic way of life, which will bring about solid development and will stimulate a conscious march towards the implementation of full human rights. At the same time, we cannot hide our dismay over the unjustly invalidated votes which have made it difficult for those voted for to take part in parliament, including devoted nationalists who could otherwise today be active members of parliament. It is of some consolation for this loss for us to know that they continue to think outside parliament for the benefit of the nation and are continuing their efforts through the press and in their political associations. The final lesson can be found in work rather than in the workplace. Perhaps people will calm down and our leaders, revolutionaries, and younger generations will temper their anger. Perhaps they will stop downplaying our glorious achievements and sullying our memories, and we will be able to step towards the task of confronting reality and its problems, and gaining the decisive will to create a better future and a more noble history.

31 May 1984

A Word to Our Youth

The election campaign has managed to compound the confusion felt by our youth as, in front of their very eyes, there flew around unfounded accusations over the past and the present, over events both before and after July 1952. Our youth have the right to wonder: where does the truth lie in all of this? Should we listen to the trustworthy hero or to a treacherous thief? Which deeds were carried out as useful parts of the general struggle and which were a waste of effort and time? Were Saad Zaghloul and Mostafa Nahas great leaders of our struggle or buffoons? Were Gamal Abdel Nasser and Anwar Sadat two warrior leaders or just two men who brought down upon us hitherto unprecedented defeat, shame and destruction?

To our youth I would say: you will not gain an understanding of history from the mouths of those involved in arguments of historic proportions. The underlying facts do not just appear when the dust of battle has settled. History will have its say at the right time, in its own way, and through people who are above any aim except that of finding out the truth – and to them I would also state that only God can have a perfect understanding of events, for man is composed of heroism and cowardice, man can do both right and wrong, and his acts will be weighed in the balance, 'so whoever does an atom's weight of good will see it, and whoever does an atom's weight of evil will see it.'[1] I would also tell them that every country's rebirth in history has passed through stages similar to those of an individual: an infancy during which the seed comes to life, and naturally it sprouts and grows, passes through its youth bursting with resources of strength and innovation into a stage of maturity which brings forth wisdom and righteousness. Then old age overcomes it and it falls into errors and weakness of judgment and in that lies its chance to be re-created, to arise again after death through new generations who take the whole cycle further on its path. So do not let yourselves be beset with doubt over your country and its history, nor over the coming generations and

---

1 Qur'an, 99:7-8. Refers to man's judgement on the Day of Judgement.

their struggle, and do not despair over the bad things you have heard about past ages and people, for every generation has done its very best under the prevailing circumstances, and there is a good and bad side to everything. Do not let the anger from past arguments overshadow the sacrifices people have made or the beautiful things created by previous generations. However many obstacles and problems we may have today, Egypt is still a country whose wealth comes from her children and they are our seed capital which, if well invested, will give a wonderful return: and here I am referring to oil, cotton, the Suez Canal and the many possibilities for progress and expansion both to the East and the West. The rewards are much greater than any lurking risks. However, the scale can only be tipped with your faith, your sense of belonging and your intellects.

7 June 1984

A Word to the Wafd Party

The Wafd Party has returned to the arena of the national struggle and occupies a respected position in the parliament. Life should not go on in its old rhythm and no doubt we will see change, and no doubt it will be for the better. It is undeniable that the hearts of the grassroots are beating with age-old hopes which they anticipate the Wafd will realise from its new position:

1. First and foremost they hope that the Wafd will base its opposition uniquely on being objective, serious, free from corruption. That the Wafd will deal with the facts as they are as the party continues its venerable struggle for the sake of the nation which has made it the nation's bellwether and to which the nation looks for leadership.
2. We hope that the party will endeavour, with all its faith in the people and its powers of persuasion, to put into action what it promised in the election platform – to restore Egypt's democratic character so that the country can tower above all its faults and finally provide a solid foundation for human rights.
3. Perhaps the Wafd does not need reminding about the problems besetting the nation as a result of its past long years of isolation in order to deal with the roots of the economic, social and cultural crisis. The party, with impartiality and integrity, needs to establish ways of treating these issues and applying all the new means it deems necessary to resolve them, to bring about reform and to achieve its aims as quickly as possible. Things have become most unclear with everyone offering up different views and solutions, all mixed up with political rivalry, resulting in the development of an unhealthy miasma which has polluted the atmosphere, and the general public can only look on with fear and confusion. The Wafd ought to set up specialist investigation committees immediately to come up with the right solutions, even if they have to give up some of their summer recess to do so.

We are passing through a long bottleneck, and the country is in urgent need of its citizens' cooperation and devotion, and of a government which knuckles down to work. I believe that the government will not spurn any useful opinion, or be dismissive towards a hand stretched out to it with love and loyalty for Egypt. We hope, with the return of the Wafd Party, that actions will move in a faster pace, that productivity will rise, and progress will be swifter and more robust for the sake of the whole nation, God willing.

14 June 1984

A Small Nation Among Giants

A small nation in a world of giants must think about the logic of a small nation, and may God have mercy upon anyone who recognises his own capability. We are a small nation. We might approach gianthood if one day we realise our Arab dream, but today we are a small nation and we have to think about the logic of reality and not of dreams. I am not calling for our surrender or debasement as the price for existence and bread, for a small nation can, with prudence and rationality, guarantee itself a dignified, valuable and enlightened life. To do that it has to bring about two essential elements, firstly: with regard to its domestic affairs, it must establish its citizens' life on the basis of freedom, social justice, science and work, for without freedom there is no dignity, without justice there is no sense of belonging, without science we cannot operate within the world, and without work we cannot assure our existence.

Secondly: with regard to its external affairs we have to know which of our aims are vital and which are secondary, and at the same time we have to know what the aims of others are, and in particular we have to know what the vital and secondary aims of the giants are. After that we have to look again at our aims in the light of what we know about the aims of the giants and then decide upon a policy which can realise as many of our hopes as possible with the least amount of sacrifice while guaranteeing our existence, dignity and security. All the options have negative and positive facets and can bring about gains or losses, but the important thing is that the chosen option is to our benefit in the final analysis. In the past the world applauded us as we fought for our liberation, but this applause was of little use to us and we paid little heed to the awfulness of the consequence. To this day we have not stopped fighting in order to find the right path to follow, to find unpolluted water to drink and to have enough to eat without incurring loans from other countries. Perhaps if we had taken on the logic of a small country at the start of our national reawakening, the national rebirth attempted by Muhammad Ali would not have been stillborn and the national rebirth attempted by Abd al-Nasser would not have withered when in full bloom, and perhaps today we would have been a nation of giants in terms of values in spite of our modest size among the nations.

28 June 1984

The Party Platforms and Our Youth

Despite the general awareness raised by the election campaign, we still have a not inconsiderable number of our youth who have no party preference or political motivation. Much has been said about this phenomenon as one of the reasons for their lack of a sense of belonging. I do not intend to raise this subject yet again, but today I would like to search for a way out of this conundrum now that our prevailing democratic life has created the appropriate climate for doing so. We hope that this climate will help us regain our psychological and social well-being and perhaps the party platforms can rekindle interest in this recovery and provide the incentive for us to reconsider matters of national interest, factors upon which our fate depends, and make us leave behind our sense of insularity and alienation. We hope that this can come about if our youth read the party manifestos carefully, even if it does not happen now, for most of those I have in mind are not on the electoral register or are too young to register yet. The crucial thing is for them to be able to compare party manifestos, to form a critical opinion and to come up with their own preferences and to be able to say so publicly. This should encourage our youth to think freely, to gain some understanding of cultural and political factors, and to make a conscious choice. This will also provide an impetus for them towards a sense of national belonging. This could be accomplished in the form of a general competition with prizes awarded to the winners, based objectively on their power of observation, their depth of criticism, and the merits of their argument regarding their electoral choice. This could be done either through a youth organisation or on television, or both at the same time. Even if this suggestion is no more than a mental sport or summer activity, it is worth consideration and being put into action.

1 July 1984

Look in Anger at Reality

Let us take a glance at our own capabilities for perhaps people have acquired a contempt for reality because they have lived with it for so long. We are nations which speak the same language,[1] breathe in the same culture and share the same history. We lie at the mid-point between the continents of the world and possess enough agricultural and potentially agricultural land to satisfy our needs as well as to produce a surplus which can satisfy the needs of others. We possess the largest energy reserves which has resulted in the massive in-flows of cash. We have more than enough manpower as well as scientific, manufacturing and various other specialised establishments. And nor do the Arabs lack brain power. They know what their aims are and the path they have to take to achieve them.

Let us now take a glance at our reality, and what do we see? We see states which are as far as can be from unity in any form of the word's meaning, and much closer to a state of competition, dispute and even war. For their daily needs they rely upon imports meaning that they import foodstuffs, science, culture and politics. They invest only a small proportion of their wealth at home and most of it abroad, although not of course with their enemies. Much of this wealth has gone into servicing debts, has barely made a dent on poverty and has not had the slightest effect on the rights of their populations or the enhancement of their own capabilities. At the same time their cultural development lurches along towards a future hedged with worry, fear and risk. Just look at the auspicious beginnings of projects and then at their wretched results and you will see that we do not lack real vision or an awareness of our aims and how to achieve them, but we do lack the true will to overcome the challenges of life and we must remember that God only changes the fate of a nation when its people manage to find the impetus within themselves.

5 July 1984

1 The pronoun 'we' here indicates the pan-Arab plural.

Between Culture and Development

Many people imagine that the most they can derive from culture is spiritual enjoyment and intellectual enlightenment. If that is the case then we are right to consider it one of the core aims which deserve attention and nurturing, for spiritual enjoyment is a rare value and intellectual enlightenment is a wonderful delight and both of these are worth no less and perhaps more than material values. However, culture has another effect on daily life itself as it helps make a person into what he is today, it helps form his opinions and shapes the way he sees himself, other people and life in general. Culture guides an individual to the meaning of his life and the message of our existence. Furthermore, it defines a person's relationship to his work as one of not just working for self-fulfilment, or profit or success, but as one whereby he can outdo himself and become an example to others and to society of fine precepts and values. That is how work and its results can have a general, national and universal meaning. That is how culture and daily life are intertwined, and the most important thing that can come out of that is the completion of our comprehensive five-year development plan.[1]

Perhaps the absence of this truth from our minds has been responsible for the absence of culture from the platforms of the political parties in the frenzy of the election campaign,[2] and for the scant references made to culture in the weighty statements issued on the occasion of numerous historical commemorations. It has become difficult for us to discuss the role of culture in life. However, no one thinks to notice the mysterious link between this fact and the alienation, self-absorption and negativity of the electorate who abstained from voting and thereby committed a great act of injustice against a burgeoning democracy. Many people have spoken about all this but made no reference to its relationship with culture.

---

1 Perhaps the five-year plan for economic and social development 1982/83–1986/87.

2 Parliamentary elections were held in Egypt on 27 May 1984.

I cannot deny that those phenomena have causes other than political and economic, just as I cannot deny the existence of a cultured section of the population who are drowning in negativity, but the negativity of the majority stems from deficient nationalist education, from a lack of political awareness and from a shallow level of culture. The importance of culture in the Third World becomes magnified as circumstances require a positive and active citizen, with a sense of belonging and an alert social conscience, a citizen who is open to sharing and inclusion, prepared to make sacrifices and to do his utmost for the development of his country as a producer and consumer alike and to carry out his duties in the service of his fellow countrymen.

There may well be a delay in creating the right political climate for us to create this citizen, and there may well be obstacles along the path to that economic success which will make the citizen's life more comfortable, but there is no means more available or effective in doing this than that form of culture which symbolises intellectual steadiness, good intentions and nobility of spirit, whose variegated roots reach out to the world at large, both in the present circumstances and in the tomorrow we hope for, and which provide the life-blood which flows to the brain and enables the emotions and the will, and which in the end enables us to know where we stand, to be people of vision and to establish a modern modus vivendi.

The state has means of disseminating this culture through all stages of education, through the various organs of the national press, through its public relations apparatus such as the state radio and television and through its advanced legislation. We will not forget how things used to be in our schools in days gone by, nor can we forget the rich cultural climate embodied in textbooks, magazines and the various bodies which perform music and poetry. That era produced generations of people who loved culture and their country as well as providing people who strove devotedly for our social development. Now we are calling for reforms to education, for it to be part of the larger picture of social and developmental aims through science, technology and planning. However, this will not be achieved through science and technology alone, but by people with work expertise. The people who carry this out should not be those who are driven by success or self-fulfilment alone as their aim, but first and foremost by people of vision, people on a mission for their homeland and humanity. The only way we can reach this higher level of social development is through culture.

6 July 1984

In Defence of Higher Values

When we study the history of the life of a nation we find that it does not lack events or higher values which can be considered landmarks in its development and the starting points of its rebirth. Examples of these are the drafting of a constitution, the outbreak of a revolution, the establishment of a national academy and so on. Anyone who looks into our history will find incontrovertible evidence of these, but he will also notice that they have not led automatically towards development and prosperity. That path has been full of obstacles, progress has relapsed and often the results have been the opposite of what was intended. Since the turn of the nineteenth century, we have been aware that our civilisation was in need of modernisation, and we sent groups of students abroad,[1] we established schools and brought about a rebirth in agriculture, manufacturing, administration and the military.

At the beginning of the century we were rewarded with a rather good constitution and it was expected that we would lurch forward with the democratic experiment, but the attempt ended badly with us having become experts at rigging elections and creating tyrannical governments which collaborated with the throne and with imperialism.

In one of the happy moments when we had faith in our own people, we decided that education was a human right, just like access to water and air. Enough time has now passed for us to have eradicated illiteracy and to have raised the nation to higher levels of expertise, but until now illiteracy still afflicts more than half of the population and we are still trying to bring about reforms in education and teaching.

So what is the secret of this disaster? We have become accustomed to blaming colonialism for this failure, and that is by its very nature undeniable, but we should not close our eyes to the bitter truth that when we were controlled by colonial powers, they found willing collaborators among us – not to mention the fact that we corrupted our own values even without the intervention of colonialism.

1 This is a reference to Muhammad Ali's policy of sending groups of Egyptian students to study in Europe.

Hence we should concentrate on our own shortcomings and weak points above all. That is the struggle we should be carrying on.

12 July 1984

The July Revolution

The time has come again for us to commemorate the Revolution. The Revolution is an irrefutable truth and pulsates within the heart of the nation. It is a topic beyond any dispute or strife, and it shelters its supporters, as well as others, under its outstretched wing. Its positive aspects have become the cornerstone of the edifice of our national rebirth by virtue of its popular achievements, its national goals and its economic and social solidity. It has proved to be an ongoing and lethal warning to the irresponsible, a lesson for those who need to learn, an impediment for the reckless, and a living reprimand for those murderers, thieves and ignorant people who spread corruption on earth. The Revolution's negative aspects might have outweighed its positive attributes and uprooted our hopes of saving what we could, had God not allowed the Revolution to endure and ensured the kind treatment of an innocent people, showing the Revolution the way to repentance, regret and reform as the bitter fight continued challenging waves of pain, patience and struggle.

The Revolution could have come to an end in the immediate aftermath of the Tripartite Aggression,[1] had it not been for international pressure. It could have been liquidated after 5 June,[2] had the masses not been able to draw strength, determination and obstinacy from their despair. The Revolution somehow pulled itself back together and managed to create days of shining revival like the 6 October[3] and 25 April.[4]

It then went through a period of prudence in which it tried to atone for past wrongs, to correct its mistakes, to recognise the people as the source of power, authority, history, the present day and hope, and to direct its efforts towards serving the people and reform, rebirth and

---

1 The Suez Crisis of 1956.

2 The outbreak of the 1967 Arab-Israeli war.

3 The outbreak of the October War of 1973.

4 Sinai Liberation Day, celebrating the final withdrawal of Israeli forces from the Sinai Peninsula in 1982.

renewal, with recourse to integrity and sincerity, security and national feeling, and wisdom. A sense of high-mindedness came into being and it became clear what could and needed to be done.

The Revolution learned its capabilities and acknowledged its positive and negative impacts.

Let us call upon God to enable the ship of state to continue its journey to the destination which every citizen's heart wishes. Amen.

19 July 1984

The Return of the Giants

The renewal of full diplomatic relations with the Soviet Union has been announced. This is a decision whose achievement stemmed from our foreign policy and is along the lines of our similar promising achievements in the Arab, African and Islamic regions. It is not prudent for us to have bad relations with a state such as the Soviet Union which, according to any benchmark, is considered one of the greatest powers in the contemporary world and we should only be in a state of bad relations as a result of our own national interest, but this would not be in accordance with our policy, with a true desire for peace, with cooperation or with an exchange of interests. The proviso here is that we keep a complete hold on our freedom, our will and our principles. In this regard we will never forget the stance of the Soviet Union with regard to the Arab cause and their support in international assemblies. We should not forget the Soviet Union's collaboration with us in developing our rebirth in agriculture, industry and defence, and nor should we forget that we brought about our stunning victory on 6 October with their weapons which matched up to the faith and bravery of our army. It is clear that the resumption of relations does not mean a change in our policy, for our external policy has its own constituent elements which are essentially based on our national interest, and this national interest is what defines our aims, what specifies the means of achieving them, and what delineates the boundaries of the path we have to follow, whether it is that of alignment or non-alignment. However, the resumption of normal diplomatic relations is the starting point for human development in the economy and culture, as well as for providing more opportunities to resolve the Palestinian issue, or to defend the suffering people of Afghanistan. We welcome the resumption of relations with the Soviet Union and congratulate the state upon this success.

26 July 1984

Those without a Sense of Belonging

The question that we should pose and for which we should seek an answer is how do we motivate the citizen who has no sense of belonging to perform his duty for his nation? That is what the present situation requires, and this is a question we should deal with without prevarication or delay. I do not say this out of desperation and nor am I underestimating the situation, but we have already said everything that it is possible to say. We caused this situation, and we have made suggestions to treat it, concentrating on the role played by the family, the school, the National Democratic Party, culture and the mass media, but it would appear that we will have to wait a long time until we see the shaping of a generation with a sense of belonging upon whom we can rely to build up the nation and deal with its problems. At the same time the urgent demands of daily life do not allow us to put off making some achievements in this regard. So how can we motivate a citizen who has no sense of belonging to give as much as he can? We have to work on detaching him from his selfishness and self-interest. We have to prepare him to do the work he has been trained for, to find him a job where his education can be put to use and to create the means of self-fulfilment in an equitable political climate. We have to provide incentives and encouragement. If the citizen then falls short in his work, is negligent or betrays the trust placed in his hands, we should not hesitate to mete out the sort of punishment which will be a deterrent to others.

That is not just the right way to treat those who have no sense of belonging, but it is the right way for all situations. This is how justice will be realised for the individual and how we will achieve our aims.

9 August 1984

Democratic Demands

Here we are practising a real, democratic life. And over there is the opposition, lurking in the parliament, waiting to spring into action and do their national duty, supported by the extra-parliamentary opposition which is just as strong and tenacious. And here you will find the government itself deeply involved in an ongoing debate with opposing opinions that pull no punches when it comes to defending what is right and true.

Just as we demand objectivity and seriousness from the opposition, we demand the government to be magnanimous and far-sighted enough to approach dialectical disagreements with due respect and equanimity. For what is democracy if not a sense of responsibility, a burden, a form of criticism and accountability? However, the government, in addition to this, must do its general duty as best it can with regard to the five-year plan for domestic and foreign policy, and with regard to solving the daily problems of the masses. However, it is my fear that opposition activity will be held against it and not in its favour and that the opposition, in pursuing their campaigns, will be accused of wasting valuable time and precious energy on the wrong sort of things.

Therefore, I am returning to an old proposal that I have long reiterated with regard to the distribution of labour among the ministries, and perhaps this becomes more urgent with every new step we take along the path of democracy. It is unarguable that our new style of life imposes on the ministers new burdens required by the masses and by their work in the cabinet and in parliament. Officials at the highest level of responsibility must be designated to carry out the five-year plan, to put it into action and supervise it, to oversee public services in the various areas so that we can put it into action with the desired speed, no matter what the conditions or circumstances.

In this manner, democracy can bestow on us what it does best for people in terms of freedom, consultation, constructive criticism, vigilance and impartial accountability. This will at the time constitute a driving force in the spheres of unceasing labour and creativity.

12 August 1984

The State Radio, Television and Culture

One of the duties of the visual and aural media is to consider itself especially responsible for our national culture at this period of time. This is a responsibility imposed on it by our current state of development as a result of the media's hitherto unimaginable power, attraction and ubiquity. In saying this I do not mean to cause despair to the written-word community, to denigrate their call for serious culture to be supported, to make light of the maxim that the book is the source of fine culture or to play down the efforts of the Ministry of Culture and its employees in their services to magazine and book publishing, the theatre, the cinema, music, mass culture or antiquities, and I certainly do not mean to underestimate the value of the reforms we hope the Ministry of Education will institute in order to place culture centre-stage among the young and to give the Arab language its due centrality and serious attention.

We will not relinquish our hope that a mature culture will find its place in our country, based on a broad level of readership and that this will extend in a general manner to providing the radio and television audience with an ever-increasing stream of information, values and discerning entertainment programmes. However, in order to achieve this, in order for us to pass through this critical cultural period which is the bitter fruit of our many wars and political, economic and educational crises, the state media must hold itself especially responsible for culture and for state-building and employ all its clout and patriotism to fight against negativity, falling standards and the risk of appealing to the lowest common denominator. I am absolutely certain that the media's message is multi-dimensional and has a multitude of aims. Being the voice and philosophy of the state, it broadcasts domestic and foreign news, it guides all classes of society and communities to our aims, and it connects the past with the present and the future, to mention just a few things. And offering culture in its specific sense is just one of the media's duties. However, we are living through a trying period which calls for a redoubling of our effort and for some superhuman achievements to pull us out of this predicament. I am not asking too much in setting out some thoughts for consideration, and I offer my apologies for drawing attention to these, but I find it important that they should be carried out for the general benefit.

They are as follows:

1. We should remove the dividing line between what are generally called serious topics and what are known as inconsequential topics. This has perhaps led us to present serious topics in too dull and dry a manner and to present lighter topics in too frivolous a manner, and we should not forget that even a serious topic may well have its lighter side if presented properly. Thereby we would gain a double advantage and I would not be exaggerating if I said that the documentaries Animal World, Sea World, or Science and Faith, are twice as enjoyable as some of the drama series. The best example of successful programming is that in which a serious subject is presented in an entertaining manner and this combination of educational, edifying and entertaining content is the way forward.
2. We should, in a planned manner, highlight the book world by giving it publicity, by making programmes about it, by holding panel shows and discussions and by public book fairs and literary competitions. I have railed on about this at length in a previous article and so I will not repeat myself here.
3. We should think about making specialised cultural television programmes along the lines of Channel 2, either by setting up a new channel specifically for this or by broadcasting these programmes on the existing channels at prime time along with lectures on a specific subject followed by serious discussions. We might even, from time to time, broadcast discussions of some doctoral theses, or show highlights from concerts, dramas and foreign or even experimental films, and here I would like to take the opportunity to restate my hope that Channel 2's broadcast signal should be strengthened and that its programme listings should be advertised correctly.

I hope that in setting out these thoughts for consideration no one will misinterpret them as some form of slight against the broadcast cultural services offered to all levels of the population and over such a long period of time by the state media organisations, and that all deserves the appreciation of the nation and the gratitude of culture lovers. I have already made public my opinion about that, but I am convinced now that we are passing through a critical period which needs a redoubling of our effort and input and which requires executives in both branches of the state broadcasting service to remember that culture, which is the basis of human development, has been entrusted to them due to their devotion, zeal and their love for the nation and its citizens.

23 August 1984

23 August

Today is the anniversary of the death of Saad Zaghloul[1] and Mustafa el-Nahhas.[2] I would not be stretching the truth if I were to say that the two were the greatest popular leaders whose names are linked with the greatest popular revolution in our history, the 1919 Revolution, a revolution carried out by peasants, workers, the artistic community and women who shook the dust of time and the residue of enslavement from their eternal and authentic core, who, of their own accord, gloriously offered themselves up in the thousands to the bullets, the gallows, imprisonment and exile, and from whose fierce consciousness there arose a robust national unity based firmly on self-sacrifice and on will-power which exuded the spirit of creativity and innovation in all spheres of civilisation, laying the foundation stone of the Egyptian economy, freeing women from the slavery of ignorance and opening the gateway of learning, work and dignity for them, resisting home-grown tyrants just as they had resisted the imperialists with their ongoing and stubborn defence of the constitution and the sovereignty of the people, fighting their mighty enemies over the course of seventeen years between 1919 and 1936, a struggle crowned by the Anglo-Egyptian Treaty of 1936 which brought Egypt honour as it represented a struggle between a defenceless people on the one hand and the largest empire in history on the other, and which must be considered a noble end even if not all its aims were realised, for it succeeded in re-creating Egypt.

As for the events which came afterwards, a new page was turned as a result of the Second World War, the development of society, and the appearance of new powers which required a new revolution in order to cope with their inconsistencies which, unsurprisingly, caused society in that critical period no end of convulsions and upheaval and which surprisingly made people forget what had come before it.

---

1 (1859–1927), revolutionary and statesman.

2 (1879–1965), five times prime minister and one of the founders of the Arab League.

Days will pass, and generation will follow generation, but the greatness of those incredible leaders and their revolution will remain a beacon which every Egypt-loving nationalist will follow in the darkness of existence, a burning ember which will scorch those enemies who envy the Egyptian people and their freedom, and a great and eternal memorial to those leaders and their revolution.

23 August 1984

The First Aim

Let us remember that the comprehensive development plan is the greatest trust that we can carry in this period of our history. It is our way out of a multi-faceted and complex crisis and our way into a sense of freedom and civilisation. It is the cure-all for all our concerns, whether they be economic, social or cultural, and it will incorporate various ramifications, such as agriculture, manufacturing, education, health and comfort.

We must not hesitate in devoting resources to studying and re-studying the plan whenever necessary, and carrying out the requisite oversight and follow-up. At the end of each year of the plan, when the annual accounts are prepared, we must publish what we have achieved in detail and faithfully, avoiding exaggerations and the hollow search for approval, admitting any errors which may have taken place, and aiming at ever more perseverance and understanding.

We must not have any tolerance for negligence, sloth, or apathy but we should have the integrity and honesty to set ourselves up as our own critics before anyone else does. We should accept criticism as a positive element in our achievements and work. However much effort we expend, it is still very little in comparison with the intended result, which is the affirmation of our civilisational presence in a world rushing forward at the speed of light.

We should not neglect deciding upon what is necessary for us to free ourselves from the burden of aid and loans, taking into account our integration with Sudan and the needs of the youth in their various educational and vocational stages as well as the sacrifices which each citizen much make according to his ability. There is no shame in considering ourselves to be in a predicament, and we should give all praise to those who are suffering in this predicament with solidarity, cooperation and sincerity in their work and who have raised their outlook and emotions to the level of the stubborn challenges.

These challenges are contradictory forces in whose vast open spaces civilisations are renewed or disappear, and we must choose existence and not a substitute for that.

30 August 1984

The Minister of the Interior Begins the Battle

What is taking place in the streets of Cairo is a phenomenon deserving of consideration. It is dispelling the gloom and doom and bringing new hope. To put it bluntly it shows that the good will of humanity is more powerful than any challenge. So ask me, as I am such a great expert at walking through Cairo every day from its outer edges to its centre and then back again, as to what I come across every day among the people in terms of toil, concern, distress and deep-rooted chaos, as well as cars bumping into each other all the time.

I do not consider the street the be-all and end-all of the minister of the interior, but as one of the many sub-departments of the ministry of the interior. The street is just an example of what will happen, and what must happen in terms of productivity, consumerism, education and culture, electricity, water, telephones, housing, dialogue between the government and the opposition, cooperation between the state and the Arabs, our policy towards Israel, Africa, the United States and the Soviet Union.

Let us make what is happening in the street today a watchword for the implementation of deeds and not just the home of cheap jingles. Let us make it a symbol of a new life of challenge and victory. Let us all remember that even if one part of our progress requires loans and aid, another not-insignificant part can solve our problems through good will, planning according to lofty ideals and unyielding resoluteness.

Let us all remember that if we succeed in this, and we will inevitably succeed, we must not wonder in confusion tomorrow why our children excel abroad and are unable to find employment at home, or why their feelings of belonging to their sacred homeland have weakened.

6 September 1984

We Have the Power

There is something within our very nature that equips us to confront the modern age with all its challenges. I do not say that out of some emotional sense of chauvinism, nor out of some imaginary or dream-like sense of security, nor do I say it heedless of the mistrust that is tearing us apart, nor out of a lack of solidarity or indifference to public opinion and action. I acknowledge that we have passed, and continue to pass, through a period of moral and economic hardship as well as consecutive wars and their squalid consequences, and although they have their reasons, these will eventually fade away and there is no point blaming our instinctive nature or our own particular approach to things. I have hard evidence to invalidate the shortcomings we appear to suffer and which actually points to the very opposite. I do not have to go very deep into history to present some situations and examples, so just let me mention what our émigrés have achieved and how they have risen to the top in various scientific fields, and allow me to mention the victory we achieved in a very short time and with relatively limited means in the 6 October war. Moreover I can actually feel the steadfastness and the social spirit in their daily social manifestations such as the way a majority of us are devoted to our families and will sacrifice anything for them, and the way we give ourselves over to the larger social units in a way which overcomes self and pays no heed to the consequences thereof. We also have a tradition of revenge, which is a despicable tradition. It has outlived its time and sometimes ends up in the destruction of whole villages except for the women and children. It is an ugly and despicable tradition, but it bears witness to this sense of perseverance and to the preparedness of many people to sacrifice themselves for something they believe in, even if they do so erroneously. Thus we do not hesitate to sacrifice ourselves if we believe in the sanctity of what we are doing. We are a people who do not lack perseverance or strength, and we do not find it difficult to sacrifice ourselves for the common cause or for our values. Perhaps we do need justice in our human interactions as well as good guidance and education so that our strengths can be channelled to new aims. We are like cacophonous strains of sound just waiting for a skilled conductor to turn us into a wonderful, powerful and beautiful symphony.

20 September 1984

The Media and the New Class

The gateway to earning a living wage has been opened for the peasants, workers and artisans who make up the toiling masses of our nation and their income has risen by unexpected degrees, enabling them to escape from hardship being endured by those on fixed salaries. This has come about as the result of the liberalisation of the economy and emigration, and not as a result of any reforms or revolutionary planning. However, the improved fate of the masses has been the subject of much aggrieved comment by others. In my humble opinion, no matter how our opinions may differ regarding the liberalisation of the economy and emigration, we should not differ over this happy outcome which is of so much benefit to the toiling masses. This in itself leads us on to think about other social evils, for it was always the dream of the liberals of our generation to liberate the working class from poverty, disease and ignorance and it seems that the first of these two aims have been achieved. However, when it comes to their under-education we still need to invest more effort and to find more patience. We are most dismayed at seeing the creation of a new class of citizens who are being driven unrestrainedly into the arms of consumerism, with some of them now turning to drugs after years of living in deprivation, not having been instilled with any social awareness or having received any support. They represent a not insignificant part of the nation. They scrape their way through life relying on their instincts, heedless of tomorrow and ill-prepared for any potential or sudden change. I have not noticed the media paying any particular attention to this section of the population, despite the media's undeniable service to other sections of the population. These are the people who ought to be made constantly aware of the dangers of unbridled consumerism and of drugs, they need to be made aware of potential changes to the economy in the near future and of the need to put something aside for a rainy day. There should also be some popular cultural programmes to guide them towards our traditional values in daily life. Our mass media should really be dealing with this important aspect of our modern life and it should be an integral part of its programming. This would reflect well on the programme makers and have a beneficial effect on society. We should not neglect our underclass now that their lives have become a little easier, the way we neglected them in the past when their lives were so grim. It might even be said that their need is just as great as ever.

22 September 1984

6 October

The day of victory has come around again with all its memories. Its bright light shines in our ether which blazes away with the heat of our earnest existential and civilisational struggle. It brings a smile of happiness which eases our troubles, and makes us think more deeply about how to solve our problems. For the diligent, it opens up new windows of hope that we may again defeat the challenges facing us, so let us remember with love and gratitude the thousands of people who died in order to save the Arab spirit from the quagmire of 5 June,[1] who restored its confidence in its own strength and its determination to continue the struggle by a great act of self-sacrifice with the hero of the day itself, Anwar Sadat, at the forefront. The fates decreed that he should be at the head of the column of martyrs as he celebrated both this victory and the memory of its martyrs. In addition to all of that, this historical day represents the start of a new policy – a policy of comprehensive peace and constructiveness which has brought us out of the morass of no-peace no-war that the war of attrition had imposed on us, draining our blood and money to no avail. This day also represents the birth of a new generation, who, with honest courageousness, face challenges with integrity, patriotism and learning. And now the day has come around again and it finds us in the midst of a battle even more ferocious than the battle we won on the same day – the battle that has opened the third year of our five-year plan, which has met undeniable success, and we look forward purposefully to its eventual triumph, God willing, and to a situation where citizens can channel their endeavours in an atmosphere of democracy, human rights and self-discipline, which promises to face the facts, to publicise and deal with them with all the necessary resolve, self-sacrifice, patience and solidarity. From this moment on, let no voice be louder than that of the nation, and let there be no slogans except those in favour of the well-being and progress of our nation. Whenever the going gets hard, let us look

1 The outbreak of the 1967 Arab-Israeli war.

to the lexicon of 6 October to find definitions for our concepts of resolve, hope and victory.

4 October 1984

6 October

We will remember 6 October above all the bright days of our long history. When we look at it within the context of our modern history, it represents a victory which came about in the aftermath of a string of military and political defeats during the course of our long struggle against European colonialism and the challenge of Israel. For this reason, its unlimited moral affects are greater than its limited material successes. It is as if that day was destined to resurrect the spirit of Arabism from its long slumber, to inject it in full vigour back into the course of history after it had almost been swept out of existence, and to place Egypt in its new guise on the throne of trust and decisiveness, where it will forever remain as a symbol of the steadfastness of its people, the valour of its army and of individual bravery. No matter what differences of opinion there are with regard to this victory, there is no difference of opinion over the debt owed to the people in achieving that great victory. It was a day fit to be the starting point for incredible development and a complete cultural rebirth aiming to bring all aspects of life and civilisation to the peak of progress and comfort. However this bright day has been struck by hurricanes and storms, beset by unfortunate and precocious old age, and so exploited by people who are smitten with the evil qualities of selfishness, greed, recklessness and myopia. The memory of this day has been wounded with blood and threatened with oblivion – something which tells any rational person that a preponderance of unfounded criticism can outweigh the truth, can turn history on its head and can end up consigning the hero of the victory and peace to unwarranted ignominy. And we find ourselves celebrating this great anniversary, the anniversary of victory and heroism, after all the trials we have lived through and the negativity which has been so heavily heaped upon youthful resoluteness. We are carrying on the challenge of living out our mistakes and ill-fortune, and we have it within ourselves to affirm this victory through work, learning and faith so that we can pass through this stage of backwardness just as we have passed beyond the defeats of yesteryear.

4 October 1984

Our Lives

The real value of a nation can be measured by its achievements in the fields of science, thought, culture and the economy, and innovation in these fields can only come about within a society based on justice, freedom and respect for human rights, a society whose individual members can be characterised by a moral strength which has absorbed those sound religious values and principles which create human-beings deserving of the name. Perhaps the thing which separates an undeveloped society from a progressive one is that the former comes across as deficient in the disciplines listed above and reliant upon others for innovation, whereas a progressive society is one where people are on an equal footing, a society which is productive, creative and generally constructive, no matter the size of its population or territory, and no matter how great its history may be. That is why a country the size of Sweden can outperform a nation as large as Indonesia or India.

That is the primary and supreme aim of any nation that wants the best for its people, and it is an aim which should not be absent from our minds for a single moment among the welter of other events. We have become distracted by various problems which become so pressing that we think solving them is an end in itself. We may well dream of our past glory and imagine that this can help us in the world of today which is actually indifferent to it. We may well look to fantastic leaders who drain our resources but effect no real gain for us. It is undeniable that our problems require us to mobilise our powers in order to solve them decisively. It is undeniable that our past glory is a force for enlightenment and that leadership is a valuable commodity in a meritocracy, but our long-term planning for the future must at the very least take into account our greatest ambitions and keep them in mind at every stage of planning and activity. Our planners must always remember that they are working with the purpose of constructing a better society and a more rounded individual, of producing a climate which fosters creativity and innovation. They must make use of all the modern means available to them, not forgetting our inherited values, and they should profit from the experiments of other nations and of historical studies. Life is not a mere whim, nor is it empty rhetoric or blind opportunism, but an infinite process of learning, of never-ending work, of unceasing thought and non-stop effort. The choice ahead of us is to be, or not to be.

11 October 1984

A Good Start

Our democratic life has got off to its official start and the signs are that it will thrive and prosper. On the one hand, this calls upon the state and the opposition to play their part in confronting challenges and solving our greatest issues, while giving them a prestigious place among the parties and popular associations and in so doing we will have accepted that the opposition is not the enemy but just another of the people's voices, a grassroots element, whose opinions may differ from those of the majority but which has an identity of hope when it comes to the welfare, progress and happiness of the nation. On the other hand, the opposition has carried out its duty, offering up the best of its knowledge, expertise and enthusiasm, committed to objectivity and well-mannered debate, and joining with the majority when it sees that the general welfare of the country requires a unity of opinion and rank. In so doing the opposition has accepted that the government is not the enemy, that governance is not an end in itself, and that the opposition's duty above all other things is to uncover the truth, to support what is right, to offer up advice and to battle against complacency for the benefit and welfare of the country. I do not want to see things move in this vein for evermore. We need to be ready for the occasional outbreaks of fierce quarrels, but I am neither fearful of this and nor am I against it. In fact, I welcome it, as it is in the nature of things, made necessary by differences of opinion. However, under all circumstances it is important for us to preserve our objectivity, our well-mannered debate, and the integrity of our aims. As a result of all of this, the reports of parliamentary proceedings in our press have become much livelier, are seen as more important, are more widely read and have highlighted the new stars of the opposition and the majority party, including the speaker of parliament himself in terms of his respect for, and leadership of, freedom, and in terms of the spirit that has returned to our parliament and offers encouragement for the path of belonging, cohesion and the realisation of our hopes.

18 October 1984

Support for a Society of Freedom and Justice

State support is a necessary step taken to help certain groups of people to cope with the inflation which is beyond their limited resources, and in that there is no sin. Just as their right to foodstuffs, clothing, shelter, education and the other essentials is a human right which is beyond discussion, there must be no discussion of state support in these areas. We live under the wings of a state which is the heir to glorious revolutions waged for the sake of freedom and social justice. Any investigations into the matter of state support should be directed to the following aspects:

1. Defining the groups of society who deserve support, how to give them that support, and the best suggestions for doing that;
2. Removing the subsidies from non-essential items, and allowing prices of these items to fluctuate according to market forces;
3. Closely scrutinising expenditure so that not one piastre is spent unnecessarily;
4. Improving the government's tax-collecting capability and making non-payment or evasion a serious crime which in our current circumstances should be no less than high treason;
5. Expending every last effort to increase productivity, to improve administration, and to make the public purse accountable by reinforcing the powers of the ombudsman.

Finally we must view the problem of subsidised commodities as the gateway to serious discipline in balancing social justice and as a sincere attempt to steer society away from apathy and towards a system where we all work together, as it should be.

25 October 1984

What a Political Party Means

Any party worthy of its name has a job to do and a message to deliver. Its job is to participate in political life either by giving its support or its opposition. The message is its voice which pulsates with its principles and which is channelled through a whole variety of means to the people in general and to the youth in particular. If you want to set up a party, look to the youth to show you its real force and its real future qualitatively and quantitatively, to show you its strength of belonging, positivity, the power of its consciousness and its visceral enthusiasm. The power of the youth in the long term is more important than any distinctions of power, executive authority or professional rank.

The message of a party is greater than its size and spreads among the masses, educating them along a particular form of politics while moving them towards commitment to society, values and the highest standards, preparing them to shoulder responsibility guided by both an individual and social conscience, and protected from recriminations or accusations of acting out of self-interest.

It is from this point that a party can become patriotic in its full educational sense, and humane in its exalted values, creating for itself a role in building society, shaping its citizens and consequently becoming an institution every bit as vital as colleges and universities.

For a party to perform its duty in this risky area, it must get its message across and furnish it with an identifiable and internally consistent philosophy. The party must set a good example of believing in its own philosophy, of showing devotion to said philosophy, and of making self-sacrifices for its sake. In order to attract support, it must not hesitate to make use of its public relations resources, employ its own press and distribute flyers written by its theorists, lecturers and preachers.

Party-political life is a lofty and endlessly busy one. It is not restricted to policymaking in parliament, but is, first and foremost, a vital and open call to the coming generations. It aims to make of them a new form of human being, to give the future a new shape, and its ultimate goal is the creation of a better society and more rounded human beings.

8 November 1984

Decisive Years

The next five years are considered one of the most important periods of Egypt's existence. The first five-year plan will come to an end in this period, and we will embark on the second five-year plan, bringing about solid development in all areas of life, including industry, agriculture, society, education, science and culture. We hope that the man in the street will feel a tangible improvement in his circumstances and have the firm conviction that the situation can only get better. Over these five years new parties will emerge and we will see the birth of democracy in practice in state institutions and public relations apparatus. On top of the list of what we anticipate from the government and opposition is the cleansing of the face of our democracy from the emergency and revisionist laws which sully it, even if this necessitates a new reading of the constitution to bring its sections into line with the reality of our lives, which I believe has gone beyond the constitution with its prevailing lofty spirit of nationalism, its clear inclination towards freedom and respect for human rights. We will have a renewed and unique opportunity for a debate among the parties on the one hand, and the government on the other, as well as an inter-party debate. It is my belief that if we think cleverly, there may come about a natural shift among the parties based on some affinity of principles. We may end up with a smaller number of parties, but they will have clearly defined platforms and defined aims. All this will help the citizen make his electoral choice without confusion or hot-headedness. This move, I believe, will make the forthcoming elections a more genuine expression of the grassroots and will offer a greater sense of positivity and belonging.

Egypt must be a calm example, in the region, of stable progress in science and in belief, and of democracy based on social justice and human rights.

15 November 1984

'13 November'

This is one of the great days of our history: it was the day when three men – Saad Zaghloul, Ali Sharawi[1] and Abd al-Aziz Fahmi,[2] went to the British High Commission to discuss the fate of Egypt following the declaration of peace at the end of the First World War.[3] For the people that day stands out as a symbol of their struggle against colonialism, despotism and autocracy and hence it became known as *Yawm al-Jihad* (the Day of Struggle) and people shouted themselves hoarse praising it year after year until its place was taken by another 'Struggle' in 1952. We must not forget this day, for history is the memory of a people which preserves its singular experience. Nor should we forget it as a rhetorical concept and a value, for the vitality of nations stems from their sources of rhetorical concepts and values, and this day has a solid and cherished place in the history of our struggle. It has a connection with the revolutions and sacrifices that preceded it and it ushered in the revolutions and sacrifices that followed it. When I speak of this day, I do not mean to suggest that it should be a national holiday at the expense of work and productivity, but the very opposite of that. I mean that we should draw strength and tenaciousness from that day as well as any other concepts that can support our resolve to face challenges and overcome difficulties. This day previously had the power to be a torch for revolution, it inculcated a sense of devotion to independence, democracy and national unity, and has been the inspiration for our greatest popular leaders as well as the driving factor for waves of creativity in the fields of the economy, literature, art, education and honouring women. Today this day should breathe its spirit into us so that we can confront the challenges in our economy, our

---

1 A wealthy landowner, leading member of the Wafd party and husband of the celebrated Egyptian feminist Huda Sharawi.

2 (1870–1951), politician, jurist and intellectual.

3 On 13 November 1918 they were granted an audience with General Sir Reginald Wingate, the British High Commissioner. They demanded complete independence with the proviso that Britain be allowed to supervise the Suez Canal and the public debt.

culture, our essential infrastructure, our population explosion and the dangers staring us down at home and abroad. It should help us gain what we desire from the modern age and allow us to participate in its achievements. For all those reasons, we should commemorate the 13 November 1918.

15 November 1984

The National Democratic Party and Culture

The National Democratic Party has a role in the domain of culture. Culture in the usual understanding of the word means the essential and constructive elements which together form a person's character. Culture is the light of the enquiring spirit, it is the beauty of thought and art, the wisdom of traditions and individual and popular customs, the embodiment of religious and social modes of behaviour and it encompasses sport and our eating habits. The fact that culture was ignored in the party platforms during the election campaign is a disaster which, if it signifies anything, signifies that we waged a materialistic battle and paid no attention to our values. It was as if it is a luxury which can be put off for another day. Culture is not the monopoly of some ministry or state institution. It provides power to the very core of every party for there can be no such thing as a party without a philosophy or vision of life. Hence it is incumbent upon a party to translate its philosophy rather than just mouthing the party's principles. As well as having direct interface with the public and offering constructive criticism of our intellectual and artistic life as represented by books, on the stage, in the cinema, and on the radio and television, a party must – in the pages of its own weekly newspaper – offer comprehensive coverage of its philosophy. And here I should like to praise the activities of the Tajamu' Party for its coverage of culture in the *al-Ahali* weekly, and for publishing a magazine on literature and criticism, in addition to its series of thought-provoking books. In doing all of this, the party is reaffirming the significance of its existence and goals and its weekly newspaper has played a great role in disseminating the party's message. No political party should constrain itself simply to winning the elections. All the parties should work tirelessly towards putting the character of the Egyptian people at the core of their philosophy and programme. Decades ago, before the July Revolution,[1] the two most important parties, the

1 Of 1952.

Wafd and the Liberal Party, were the two foci of our intellectual and literary rebirth, and they educated generation upon generation of our youth with their two magazines, *al-Balagh al-Usbu'i* and *al-Siyasa al-Usbu'iyya,* in whose pages there raged the greatest intellectual debates of the era. The National Democratic Party must be a party in the full meaning of the word in this age of space travel and data.

22 November 1984

The Ministry and the Festival

When a country bids to establish a film festival the first thing that comes to mind is that the film industry in that country must have the requisite infrastructure. It is unimaginable that a festival of cinema could be held in a country without a cinema studio worthy of the name and qualitatively and quantitively low levels of production. Nor in a country that only produces a handful of decent films throughout the whole year. It would not be a bad thing if the film festival was being organised by a non-state organisation, such as the Association of Critics for there is nothing to stop it doing so. We should remember how successful it has been at holding festivals, year after year, nor overlook all its success in the academic, public relations and tourism fields, and for that it deserves appreciation and gratitude. The Association of Critics is not to be dismissed out of misplaced nepotism and nor should it fall victim to the general dismissiveness from which nothing in this country can escape. In any case it has been decreed that the Ministry of Culture and the unions should supervise the work of organising the festival so that it is done in a manner worthy of the name Egypt. We welcome any step taken whose purpose is general reform and organisational improvement, but I am lukewarm when it comes to the Ministry of Culture deciding that it will be the exclusive organiser of the festival. I am also one of those people who thinks that a ministry should get its own house in order before extending itself further afield. The Ministry of Culture has undeniably provided many valuable services to culture in its various manifestations, but when it comes to the cinema extra special care needs to be taken. It would be better for us to invest whatever funds are available in supporting the Egyptian cinema's essential infrastructure and institutions, in raising its production values to a point where it can really be considered part of world cinema.

29 November 1984

The Majority Party

I do not mean the official majority party, the National Democratic Party, but the other party which works in the shade, far from the arena of politics and daily life. Its influence has spread so much into both politics and daily life that we are aware of it without even trying and we can sense its presence in public spaces. We can observe its apparent effects in rejectionist movements and among exiles. We can observe its abusive behaviour, its neglect and disrespect of values, its disregard of political positions and events, and so on. We even have statistics about it in the lead-up to the election, suggesting that it is an enormous party with more than twenty million members, including a large number whose names are not on the electoral register, and a number who, despite being registered to vote, do not bother. Even if we assume that in this enormous party there are people who do not vote for some logical or arguable reason, it is beyond question that the overwhelming majority do not vote on grounds of negativity, apathy or some mental block. When it comes to the reasons for this plague having spread to such a great extent, it has been said that it is the unavoidable result of totalitarian rule, of wars, of the rotten economic situation, and of a lack of patriotic education in general. It can also be said that this plague of negativity, for its part, has been one of the reasons for the increase in corrupt behaviour, such as the prevalence of opportunism and selfishness, arson, the collapse of the conscience and the ill-treatment of the masses in government offices. The only way any real treatment can flourish is through general reform, democracy, productivity, by raising the level of services in all areas, and by intensifying educational campaigns in schools and the media. The parties have a role to play in this arena and a party aspiring to real popularity must know how to get to the heart of that absent human mass. It must have some force of attraction in the national and intellectual example it offers and in the activity of its cadres across the provinces. We will be able to judge the results of this when we see the statistics of new names in the electoral register and we hope to see these disparate forces immediately turned into constructive forces for the good of the nation.

13 December 1984

Party and Development

A party must have a role in our comprehensive development that goes beyond its significance as an opposing force. It is actually the government which has put the five-year plan in place and is responsible for carrying it out. However, development is like the air around us and no individual or group can avoid interacting with it. Development is carried out by the labour of people. It is their eyes that watch over it, and they are its beneficiaries in all of its agricultural, industrial, educational, cultural and health aspects, among others. Development is a comprehensive activity that cannot be limited to just one government authority. It is up to every individual to play his defined role according to his status as a producer or a consumer. Consequently there is some importance in the way support is offered and education is structured for development, with the state doing its duty in this regard – and the state must also do all it can within its own realm and so must the party among its adult and youth members. It must call upon its membership to draw up plans for investing in productivity within the remit of the five-year plan. It must also call upon others to be as prudent as possible with their spending, and it must call upon the grassroots to show some restraint in their consumerism and encourage national productivity above everything else. The National Democratic Party has acknowledged experience in this arena, and similarly the Wafd Party in its new reincarnation has lobbied for the establishment of a development bank for those with disabilities. It is only fitting that it should enlarge its activities in this domain for the sake of the present and the future, and last but not least, for the sake of civilisation and progress. I would like the Wafd Party not to prevail upon the opposition to postpone the good results for any reason or excuse. The Wafd has only experienced power for approximately six years in total during which, we should not forget, they provided great services to the nation, but these can be considered minor exploits compared with its long-lasting effect as a school for nationalism and democracy, persevering in spreading its innovative and worthy spirit among the masses. What we demand today is simply that it continues its work of old, that it becomes a source for the expansion of freedom, national unity, morality and innovation for good and among the masses in the cities and the countryside.

20 December 1984

Back to the Electoral Law

There are myriad occasions in which the new electoral law is subjected to criticism: in parliament sometimes, in the press very often – with the criticism often uncovering many lacunae in the law, and there is a growing emphasis on denying independents the right to be elected and to vote. I may differ from the critics of the law on this point, and perhaps I believe that denying independents the right to participate is an important part of the law. Whatever the case, I am one of those people who support an election based on proportional representation, for that way no vote is wasted, and the election becomes one of principles and parties and not one of individuals or tribalism. It offers citizens a better form of political education, but I naturally object to the 8 per cent limit and I do not just think that this should be lowered, I hope that this limit will be completely overturned on the grounds that any grouping of people should have the right to be represented in parliament according to the number of people who vote for them. Moreover, I admire a system that takes in the whole country and allows every party to translate the number of votes it gains into a proportionate number of MPs. It is not deleterious for a party to become stronger as a consequence of this, and for it to extend its dominance over its individuals. There is no contradiction between a party and its members as it is an aspiration of democratic life for a party to be strong. The independents should have no issue with this because otherwise they would have no representation. Provided their principles are within the law and membership is free of any coercion, as it should be, it is both natural and logical that an individual member of any party should find in that party his appropriate or nearly-appropriate political and social home. That said and done, for those who wish to undertake political activity, being an independent should not imply an inability to think, a disdain for it, a fear of declaring one's opinions or having to seek a safe place in order to work with the public. Such an attitude is the manner of opportunism from which we have suffered in the past, and we do not wish to see it repeated in the present or the future. We need not only to reform the law, but to take another look at the constitution with a greater idea of justice, freedom and maturity.

3 January 1985

Parliament and the Media

Parliament has recently reconvened, beginning a new cycle of its life and continuing its effective contribution to governance and the establishment of democracy. On this happy occasion, we assert that our national assembly does not enjoy its full rights in the press, or on the radio and television.

It enjoys an undeniable interest, but has not reached the necessary coverage appropriate to its place and value in our lives. You just have to see how much space the media dedicates to the coverage of the national assembly compared to the space given to the executive authority or sports features.

We often sing the praises of democracy but do not provide the means for either the voice of the government or the opposition to be disseminated and reach every heart and mind. We should view what takes place in parliament as a historic, glorious and hallowed debate whose every sentence should be conveyed in an unbowdlerised and unexpurgated manner to the people, like the minutes of a meeting, or the text of a play, along with a record of the various reactions that accompany it such as laughter or shouts of objection so that the reader or viewer can experience the words spoken and the atmosphere, and feel that he is actively and emotionally part of our parliamentary life.

This is the right of the parliament, and the right of the people who have elected it, as well as being the duty of the various organs that, in the final analysis, are subject to the parliament and the people. To this end, I should like to mention that during the Second World War, with the declaration of martial law and the imposition of total censorship, a law or decree was issued excluding the parliament from any type of censorship. Parliamentary proceedings had to be published, parliament was a free space, and we were informed, inasmuch as possible, about what was going on there and the views of the opposition. Parliament's right to that was not a subject of discussion and it must demand its right if it finds it is being overlooked, for the parliament is the guardian of everyone's rights.

We are simply demanding that the parliament should have equality with the government and with sports matches and that's not a lot to ask of democracy.

7 January 1985

Culture between Criticism and Anger

We often subject our cultural life to discussion and criticism, sometimes even bitter criticism, out of a sense of devotion to both culture and the homeland. We feel boldly inspired to face challenges and we campaign against the underlying causes of weakness and failure. However when an Arab poet writes in an Arabic magazine that he has been forced to emigrate from Egypt because the country's intellectual life and capacity for innovation have died out, that after the 1940s it lost everything of value and all we have left here in terms of intellectual life is Ahmad Adaweyah,[1] this must be his attempt at a joke but in fact shows up his lack of empathy and complete absence of objectivity. In fact Egypt is suffering from the consequences of five consecutive wars but this is what happens to a nation when it is attempting in as determined a manner as possible to dig itself out of the abyss into which it has fallen while defending itself and the whole Arab nation. Should we thus be surprised that the effects of doing that might be reflected in the cultural climate. However Egypt still has a wealth of thinkers, scientists, writers and artists who are working their fingers to the bone to publish the fruits of their genius in our specialised magazines and daily newspapers, thereby enriching hearts and minds with philosophy, history, science, literature and art. Were these publications not so numerous I would list them, but the space here will not allow that. From Egypt's most accomplished to the up-and-coming writers, they all produce reams of material and, despite the difficulties in getting the Egyptian public to read more when they have to spend so much of their lives dealing with practical concerns, there are some in the creative industries whose works are known abroad and whose works have firmly established themselves as some of the best books and magazines

1 Ahmed Adaweyah (b. 1945), is an Egyptian singer of popular music who achieved great fame with his song *zaḥma yā dunyā, zaḥma* about the overcrowding in Cairo streets. The lyrics of some of his songs in the dialect of uneducated Cairenes are crassly populist, but they, along with the driving, hip-gyrating *sha'bī* rhythms, represented a revolt against prim middle-class means of expression.

published in our fraternal Arab countries. Egypt does not lack thought or creativity. It can be proud of its cultural leadership, just as its people are proud of Ahmed Adaweyah and other celebrities whom the street has made famous. That Arab poet might have emigrated from Egypt for reasons other than those he stated. He may yet see sense, temper his ire and come back to having a reasoned point of view.

10 January 1985

Mass Suicide

The night at the home of an Egyptian artist which ended with the death of a Moroccan woman was not just a party, nor was the home just the home of an artist, and nor was the death just the death of a woman. They are all in fact highly eloquent witnesses to an age and address more than just the people involved. They are the witnesses to an age of consumerist liberalisation and symbols of its opulence, extravagance, dissolution and singular manner of interaction and morality. They bestow extra artistic dimensions to traditional truths. They rub salt into our wounds. When viewed by right-thinking people, these symbols simply cock a snook at the ever more acute housing crisis which does not have to enter the consciousness of those who can party all night long. These symbols also slap the deprived masses in the face with their conceit that the world is fine, and that its villas are stockpiled with illicit alcohol and luxury articles imported with impunity from the furthest reaches of the Arab world. At the same time, the all-night party throws into relief the lot of the elite of the retired military and legal people who have dedicated their lives and their learning to the service of the dissolute and who now just scrape by. So what can be said to those who undermine society, and who is so without guile that he can be present among such decadence and not become corrupted by it?

In my opinion a night of boundless pleasure spent in the house of a famous artist actually represents the massacre of character, values and money and is an insult which sullies the Egyptian masses who are broken by inflation but carry on eking out a living to support their families, the nation and God.

10 January 1985

The Nile and the Law

It is an axiom of the state that the law should prevail and be respected, even if it does so quietly and behind the scenes. There can be no exception to this, and nor can it be taken lightly, for the law is the face, the conscience, the will and the dignity of the state. A fuss has broken out over the alluvial deposits of the Nile and the assaults on the river which have sometimes been carried out with the permission of people who do not have the right to grant such permission and at other times with sheer recklessness, as if the land does not have an owner. This fuss has had an effect with the administration having taken steps to put an end to these encroachments. The excitement has calmed down and the enthusiasm petered out, with apologies being published and statements issued to calm the situation. The issue is both simple and dangerous at the same time: simple in terms of clarifying the means and the end, and dangerous in terms of this all being connected with the Nile, the dignity of the state and the rights of the people. There is a ministry which has the most expertise in the matter – and that is the Ministry of Irrigation according to what has been stated in the press, and this ministry must read the law dealing with the River Nile, or revisit it, and then it must apply the law down to the last letter so that what must stop stops and what should remain remains if there is good reason for it to do so. Any delay in carrying this out can only be deleterious for the river, against the law and an infringement on the rights of the people, but this should not take place without accountability, and anyone who has granted permission or signed a contract without the right to do so should be put on trial, as should anyone who has allowed encroachments within his circle of expertise without taking the requisite steps to rectify the matter. Those who have infringed the law should not be above a deterrent punishment even after their infringements have been rectified, and no individual, association or institution should be excluded from this just because the people and government will accuse each other of mismanagement, corruption, injustice and diminution of confidence.

24 January 1985

The Day of the Police

Every decent citizen should take delight in the Day of the Police and consider it a public holiday, for the police are the cornerstone of security, security is the pillar of stability, and stability is the cradle of civilisation. We might live, even just for a day, without bread, but we cannot live securely even just for a day without the police. The need for the police grows ever greater in a society like ours whose life circumstances decree that we must live through a tricky transitional period in the calamitous aftermath of consecutive wars, totalitarianism, terrorism, sundry systems of governance and the blind rush to liberalise the country's economy, with the resultant budgetary imbalance, the shock to its values, the emergence of opportunistic and depraved groups, the threat of selfishness and apathy and the extremist trends rocking the calm waters of its infrastructure. All of these require the police to keep a watchful eye, to be ever on the alert and to have an iron will to cleanse the country of troublemakers and discourage nihilism and hopelessness. There was once a police slogan which stated: 'the police are in the service of the people' and I would like to substitute this with a new slogan which states an old truth: 'the police are in the service of civilisation' which is more appropriate for their history and the history of civilisation and which should be an ever-present watchword in the conscience of the police, defining a policeman's goal and method at one and the same time and reminding him that as his goal is to bring about civilised behaviour, his method must be inspired by the same and that he must never waver from it even when he is pained, when anger flares or when faced with provocation. His deeds must accord with his aim and the way a policeman defends another human is part and parcel of his respect for human rights.

Furthermore, I am looking forward to the day when real security springs from within society and its conscience with no need for guards or deterrence, a day when society loves its children, and exchanges rights and duties for affection and dignity, a day when sincerity is the elemental force of conversations, when people work out of a sense of devotion, and when love among people supersedes the law, as our leader of everlasting memory, Saad Zaghloul said. That day is coming, God willing, by dint of faith, knowledge and work, and on that day we will fondly remember the police for having single-handedly shouldered the burden during these trying times.

31 January 1985

A Book Display in Every Home

We are on the verge of finding a solution to the problem of the cost of book-printing and the difficulty of book distribution in the Arab world. Then we will be left with another problem which is how we publicise books here in Egypt and how we make sure that the various branches of Dar al-Ma'rifa display new works in an attractive manner so that someone looking for a particular new title will be able to find it easily and so that the display catches the eyes of the itinerant book-lover. I should like to express my complete appreciation for the efforts that the Ministry of Culture and the cultural administration have made when it comes to books, such as the Mass Culture Programme, mobile libraries, permanent book displays and annual book fairs as well as having established a magazine specialising in books and printed material in the Arab world. However, I should also mention the scarcity of public libraries and how they are gradually disappearing amid the cut and thrust of modern life. I should also state the difficulty of book borrowing in general, the distance of state-funded libraries from town centres and the lack of public transport to bring people there. As a result of all of this, I suggest that we should produce a general reference work listing all the books available in Egypt, organised according to the various subject headings, and providing a general reference to new as well as out-of-print works as well containing a comprehensive listing of all bookshops and public libraries. This reference work should also be cross-referenced by publisher. Once we have managed to settle on the reference work's layout, we should attempt to convince every publishing house, Egyptian, Arab or foreign, to share in the printing costs. The work would then need a small annual update to be produced containing newly published works. This reference work would be a permanent record of the books available in Egypt and would be available to the book industry as well as the general public. Perhaps Dr Ezzeddin Ismail[1] will look at this proposal with interest, as he is well down for his devotion to his work and his zeal for culture.

7 February 1985

---

1 At the time, head of the Egyptian General Book Authority.

Execution and Life Imprisonment

Our country is going through a wide-ranging crisis. Not a day passes without us reading or hearing all about it. It is indeed wide-ranging, with no single utility being exempted, and no single individual escaping from its painful ramifications. For its part, the state is busy mobilising all its expert forces to confront and overcome this crisis. Every individual has been summoned to take part in the struggle, each according to his position, regardless of whether he works in the governments, the public or the private sector, at home or on the streets. This moral awareness is half of the success we are aiming for, but we can only attain complete moral awareness and build up the requisite manpower by means of long education, respect for human rights, and anchoring free and democratic life on a sound a peaceful basis and that is hardly going to take place overnight. Alongside our continuing efforts to create a healthy and appropriate atmosphere for the emergence of the perfect citizen, we must also deal with corruption, apathy and sloth with the necessary resoluteness, and particularly with that form of moral corruption which threatens the very essence of society.

Indeed all forms of moral corruption must be wrinkled out, but there is a difference between that which harms an individual or an organisation and that which harms the general national effort, particularly under the trying conditions we are currently living through. Stealing from someone is a crime, but tax evasion is a greater crime because it threatens the nation with bankruptcy. It is a crime for Zayd to kill Umar, but for him to smuggle drugs or distribute them is a more heinous crime, because it threatens to destroy a whole generation of our nation. And you can say the same about any form of moral corruption – that it harms society. We must take the matter most seriously, list the forms of moral corruption of this type, and the ringleaders should face execution with their partners in crime receiving life imprisonment. Death should be the punishment for smugglers, tax evaders and people who adulterate the nation's foodstuffs, with life imprisonment for those who collaborate with them. There is nothing harsh in what I have suggested, but there is something harsh about leaving the nation to suffer under the mercy of a band of morally corrupt people, and my suggestion, moreover, is based in tenderness and love for Egypt and Egyptians.

14 February 1985

The High Dam and the Necessary Conference

Whenever I believe that I have finished thinking about the High Dam, or whenever I think that I have managed to settle the questions about its present and future, letters from experts and other people involved make me think again. There is a letter written by Abd al-Hamid Ragih Muhammad about a practical reform plan with the suggestion that this could be carried out at the same time as the Jonglei Canal Project.[1] Abd al-Hamid, an engineer, states that he sent the letter to a major newspaper which ignored it.

Here is another letter from Gamal al-Din Ahmad Suleyman of the Bank of Credit regarding a project to treat the silt problem by setting up enormous turbines which revolve when the temperature reaches 45 degrees in the summer months. To begin with I should like to praise those people for their interest, which is no surprise, for the High Dam today controls the River Nile in Egypt, and the country benefits from all its positive aspects just as it will suffer, sooner or later, from its negative aspects if they are ignored or left untreated. Perhaps it would be more appropriate if the people who have opinions were to send them to the relevant expert organisation in order to save time and avoid confusion in getting something done. In this case I can do no more than suggest to the relevant organisation, the High Dam Authority or the Ministry of Irrigation, that they should hold a conference for engineers to enable a comprehensive discussion on the subject of the dam with no item, small or large, left off the agenda. The conclusions should be published in order to reassure every Egyptian about his Nile and the future of his homeland. At the same time this would resolve the squabbles and problems which surface from time to time and about which we just hold our heads in our hands. We convene conferences on many important topics, but the subject of the High Dam should be number one.

17 February 1985

---

1 A project to divert water through the wetlands of South Sudan in order to deliver more water downstream to Sudan and Egypt for use in agriculture.

The Case of Dr Ahmed

The case of Dr Ahmed Shafik hit the news suddenly and grabbed everyone's attention despite it happening right in the middle of a series of other sensational cases. Perhaps it gripped everyone for all the right reasons rather than being purely sensationalist or headline fodder. It is a case of scientific research in a country which calls upon the academic community to come to its rescue during this tricky period of development and growth. You may perhaps have heard about it as the clever manoeuvring of a man greedy for publicity and fame, or you may have been informed that it is a sort of sad display of academic rivalry and one-upmanship, or that it is the visible face of the voracious battle for market-share being waged by multi-national drug companies. Actually I am not interested in whether these are rumours or whether they have in them a scintilla of truth. What really interests me and what should interest every citizen who loves his country and reveres learning is the subject of academic research itself, the sponsorship and encouragement it should receive and the boundless appreciation that those working in the field deserve. It is a fact of life that in order for a new drug to prove its effectiveness it needs to undergo certain scientific and ethical procedures within an established framework which is there to protect people from any potential harm. And it is these procedures which, in the final analysis, record scientific innovations and protect the rights of the research scientist. However we should not be diverted from the essentials of the Shafik case, by which I mean that any new drug which must be trialled in a purely scientific environment free of the sort of disagreements that can arise as a result of undue haste or sloppiness. Disagreements may take place between individuals involved in creating a new drug, but that drug itself is for the benefit of the whole of humanity. We can discipline someone for less than professional behaviour without this meaning that we are closing the door on scientific innovation. So whoever does an atom's weight of good will see it, and whoever does an atom's weight of evil will see it.[1]

21 February 1985

---

1 Qur'an, 99:7–8.

The Master of the Cause

We should have a clear vision of a solution to the Palestinian cause, and it should have the complete agreement of the Arabs so that we can be sure that we have taken the first decisive step on the path to the desired goal. However in reality there is more than one unannounced plan for a solution, and much time has passed without a deed, or an opinion, or an agreement being able to pave the way towards easing the foul treatment meted out to those living under such suffering. Much time has passed unnoticed, each day making the losses greater and allowing the creation of a new and intractable reality. Even the legitimacy of the Palestine Liberation Organisation in representing the Palestinian people has alienated one or more of the Arab nations. Finally we have heard news of the agreement between the PLO and Jordan which has come like a flash of hope in the cloud-laden skies. What I fear is that it will be subject to horse-trading, that it will become the butt of attacks and accusations, that it will drown in the Dead Sea, in a sea of silence, stasis and apathy, and I wonder where the Palestinian people are throughout this time of crucial trial for it is their cause and they should have the first and last say in the matter. Why do we not go back to the Palestinian people to extricate their legitimate representatives from their fumbling around in the darkness? If there is any dispute about who represents them, then let the matter be resolved by the Palestinians declaring their opinion about that. If there is more than one vision for the solution of the Palestinian issue, then let all the visions be put on the table, followed by a plebiscite within their land and abroad, held under the supervision of a UN agency, and thereafter everyone will be obliged to recognise the result and the outcome can rightfully be put into effect without hesitation or prevarication. It is the Palestinian people who are suffering the consequences of occupation and the alienation of being in the diaspora. It is the Palestinian people who are hemmed in by catastrophes and whose security is under daily threat. It is the Palestinian people who in the final analysis are the stakeholders in their own cause and who should have the final say in determining their destiny.

28 February 1985

Civilisation and the Holes in the Road

It is a very sad thing when you find one of your friends hospitalised. It is even sadder when the reason is a road accident. The saddest is when the accident happened because he drove his car at night into a hole in the road and ended up with a broken rib and a crushed collarbone. The holes in the road may have been dug by a company commissioned to carry out a task, and it may have carried out its work with the requisite precision and care, but the company did not bother to put up a barrier or light to to warn pedestrians or drivers. Everything may have a value and a worth except a human-being, who has no value or worth either in the eyes of a company or of the authorities. Perhaps the matter does not arouse much astonishment or surprise, not due to its insignificance but because of the sheer number of pot-holes, bumps and exposed electric switching boxes etc. that a citizen sees in the street, but we still have those experts who visit foreign countries and tell us all about the amazing signs of cleanliness, neatness and beauty they have seen there, emphasising the way people abroad take particular care to look after the environment with respect, not just on the constitutional level but in their daily activities, whether on the road or in state buildings. Abroad, the state, the law, the system and convention vie with each other, in a manner that beggars our imagination, to serve the citizen, to keep him comfortable and to reimburse him for any harm that comes to him. Despite the cold weather, the atmosphere abroad is warm with the love of humanity, and the individual there occupies his appropriate place with a humanity that is his in law and in practice. It is not surprising therefore that the individual abroad returns the love he receives to society, offers care for the care he receives, and evinces a sense of belonging. If you want to judge some civilisation or other, do not tire your eyes by going over the constitution and the laws, and do not bother listening to slogans and communiqués. Just follow an individual as he deals with the state, with any of its officials, and for any reason or reasons. Follow what sort of conversation, referral or behaviour transpires between them, and you will see the real face of that civilisation. My apologies for defending a human-being whom

God created in the most perfect form, and to whom he ordered the angels to prostrate themselves except for Iblis who refused and was proud and was a disbeliever.[1]

7 March 1985

1 This is a slight reworking of verse 2:34 of the Qur'an: And when we ordered the angels: 'Prostrate yourselves before Adam,' all of them fell prostrate, except Iblis. He refused, and gloried in his arrogance and became one of the disbelievers.

Art and Censorship

For art freedom is like the sun for a living creature. Art is born, grows and flourishes under freedom's bright rays, and it withers, wilts and dies in the darkness of oppression, submissiveness and subordination. It is expression, creativity and adventurousness whose path has been strewn by nature with those difficulties and challenges which arise essentially from art's need for innovative talent, for a special sensitive language and for the requisite inspiration, tenacity and patience. So how can we add to that forces which are alien to its content or role, which threaten art with admonishments and force and which clip its wings, often in the guise of protecting empty traditions, of imposing a deluded vision of what is right or attempting to subjugate art to hypocrisy and stasis. I was on the point of rejecting all forms of censorship whatsoever as unmitigated evil except in rare situations such as during a time of war or revolution, but I have tempered my stance out of disgust at the ailments I have seen sometimes afflicting freedom. The symptoms include fecklessness and giving free rein to the evil in human nature. These ailments consequently transfer their contagion to art, it becomes involuntarily side-tracked and can become a destructive force for human values which prevents them from soaring freely upwards, particularly if these ailments act like an epidemic among a mostly illiterate population and then lead to the wellsprings of culture drying up. Consequently, I have convinced myself of the value of censorship in the field of the popular arts such as cinema, radio and television, and other forms which are created by people generation after generation. I apologise for my stance to myself and to others, but what I mean by censorship is rational and politically aware censorship. So just what is that? It is a form of censorship which perceives the power of the human need for art, which cloaks art with love and appreciation, which believes in it as a divinely-inspired activity, that it plays a vital social role and helps in the human mission of elevating standards and goals. The worst thing about censorship is that it considers itself a separate species from art, an opposing force, or a supervisory authority, all things which can bring about timidity or distorted ways of thinking and then lead to animosity and hatred.

What I mean by censorship is that which believes that the very essence and aims of art are good, that its baseline is freedom of thought, and that it has the right to attempt to reach out to the emotions of the individual and the masses, and to enlighten and provide enjoyment.

What I mean by censorship is that those services are for the protection of both art and society and not society alone, for the type of degraded art which threatens social or human values generally comes about for commercial reasons, as a result of striving for success in the cheapest of manners, or as a form of flattery for base impulses or crude chauvinism. This commercial degrading of art hurts art itself primarily, and sullies its beauty and purity, it sensationalises crime rather than studying it, and uses sex for titillation rather than as a topic of education and enlightenment. The objection here is that censorship should be used to protect art, just as it is used to protect society and the individual citizen. Censorship should be in the service of art just as it is in the service of a politically aware authority. Perhaps the real test to which censorship should subject its decisions is that it should be used for the benefit of art just as it is used for the benefit of people and their values.

Provided the articles of censorship are restricted to general, specific and defined principles, they will be provide a gentle lamp to light the censor's path without any shackles hampering his thought processes or movement. When these articles of censorship multiply out of control, they can only become so confusing for the censor with all their ever-changing details that they should not be applied to any texts for they only represent a means of stagnation and of holding things back. The censor needs to feel that he has freedom of operation and behaviour so that he can keep his finger on the public pulse, and that he can work free of bureaucratic procedures and fear. The worst thing that can happen to him is that he is passed over by a new era and the dynamics of national development and that he remains bogged down in the sort of mummified nit-picking that is no longer appropriate to this day and age. So we should whittle down the principles of censorship to a few fine sentences and leave the rest to the censor in his role as an arbiter of public taste and sensitivities. For that reason it would be most beneficial if regular meetings were to take place between those commissioned with carrying out censorship and the artistic, literary and intellectual community for an exchange of opinion and to debate the subject anew so that the office of the censor can be carried out in a benign and credible manner, as a beacon for the nation and not as a malign influence on art and life in general.

Some people may also think that censorship should be extended to the artistic level in an attempt to create the right climate for the creation of good artistic output. Good art does not come about in the shadow of directives even if they can be described as rational or well-intentioned. Art is a branch of activity over which judgements and tastes differ and clash and it cannot be based on just one view or way of seeing and any attempt to impose a particular view on art can only lead to differences of opinion, insults and hurt feelings as well as to attempts not backed by legislation to assert control over the creative community intermingled with wishful thinking and inanities. These all form a new sort of double-dealing in addition to that which has so inundated the creative and innovative community that they have almost been brought to a standstill at various times in the past.

There are other ways to bring art to the fore of which we are well aware and which we practice occasionally. First and foremost is the encouragement of new works of literature and plastic arts, broadcasting the best examples on television and leaving the other works to be judged by the critics, by the public and by time itself.

Finally, censorship is engendered by the state of emergency and we have to work with it cautiously and prudently.

Literature... and the Cinema

There is a great difference between the language of literature and the language of the camera which translates literary works into scenes which tell the narrative of the story. Literature for a reading public only needs one person, that is the author, who is a person who enjoys complete freedom and can publish whatever he decides to publish. However, when it comes to the cinematic interpretation of literature, it is part of a process of production in which a large number of people take part.

If the cinema has any influence on literature, its influence comes in the area of the fast pace and abridgement of the narrative, and that is cinema's main influence on literature. However, I am mainly interested in preserving the core subject matter around which the story revolves. I do not write with an eye on a cinematic version of my work, for literature has to be for the sake of literature even if the large screen has in fact presented a number of my works in a fitting manner, such as 'The Palace Walk Trilogy', 'The Beginning and the End', 'Chatter on the Nile' and 'Karnak'.

However, 'The Palace Walk Trilogy' is one of my own favourite works and before writing it I read many works on the art of storytelling among which were novels dealing with three generations of a family and then I decided to write a novel of this genre in which I would present a depiction of Egypt. My preparations for this work lasted about a year during which I read some world literature in this genre such as 'War and Peace', 'The Forsyte Saga' and 'Love and Man',[1] and then I started making copious notes on the characteristics, and my impressions, of the characters. All in all I spent three years preparing to write the trilogy.

In addition to novels and other literary works, I read works of non-fiction recommended to me by my friends just as I take care to read the works of young writers in order to stay informed about their work.

Arabic Literature

My knowledge of literature outside Egypt is unfortunately rather limited due to the circumstances and the non-existence of a common market between us – and this applies to all the Arab countries, as their works do not reach us here even though there are works of no lesser quality than the world literature which we read. These writers include

1 The Arabic here is an obvious mistranscription.

Tayeb Saleh,[2] Hanna Mina,[3] Siba'i Othman[4] and Mohamed Alwan.

The great burden of the problem of reinvigorating our Arabic literature and turning it into world literature has fallen on the shoulders of the young generation of writers. En route to that aim they will have to be more true to themselves for true and good art comes from inside the artist, and in addition to them having to search their souls we also need better publications, good translations and public relations. The day we can bring all that about is the day when we can say that we are offering real Arabic literature to the world.

I believe that every generation has its own marvellous forms of creativity, down to the fourth and fifth generation. We do not have a crisis of productivity for we produce a vast number of entertaining works of different genres, but the crisis lies with reading and the readership. I am of the opinion that a flourishing literary and cultural life is always dependent upon the renewal of life and its development in a manner which drives innovative and creative works to ever greater development and renewal.

Man's hopes change at every stage of his life. At the outset of my life, I and my generation were taken up with the cause of independence and freedom.

After that I have been deeply involved in trying to raise the cultural level and get our Arabic culture seen internationally. I am still waiting for the day to come when Arabic literature attracts the attention of critics, commentators and teachers all over the world. I believe that a man is more creative when he feels a sense of loss or sadness.

Taha Hussein[5]... and the West

It is the opinion of some people that Dr Taha Hussein was an imitator

---

2 (1929–2009), Sudanese writer, whose best-known work in English is his 1969 book *Season of Migration to the North*.

3 (1924–2015), Syrian writer.

4 (1937–88), Sudanese short story writer.

5 (1889–1973), one of twentieth-century Egypt's greatest intellectuals and authors.

who gave credence in his work to some orientalist views, that his western culture shone through his work, that he followed the method of Descartes and that is to doubt absolutely everything until its veracity can be proved. Even if that were the case, it would be no great sin. Taha Hussein brought western culture to us and stood for intellectualism. His influence on us, as an oriental man and through his works on Islam and his literary and patriotic works, has been enormous, and no thinker can avoid being directly or indirectly influenced by those who precede him.

Taha Hussein wanted us to be people who embody both the past and the present, and this admixture was evident in his character. He was a sheikh[6] at al-Azhar, when we wanted him to be that, as well as being a European, and therein lies his greatness.

The Campaign Against al-Afghani[7]

Jamal al-Din al-Afghani was a great thinker and ideological activist wherever he was at the time, in Egypt, in Iran and in India. He brought the spirit of Islamic revivalism to every country he visited. His life-long aim was to rouse the East from its lethargy. He worked for its unification and to remove the foreigners who were exploiting it. Many people who played the greatest religious, political and social role in our life were among his disciples.

When it comes to the campaign waged against him by Dr Louis Awad,[8] it involved very little objective thought. There is no harm in every generation re-evaluating the preceding generations and sometimes it is rather difficult to forge a path towards a new way of seeing, but the discussion about what was said and the response should have been carried out in a much more objective and academic manner than it was.

15 March 1985

6 A term used for a respected teacher of religion.

7 (1839–1897), political activist and Islamic ideologist.

8 (1915–90), Egyptian intellectual and writer.

Crime between Punishment and Cure

No crime has aroused as much concern and disapprobation as the crime of rape. It represents for Egyptians the epitome of the most heinous elements of perversion such as the degradation of a woman's reputation and an assault on her honour as well as being an attack on what humanity holds dearest.

Public opinion became incensed and the whole of Egypt jumped to the defence of the victim, demanding that the perpetrator should be given an immediate and deterrent punishment with no mercy being shown to him. If that proves anything, it shows the dynamism of the ethical tradition which lives on within us all, even during eras when perversion and indifference run amok. I wish we could take the same ferocious approach toward any form of moral perversion, particularly those whose squalid repercussions fall upon society as a whole, upon its present and future, its growth and security, its progress and success and in this I make no differentiation between economic, political, cultural or intellectual perversions.

I also hope that we can take a position like this with regard to all the criminality that is taking place, and that we do not just track down the criminals, arrest them, put them on trial, punish them and enhance public security with everything then going back to its normal course.

We must turn our sights to uncovering the weaknesses and mistakes in all corners of our complicated lives and direct our attention to carrying out the plan of hunting down corruption and reinforcing the foundations of democracy and justice. We need to improve our policies towards the youth, their education and equip them to face challenges and frustrations. That should be the all-encompassing task of the state and the parties who should put all their authority and experience into this. Then there is also a problem about which we should not remain silent and that is the celibacy imposed upon our youth as they reach adulthood for numerous reasons, such as the length of education in the modern era and the unfeasibility of getting married at a young age or even at a reasonable age due to the economic and housing crises.

The void can indeed be filled with worship, culture and sport, but the problem will still loom large and needs some dedicated attention in order for us to arrive at a rational solution, first and foremost on the part of the clergy who are those primarily responsible for the purity of our souls and our decent behaviour, for if you are guided by your religion you will not be disillusioned.

21 March 1985

The Third Way

Many thinkers ascribe any defect in our economic or political life to our following a fluid policy which is not constrained by any one clear plan and which sometimes appears to follow right-wing guidelines and at other times is so left-wing that you would think there has been a great lurch to the left.

The advice which they propose is that the state should choose its own way and that it should either watch over every single component of the economy, whether large or small, or that the economy should be free from state intervention. They read the page of our life line by line through this magnifying glass and use it to explain any downturn in any area of economic activity, such as a slow-down in productivity or a price hike, a fall in the value of the Egyptian pound, etc. It is as if the policy of nations has just two contradictory paths which never shall meet and our attempts to reconcile them have only exacerbated matters.

However, if we take a look around at the world, and if moreover we remember the social experiments we have been subjected to under the aegis of the July Revolution, it is clear that there is a third way which could be described as the middle path and which will provide some relief to both the private and the public sectors and which many countries such as Sweden have the good fortune to enjoy. I am not exaggerating if I say that our overwhelming experience augurs success only in the long term. Have we only turned away from economic isolationism after our economy almost hit rock bottom, and have we only put an end to our reckless economic free-for-all now that it has turned our country into a circus for opportunism and banditry? Now we are embarking on our experience under a third way, under the aegis of ever-growing democracy, carrying out the five-year plan with undeniable success, with respect for the rights of society and encouragement for the entrepreneurship of upright individuals.

I cannot deny that the work is marred by slips, mistakes, a lack of clarity and haste, but an atmosphere of democracy and press-freedom provides objective criticism, offers a well thought-out timetable and a sense of what people should and should not do, and this criticism is what is keeping us on the straight and narrow and eradicating any glitches.

We must offer the third way all grounds for success, and help it with all the power we possess. It is the path of the best of the July Revolution and may it be blessed with the spirit of merciful peace.

28 March 1985

A Frenzied Crime

If the crime of murdering one's parents were the first of its type in our history, or even if it were the last, it would be sufficient to break our hearts and pain our consciences. As soon as this crime was reported, the killer was accused by everyone of being mad, as if insanity is all we need to rationalise the situation, despite what was reported about the killer being in possession of his mental faculties, being a balanced person but having lost his religious faith. No possible explanations nor distorted thinking about human nature can justify this vicious crime, and it cannot be explained away by references to fratricide at the beginning of human history nor by recourse to fanciful modern psychoanalysis with its Oedipus complexes, nor by what has been written about materialism and the loss of spiritual values or about the economic, ethnical and political crisis which society is constantly undergoing, nor by the break up and alienation of the nuclear family and nor by the lack of a sense of belonging, by aimlessness, faithlessness or hopelessness.

Many people go through hard times in their lives and they may become involved in nefarious activities or even commit suicide, but they do not commit this particularly odious crime. It may be that the perpetrator fell prey to a form of despondency whose strange logic made him see the crime as a mercy-killing or a form of punishment, with evil whisperings taking hold of a heart in which the springs of humanity had dried up.

We should regard this crime as a singular event and we should not waste our time trying to find erroneous interpretations or baseless expectations.

It is true that our lives are replete with innumerable frustrations, but they do not lead to this crime nor justify it. We should be cautious about ascribing our anger to existentialism or some other philosophy, for among the existentialists we find people who call for faith just as there are those who call for atheism, but none of existentialism's followers have murdered their parents.

We should not accuse a philosophy the way we accuse television or the cinema whenever we cannot find a way out of something, or when we are afraid to confront the real elements of negativity which lie behind a crime or anti-social forms of behaviour. Philosophy, art, television, the cinema and all the other negative facets of society are innocent of this frenzied crime.

4 April 1985

A Return to Language

Yet again the issue of our weak knowledge of, and contempt for, Arabic has raised its head. Language is a container for thought, a means of communication and understanding. It binds a nation together as well as being what connects us to our religion. We cannot mention the state of Arabic without it leaving a bitter taste in our mouths. Perhaps an explanation for this is that one of the many interconnected symptoms of the whole disease is the crisis that society is passing through at this stage of its development, as stated by Dr Zaki Naguib Mahmud.[1] He is correct in his opinion, but we cannot wait and do nothing until society is cured of its disease, until it regains its health in agriculture, manufacturing, science, culture and Arabic. There is a cure for each symptom when viewed on its own, just as an epidemic can spread across a country affecting a great number of the population without that preventing an individual from taking appropriate measures which do not conflict with the general resistance to the epidemic, and at this point we put forward any suggestions we have in the hope that we may be able to bring our language back to a good state of health:

I would have started with a suggestion about limiting the number of classes students have to go do, but I have found that this needs to wait until we have overcome the general crisis so I am putting it off until then. However it is not within the realm of the impossible for us to train efficient teachers, especially as we have had great success doing this in the past as evinced by former graduates of Dar al-'Ulum[2] and al-Azhar. These included our teachers at both the elementary and secondary levels and we were so impressed by them that we used to think that their knowledge of Arabic and literature was flawless. They had a great familiarity with teaching and education, and an unsurpassed

1 (1905–93), an Egyptian intellectual and thinker, known as 'the philosopher of authors and author of philosophers'.

2 An educational institution designed to produce students with both an Islamic and modern secondary education. It was founded in 1871 and is now a faculty of Cairo University.

love of the language, and could come out with never-ending quotes of the best Arabic prose and poetry. It was they who made us fall in love with the language and its treasures. They even got us to understand the intricacies of grammar and we all gained a reasonable level in it. How were these teachers prepared? I don't think that the matter is in need of foreign expertise or missions, or hard currency. Let us first of all submit that an efficient teacher is the foundation of any successful education. Teachers also had recourse to a school library and its magazine, and it was our good fortune as children that we could benefit from all that, and in our free time we used to read the classics, and books on science and the latest inventions. We published our first words in the school magazine and it may be a luxury then for me to mention the acting, speaking and singing clubs.

Let us now turn to grammar and its rules and submit that it is vastly complicated, and that the secrets of its beauty and expressive force can only be acquired after the sort of long hours of painful study for which students today do not have enough time, given that they have to absorb massive amounts of scientific, mathematical and literary material. So why have we made no progress at all in simplifying this all for them? This has become a most pressing need and has the support of people whose devotion to the language and the religion is not in doubt, and would it not be so much better if people could read the Holy Qur'an directly without having to make use of an interpretation written in the margins. Our language has to make use of all the tools available to other languages of the world and its teaching has to be adapted and updated to accord with the unceasing march of time.

If we can do that, and even if we cannot, we must fundamentally change the method of language teaching, particularly with regard to reading and literature. The teaching of literature is based on a study of selected prose and poetical texts. We should start off by teaching starter texts which deal with modern life, and then as the student progresses we should make the texts harder and harder until they reach the pre-Islamic period. I would suggest that teachers should be able to make a free choice of texts, and that they should not be restricted to the needs of examinations, by which I mean that students should be given a book of poetry for example and the students should choose the designated amount of text themselves. In the class the students should each read the pieces they have chosen and explain them, along with the reasons they have chosen them in accordance with their age and their degree of culture. The end result of education along these lines is that the student will be considered to have completed his course in literature without having to sit a useless examination.

We should also follow a new method in reading, with students reading a book, or a novel, chapter by chapter at home. Then they should give a verbal precis in class in Classical Arabic, inasmuch as possible, of what they have absorbed from the book, and at the end of the school year each student should write his own outline of the book making use of a suggested wordlist. That is how a student can be a success at reading, and we would benefit from this in two crucial areas:

Firstly: we would be able to separate literature and reading on the one hand from the hateful atmosphere of examinations.

Secondly: we would be training the students to be critical and to develop a sense of taste and love of reading. Thereafter we could hold a special weekly class where anything can be read, followed by a general discussion in Classical Arabic which will build up the students' self-confidence and help them to express themselves correctly and with good pronunciation.

As for the examination, it should only deal with grammar and composition. Finally I have not forgotten the role which both branches of the state broadcasting service, i.e. the radio and the television, should perform, providing its audience with well enunciated and carefully phrased Arabic. They have already made great inroads in this area with Qur'anic programming, their programmes in good literary Arabic and in training their programme hosts, not to mention the special programmes they make on culture. I do not think I am overshooting the mark it I were to suggest that they should have a short daily programme on the common mistakes in writing and how to correct them according to the rules of grammar and pronunciation.

I am not sure whether I have laid out everything I would like to see put into the service of our beautiful language. Perhaps I have expounded too many thoughts here, but we really need to make a great leap forward in carrying these out.

5 April 1985

Blossoms on the Path of Patience

Comprehensive development is no more than a new name for what is known to history as a complete rebirth, particularly when it concentrates on the root and branch and not on temporary placebos, and when it aims to bring about the best in society. Effecting this will take a long time, or at the very least it will take no short time.

The majority of our nation is weighed down with the daily problems of life and inflation, the bottle-neck in public services, and an inconducive climate. They reach out eagerly for anything that can lead to change and reform but if they have to wait too long for any actual results, and we cannot blame them for this, they start to think the worst, their confidence is shaken and they fling accusations about the heedlessness of the best of plans or the effort that has been expended.

Hence some quick successes are vital when it comes to the lack of development on the smaller issues around the major goals as these have a positive and speedy effect on the mood of the citizens and should be carried out without hesitation or delay and with continuous, alert and decisive supervision. In this domain there should also be vigilance about following the letter of the law, particularly when it comes to the security, safety and comfort of the citizen and the citizen should also be treated well and not confronted by red-tape all the time. There should be respect for the personality, time and effort of the individual, with respect for the law being imposed in the streets and elsewhere, and most importantly there must be support for democracy in state institutions. In order to do all that we must look again at the constitution and annul laws which have caused so much irritation so that people can breathe in a healthy and conducive climate with the burdens of life lightened. This will create a sense of trust between the citizen and the state and will give the citizen the patience to wait out the requisite time that things take. Everything I am calling for can be considered part and parcel of comprehensive development, but at the same time they are factors supported by and shored up by the opportunities for success.

11 April 1985

Our Real Wealth

The statements of the minister of education have convinced those who read them of his sincerely, his realism and his awareness of the dimensions of the educational crisis we are facing. His appointment has brought with it great trust which in a nutshell means the investment of the real wealth which we own, i.e. manpower and consequently the future of our country and the valuable life we hope for in these modern times. I have pondered what we need from the ministry of education and come up with the following:

That primary education should include every male and female child, and that they should complete the whole course of primary education as it seems that we have no other means of eradicating illiteracy, even if this takes another generation.

That the uptake rate of secondary education should be controlled to match the actual availability of university places thereby making our university life flourish again and creating the right climate for the production of graduates with specialisations.

That students, not accepted for university, should be sent to technical and training colleges, with the aim of preparing a workforce equipped for the complications of modern industrial work.

That they should work to change the teachings methods from those of learning by rote with the aim of creating the sort of independent thinking that will lead to an outrush of intellectual and emotional creative forces.

That religious and cultural education should have a special prominence at all stages of education.

That there should be more hours of teaching during the year, and there should be more civics courses to enable students to face the challenges of modern life.

If all of that is put into practice, we will be able to transform the ever-increasing number of our population into something worthwhile and we will have everything we need for our comprehensive growth as well as all the expertise we need for any situation. That is our true wealth and it will not dwindle over time. Its value can only increase.

18 April 1985

The Long-Lasting Case

Have you heard the story of olden versus modern times? That is our favourite topic, our only topic or even our longest-lasting topic of conversation. It has gone on for generations without let or hindrance, as if it is a religious duty or one of the inherent properties of the Arab mind, as if it stems from a philosophical basis like human fate, the meaning of life, the meaning of existence, the riddle of life and death, or of good and evil. These are all questions which impose themselves on us and beg for consideration despite the difficulty of the questions and the impossibility of coming up with answers. If philosophical questions find their justifications in having sprung from the life of an individual or from being so intrinsically part of his daily or public life that he cannot forget them no matter how much he might try, what then is the justification for the tenacity of this issue being quasi-insolvable, as if we are the first nation on earth to confront it? Why have we been so obsessed with repeating these questions like one big refrain over the years from the time of al-Jabarti[1] up until our contemporary thinkers, through Muhammad 'Abduh,[2] al-Kawakibi,[3] Lutfi al-Sayyid,[4] Taha Hussein and Salama Musa?[5] Every new generation asks itself: Are we basing our lives on the examples of our pious ancestors? Are we throwing ourselves headlong into the arms of unbridled western culture? Are we choosing from the old and the new those things which blend in with our culture and which can be used to build a new and solid edifice? How many articles have been written on this, how many books, and how many conferences have been held in the East and the West. It appears to me sometimes, and God forgive me if I am wrong,

1 'Abd al-Rahman al-Jabarti (1753–1825), Egyptian scholar and chronicler.

2 (1849–1905) Egyptian Islamic jurist, religious scholar and liberal reformer.

3 'Abd al-Rahman al-Kawakibi (1855–1902) Syrian author and Pan-Islamic Arab solidarity supporter.

4 Ahmad Lutfi Sayyid (1872–1963), Egyptian intellectual, anti-colonial activist and the first director of Cairo University.

5 (1887–1958), journalist, writer, advocate of secularism and pioneer of Arab socialism.

that the secret behind this is that we are wary of real thinking or shy away from it for one reason or another, but I am not saying that we are incapable of that, God forbid. So we cover our inaction with the only permissible action, and that is for us to think about the thought itself, to think about what we should do if one day we were to decide to think or act, and thus we end up with the appearance of thought without really taking its true ramifications into account, trying to test its trustworthiness or thinking through the consequences which means that we have not managed to advance at all in creating a true Arab philosophy based on a pre-existing or contemporary basis or anything in-between. To do that would take a lifetime of isolation, away from the limelight and in a fortress of abstemiousness with its culmination possibly being some book or pamphlet. We have not tried to create a new political hypothesis inspired by our history or our present, or based on our intense experience of rule and administration and benefiting from the experiences of others. That also would need independent thinking, deep consideration, a whole lifetime and generally the sacrifice of fame and money. We have not come up with an original thought on the economy which has been drawn from our own lives and traditions and inspired by the East or the West or even the two together, or even going beyond those three combinations and coming up with something new. If we could go beyond just preparing to think about this to actually thinking about it, if we could throw ourselves into that unknown sea of adventure and innovation, we could come up with opinions, thoughts and theories which we would be able to examine in the light of the current situation and our experience in implementing them. The population would then become engaged with them and they would be an important new element for evaluation and judgment. That is how we could come to know the best way, through the power of thought, action, and mass mutual interaction. That would be a thousand times better than the repetitive and barren invective which we repeat again and again like the name of God in a Sufi ceremony or a section of the Qur'an. Perhaps literature is the only area where there has been room for adventure and in which creativity has been able to flourish accompanied by concomitant criticism and argumentation, giving existence to perfect classical and modern works of poetry, plays and adapted or semi-adapted short stories and other experimental forms of Arabic writing as well as our furious attempts to place form ahead of content. However it cannot be denied that literature and authors have been created and there has been a public who either accepted or rejected their output. If I were to follow what has appeared in other magazines, we would today only have works on history or the present day which do not bear witness to any artistic creativity. But what of literature alone? Perhaps because of the victory of the abilities of literary talents over those of other intellectual or philosophical talents, or the attractiveness of art and its literary and material rewards, or perhaps because it takes less pain and self-sacrifice, literature is guaranteed some results. However what sort of way forward in life would we have unless these are based on thought and its application, and when will we draw aside the curtain on this crucial issue and set our minds free to think and do serious work? Have we not had enough time to bring the nation from the abyss of backwardness to the apogee of developed nations?

19 April 1985

A Day of Wisdom

Today is a celebration commemorating the liberation of Sinai, or the liberation of Egypt if we consider that its territory is indivisible. Sticking to this principle, we are still waiting to recover Taba[1] no matter how small or insignificant the area is. The first thing that comes to our hearts is that we should offer prayers for those soldiers, officers and citizens who died during the liberation of Sinai, that we should remember Anwar Sadat with admiration and reverence for his wonderful national achievements, and that we should call upon others to remember him just as they point out his negative sides at every opportunity. Let us remember the policy of no war no peace, or that he used war as a path to peace, and how he regained part of the nation which had been lost to us for long, sad years.

Before that we had a different policy which aspired to liberate countries, claimed to speak for other nations, challenged states, a policy whose efforts were wasted and which brought us to the critical situation in which our greatest hopes were to regain the lands we lost after 5 June, a policy which occasioned a violent shift from sovereignty to begging and produced generations of young people immersed in sorrow, bitter despair and injurious apathy, a policy which caused the breakdown of the individual, family, and the social values we hold so dear. So let the past be a lesson whose light can guide us towards the path of peace and rebirth, and let us learn from the past that a worthy life is based on wisdom, learning and work and may God have mercy on those who know their own worth. Today the face of Sinai is changing with the hustle and bustle of construction and development, tracing out the outline of a better future in-keeping with its agricultural, mineral and tourist capacities.

We spent a long time fantasising and daydreaming until we faced up to the brutal reality but with wisdom and realistic policies we managed to drag ourselves out of the pit of destruction and onto the right path,

---

1 Taba was the last section of Sinai to be returned to Egypt by Israel. This took place in February 1989.

the path of democracy, learning and work. The less precipitously we act, the more wisdom, learning and work we achieve.

25 April 1985

The Peace Track

Since time immemorial Egypt has only enjoyed real independence and the capability to decide her own fate in the aftermath of the July Revolution when her will was liberated from any legitimate or illegitimate foreign power, when Egypt's sons took on her governance and sailed the ship of state through stormy waters in search of a safe harbour. I shall not tell you about the history which Egypt made in that era, for you yourself can no doubt recall what was built up and what was destroyed, you can remember the battles lost and won, development, stagnation and the restarting of development, you can recall the attempts at governance that moved from authoritarianism to authoritarianism tinged with democracy to unhurried democracy. You can remember the hardships of isolationism, economic liberalisation and its catastrophes, the middle way and its bedfellows, you can remember the great hopes which the people became intoxicated with and the bitter frustrations which swallowed them up. You can certainly remember inflation, debts and our begging for loans, the class imbalance, the explosion of corruption, the maladies of the youth, and the afflictions of the old.

It is a history full of pain and lessons, brimming with memories some sweet, some as bitter as Coloquintida[1] and some more venomous than fast-acting poison. We have borne and suffered this history perhaps not only as an unavoidable test for our new-found independence but also because we are fully prepared to take it on as a harsh test on our route towards the path of rationalism and rebirth as we attempt to divest the nation's tortured spirit of negativity while raising our eyes to a morrow which promises goodness, blessings and honour. The third aspect of the July Revolution, the aspect of democracy, renewal and purification, must affirm that – not with words, communiqués or promises, but through serious, continuous creative work in an atmosphere of freedom, quality, the rule of law and virtue.

We do not have copious amounts of time or choice. Either we head

1 Mahfouz says 'bitter gourd', the extract of which Shakespeare refers to in Othello by its Latin name.

for success – there are auspicious glimmers of this on the horizon – or we backslide into ignorance. For God is with those who strive to achieve things for themselves.

9 May 1985

A Wonderful Movement

In our Arab region a spark of vigorous activity has emerged and we hope that it will not be snuffed out before its aims are achieved. It shows that we have long suffered from a state of waiting and negativity, and that we have now resolved to confront the future with practical thinking and fruitful dialogue, to take the task on for ourselves and for the coming generations. I hope that whatever it is that has motivated this wonderful movement does not restrict itself to seeking out the means of resolving the Arab issue in a just and comprehensive manner but also re-examines our cultural-developmental state in light of the demands of the modern age. In other words, I hope that all the thought going into a solution of the Arab issue will also be translated into the wider issue of progress and rebirth in our economic, political, social and cultural life.

We are still standing at the feet of a great mountain of scientific innovations, social development and a new vision of humanity and existence, like some country cousins at the entrance to a modern city full of wonders. We have to plan for this new life on a totally scientific basis and come to terms with the most leading-edge developments, otherwise we will miss the train and be no more than the remnants of an age gone by or exhibits from a dying era. In any case, we are not starting from zero for we have indeed made achievements in agriculture and industry. We have a privileged position, we have the manpower and the expertise in various fields of activity and beyond all that we are the inheritors of robust and stable values which are the best guarantee for a decent life.

Moreover we[1] still have the oil revenues which we can invest properly and productively which can help develop the land, our brainpower and our will. We only have to admit that we have lagged dreadfully behind and that from now on we have to make the most of every minute and second for the sake of the present and the future.

16 May 1985

---

1 When Mahfouz speaks in the first person plural, it is the pan-Arabic 'royal plural', i.e. he means 'the Arabs'.

Independence in Jungle Life

I understand that we guard our independence with great care for that is a subject inculcated in us from the cradle, one which we have struggled for our whole lives and which we have achieved with blood, sweat and tears. What I do not understand is that we either neglect to nurture it, or that we are complacent about it and deem the responsibility too great.

There is a clear way of preserving our independence in our time and that is for us to be so self-reliant that we do not need to request help or throw ourselves upon the mercy of others. We should be self-reliant no matter how much effort or sacrifice it takes. We should organise our budget so that not one piastre is spent unnecessarily and we need to put the motor of productivity into first gear. We should make the most of our whole work force and of all the time granted to us on this earth. We should do our utmost to improve the durability and aesthetic quality of our products even if they are a degree or so less good than similar foreign items. We should empower the state to collect tax from everyone according to his ability, and we should preserve the purity and virtue of work while mercilessly pursuing those who give themselves over to corrupt activities. Any deviation from this plan is tantamount to high treason, both against us and against the coming generations.

We need to balance our budget and our spending so that some individual, social and moral equilibrium can come back into our lives.

If we do all that, and still find it difficult to achieve our aim, or if achieving our aim takes a long time, if we knock on every door and try every means but still end up in need of foreign aid, we must remember one essential and fundamental truth, no matter how bitter it may be, and that is that international relations between states are not based on magnanimity, chivalry or mercy, but on the principle of mutual interest. Anyone who wants to take must give, anyone to wants to ask for things must give something in exchange. That is part of the sacrifices that we must make at every stage of our development, even if reluctantly, and we must do this without complaint, protest or hollow anger.

The path of life is full of difficult things which we would prefer not to do but we must move on with energy, seriousness, resolution and remorseless sacrifice.

The path of independence is clear, and anyone who wants to protect it must play his part in order to enjoy it fully.

23 May 1985

The Spectator's Confusion

I think I am well aware of the struggles faced by the state in our present life: the dilapidated and moribund infrastructure, the funding required by the comprehensive development plan, the problems of overpopulation and inflation and the subsequent dissolution of nerves, hearts and values. I am aware of all of that and I am following the battles we are waging to set it all aright, to renovate and renew or reconstruct. Then there are the things whose secret I do not know. They are the unpleasant complications that we add to the woes we have inherited as a result of expenditures which beggar explanation or comprehension, particularly when this has to do with our economic activity. This is a highly sensitive and very risky area whose actions have almost immediate consequences. Over the course of three months, declarations were issued, based on long slow study and subjected to many revisions, which have created a worrying clamour which is somewhere between light resignation and overt rejection. Ten days later new amended declarations were issued, and the worrying resignation-rejection clamour has continued, and in the meantime a volcano of accusations has erupted, with some of its flames enveloping the guilty and the blameless alike and other flames pointing to the complete responsibility of a minister as the cabinet member most involved. The matter has now come to judgment, and the legal considerations include criticism of impunity and working methods. At this point one minister departs and another one comes, and new economic declarations are issued which are deemed to supersede those which were issued after such long slow study and which have a slight element of reform in them. What can a spectator of this drama say, particularly when you remember that the cabinet has an economic sub-committee made up of PhDs, in addition to the parliament and the Consultative Council and the various specialised sub-committees? They all go on discussing what has adversely affected the market, manufacturing and the country's reputation, but they offer no explanation, no accountability and no sanctions. What is there left for me to say?

30 May 1985

The Missing Constitution

I have reached an advanced stage of my life in this world. I have lived through a myriad of happy and painful experiences – but this is not the place to speak of them, although there may be enough space to mention a few highlights which could be considered to symbolise the values without which life would hold no meaning. First and foremost, among these is faith in God and his prophets along with the sanctity and enlightenment this grants to our world notwithstanding all its faults and setbacks. This is closely followed by a love for our homeland, its people, history, hopes, pain and its essential pillar which is that all Egyptians should pull together with a sincere and real sense of oneness that does not differ from person to person for reasons of belief, opinion, skin-colour or race. National unity and nationalism are two names for one concept and are the pulse of one and the same emotion – for there can be no homeland without unity and no unity without a homeland, and any attempt to re-write history is an atrocious attack on the country's sanctity, which, in religious terms, would be tantamount to polytheism.

There is also the issue of faith in Arab unity which in itself is a call for harmony, cooperation and cohesion directed towards the branches of one large family who have been kept apart by its sons' ambitions to rule and by the politics of exploitative colonialists. In reality there is no contradiction between patriotism and Arab nationalism, just as there is no contradiction between those two concepts and general human unity if our hearts were only ready for that, if circumstances allowed it and if this also included a belief in freedom, and you know what I mean by that. We have practised this in the name of democracy in days of yore as well as more recently when we were able to imagine what the relationship between the ruler and the ruled ought to be, how the ruled should relate to each other and what social justice should be. We have been able to conceptualise equality before the law, the opportunities granted by life, and we have put an end to abusive financial privileges. This has been the gift of the July Revolution to our people and we should not let this slip through our fingers no matter how varied our paths. I would also include faith in the intellect and the legislated right to seek the truth in nature as well as in what lies beyond nature. This should be considered sacrosanct and be a protected right of all humans. Anyone who hinders the intellect and its rights even to the smallest degree is actually wounding humanity to the quick and destroying our identity and dignity. Last but not least, it is an attack on the value of art, aesthetics and the innocent human enjoyment of talent and vision.

This is the outcome of this stage in our values, or perhaps it is the most important or the one most worth mentioning in this brief list. I am not saying that I alone have been particularly involved in this, for inequality has been the hallmark of our generation, but we have managed to live through it all, despite the trials and tribulations, and it has never occurred to a single one of us that a day would come when our society would become the focus of a wicked accusation, or be tarnished by ignorance and unbelief, but this has happened and faith alone in God and his prophets has become apostasy, patriotism has become heresy, Arab nationalism has become a trap, the intellect has been splattered with mud, and art has turned into rank licentiousness. The ground beneath our feet has been shaken and our heads turned, and the debate between us and some of the new pioneers has left us wondering: what is it that you want and just how do you see our world and your world? What sort of unity, freedom, people, intellect and art do you have? And we have not yet received a full answer. Is it some sort of secret? Has the answer not yet been formulated? We have been drip-fed partial answers, obfuscating and condescending answers – as if in an attempt to mollify and silence those doing the asking.

I cannot recall having read research on minor issues where the researchers' views differed but where there was no general conclusion. Moreover the existence of various unbridled types of Islamic rule in the countries of Pakistan and Iran has not revealed just one form of truth, and their many differences in vision and relations are ugly and unbrotherly, leading to an increase in the causes of confusion and confirming the need for us to define more carefully the call to Islam and all its features, dimensions and divisions. This call has been sounded in Egypt for more than fifty years and it has been repeated in varying degrees according to the prevailing circumstances, but is generally restricted to calls upon our conscience, to preaching and offering guidance, to drawing lessons from the conduct of our early and righteous Muslim ancestors and only occasionally have some partial studies dealt with the system of governance or the economy.

It is high time for us to issue a comprehensive, pre-emptive constitution to clarify the new system of governance in all its details, the suggested economic methods, rights and duties, the dimensions of national unity, the role of science, culture and art, the position of women and our relationship with the world and its people, so that every citizen can know his role and what his future may be, and the work he is supposed to do for the country as a whole – as an example to the elite, and that he is worth any effort made to bring this about with no further delay. Before sending it to print, the drafters of this new constitution should show it to our intellectuals of whatever religion and they should be open to any and all opinion and comment. This is more than just having a book published. It is a covenant and a life-plan, and all our hopes should be for its success, first in Egypt. This would then send out an open call not just to every Islamic state but perhaps to every country in the world if it is able to offer humanity the freedom that has not been provided by other systems of governance, and the justice that has not yet been brought about by other experiments, along with a spiritual life supported by sound human values and forms of behaviour.

31 May 1985

A Revolution and a Lesson

Sudan has given the Arab nation, as well as the whole Third World, a revolution and a lesson, having suffered from a form of totalitarian rule that was mindless of the era we live in and of its own people. It underwent a crushing economic crisis which was treated with a sudden decree removing subsidies with no heed paid to all those suffering or to the benefit of national unity, and dragged itself to the brink of civil war. It did this by hurriedly decreeing the imposition of Islamic law without any study, thought or consideration given to those of other religions. The people had had enough and there was a popular revolution to which the army responded with a sense of national duty and wisdom, immediately acquiescing to as many of the people's demands as it could and going on to prepare the way to effect their remaining demands. For all his mistakes, we should not forget the achievements of the previous Sudanese president, the services he offered to his country in particular and to the Nile Valley in general. It may be that he himself lost his position as a result of his totalitarian rule and its evil consequences for both the ruler and the ruled. And now we hope from the depth of our hearts that the brotherly nation of Sudan has found the right path to its noble goal, and we also hope that the Third World will benefit from the lesson Sudan has offered to right-thinking people. We hope that faith in democracy will be deeply, unhesitatingly and unshakingly rooted. We hope that faith in democracy will establish itself in people as the firm and only foundation of national life and the current reality. We hope that those who desire a pure Islamic lifestyle which is up to the challenge of corruption and dissolution will make it their concern to act with patience, prudence and through consultation, and come to the understanding that the lifestyle they desire cannot be decreed into existence, that it cannot be imposed upon others against their will, but that it can only come about after much education and hard work. Sudan has indeed given the Arab nation a revolution and a lesson. It should be delighted with its revolution and may it benefit from the lesson.

6 June 1985

Rationalising Rationalisation

Important decisions have been made to rationalise energy in the fields of street lighting and television transmission, and we thank those civil servants for their thoughts in this matter and we welcome their decisions. We announce our support for any rationalisation which can control expenditure and work towards the rebalancing of our budget. However, we do not want this rationalisation to take place willy-nilly or to affect the activity of one ministry and not another, or to operate on the basis of ad hoc agreements. This policy might well bring about some savings, but it might start off with something that can bear delay, it might delay what is better not put off for the future and it might overlook things that should not be ignored. For example, we could reduce street lighting and yet still go on holding wildly extravagant celebrations which subvert the wisdom and integrity of those economising decisions. The apposite policy in this matter is the one which is comprehensive, based on study and planning, whose contents are ranked according to importance and which deals with the public interest and the comfort of the masses and which saves energy and money according to a just and precise system. Perhaps out of wisdom or necessity, or both of them together, it has been decided not to issue policy statements in one fell swoop but pell-mell. However, this should not prevent any decision from following a system governed by justice and respect for the masses and inasmuch as is possible it should not push the people too hard or too far. I believe that the masses are prepared to make yet more sacrifice, to be patient and tolerant, but only if they are convinced of the value of a policy decision, its justice and its purpose for the public good. A just policy decision has another advantage which is that it underpins the bases of trust between the people and the state.

13 June 1985

An Abstruse Problem

It is no more than common sense that those on fixed salaries should possess the means to confront the daily challenges of life but at the same time they should evince an eagerness to put more effort into increasing productivity and into serving the people and the state with respect, honesty and decency. That said and done, I would not be overshooting the mark if I were to confirm the supreme importance of the role this small group of people perform in our economic, social and cultural lives, for they are the very people behind every form of activity in the realms of education, health, food distribution, communications, security, etc. The inability of their salaries to cater to their basic needs has provided the motivation for many of them to take on a second job, something which is responsible for the grotesquery which mars our administration and which is, in the final analysis, among the causes of our tortured populace's woes. More often than not the government stands as if handcuffed in face of its workers at all levels since this inability to support oneself has mired everyone in its dragnet, and since the government does not treat the matter with the utter determination necessary. The government is well aware that it does not pay its workers enough to cover the bare necessities of life and that is why productivity is shuddering to a halt, why services have declined and corruption is widespread, and yet the only means we have for reform or improvement are advice, appeals to the conscience and warnings of doom. The issue is simple enough – a civil servant is more than a large problem, he is perhaps the largest problem of all and the day we manage to bring about a decisive end to this problem, i.e. to the problem of his salary, will go down in history as one of real reform throughout the public services. We will then, without the slightest injustice, be able to supervise a civil servant's work with the requisite attention, we will be able to ask him to do his job properly and we will be able to make him account for his errors before they become great mistakes, and to increase or decrease his salary according to his job performance. At that time today's sorry state of affairs in productivity, public services, and the way the general public are treated will change.

The wheel will turn to a new rhythm and God's truth will shine upon the earth. The question is whether we will be allowed to wake up from this nightmare and find a bright new morning?

20 June 1985

The Battle of Freedom and Civilisation

We are waging a destructive battle. We must consider this truth, and believe in it, despite the announcement of a limited peace and despite the peace whose banners we strive, with devotion and perseverance, to unfurl not only over our shattered region but over the whole wounded world, from South Africa to Afghanistan. Notwithstanding all that, we are waging a destructive battle.

It is the battle to defend ourselves, to defend civilisation, to defend our heritage and history, our today and tomorrow, a celebrated battle against underdevelopment, poverty and the troubled balance of life. You can call it the battle of underdevelopment should you so wish, or the battle for rebirth if you wish, or the battle for comprehensive growth as we have become used to calling it. Our strategy aims to stake a claim for ourselves in modern civilisation and the tactics are based on diligent daily work in which every citizen takes part, from the street cleaner to the president of the republic. It is an aim for all those who are without an aim but who mouth the need for one. It is a broad and compliant ideology for those who seek to belong, and people should voice and write their support for this, the media should be full of it, and the political parties should vie with each other to support or oppose it.

Fortunately it is an open battle for human values and should not be used as an excuse for oppression, suppression or autocracy and it does not mean that no voice should be heard above the clamour of battle. It is a battle which will only be won in an atmosphere of freedom, whose achievements will only be made under the aegis of democracy, because by its very nature it needs to hear every opinion, every point of view and every thought, and will benefit from moderation just as it benefits from the right and the left, for underdevelopment is the enemy of everyone and overcoming it is the aim of every true citizen. However the battle also needs responsible freedom, that freedom which respects the system as it respects other people's views, which longs for stability just as it desires freedom of expression and freedom for those who work hard and strive for improvement with all their heart, might and will.

27 June 1985

Literature and Politics

Literature has had a rather exciting history with politics during the era of the Revolution, a history full of twists and turns, peaks and troughs, which has sometimes gone hand in hand with revolutionary planning and sometimes with the political climate and prevailing circumstances. People have had many views about this history depending on their various political and mutually conflicting positions and fads. We may not be able to extract any objective thought from this before history itself sets in and the essential signposts can be usefully seen from a reasonable distance. At the outset of the Revolution, and after its fate was decreed by absolute rule, when any dissenting voice disappeared from the state media, literature had to grope its way along a risky and uncertain path. Literature continued to express itself via symbolism, which was preferable to falling silent or resorting to hypocrisy. I do not think that the authorities are unaware of this but it may be that they have found some sort of hidden accountability in this rather than a rejection of their essential message or some radical argument against them. Or perhaps they found that the circle in which culture revolves is so narrow and restricted that it does not pose any real risk or have any effect on public opinion. Or perhaps for some reason they have seen that relaxing their grip on literary activity and letting it breathe not only does more good than harm but might allow them to use it as propaganda particularly against those critics abroad, who accuse them of being dictatorial. In the past literature enjoyed a relative freedom not enjoyed by any other form of expression, and rang out like a clarion call amidst the almost overwhelming silence for those under repression who longed to read the word of truth, or an allusion to criticism, and they devoured literature wherever they could find it. That is how enormous numbers of the victims of politics and tyranny were added to the readership of literature, people who perhaps for the first time in their lives now read novels and watched plays with a great sense of amazement and excitement, whispering to each other about the meaning of the content, and drawing strength from reading the lost sound of opposition and the muzzled struggle. It was through this extra role played by literature that it enlarged its natural reach and enlarged its dimensions, that its influence could not be held in check and that it achieved a great and unprecedented popular success that it otherwise would not have had.

Then came the second period of the revolution which brought about two great achievements, each of which had an active influence on literature, even if literature itself was not an intrinsic part of its planning. Firstly this period established what we know as the Corrective Revolution which groped its way forward in the wide open spaces of democracy, the supremacy of the law and the freeing-up of opinion. For the first time in a long time, an opposing voice was able to announce itself clearly in the pages of the newspapers and magazines, exposing things formerly suppressed such as the horror of our prisons. As a result of that literature lost the additional role it had played in the first stage of the Revolution, and political symbolism no longer had any meaning. Literature could no longer vie with the opposition when it came to daily matters and it retreated somewhat to fulfil its natural role among the literati. However at that time this retrenchment did not appear natural and many people subsequently thought that it must have suffered some sort of reversal which had undermined it and restricted its activity.

Secondly, the new era embraced a new policy towards the left abroad and at home, declaring unhesitatingly that there was no place for left-wingers anywhere in the state media apparatus. When right-wingers formed a not negligible number in the world of literature, their removal simply weakened literary activity to a degree from which it has not recovered and led to such a degradation of its standards that people blamed the authorities for having put an end to literature and doing away with writers. In fact, this had nothing to do with putting an end to literature or bad intentions, but was simply a matter of politics which are sometimes unintentionally good for literature and sometimes unintentionally damaging. Then along came the age of television, video and sub-standard education, and the matter came to a head, so to speak, as it fell into an abyss of indifference despite the creative output of the new generation and the openness of the youth to the enormous number of good and new talents.

In our day politics has taken a neutral and encouraging stance towards culture, allowing all sorts of talents to develop and bestowing prizes and appreciation and honours as well as giving their output wide coverage in the various branches of the media. It is true to say that the field is not devoid of irascible obstacles such as the problem of getting a book published on the economic crisis, sub-standard education, and Arabic language teaching in our schools, as well as the violent wave of revanchism gripping our society and threatening all forms of free thought. Last but not least, television looms as a dangerous and entrancing challenger to book reading in general, and to the literarily readership specifically. Literature must overcome all these obstacles in order to regain its natural level, or at least to preserve the space allotted to it by modern culture.

28 June 1985

The Opposition between Tradition and Renewal

The parliamentary year has now come to an end. All those who follow our political activity can justifiably regard our democratic practice as auspicious, with the calm atmosphere in the lower house allowing people to express opinions even if they go against those of the absolute majority.

The opposition has performed its legitimate duty, faced questioning and has brought up for debate important issues that should concern public opinion. Our opposition has behaved with objectivity and sometimes with precision, depth and thoroughness. It has gone with what is right wherever that may be, and in addition to that the parties have gone on to form special committees, and the grassroots operatives in the provinces have attempted to restore to the masses some of the vigour they lost during the years of oppression and authoritarianism.

However, we still demand that the opposition should make an even greater effort to stabilise democracy, and to support freedom and accountability. We hope that the opposition will complete the whole democratic journey and arrive at its pristine destination without irregularities or impediments from the past, and we expect that their special committees will offer their well-thought-through vision on the prevailing problems along with wholesome solutions for them. Just as we hope that they will hold public debates in the provinces in order to instil the desired sense of rebirth in a people exhausted by their living conditions and to draw attention to them. We want these committees to open the gates of belonging and usher our lost youth back to the ideals of patriotism and human principles. In addition to all of that, we demand that they go out onto the street and mix with the youth, take on their concerns, and urge every individual whatever his stance may be to join in the battle for comprehensive development as the form of our new and decisive rebirth so that we can leave our economic crisis and backwardness behind and set off towards the horizons of this dog-eat-dog world. Far from being satisfied with an energetic opposition that spouts just hot air, we want it to be real, creative and innovative and a popular leadership that takes us towards a better tomorrow.

11 July 1985

Between Awakening and Deviation

Religious awakening is a healthy revivalist movement, a spiritual release for resisting physical annihilation and the breakdown of God-given values. As such, this encompasses the whole world and not just the Islamic world, even if, in the Islamic world especially it is accompanied by a wish to return to a sense of authenticity and personal independence in the wake of its liberation from the claws of colonialism. It essentially serves as a foundation for building up a complete character – one that is up to confronting the problems of the age and of setting oneself on a higher level of giving and taking, but with a reliance on traditional religious obligations. At the forefront of these is a reverence for knowledge, labour, solidarity, brotherliness and a complete respect for human rights without needing to fear for our national unity, our modern aspirations or our dreams of the future – with religion serving as a permanent revolution against ignorance, extremism and corruption, as something ever open to anything that benefits humanity and drives us forward in the areas of power, knowledge and values. This should be completely unsullied by any sort of deviationism, violence or terrorism, or by ignorance of the present or the past. The secret of our tragedy lies in the fact that pure religious awakening has encountered conditions along the way that caused exhaustion and which generally go back to systems of authoritarian governance which are characterised by incapacity and corruption. This made problems pile up, causing our youth to lean towards ignorant, violent and extremist voices and to participate in moribund ways of thinking which came into being in times of yore as a result of defeat and oppression. The cure will only turn up after we have eradicated the reasons and causes of the illness, by offering a convincing and useful example of doing serious work that contributes to productivity. That is what we need to do in order to extricate ourselves from the bottle-neck and to regain a life with a sense of balance, in which our hope is renewed and people return to the wholesome form of thinking that can be brought about by a real spiritual reawakening.

1 August 1985

23 August

In recent years, the anniversary of the death of two glorious leaders, Saad Zaghloul and Mustafa al-Nahhas, has been crowned with victory in the shade of triumphant democracy, solid national unity and firmly established independence – reminding the millions that the efforts of these two leaders achieved their goals and that we are now enjoying their fruit. It is perhaps a natural opportunity for anyone who wishes to speak about our popular and eternal revolution, the 1919 Revolution, and about the nobleness of hard work, the power of self-sacrifice, the gauntlet thrown down to the greatest empire known to history and the oldest throne in all human existence – although everything there is to say about it has already been said and written down in memoirs and books. I would just like to ask, as I did on the anniversary of the July Revolution, what we should remember of these two leaders in terms of an eternal message to be renewed in every new generation and which we should heed with devoted loyalty. The most important legacy is our national unity which has turned the sons of Egypt into a cohesive nation living with a sense of belonging, on a firm footing of equality of rights and responsibilities in the shade of a cohesive and un-schizophrenic unity regardless of any difference of vision, belief and thought. This is not some fantastic dream, for it has become reality and has set a fine example which was aspired to by the efforts of the twentieth-century saint Mahatma Gandhi. This has been followed by something just as important in terms of democracy, that is rule of the people by the people and for the people, the rule of dignity and pride, and the carefully prepared path to purity, progress and social justice. How many victims died for the Revolution over the years until the July Revolution took place, and even after it, all with one aim in mind during their struggle: that of freedom and government by the people. That is what we should remember of the 1919 Revolution and its two glorious leaders, Saad Zaghloul and Mustafa al-Nahhas, and their names should be a byword for freedom and national unity.

22 August 1985

The Necessity of Culture

I was delighted, as was undoubtedly everyone in the cultural community, at the great attention lavished on books in recent times, and we have the Book Union to thank for that, as well as the Al-Ahram Book Club on the one hand, and the responsiveness of the state and the minister of culture on the other hand. It has been made much easier to import and export books and the *Al-Ahram* newspaper has started a book club for its readers in all branches of knowledge, and a project to publish a thousand books looms on the horizon along with a number of cultural magazines for children, youth and adults. This has taken place in a period when we have the greatest need of culture, despite appearances to the contrary, and we should be giving priority to making ever greater efforts in the struggle for development and overcoming our economic difficulties. However, that in itself calls for more interest to be paid to culture as the basis for not only constructing the character of a person but also bringing the necessary equilibrium to people who have been set off balance by the crisis and diverted from their traditional course. Today there is no time to do anything but eke out a living, put food on the table, and try to stave of the fears of tomorrow. It is a struggle whose hardships have made us lose much of our sense of compassion, values and human emotions, of our taste for beauty and virtue, of our love of introspection and thinking. We seem to be living in order to eat rather than eating in order to live, and we have extended the dimensions of our life in every which direction. It is unthinkable for us to have to live with this form of degradation until we overcome our troubles and master our own fate. We are in the greatest and most urgent need of something to protect our humanity from the elements of stagnation and corruption, and in the greatest need of something to wake up our sense of goodness, aesthetics and thought. In other words, we are in the greatest need of culture in this uncultured period as a defence for our own humanity which is threatened with perdition. Our cultural institutions and media organisations should accept this and set to work at full power with all the expertise and dedication they possess.

29 August 1985

The Unretouched Picture

It is a race between a force which invests all its capabilities in trying to bring about comprehensive development with the aim of defeating the crushing crisis and achieving a natural degree of equilibrium in order to bring about progress and comfort, and a second force which lurks around waiting to exploit any mistakes and the woes of the masses and which is ready to pounce at the any moment. Between this rock and hard place the people live out their lives, with their inborn and traditional patience as their bedfellows as they are buffeted by frustration and hope and affected to varying degrees by the extent of their awareness of the enormity of the ferocious battle raging around them. Perhaps the greatest impediment in the path of the first force is the fact that its target is so unreachable and that its aims will not be realised any time soon, for it has inherited problems of extreme complication and number, problems that will need billions of pounds to solve them and may need two five-year development plans or even more before the ordinary ground-down citizen benefits from the fruit of their ongoing efforts, not to mention the world crisis which has accompanied our development plans and whose effects have been reflected in the domestic sphere. This has aggravated and exacerbated the situation, and consequently there has been a need for new and more painful procedures to be instituted. Despite the gloomy picture, we must expunge despair and its synonyms from our dictionary and hold onto the belief that there is no alternative for steadfastness, patience and success because other people do not possess magic solutions and in these modern times we must preserve the unity of the nation and its future cohesion with all its inherited glory. For that reason we must work together with the great minds who are seeking out the shortest and best route and who have the power of self-selection, of correcting mistakes, of confronting truths, heeding nothing but what is right and correct, for the welfare of the country lies in sincere faith in God and man.

5 September 1985

A Cure for All Eras

We must believe truly and practically that depending upon one power alone in confronting the challenges of varying opinions is an abortive policy of which I cannot recall one successful example in history, whereas history is brim-full of examples of its failure. As long as we believe in freedom, we must open our windows to its limpid air, particularly since wisdom dictates that we must see things as they are and acknowledge the existence of their challenges rather than allowing these challenges to be overlooked through ignorance or insouciance. For that reason I would state that the time has come to throw off the spurious shackles which hobble the freedom to constitute political parties. It is the right of every group to agree upon a platform, to become a political party and to present this platform to the people in free elections. In this manner it is the right of the people to be presented with the platform of any association in the form of a comprehensive programme which covers points large and small, such as the system of government, the economy, foreign policy, education, culture, the role of the minorities and of women, and so on and so forth. One of the results of that is that political activity will come out from the dark into the light, from the obscure to the transparent, taking up its legitimate right to organise, giving the people their right to know about these parties, what they want and what they are offering. As a consequence of that some parties with similar outlooks may coalesce and gain strength which might even spur all the other parties into renewed activity and motivate them into doing more for the people, into coming together over the problems and polarisation of their young members and offer goals which grab people's hearts, move their wills and engender a sense of belonging and enthusiasm. This suggestion actually accords with the meaning of freedom at any time, but it can be considered a pressing necessity in the prevailing conditions and it should neither be delayed, nor should its call be ignored. When it comes to power, a free person should only have recourse to it in defence of freedom and as the final means of working together with those people who reject discussion and wield power.

12 September 1985

The Role of the State

Perhaps the role of the state in the rescue and rebalancing of the economy will remain the foremost issue under all circumstances and in any situation. By this I am not only speaking of the party of the majority, but I must also include the opposition parties which participate in governance in the parliament. It, that is, the state, will be able to deal with everything that threatens the welfare of the nation if it overcomes the current crisis, solves the problems, and brings society back to a state of equilibrium and well-being. We have previously stated that the success of the five-year plan will take no end of time, and that we will need more than one successful five-year plan before we reach a safe harbour. We only need to gain the trust of the people, achieve complete transparency, present good examples to follow, and offer complete social justice and law and order. What offers the soul some hope in this gloomy atmosphere is that the state has in fact started to look again at the problems facing it with a sense of realism and decisiveness when it comes to the government apparatus, the public sector, overspending, the eradication of corrupt practices, the reform of the education system and working practices to get the populace involved in the issues of national development – wherever there is a need. Gaining the people's trust is not an easy task, but it is not completely impossible if we are well intentioned and of strong resolution. Moreover, there is another area of achievement and performance which neither needs foreign funds nor loans, but it most definitely needs resolution, determination, dedication, supervision, follow-up and continuity. We have a visible and successful example in the work of the Ministry of the Interior and its minister, and we just have to believe in duty, respect and the citizen, his human right to decent treatment and government services, we have to safeguard his integrity and well-being, to provide him with the truth about matters and avoid making ethereal statements. That way the citizen will be ever ready to face challenges with the requisite patience and steadfastness. If you provide the people with work, treat them fairly and with integrity, they will pay this back with trust and they will work with the government responsively and with a sense of loyalty.

26 September 1985

A Five-Year Plan Which Never Stops

Last but not least, I am returning to an old subject about which not only have I written time and time again and of which I never become bored, but which comes up again whenever we hear rumours about a cabinet reshuffle, or when some matter or other threatens internal or external security and which polarises the work of the civil services and adds new burdens to their workload notwithstanding the enormous number of tasks and the ever-increasing number of problems they have to deal with. In a nutshell: the five-year plan should continue without let or hindrance, and it should be carried out on a sound scientific basis with meticulous supervision and follow-up. It should move forwards whether we are blessed with stability or whether we are exposed to some minor issues, whether we have an atmosphere of calm or unease, whether things are quiet or troubled. Moreover, it should move forwards in war and peace alike. It should not be subject to any delay, sense of complacency, or be neglected for even an hour of our lives for it is our present and future life. For that reason, there is no escape from setting up a special unit for the five-year plan which should be solely concerned with carrying it out and checking on its progress. This should be a unit which does not change when there is a cabinet reshuffle, which does not stop and which is not affected by events. It should be made up of specialists from every ministry who have a high level of efficiency and integrity, headed by a permanent and dedicated representative, or the deputy minister, who works under the supervision of the minister in normal circumstances. He should have the automatic right to make decisions independently if the minister is otherwise occupied with general or urgent matters or when there is a cabinet reshuffle, as happens from time to time. This plan will have enemies who feel harmed by its success, as we sometimes see here, and they may concoct reasons to frustrate it. But we should not empower them to achieve their aims, especially since the success of the plan is our primary aim at this important time in our development. I beseech God to realise our hopes and to save our homeland from disintegration.

3 October 1985

Can the Reward for Murder Be Anything Other Than Death?

It would appear that the danger from drugs has become so rampant that it is no longer commented upon at the national level. It is a sudden and destructive tsunami with speedy and evil consequences which can seriously handicap the flower of our youth and our workforce, and which has more serious repercussions than those engendered by war, the economy and revanchism. My memory takes me back to the middle third of this century – the twentieth – when I used to see some victims of drugs among our youth skulking like skeletons at the roadside. My memory also takes me back to the furious press campaigns warning the youth and urging the government to take serious measures to eradicate this dreadful plague, and I remember our school visit to the Fuad the First Museum of Hygiene & Medicine to see the visual representations of how a disease affects the brain and the nervous system along with examples of its victims which has affected me until now. The police acted speedily and resolutely in pursuing smugglers and drug pushers and the national feeling of responsibility has put an end to the traffic in drugs in an exemplary and short time, and the country has been saved from its evil. It is now no more than a hellish fable from ancient times. At that time the police provided a vivid example of their devotion to work and nationwide vigilance for which they should be remembered for a long time to come. It is undeniable that fighting drugs needs a general policy stemming from educational, political, cultural and media principles, one which needs to go on for the long term, not to mention that confronting this destructive danger requires the taking of urgent and immediate measures. If we take a look at our policemen, they are no less zealous, nationalist or responsible than their forefathers and in fact they are better than them in terms of expertise, science and innovation, particularly as they work under the leadership of a man known by everyone for his decisiveness, resoluteness and capability. We should also make sure that the criminals receive no mercy from us and the sentence for importing or pushing drugs should be that of death and it should be carried out without delay as a salutary lesson. The issue can be summed up in a simple phrase: whether death or suicide, God is the helper of man provided that man is the helper of his brother.

24 October 1985

Towards a New Citizen

We are a nation suffering from overpopulation and overcrowding and the concomitant poverty and underproductivity, but through rational teaching and education this overpopulation can turn into an uplifting human value, for if our homelands do not have enough to offer our people, they will find space for themselves anywhere in the world. These days education and culture have become pressing concerns which are never far from the minds of officials and have taken their legitimate place among the essential recommendations which were the mission of the last Ministry of Education. We can rightly say that these were always part and parcel of comprehensive development, that they were recognised as one of the rights of the citizen and that huge achievements were made in those fields. However, education in itself has faced grave elements of negativity as regards schools, teachers and pupils and has produced generations of underachievers in terms of knowledge, culture and education. We should be lamenting this catastrophe in all its elements, and concentrating on the core aims of education, acknowledging the value of the intellect, the influence of learning and the fruits of culture and education. That means, in the final analysis, giving our all for our children and the general educational environment. We should now be going at top speed in providing the appropriate number of schools to absorb every infant, as that is the quickest way of eliminating illiteracy and producing a citizen capable of dealing with the challenges of modern life. We need to change the teaching system from that of rote learning to one of free thinking in order to be ready to participate fully in the era of science and innovation. We must make sure that the new generations are imbued with lofty principles, with a sense of belonging and with the sort of developed taste which can be instilled by a religious, nationalist and liberal education. For life will surely be less of a burden upon people if they are possessed of these noble qualities.

31 October 1985

Between Two Eras

We are fated to experience two unimaginably contradictory periods simultaneously: a period of modern civilisation some of whose achievements we can experience in our country and the rest of which we learn about from the aural and visual media, from the television, from books, magazines and the daily newspapers. We can now enjoy the utmost of human progress and development in science and the application thereof, whether here on earth or in space. We have witnessed what is tantamount to the miraculous in medicine, engineering, the humanities, systems of governance and human rights though we are aware of the downsides of this modernity such as the imposition of tax on any new discovery or development.

The other period is that of our reality and of all the suffering our country is experiencing during this period of its life as it bandages its wounds and tries to get back on its feet again. We learn all about that as we go about our daily lives and from the media. We see a people ground down by wars, laid low by poverty just as much as they are depredated by pockets of obscene wealth. Their sense of belonging has been shaken to the core, their morals corrupted. They are beset by the chaos in the country and by pollution. The streets are choked with traffic, the sewers are overflowing, and the national debt goes sky high.

We look at both these periods of civilisation. We compare them and ponder. We remember and dream, but the reality is inescapable and unavoidable: we have to un-corrupt the corrupt, straighten the crooked, pay off every last loan and overcome every obstacle, not just to provide firm foundations for our infrastructure, but so that we can continue catching up with the world of the space age and contribute and benefit from it in terms of thought and work.

This is a task of monumental proportions, and in truth it needs a miracle to bring it about. However, that miraculous force does exist and its name is our people, our people with their intelligence, will, faith and drive.

That is how the dream will turn into the actual and the impossible into the achievable.

21 November 1985

The Coming Years of Hard Work

Over the last four years we have correctly diagnosed our economic and social diseases, and come to know how to treat and cure them. We have set off along this path with undeniable effort only to be beset by accidents which have taught us a bitter lesson and brought us to realise that the effort expended on work was not the right or necessary effort, and that the issue is not one of carrying out the five-year plan but is actually a practical and ethical revolution to be achieved through self-reliance, whose aim is freedom from dependency and self-realisation in the present age based on a sense of nationalism, dignity and patriotism. We have the choice of a dignified life of innovative struggle or we can go around with a begging bowl. We cannot just gain what we wish for with fine words, slogans or meaningless zeal. We need to gain it with firm resolve and serious work, by changing our outlook and the way we see things. We need to face up to self-sacrifice and toil, and by this I am not speaking about the class which has been forced into self-sacrifice and toil over long years, without any choice in the matter. Thus we must take another look at everything without discounting the work which has already taken place. We must consider forcing people to do things a form of curse, and continuing to do so a crime. We must put a stop to it at whatever cost. We must consider every piastre spent wrongly to be an act of treason and anyone doing so should be ostracised. We need to redouble the amount of work we do, and we should not countenance sloppiness or laziness, even if we have to change the labour laws. We need to modernise the administration and services, making sure they are run properly, and we must show no mercy to those who bend the rules. We must redouble our resolve to dismiss those who behave as a law unto themselves in order to restore trust between the people and the government. We must treat our citizens with justice and equality and remove all blots from the escutcheon of freedom. We must break the shackles and irregularities that stand in the way of the will of the people. We face a period of hard work, but in order for the people to participate in this with all their hearts and souls, they must seize their rights and regain their trust in our values and our politicians.

28 November 1985

Confrontation without Hesitation

As far as I can see, renewed vigour is something a person gains from sleep or from habit. It motivates a man to be more active and innovative, to face up to difficulties and to achieve a higher level of human perfection and it brings with it a lantern which lights up everything around him. He can then see how he is living, which values he should embrace, which path of life he should prefer. He sees his own soul with a new clarity, enabling him to face what is negative or has been holding him back. He realises how much his behaviour has kept him back and he then sets to work redeeming himself through change and constructive action. When I look into the light of the lantern, I see first and foremost that we yearn for a modern lifestyle, but we only choose the comfortable means of attaining this. We depend upon ourselves but avoid doing too much whenever possible. We exploit our capabilities in a gentle, forbearing and tolerant manner, making up for what we lack by relying upon others for expertise, loans and aid. Alertness should primarily mean self-reliance and refusing to go about begging in any form or manner. It should also mean that we look at our current situation with a new eye and with new resoluteness so that we spend public money without waste, so that we have meticulous oversight over expenditure to the point of robust austerity, and so that we can increase productivity like a man fighting for his life. If, thereafter, there is still a gap between income and expenditure, we will have to rein in our ambitions with the proviso that we organise our activities according to their importance with regard to our development so that we make do with less, albeit with full respect for justice and social inclusion so that everyone does what he is capable of doing. Then we will accept with maturity and patience the sacrifices imposed on us by our spiritual wakefulness as well as the pains which will wrack our whole system but which have the potential to create new men and a new nation out of us. We will never deserve a new and noble life until we pay our dues without shirking. That is what renewed vigour means if we are being truthful with ourselves.

5 December 1985

A Discussion about the Future

I believe that thinking has already started about putting the second five-year plan in place, and perhaps it is advisable for us to depart from the traditional route in setting it out and studying it, by which I mean that it is not sufficient for it to be discussed in the cabinet, by the majority party and the parliament, but it should also be presented to the parties which have not managed to gain representation in the parliament, such as Tajammu[1] and the Liberal Party, as well as the political associations which have not yet been recognised as parties. It would be even better if the plan was also presented to the students union with the aim of hearing the opinions of the youth, getting them involved with the nation's problems and obliging them to give them some serious thought. After the end of the academic year I would also like to see students invited to a general conference for a discussion of their various views so that some elements of the plan will at least represent what they can agree upon and the publication of the plan will not diminish the value of the discussion over radically contradictory visions. We know from the outset that there are some among us who believe that we can build our economy on both the public and the private sectors, just as we know that there is a group who believe that the private sector should be restricted or abolished as well as a group who believe that the public sector should be restricted or liquidated. However, even if we differ with this group or that over their universalist or integrationalist views, we can benefit from their opinions in enhancing either sector. In any case it would be a wonderful opportunity to find out which domestic or foreign matters we can agree upon, so that we can then set off realising them more robustly and with greater confidence. In addition to that there are matters which keep us awake at night or which ought to do so, and for which it is not so difficult for us all to agree upon finding a decisive solution such as liberation from economic subordination, the debt problem and cleansing democracy of the exceptions and shackles which have accreted to it. If we do this,

1 The National Progressive Unionist Party.

the discussion will be an opportunity for a comprehensive national debate which might yield more fruit.

12 December 1985

No Love from One Party

There is a subject which keeps coming back to my mind involuntarily. It is that of a sense of belonging. Perhaps it is the inevitable result of following what is transpiring in our daily lives. In my early life I had a sense of belonging. This only reappears when the primary reasons for its existence flood into our souls in the aftermath of a great national revolution or when everyone agrees upon the same goal such as that of independence. However a sense of belonging cannot just be the echo of great events alone, it is the very essence of social life in all times and in all circumstances.

All it takes is a very small number of fellow countrymen, and a degree of social conscience, to push an individual to be concerned about others and he will also be concerned about his own affairs. That is to say that any amount of general loyalty will also accompany a person's loyalty to himself, and I wonder who can create this modicum of a sense of belonging? This question also makes me think about matters which we should not overlook:

1. It reminds me that love cannot be love unless it is mutual between two parties. There can be no love from one party alone. Hence society should shower love on its individuals if it wants them to love it. It should respect human rights and accord them respect on the street, in business, at school, in hospital, etc.
2. After we manage to achieve that, or at the very least if we attempt to bring this about for all bar none, it then becomes the duty of nationalist education at school and of the media to be based on the truth and to avoid hollow rhetoric.
3. We need to give our youth a clear aim to aspire to, and perhaps the best aim in our era is that of throwing off our backwardness, something which will only come about through the supremacy of science and by cleaving to our values in the shade of complete democracy.
4. Our leaders should set an example of a sense of belonging, that

is an example of dedication to work, integrity and honesty, for they are the lanterns that lead us towards peace and repentance.

5. Last but not least, the political parties should spread their message among the masses, and particularly among the youth in order to mobilise them into working in the service of the nation. Without work we have no life, and there can be no work without a sense of belonging.

19 December 1985

Between Reality and Dream

In our lives we have a reality, and in our lives we also have a dream. Reality is a group of truths which shape our domestic and external path through life. A dream is what we should like to be in the near or distant future. There are many nations similar to us in this respect, but perhaps we are the only ones who sometimes do things inspired by our dream rather than by our reality, and thereby encounter unavoidable problems. What is our reality? And what is our dream?

Our domestic reality is that we are fighting pre-existing challenges with patience and resolve, challenges such as the dilapidation of our essential structures, the frightening imbalance between national production and consumption, our debts, our steady population increase, and our social evils... Our reality abroad is that we have a special relationship with the United States, a peace treaty with Israel, and a quasi-total boycott by the Arab states. When it comes to our dream, it is that we should bring about our national rebirth on the one hand, and restore our historic Arab role on the other hand. As I have said, it is natural that a nation should have a reality and a dream, and it is also natural for it to strive to turn this dream into reality, while at the same time not shedding all the positive aspects of the nation's recent past. What is not natural, however, is that work should be inspired by a dream considered reality, or that the reality should be overlooked.

It is our right and our duty to protest against any act of aggression, to become angry over any violation of international law, and it is our right and duty to act on our good emotions and offer our special advice. Moreover, we should strive for the good wherever we find a way to do this. This should always be within the framework of reality, however, based on the truth of a matter, with our complete concern for the general welfare, for the stability of the nation, and for its security, safety and dignity. We should do this without becoming involved in any fact or stance that causes us to set aside a real friend in favour of a potential friend, or to upset the prevailing reality in favour of an as yet unrealised dream. This does not mean that I am unreservedly in favour of our current reality, or that I am unreservedly against a dream, but my sense of honesty and sincerity has dictated what I have just written.

2 January 1986

Arab Nationalism between Reality and Dream

Arab nationalism is the dream of every sincere Arab. When it comes to the Arab reality, it is what you see and what you hear, and I do not need to expound on that. Arab nationalism has enemies abroad whose strength should not be easily dismissed, just as it has opponents within every Arab country for various reasons. As a consequence, some provisional steps are needed so that it can become stronger, and so that its philosophy can mature and become firmly rooted in everyone's hearts and minds.

Unfortunately, the Arabs have gone through shaky historical circumstances, mistaking a dream for reality, ignoring bare facts, and they have always ended up as the losers. They did this in 1948 when they announced that they were going to war to defend Palestine, relying on the fiction of their unity, and ignoring the fact that they were in reality separate countries and the puppets of more than western imperialism. Had they remained within the bounds of reality, the Palestinians in Palestine would today be in Palestine pursuant to whatever agreement they might have come to with the Jews, the mandatory authority and the international community, and even if this had entailed some small or large amount of injustice it would not have lasted. You just need to recall what is going on today in South Africa. However, living in a dream-world is what lost Palestine and led to the dispersal of the Palestinians and the great defeat that befell the whole Arab world. They did that under the influence of the leadership of Nasser. The voice of unity was so loud that our enemies thought it was close at hand. It drowned out many other voices that were muttering here and there, advising caution against hostilities, resulting in the tragic and shameful defeat of that dark day, 5 June.

The best thing we can say to the Arabs in their pathetic current state is what the great Socrates said: 'Know yourself.' And the best thing they can be reminded of is what God Almighty has stated: 'Indeed, Allah will not change the condition of a people until they change what is in themselves.'[1] What they should remember first and foremost is that Arab unity is the desired dream and not the reality, and that their role today is to bring about peace on the basis of reality. They need to work out what they agree upon and work from that with devotion and assiduity, for this will not come into being like something in the domains of culture or economic integration. The rest should be left to time, for time is the wise healer when it comes to setting broken bones, dressing wounds and regaining lost rights.

9 January 1986

1 Qur'an, 13:11.

Towards a New Arab Unity

Our long history shows that our position in the centre of the Arab world has made us the crossroads and starting point for its conflicting trends. This has also imposed on us the role we play in even the furthest flung regions, helping those areas not to be swallowed up, or at least in keeping harm away from them just as if we were defending ourselves. If you want more proof of that, look back to the Fatimid era, or the Ayyubid era, or that of Muhammad Ali or Gamal Abdel Nasser. Or if you wish, look back to the Pharaonic era.

That is why we can rightfully say about our role in Arab unity that it is our inescapable fate. Today's world has superpowers whose strategic interests cover the length and breadth of the world and whose responsibilities and interests cannot be contained. The stage has been set for a new narrative, and consequently roles must change, and the small nations must wonder what sort of role appropriate to their size and status is left for them in the new world.

It is because this question was not taken on board by either Muhammad Ali or Gamal Abdel Nasser that they both brought about setbacks that destroyed them and almost destroyed Egypt. The last place we should be looking at for what is suitable for us is within the domains of leadership, power or politics. We should look to our civilisation, both past and present, for its real value is the creativity of which we should be proud. It is within the field of our civilisation that our concerns should be measured – not according to their volume, density or force, but by their value, usefulness and effectiveness.

Our true role is to learn, to become cultured and to innovate, to give back to the world what we take from it. You should not think that I am calling for us to isolate ourselves from the Arab nations, but I am calling for a unity to arise founded on economic, cultural and scientific integration, far from challenges or provocations, and not just based on the exchange of money for useless items. We should know what role we have to play, and we should perform it properly. We need to shed those dreams whose time has passed and believe with all our might that our new role is greater and longer-lasting than anything that has gone before it.

16 January 1986

The Truth about Suleiman Khater

Suleiman Khater has appeared in our lives to show us up, even if we are not in need of that, and were our infrastructure not in such a dreadful and dilapidated state this would have been just another ghastly piece of news of the type that shocks us daily and then fades into the generality of events – a crime on the border that is being investigated and that will be dealt with in due course by the judiciary. At that point the relevant circumstances and motives will be discovered, and the truth will be revealed in a form that every citizen can clearly understand. However, what has happened in reality is a cause of astonishment and surprise. Intense debate has broken out about the man and his action in a form that usually only goes on around complicated metaphysical problems. He was an unusual guy who was killed without us knowing how he was killed. Some people have said, moreover, that he was a trustworthy guard who set out to defend our borders. Other people say that he was a national hero who faced up to Israeli provocation, and still others declare that he was a fighter for Islam who raised the banner of Islam. Regarding his sad end, some people say that he committed suicide, but others are sure that he was killed, and others believe that he was driven to suicide. From all this uproar, I have drawn two results:

Firstly: we live in an atmosphere that has lost a sense of honesty and trust, and which subsists in murky darkness. It is an atmosphere bereft of the essential human understanding and logic required for the minimum of interaction between people no matter how different their views.

Secondly: Egyptians have received unexpected and unimaginably painful blows that have wounded them to their core. They have become tired of dressing their wounds and trying to convalesce. When one group of people called Khater a hero, this gained some traction and people spoke of the mistreatment he had suffered, and that he was a hero who had taken a stand after the confrontation and rejectionist states sat by and watched the Israeli invasion of Lebanon and the Israeli raid on Tunis.

In this way they see the dead soldier not as a man but as a

phenomenon through whom God, the Omniscient and Wise, wished to remind us of our souls and our lives. We must take this opportunity to cleanse our atmosphere of its poisonous content before Suleiman Khater rises from his grave and points his gun at us this time.

23 January 1986

Democracy between the Opposition and the Government

Democracy is a fruit that can only be picked by a people who are prepared to struggle and shed their blood. This was the oft-uttered adage about democracy before the July Revolution. The few years in which democratic rule prevailed were only achieved by snatching it from royal dictatorship through struggle and with bloodshed. As for our current democracy, it came about at the initiative of authoritarian rule which saw it as a historic model whose lessons could be beneficial. Praiseworthy efforts were made to work along with the people and we changed course towards a multi-party system and the rule of law.

We can rightly say that democracy emerged from those circumstances and that the government and opposition needed to undertake special and appropriate practices for its consolidation and to root it firmly within our traditions.

There is no need to say that this reality bypassed the era of President Sadat, which is one of the things that has brought us to catastrophe. Democracy needs prudence in every step it takes. It imposes obligations and prohibitions on both the opposition and the government and the best thing the opposition can do is to hold on to objectivity in their thinking, to remain calm in their argumentation, and to be precise in their accusations and judgements. They need to face up to the problems and let their experts deal with them, suggesting solutions and avoiding, inasmuch as possible, sensationalism or anything that goes against our beliefs or decent behaviour. They need to see themselves as the conscience of the nation, to shine a light on the government, and to call upon our youth in all four corners of the country to think and work along with them through a sense of belonging. That is how the opposition will be able to set itself up in the eyes of the people as an indispensable nationalist force, and how it will bring people to have more faith in democracy and encourage them to provide the elements that are still absent from our democracy.

The best thing for the state in this situation is to do what is expected of it, to rescind the emergency laws, to give us the opportunity to bring the constitution into conformity with life as it is today and as we hope it will be tomorrow, giving the people their full rights and providing a robust foundation for stability. We must all understand the meaning of the historic journey we are undertaking and dedicate our work to making the country a better place in the long run.

30 January 1986

The Opposition's Message

The methods of the opposition may be various, and its tactics may oscillate between attack and defence, but its ultimate aim is contingent upon it achieving power. That is the legal right of an opposition within any democratic system. Elections at the appropriate time are the means of achieving this, as stated in the constitution. Governance should be the aim of every party, just as it is the legitimate way of realising its message in the service of the nation. Among the things being said of the opposition in Egypt today are that it operates with the frustrating feeling that it will not achieve power due to special conditions and circumstances. If we were to accept this argument, would that mean that the opposition is useless and serves no purpose and that it has refrained from doing any useful work?

I cannot deny that accepting this situation is an impediment to the endeavours of any party that really believes in its message and wishes to be accorded the legitimate opportunity to put itself in the service of the country, but this does not mean that it has no national role at any time or under any circumstances. What I most fear is that the opposition, in despair at ever coming to power, will resort to rabble-rousing, creating incidents, inspiring violence or provocative actions, arguing for the sake of arguing, and evincing a completely hot-headed 'bring-it-on' attitude.

The opposition must always proclaim its heritage as the child of Egypt's nationalist movement. It must behave as if it is here for the long-term, and it must believe that sacrifice is no less noble than good work. It must accept that there is enough room for it to be of service by doing any positive deed it can, by drawing our attention to the government's failings, by supporting those who try to do good with advice, by studying our problems and offering solutions, by uncovering deviation and apathy, by waking the people up and by calling upon our youth to think and act. All of that should be an example and a model, a harbinger of constructiveness, morality and seriousness. The opposition has a message which is no less weighty for their not being in power.

6 February 1986

The Direction of Democracy

May God grant us success in living with democracy without too much ado, in experiencing freedom without too much grumbling, and in working with opposing opinions without too much rancour. God has taught us that there is nothing better for us than to write objectively and moreover the magnitude of our problems and our risky conditions are the very things that require us to be objective, to take a serious approach and to avoid confrontation and arrogance. However, we need to remember that every nation has its own rationale and emotions, and that we should face reality with the requisite perception and tolerance. In addition to all of that, the law in general offers protection to all, protects the right of the innocent, and holds people accountable for their errors. It saddens me greatly to see criticism of the methods of debate applied indirectly to democracy itself, as if we begrudge its blessings upon us or are trying to contain it.

No, ladies and gentlemen! Criticism of the methods of debate is a long-established element of freedom. Moreover, debate itself – no matter how harsh, off-centre, or violent – is nothing in comparison with the slightest element of dictatorship with all its defeats, corruption and transgressions against human rights.

Perhaps what may reduce the impact of some of the methods of debate in Egypt is if we cast our minds over methods of democratic practice in countries where this has been long established, and where there is an astonishing freedom of criticism, thought and behaviour, along with a plethora of ways of protesting and expressing one's opinion. We should note the way they have established deep respect for human rights. If we compare this to the Egyptian way, it all seems to be a model of self-discipline and self-control, even if it means things move forwards very slowly. Finally, we should remember that all the crises we suffer in our economy, in our infrastructure, our debts, our national fatigue, our apathy and indifference, are all no more than the bitter fruit of dictatorial excesses, and that the excesses of democracy are almost completely negligible. When all is said and done, we hope that our democracy will be one of complete freedom and rationality.

13 February 1986

Crisis… Strengthen and Be Gone!

We seem to be approaching a new time of tension in our economic life. We have been warned of this by an official in his comments about the looming crash of the oil market. This approaching crisis by its very nature calls for additional self-discipline and requires our citizens to remain patient. So how can we confront the challenges, both old and new, in a serious manner befitting a civilised nation? As a preliminary step I would say to the opposition that it must view the crisis as a general, nationwide time of trial which calls upon them to think and act in order to eradicate this scourge and rescue us, not in a way that exacerbates the situation or scores points against their opponents. My faith in the opposition's sense of national duty and prudence brings me to expect that good will come of them.

On the other hand, it is incumbent upon the government to try and convince people of its serious approach, to set a good example for them, and to make as much effort as possible to clamp down on all manifestations of extravagance. It must redouble its efforts to collect tax revenues and simplify the tax regime so that it can function efficiently and with impartiality. It must revitalise the public sector and free it from red tape. It must have oversight over the public sector's leadership and increase productivity by incentivising those who innovate and by punishing those who are in it for their own good. At that point alone will the government revisit the issue of whether to keep subsidies in place or to raise the price of some commodities – without hurting those on a fixed income who are incapable of making any further sacrifices.

One of the ways for confronting this comprehensively would be to appoint a number of opposition figures as ministers, so that they can actively shoulder some of the responsibility, and this coalition could include parties which do not have representation in parliament, even those parties who have not yet legally formalised their existence. The situation perhaps demands something greater than all these formalities; in particular, it will no longer be concentrating on trying to stifle any dissident voice, for even the MPs from the majority party sometimes speak against the government without that adversely affecting their party affiliation. As the crisis is starting to take on alarming proportions, we can do nothing less than pull together as one in order to deal with it.

20 February 1986

A Violent Battle

A corrupt country is not one that seethes with thousands of corrupt people, but one that puts up with a single corrupt person. Among the Egyptians I mix with, I have not felt such happiness as when justice catches up with corrupt people. I can think of nothing tantamount to that sort of real happiness, except for when we managed to cross the Suez Canal in 1973. I state this not out of a sense of gloating, or out of a sense of revenge against people who have been undermining Egypt as it faced unprecedented challenges, but as an auspicious sign of the good conduct which is the foundation of governance, as a sign of our aspiration for the sort of calm that can only prevail in an era of shining decency, and as a hope for an un-corrupt and capable administration that is able to launch a successful campaign against the torrents of crises and problems. That is why this wonderful dynamic must go on until it reaches its goal and it should not stop until it immobilises every hand that has acted with evil intent against the country making progress and pushed us into the critical state from which we are fighting to extricate ourselves.

The people could do no more than suffer and look on from afar as the corrupt enjoyed the fruit of their criminal actions, but today the people have regained their faith in themselves. Seeing the wrongdoers behind bars has strengthened the people's spirit, reinvigorated their dynamism, and kept them moving forward. This new strength has given them a new sense of belonging and an improved work ethic. Today the budget is balanced and life has regained its meaning, bringing to mind two verses from the Holy Qur'an: 'So whoever does an atom's weight of good will see it, and whoever does an atom's weight of evil will see it.'[1]

Hence it is only fitting for us, in the aftermath of this great leap forward, to renew our loyalty to President Mubarak, and to put increased trust in the legal and security establishment. Our salvation is not contingent alone upon engineers, economists or those who work

1 Qur'an, 99:7–8.

in the cultural sector, for they would all be superfluous without the support of the legal and security establishments, without the systems of reward and punishment, and without the sweet aroma of a life lived with the morality imposed on us by God and for which purpose he sent his messengers to bring good news and to deliver warnings, giving this confused and confusing life a meaning in which our hearts can find shelter in our never-ending struggle.

27 February 1986

The Five Commandments

An incident has shaken us to our core. People have counted their losses in all sincerity, and people have boasted of their profits, also in all sincerity. The time has come for us to face the consequences and to do so decisively and with perception.

Firstly: we need to dispel any ambiguity about what has happened. We need to know the truth about what is apparent and what has not yet been known. We need to apportion responsibility without prevarication or self-deception. Now that we have identified a symptom of the disease, we need to put it into reverse and profit from the frightening warning that was given to us while we were in a complete state of inattentiveness and which can only be redressed with hard thinking and work.

Secondly: we need to think again about how to rebalance these unforeseen losses, how to deal with the setbacks of an old crisis, how to stop our expenditure from haemorrhaging, how better to collect taxes, how to improve working habits and set new national targets for those of us who are capable of work. This should all be accompanied by patience, perseverance, austerity and a sense of solidary for the people as they embark on these ordeals.

Thirdly: we need to take decisive steps towards making our democracy more robust, supporting the authority of the people and giving them oversight now that it has become plain as daylight that these errors only bring about uncontrollable consequences when they are left, unadvisedly, to run their course and not subjected to true democratic methods.

Fourthly: we need to continue relentlessly removing those who are corrupt. We need to fight against smugglers, drug dealers and loan sharks now that everyone has seen that they are a source of brutal provocation that could plunge us all, friend or foe, into a catastrophic maelstrom.

Fifthly: we should answer the nationalist call to become united and to form one rank in the face of the storm of upcoming events, and I would repeat what I said a few weeks ago when I stated that all the parties should be represented in the cabinet, by which I do not mean that opposing views should be silenced, but that they should be given free reign, away from party-political restraints or accusations of evil intent or jockeying for position.

It is those who work who will see better results.

6 March 1986

Stability, Development and Humankind

True stability for a society means that it has managed to satisfy all its basic needs, that its governance is on a firm footing, and that it has become a free society which guarantees human rights. It also means that public services are available, first and foremost as the infrastructure that leads society towards the sublime aim by which life is directed. We must acknowledge the great effort undertaken by the state in accomplishing these goals as represented by the achievements of the first five-year plan, as well as by those projects which are still being carried out as I write. However, we must also accept that the majority of the population still undergo great hardship in simply staying alive in the face of an all-encompassing crisis. It is perhaps the feeling of the majority with the daily grind of their lives, along with the democratic freedoms they enjoy and the nationalism, impartiality and concern for values shown by their president, that has enabled them to face the greatest disaster to occur with respect to their security. And they have faced all this with a sense of stability and are overcoming all of this with faith and resolve.

The state will doubtless continue on the path of reform with redoubled dynamism, but it must concentrate on the principle of satisfying the basic needs of life and it must do so without resorting to half-baked measures. It must provide every citizen who serves the state with the very minimum needed to bear the burdens of life while preserving his dignity and pride, for it is that very citizen who carries out our development projects. It is that citizen who, if he can provide for himself and his dependents, will apply himself to his work with assiduity and devotion. It is that citizen who, if overcome by worry and anxiety, will become diffident, indifferent, accept bribes or embezzle, and when times get hard go mad or explode. Many people may ask where we can find the money for this? Fine, let us hold back on our expenditure, let us improve the collection of taxes, and increase the burden on those of us capable of doing more, for how can there be a society if we do not pull together? And if none of that has any effect, then let us reshape our development plan to manageable proportions, for 'God does not charge a soul except with that within its capacity'.[1] Surely it is better for us to cut back a little on some parts of the development plan than to victimise the poor, overburdened man for whom the plan has been formulated in the first place. If we do not do that, how much further away will stability and development be?

13 March 1986

1 Qur'an, 2:286.

A Soap Opera of Suffering, Sabotage and Arson

The unfortunate events of 25 February are nothing new. What is new is that this time the riots broke out inside a facility of the security apparatus itself, stirring up great alarm and fright, but the motivation and consequences comprise the final episode in a long and pain-inducing soap opera which has been eating away at our society for decades. The fundamental illness can be summed up in the forbidding word: suffering. When it comes to the consequences, they follow on in forms which we have learned by rote, such as having to do extra work in order to eke out a living and the prevalent negligence, apathy, bribe-taking, embezzling and manipulation of tenders. This shows itself in the form of serious sabotage, such as when buildings collapse upon their trusting tenants, or in the form of the fires which break out at inventory time, destroying commodities and public buildings.

The soap opera of uprisings, sabotage and arson has continued to spread unchecked with the latest contagion breaking out in a facility of the security apparatus itself. This caused great consternation and alarm, not because it was a new phenomenon, but because the rioting broke out this time in a site that is entrusted with our safety and security and with protecting human life and assets, and also because the uprising was intent on using overt and public means and not the secret or underhand means used by civilians.

One component of the soap opera is represented by the morass of suffering we live in, where the poison of sabotage and arson spreads with its evil consequences aimed directly at the people's present and future, impeding and severely limiting the comprehensive development plan upon which their lives are based. This is not some transient phenomenon specific to the security forces, and it cannot be treated by renovating or rebuilding a police facility. It is suffering which is the primary enemy of the people and the enemy of its national rebirth. I do not deny, and no reasonable person would, what the state has done and is doing to support those on a limited income to reduce their suffering. However, the matter needs a decisive cure no matter how great the sacrifice in order to preserve social peace without which the lives of those on limited, or unlimited, incomes will not be improved.

20 March 1986

Who Engineered the Events of 25 February?

The incidents of 25 February were committed by a number of rebels, a small number of whom were killed during the clashes, with the majority awaiting trial. However, they do not actually represent all those responsible for the events of that day. Some people got away scot-free and they are neither being investigated and nor will the long arm of justice reach them. They are leading a life of calm and are pleased as punch.

Among those who are still at large are those with money to invest but who begrudge it to the state for some reason, those who have stashed their money away or invested abroad hoping in their greed for a better return, or as a precautionary measure against an uncertain future. They have all brought these events about through their selfishness. Let us not exclude all those who have gone to work abroad but have stopped sending remittances back to Egypt heedless of the consequences, and those who smuggle goods and do not pay the appropriate taxes to the state. Nor should we forget those who have betrayed their country's trust with laziness, negligence, depravity, bribery and embezzlement, and those who cannot be bothered to treat our citizens properly in government offices. Nor those who set out to provoke through their outrageous behaviour or behave ostentatiously and hold flashy parties without a thought for the overworked and half-starving people working around them. Nor those thinkers or writers who have seen an act of injustice or unfairness but pretend not to notice and stay quiet for their own benefit or to keep the peace. Nor those who know that all of these things are taking place around them but look the other way, preferring to shut themselves in and concentrate on their own affairs, as if they live in a void or do not belong to a larger group of people.

All of those people are responsible for the events of that day and have been participants in the events that led up to it. They think that they will be able to get away with their behaviour forever, but we are all in the same boat and will all face the same fate. 'Indeed, Allah will not change the condition of a people until they change what is in themselves.'[1]

27 March 1986

1 Qur'an, 13:11.

Ever in the Service of the People

The minister of the interior stated in an interview that his top priority is to restore police trust; that is, the police's trust in itself and the public's trust in the police. This is a vital and pressing need and is indispensable for a society in an existential struggle for progress, for a society buffeted by storms of crises and hatred. This trust has been blown about by a strange wind, but that has not yet shaken its foundations or touched its deep-rooted history, and nor can it make us forget the greatness it achieved in the era of Ahmed Rushdi who brought peace back to the streets and put a violent end to anti-social behaviour without differentiating between the various levels of society, and who declared an all-encompassing and unrelenting war against the drug-traders as enemies of the people. He turned the administration into a nationalist institution which embodied our hopes and dreams.

Doubtless the choice of the new minister has been made after due thought and consideration, and with full faith in his ability to reset our bones, repair the hernia and start walking again along the path of justice, resolve and purity and the defence of values.

The police should not be a symbol of fear or coercion, but the emblem of safety and security. The police should be committed to serving the people and being the guardian of human rights. The moment the police reappear and take up their position, we should welcome them back as if nothing has happened and as if nothing can happen.

We should wish to see the police apparatus continue to spread their message of restoring law and order, of the application of laws, of confronting anti-social behaviour, employing the same amount of force or even more in fighting the murderous drug dealers and anyone who even thinks of sabotaging our national rebirth or impeding our progress. Let us pray God to grant the new minister success, to make firm his footsteps and to empower him and his administration to deal mercifully with the people, and mercilessly with the people's enemies.

3 April 1986

Directness between the Government and the Opposition

The economic directives have introduced a degree of calm and moderation. They do not affect those on a fixed income. They are nuanced in their treatment of the big players and should not create a sense of resentment if their desired aims of reform and justice are realised. Having said that, we should demand more and the citizen is correct to ask why these directives were not issued at an earlier stage of the loan, or at least before we plunged into it? And why did we not take it out before our debts piled up so high? Would this not have absolved us of our debts or reduced them to the absolute minimum? It would appear that we do not move towards taking any decisive decisions until problems show their ugly face. There have been some members of the opposition who are of the opinion that we should all form a coalition to confront the crisis, rather than this being dealt with by the majority party alone, and we all support the idea of unity in this critical time in our lives.

The parties have been holding a series of meetings to go over important matters connected with the constitution and the electoral system, but the economic crisis is no less important than the constitution and elections. Moreover, the crisis is not apart from those in terms of content and treatment and our politicians should include it in their work schedule so that they can find some standard solutions for dealing with this emergency, notwithstanding differences over strategic principles. In any case, such a coming together would bring with it an opportunity for an exchange and thorough examination of views. This would provide some impetus in coming to agreement, even on the most basic of solutions, in spite of any difference in principles. Whatever the case, this form of cooperation, if accepted, is better than resorting to criticism and half-hearted suggestions regarding a situation in which everyone just proffers an opinion. In the *al-Wafd* newspaper of 3 April, there is a reference to a directive setting out a comprehensive examination of the economic situation which will include both diagnosis and cure and which is of great importance and highly laudable. If only all the other parties would join in to achieve this national programme and to put into effect what has already been studied and achieved inside the National Democratic Party and the parliament.

10 April 1986

Facing the Facts

Having studied consecutive reports, we should not ignore any one opinion without studying it nor close our ears to any voice that is raised with a complaint or accusation. And nor should we ignore any rumour no matter how fantastic or ridiculous it may sound. In a democracy we have many constitutional institutions, we have the television, the radio and the press, and we also have the wherewithal that enables us to follow up, investigate, and broadcast the facts to the people and that enables us to fix what needs fixing before we are overwhelmed by problems or risks.

I have not forgotten that a respected member of parliament raised some questions about the Aswan High Dam, the royal family jewels, smuggled funds, and the impartiality of governance. Following his speech, a violent debate broke out in the form of an attack concentrated on the negative aspects of the pre-revolutionary era, a debate which ended with the opposition walking out. In fact, we expected any result except that of the matter ending up in a historical comparison between the negative aspects of two eras. The past is what it is, and we should not be raking it up, particularly as history has already dealt with it and opened up a new page for a new era. What interests us today is the present and the future and the challenges and problems on the way forward. That is why things should not have stopped where they did, and we should not have simply started working again as if nothing had happened.

Plainly put, the question is this: what do the queries that were raised by this respected member of parliament mean? Were they based on facts or delusion or something in between? What methods do we have for investigating the dimensions of these questions and communicating the outcome to the people? How can the government, opposition, and people, all come together to face these questions in order to guarantee our progress today and tomorrow? I cannot imagine that such serious queries can be raised without them being followed by the requisite investigation so that the people will understand that their lives still have some meaning, that their lives deserve all the thought and work being put in on their behalf as well as the dedication and sense of belonging demanded of them. And it is for the sake of this that we consider it a shared responsibility of the majority parties and the opposition to return to the subject which is one that they will be questioned about by the people and by history.

17 April 1986

Development and Social Peace

Today we have two essential demands, which are: comprehensive development and social peace. These are complementary requests, for there can be no development without social peace and there can be no social peace without development. However, the problem is that we do not possess the capabilities to bring about both of these aims at the desired level. Development uses up any surplus we may have, as well as bringing with it loans and subsidies, and social peace requires the realisation of the right amount of social justice to do away with suffering and to offer a sense of security to those who work hard, or are capable of working hard. Moreover, we all yearn for the day when we will need no more loans, and we hope that this day will come in the near future. So what must we all do to realise these goals without further delay?

We may well act in good faith regarding the pressure of our expenditures, tax collection, and increasing our resources, but I see no harm, and I am sorry to say this, in cutting back our development plans, though perhaps not even that will enable us to achieve what we want. There is no alternative to demanding those capable to work as hard as their national duty requires. We should ask them to be nationalist economists and not just economists. They must invest their money post haste. They must not abandon the nation in its time of need, especially because we are not asking them to make a sacrifice but rather to help increase productivity and legitimate profits. They must undertake the greatest duty of development thereby enabling the government to perform its duty with regard to social peace. They must feel the enthusiasm and desire to work before they can fulfil the conditions for demanding privileges and concessions.

I am addressing this to the rich of Egypt, to Egyptians working abroad, and to those who have money stashed away somewhere. A nation should not stumble along at a time when it has an abundance of people who are capable to an unprecedented extent and degree. You have to face up to your duty, as befits any people who enjoy the blessings of democracy and the rule of law. You must remember that each and every citizen is responsible for any ordeal that befalls his country, and that his responsibility is of necessity proportionate to his ability and capabilities, for '...whoever does an atom's weight of good will see it, and whoever does an atom's weight of evil will see it.'[1]

24 April 1986

1 Qur'an, 99:7–8.

May Day

Today is a holiday, the festival of workers and work, so let it be a happy day, an auspicious day for everyone who works hard, a day that smiles down upon the struggle for productivity. Previously workers at the national and international level underwent varying degrees of oppression which stained periods of civilisation with inhumanity and darkness. Then, from the gloom of those eras, lights started to emerge, presaging justice and calling for the establishment of a new model of human relationships to create a better life for society and to offer society increased vigour for its rebirth and progress.

In Egypt, ever since the 1919 Revolution, the workers have formed a popular force that has done all it can as the vanguard of a strike force in the arena of national effort and productivity. The workers were the fuel of a bloody revolution for independence. They were the cornerstone of the struggle to defend democracy for the supremacy of the people. They gave much and took what was permissible for an era of rule by the people in recognition of their hard effort and in support of a general national rebirth. After the July Revolution there was an increased movement towards industrialisation, and the grassroot workers became more efficient and stronger, performing a significant role in this new life, participating to a great degree in building the Egypt of the future and achieving the just treatment, rights and privileges they deserved and had earned.

The grassroot workers are called to the most noble duty which they share with other groups of people – that of dragging the nation out of its predicament, saving it from its critical situation, and steering it along the path of survival and civilisation. No matter how many directives we issue regarding limiting our expenditure, increasing our resources, budget reform or improving work discipline, productivity will remain the primary support and the final aim of our rebirth and progress. It is the proven method of increasing food supplies, of construction, of staunching our debts and improving all our facilities, of playing our part in the final analysis in creating innovation and civilisation, and it is the workers who are the vanguard upon which the whole nation depends.

It is the workers who will take us forward with their strength, intelligence and hearts, and they should be a good example for all.

Our greetings go to the workers on the occasion of their holiday, and to the nation for its workers.

1 May 1986

Religious Education

What do we want from religious education? We want it to instil religion in the thoughts and principles of the individual. It is normal for us to start by teaching a child the basic elements of religion and how they should be performed. Then we have to plant in a child's mind the principles that exemplify the Prophet's message, that have enabled believers to build an abode for religion and to build that abode up into a civilisation with culture and learning. As a consequence, we have the principle of government by consultation, the sanctity of mankind and freedom, equality among men regardless of race or colour, religious tolerance, the conditional trusteeship duty of care that God has placed in humankind, the religious duty of thinking and seeking knowledge, of work being considered more meritorious than praying, and a sense of human solidarity in society.

These are the principles which should go into shaping a child's mind year after year, with the help of sacred verses, historical events and facts. A child should also not be tested on them with a written examination, or with a written examination alone, but by observing his general behaviour in school and how this is reflected in the way the pupils interact with each other and with the school, how they react to being given tasks and to all the new things they learn. What we want is for education to instil religion in every pupil, in the way he speaks, acts and behaves, in how he sees the world around him and how he interrelates with the rest of humanity. We want to see it create a new generation for us, a generation of people who have a real and sincere sense of belonging and duty, a generation willing to learn, work and think, who value human and social rights.

No religious nation should evince negative qualities such as laziness, complacency, apathy, injustice, bribery, exploitation or special privileges for the few. If these exist, that means that the nation is not avowedly religious. Or if it is, then it is for outward show. If it is truly religious, then its faith is not being translated into action and it is being slack about teaching religious principles to its young. Religious education does not mean listening, learning and reciting. It should be a sincere attempt to bring the individual back to the divine foundations that will help him face up to his challenges as he goes through life, and that will keep him on a balanced psychological, intellectual and ethical course between the requirements of this world and what awaits him in the afterlife.

15 May 1986

The Most Beautiful of Times

In our past before the July Revolution, and in a dark period in which violence, corruption and injustice were rife, some devoted reformers dreamt about an enlightened autocrat filling the earth with light and justice. Their dream was not an expression of despair at the sterility of democratic rule, for in reality violence, corruption and injustice only run rife when democracy has been tampered with, such as under the former monarchical regime which was a puppet of British colonialism. Those reformers must have been dreaming about a firmly established democracy. Even more incredible is that their dream, or nightmare, has a parallel with a very great historical event, one from the era of Umar ibn al-Khattab, who, in the distant past of the Islamic era, shone so brightly as a unique example of enlightened rule that many people still think of him as a paragon ruler.

The truth is that Islamic history has not known another ruler like Umar ibn al-Khattab who took consultation as a cornerstone, principle and constitutional basis for his rule. History tells us that whenever he had a problem regarding his rule at home or abroad he would convene a consultative council in the mosque of Medina, expound the issue to them and then listen to every opinion without differentiating between the old and the young or between man and woman until they came to a solution. Then he would make his decision and put his faith in God.

He was, in the language of our age, a man of democracy, not of autocracy, a symbol of freedom, not of oppression or abstruseness. That is what makes his age stand out above others, flooding it with light, justice and achievement. In truth nothing is more diametrically opposite than autocracy and justice. Autocracy is based on the opinion of one person to the exclusion of all other opinions, and justice by its very nature affords a hearing to every last person. We should remember this, but at the same time we should also remember that the most beautiful period in our history has been the era of democracy.

22 May 1986

On the Question of Ethics

Our loss of ethics is at the forefront of all our losses. We are beset with bitter concerns, such as mounting debts, an acute rate of population increase, a rumbling administration, deteriorating essential infrastructure, a budget imbalance, and creaking industrial and agricultural sectors. Amidst all this turmoil we forget about ethics. We fail to see that those concerns are all tinged by corruption, or we do not judge them negatively enough for they essentially lie hidden within the establishment, breathing out their poison. I do not state this out of sheer despair, for I am not unaware of the sincere effort being expended on renovation, renewal and reform, nor of the science-based planning or consultation, inspired by nationalism and faith. However I recognise and restate the actual situation which is that there can be no success or progress without solid and un-corrupt ethics to provide people with resolve, perseverance, a sense of belonging and altruism, as well as a sense of loyalty to the homeland, to our fellow citizens and to sublime values.

In fact, there is no society completely free from corruption, but this is generally practised so far out in the margins of society that it does not affect the welfare or safety of that society. Our society, on the other hand, has been exposed to raging plagues as a result of dictatorial rule, grinding wars, economic crises and a whole series of frustrations. Our society has forgotten itself along with its noble traditions, it has turned away from its principles, it has fallen into opportunism and selfishness as it rushed towards cheap success with brazen disdain and pathetic indifference. Were you to investigate the reasons for our losses, you would find that they are rooted in corruption just as much as in other frustrations. Hence we have failed in our challenges as a result of greed, and our five-year plan alone will not serve us unless helped by a strong, believing, belonging, and ambitious personality who upholds the right, the good and the beautiful.

Fortunately, the atmosphere has changed in favour of a moral resurgence thanks to a democracy that respects human rights, that is an example of leadership, a paragon of un-corrupt behaviour and national sentiment. Last but not least, there has been an effort made towards the correct practise of faith, which shows a burning desire for clear thought. We must do nothing other than support these positive aspects to continue, not to be truncated, in order to bring our citizens back to a decent moral standing, for they are our real treasure and they are the people we have to depend upon in our long journey.

22 May 1986

5 June

This day should not pass without us stopping and thinking. Not in order to feel renewed sadness, to torture ourselves, or to become antagonistic, for that we have never been and never will be. However, there has been a setback for our national rebirth, a blow to the hopes of a nation, a deep wound in the dignity of a noble people, and the least we should do is to call to mind the reasons that have led to this, or that have eased the way for it to come about in such an ugly manner. People have tried to excuse this setback by saying that it has come about as a result of an international plot concocted over a long dark period in order to destroy Egypt as a symbol of Arab revolution with its ongoing call for liberation to subjugated nations. This excuse is unacceptable, and the least that can be demanded by the Arab world of the unified political leadership is that it should expect attacks, be aware of plots and be ready to foil them. This is the opposite of what we experienced as we rushed headlong into the arms of a plot without planning or evaluating the consequences. Furthermore, let us ask ourselves: did we possess the power needed for challenging a wicked and tyrannical world when we swore an oath to liberate the oppressed of the earth? Should a politician not look before he leaps? Is the issue one of romantic aspirations and individual chivalry, or of assuring the existence of a nation and insuring its future?

I would add to that the corruption which events have uncovered among people who hold great responsibility, the apathy coursing through their veins, the coercion, damage and brutality meted out mercilessly and inhumanely to the opposition, in addition to the ongoing negativity and indifference inflicted by authoritarian rule on a whole people.

Therefore we should remember 5 June in turn with the necessary sense of awareness and alertness, and with an unexaggerated image of ourselves. It should remind us to adhere to our ethics and values, to respect human rights and to place our faith in the fact that there can neither be a national rebirth nor a life worth living when the people do not have their full rights or live up to their obligations.

5 June 1986

Values Fit for All Times and Places

There is nothing new in what people are talking about today. It is a subject that every Muslim is familiar with, whatever his degree of religious culture. It is a subject set out by its proponents and intellectuals in various forms justifying their argument with recourse to the Qur'an, the reported sayings of the Prophet and the early converts to Islam, as well as to the deeds of just rulers. So what are they all talking about?

It has been said that the central pillar of faith, which is the uttering of the statement that there is no God but God, implies the liberation of man from any mundane authority, and that a Muslim is indeed a free person who is not enslaved by any individual, regime or urge.

It has been said that Islam promotes learning, that it respects those who study and accords them an honoured position, and that a Muslim should really be a learned person or a person who respects learning and scholars.

It has been said that Islam calls upon man to think and meditate, and sanctify the intellect, and a Muslim is indeed a thinker, or someone who considers thinking as a lantern to guide him through life.

It has been said that Islam unites all mankind in its vision, with no differentiation between people based on race, colour, ethnicity or class, and that a Muslim is essentially a person who respects people for their humanity, values, piety and behaviour.

It has been said that Islam respects all religions and allows the conscience freedom of choice. There is no compulsion in religion,[1] and God guides whom he wills,[2] and a Muslim is in fact a person who can live alongside all other religions in peace. This is said by proponents and thinkers who provide support for this statement from the Qur'an, Islamic tradition and history.

And as I have stated, no Muslim is unaware of this fact regardless of how much he knows about his religion, but we have been losing those

1 Qur'an, 2:256.

2 Qur'an, 28:56.

values in our daily lives, or we might say that they have lost the position they should have among a people known since time immemorial for their religiosity and piety – as if the principles are some ancient cultural artefact discovered by researchers who then move nonchalantly on to other matters. In fact these values should be firmly implanted in the hearts of our children from a young age, they should course with the very blood in their bodies, they should be in every breath they take, so that they are reflected in their daily behaviour and personalities. This is the task and message of education. This is the primary duty that should be carried out by the Ministry of Education, by the media and by parents. In that manner we will be correct to say that Islam is valid for all times and places.

12 June 1986

On the Question of Change

A ferocious battle has broken out on the question of change, and as usual the core issue has remained obscure with the attacks focusing on the negative aspects of our life before the Revolution, as if life is a series of inevitable woes which appear one after another. The real question is that of change, or of establishing our political system on new foundations more suitable for our present and our future. Surprisingly the need for change itself has been agreed upon as a principle, and I have not read a single word against this, but the differences of opinion have revolved around the appropriate timing.

Some people think that the present moment is not the appropriate time due to the sensitive times we are living through, and out of fear that it could be a distraction from the crushing crisis and even exacerbate it. Hence they suggest putting it off indefinitely, or for the two years they think it will take us to restore economic stability.

There are also people who think that there is no point in any economic reform if it is not preceded by a comprehensive political reform that grants the people their human rights and which consequently would be more capable of confronting our challenges, or making sacrifices, and of carrying the burdens of allegiance and belonging.

Both of these opinions have a certain amount of validity and credibility, but perhaps we could achieve a compromise between those who wish to act speedily and those who want a delay. We should start by allowing people the unconditional and unfettered freedom to form political parties, and we should agree on a period of years which the new parties can spend establishing themselves, setting up branches across the country and shaping their publicity apparatus. At the same time, the old parties should review their positions in the light of the new political map and what the situation calls for in terms of the compilation, integration or clarification of their intellectual content. This would then allow elections to take place with all the agreed upon guarantees. Then it will be the first task of the new parliament to draft a new constitution that accords with the desire of the people as evidenced by the results of a free election. During this period, development work should not stop for a single second and should remain completely untouched by the calm and respectful political discussion taking place in parliament. Then work should carry on again in the same manner, or in a new manner. The people will have to deal with the responsibility of their free choice, and they will have to do so with their characteristic patience and resolve.

19 June 1986

Why Subsidies... and Why Education?

I do not understand the wisdom behind subsidies and free education having become the topics of public debate. Neither bears the responsibility for the imbalance in our budget, and reorganising them will not plug the gap. But let us ask ourselves what purpose is served by subsidies and free education.

The average citizen is beguiled by hopes that we might mention here. He hopes to see the state reduce its current outgoings without exception. He hopes that the state has drawn up a plan to collect every last penny in tax and to tighten the dragnet around every last tax evader.

He wants to see how the deficit can be removed from all forms of expenditure, whether in the form of free education, health services, communications, law and order, defence, investments, etc. The debate should not be about principles, for we have accepted our popular revolutionary achievements as irreversible rights, but the debate should be about how we confront this question: how can we reduce the deficit in those firmly established categories of expenditure? How can we find a temporary solution for the current emergency and the crippling economic crisis?

The burden of sacrifice may fall more heavily on one category than another, and moreover some categories may be completely excluded for unavoidable reasons. But this should all take place far removed from any consideration except that of complete justice and the general good. This should all take place in the open, with the participation of the people or within their purview, so that they can be persuaded to shoulder the requisite sacrifices without the slightest doubt about the need for them.

Our nation is equipped to confront challenges. It is capable of giving and of being patient on condition that it sees devotion and fair treatment from the government and that people are treated as human beings and not as sacrificial victims.

10 July 1986

Towards an Ethical Plan

Last week we spoke about our national target and the effort being expended to achieve it. We also spoke about the lack of knowledge of this target despite it being very clear, about the denials of the effort being expended, about suspicions surrounding it, and about the fact that it has not received the requisite enthusiasm, not to mention all the corruption and mismanagement that this has caused.

In truth, the opposition has been taken up with these two plagues, specifically that of corruption. I have to admit that I have been taken aback by the ferocity of the campaign, not because I have any tolerance for corruption, but out of the fear that the efforts, which must be made to face these challenges, may be diverted to side issues that can be considered secondary in comparison with our most significant enemies, that is, backwardness and mismanagement. I have been horrified by the reticence of our youth, which has affected both the populace and the workplace, and the last thing we should be doing is to have a plan that works for us or increases employment without giving our youth a chance to offer their sincere support and faith together with their enthusiasm and sense of belonging, one that does not see them either pushed into apathy on the one hand or extremism and violence on the other. The catastrophe is that our current situation is continuing as it is – in spite of our having established democracy – and thereby preventing us from having an un-corrupt national leadership to serve as an example. And why do we not have this?

The youth's answer to this is to ask how we can demand increased employment when there are so many impediments, when high-mindedness is shackled by bureaucracy and mistreatment, and how can we demand sacrifices in a country mercilessly and unconscionably pillaged by a minority? This is their gut feeling and it has become stronger as the crisis has further exacerbated. This has led me to become convinced that there is no purpose to employment if it is not preceded or accompanied by a general purge of corrupt activities overlooking neither old nor new misdeeds, and that this is the only real way to convince the people of the seriousness of work and self-sacrifice.

We are a religious people, or to put it in other words, we are an ethical people and the only way to our hearts is by satisfying our ethical sense for we feel as strongly about ethics as we do about issuing economic directives.

13 July 1986

The Present between Anger and Perfection

Our democratic life stands accused and faces attacks and protests every day. Our patience has run out and we can no longer remain silent about the crucial issues or their negative aspects. I cannot say that our democratic life is perfect or that I am one of those who do not wish to see it as perfect, and for a long time now I have been demanding that unfair laws should be rescinded and that we should take a new look at the constitution, but at the same time I do not belittle or disparage what has been achieved.

Political opinion has never been as blessed with freedom as it is today, whether in the press, in parliament, or in what is said across all the television channels.

The opposition fulfils its duty the best it can without being subject to any restrictions on its opinions or on its time. You should not expect the majority party to abandon its role in the government following some questioning, for the National Democratic Party and the government are an inseparable whole, united by an identity of opinion and vision. Being transferred to the order paper does not mean that the efforts of the opposition have been for naught or that their statements have become no more than wisps of smoke dispersed in the air, for the opposition's effect can be seen indirectly within the government itself even if it is not immediately apparent. It has established itself in people's souls and has played its expected role in forming knowledgeable, effective and efficient public opinion.

Our quest for perfection should not incite us to disparage the present, or obstruct us from working with all our strength and perseverance with the positive aspects of democracy, or from recognising those eminent people who guide us in the field of decisive work and job performance.

It would be a good sign for us to call upon the government and the opposition to come to an agreement on the challenges they face as we go through a grinding crisis which requires self-control, self-sacrifice, and a redoubling of work for the sake of the country alone. So let us all agree to staunch our anger and despair and work for victory, with the help of God.

17 July 1986

The Occasion of the 23 July 1952 Revolution

The July Revolution took place at a historic moment when royal autocracy and social injustice were running rife and when corruption was widespread. The people knew instinctively that this was the natural reaction to their suffering and they unhesitatingly flocked around the revolution, expecting it to come up with the panacea for all their ills. The Revolution did realise their expectations in the fields of social justice with a strong list of achievements such as agricultural reform and advances in the fields of industry, agriculture and services, and a hard-working people generally felt that they had become the focus of attention and care for the first time in their lives.

However, the Revolution proved to be no more than an extension of the monarchic regime in terms of how it dealt with authoritarianism and corruption, and going even further in that regard in terms of the unprecedented violence and draconian harshness that ensued in its aftermath. It was then dragged into international challenges for which it neither had, nor could have had, possessed the necessary power and was driven along by romantic dreams and a sense of national chivalry with no thought given to the consequences, until that fateful day, 5 June 1967, marking the end of the Revolution's first epoch and the start of a new chapter as it moved, under the pressure of incidents, storms and bitter experience, towards democracy, the rule of law and a state of law and order. It then achieved its greatest success on 6 October 1973 but became bogged down in consumerism, stoking the flames of inflation and a budgetary war, freeing the ghouls of corruption to rain their curse down upon the earth, up to the point when in September the setback emerged in full force, ending the Revolution's second chapter with the catastrophe brought about by its leaders. Then came the third era which attempted to restore order amid the bloody conditions and inherited the worst thing that a government can inherit – a country in ruins, burdened with debts and corruption. It seemed that the country was destined to start again from scratch, just as Ancient Egypt did after a period of drought.

There is no room today for romantic dreams, false chivalry, or narcissistic fecklessness, for this is the era of the intellect, of science, work and consultation, of wisdom, of un-corrupt behaviour and patience. Undeniable achievements have been made, and no day passes without something memorable being achieved, and perhaps what we lack and what burdens us cannot be traced back to neglect as much as to our misfortune of having inherited a tainted legacy that needs time and patience to be cleansed. We may be undergoing hard times, but we still have hope which glimmers in the distance and demands that we resort to an increased amount of intellect, knowledge, learning, consultative procedures, wisdom, un-corrupt behaviour and patience.

24 July 1986

We Are Not a Nation without an Aim

Whenever the general morale is at a low ebb due to indifference and many people being unable to meet their daily needs, intellectuals hope to find a decisive cure in setting a national aim that can win over people's hearts and concentrate everyone's efforts – an aim which should act like a lighthouse on the horizon to guide ships in the swirling dark. I am really surprised that anyone has to ask about a national aim in a country suffering so bitterly from underdevelopment while looking forward to the progress that is flourishing so close by, embodied in science, scholarship, culture, industry, agriculture, and refined human relations, in addition to what our history has produced in terms of sublime values and parables for all ages. If all of that is not a worthy aim, then what is our aim? And what should it be?

The aim is there for all to see and moreover we expend a huge amount of effort to arrive at it, in terms of plans, labour, the healthy and democratic atmosphere we have created for it, the rule of law and the removal of anti-social behaviour. So why is it not working its magic on people, preparing the stage and the actors for a new and historic performance worthy of the people and their history?

Perhaps it does not yet possess the adequate care it has crystallised in the people's consciousness, perhaps because they have a fog in front of their eyes, a fog of pain and lost trust, a pain incubated by the economic crisis and a trust lost to the ocean of corruption. As a consequence, the sincere effort expended has not received the recognition or backing it deserves, and the people and their achievements have been subsumed by the musty odour of doubt and suspiciousness. I am writing these words with ever-growing sadness and sorrow, but I hope I am mistaken in my depiction, and that the actual situation is more conducive to optimism. Whatever the case may be, we are today in great need of reforming our administration so it can re-emerge in a form based on science and dedication, and we are in great need of a complete purification to weed out past and present corruption. This is a national task which can brook no hesitation or delay so that we can breathe new faith, enthusiasm and a sense of seriousness into our waning souls – for we will rise again.

26 July 1986

The Role of the People

When it comes to confronting our most insurmountable challenges, the people must take their place at the head of the struggle. They have to support the state and not only drive it forwards but they must be at its head. There can be no real national rebirth if the people do not support it with their manpower, their intellect, their hearts and their words.

The state still takes upon itself the greatest role in comprehensive development, and that is a weighty role, with bumps along the way. At the same time no one can deny the achievements that have been, and are being, made. When it comes to the people, and particularly our youth, their response has not yet been as we might have hoped, and they are still riven by indifference on the one hand and by extremism and violence on the other. To know the causes of this is not to excuse it, but one should mention that they piled up during the long years of authoritarian rule which stripped the people of their efficiency and turned them into onlookers. There is a similar case when it comes to the corruption which took on plague proportions, disincentivising people and spreading a mood of defeat and opportunism. We can never forget the forces that lay in wait for us at home and abroad, exploiting our grinding economic crisis in order to provoke unrest whenever there was an opportunity or when we were preoccupied.

Let us not be content with official work alone. We must take serious initiatives to cleanse the atmosphere, regain trust, and dispel indifference. We must contain violence and anger for the time has come for us to set up the firm supports of a complete democracy and to eradicate red tape from our political lives. We must give the people the unconditional and unfettered opportunity to express their opinion. The anti-corruption campaign must be extended so that corruption is completely uprooted and every Egyptian citizen can enjoy the blessings of law and order and equal opportunity within the protection of the rule of law. The media must continue its rightly guided policy of giving the public correct information and it must offer airtime to all without distinction. Moreover, the media should not present events as a Potemkin village, but should show developments in the cold light of day while, at the same time, requesting the public to be patient and to work even harder. In so doing, we would hope that the people will regain their historic and authentic spirit, that they will spring back into action, and declare their strong will in the face of challenges, just as they have in the past when confronted by the greatest empire known to history.

31 July 1986

Towards the Other Shore

Apathy and radicalism – they are twins. They appear to be opposites but their apparent difference stems from a shared peculiarity, that is, extremism. An apathetic person stands at one end of the connecting line, just as the fanatic stands at the other. If we take a look at our particular circumstances, we find that they both stem from the same cause, which is corruption. It stretches apathy to the point of hopelessness about everything, and extremism to anger about everything, both of which are deviations from the norm. Apathy may cause its proponents to become involved in corruption, and extremism often leads people to violence and breaking the law. This unfortunately results in corruption becoming generalised and takes in the corrupt along with the angry and the apathetic. A corrupt person may get away with his crime due to insufficient evidence or because he takes precautions before committing his crime. An apathetic person often fails due to his lack of expertise, and an extremist because of his precipitousness. No amount of pontificating, nor even free discussion, although this has its benefits, will save us. First and foremost, we must put an end to corruption and root out corrupt people, and we must set a good example. All those people investing effort and funds rooting out the corrupt and preparing to take action against them, would spend half of that effort and funds if they were to scrutinise the way the administration uses the labour force inside and outside the civil service, and they could rid us of those who exploit people, of those who have their fingers in the pot, and of those who adulterate foodstuffs. They should cleanse our lives from the flaws that disfigure us and that sully our reputation so that people can trust again, so that people can regain their spirit, and so that the work expended on comprehensive development can have the credibility it deserves and the support it merits, so that with the blessings of being an un-corrupt, dedicated and serious society, we can all be brothers working together as we face the challenges imposed on us during the night of ignorance, cruelty and vanity. It is unavoidable that the innocent rather than the criminals will be those who atone for this, but there is no alternative if we want the ship of state to arrive safely at its port.

7 August 1986

Democracy Is Wonderful Despite Its Errors

Much has been said about our democratic life, and the more the opposition practise it, the more is said and the harsher and the more strident the comments become. The image reflected in the mirror of parliament and the press may appear to be far from what those who wish for perfection want to see. What we really hoped for was to see debates taking place with greater objectivity, that excitability would be tempered with a sense of calm and self-control, that the opposition would act with greater wisdom and that the majority party would be more open and responsive. Despite all of that, I am an optimistic admirer of our democracy and judge it to be energetic, lively and functioning. It does its job in terms of monitoring conditions in the country, offence and defence. It attracts people to the public arena, enables them to feel a sense of belonging, creates the necessary meeting point between the rulers and the ruled, and cements the values of freedom, justice and the sovereignty of the people.

And nor should you forget that our democratic practice must offer a pure reflection of the mood of the people and their lifestyle. We are a hot-headed and excitable people who often get carried away and it should come as no surprise that our debates around all of this have both positive and negative side-effects. By this I mean that we often become swept along by our own rhetoric, we use harsh language, and we raise our voices and gesticulate. I do not approve of any of that, and nor do I defend it, but it is a fact of life, just like the skin colour or weight we have ended up with, or like our blood type, and we should not anguish too much over it, attempt to explain it away or be hypercritical or beat our chests over it. I have seen many parliaments around the Mediterranean basin descend into violence and abuse but thank God we have not yet sunk to that level.

Whatever number of flaws there are in a democracy, they are completely trivial in comparison to the crimes carried out by a dictatorship and its strongmen which have left us with a legacy of defeat, anguish and debt. I hope that you share my admiration and optimism and that we will not be diverted from our quest to improve our democracy.

14 August 1986

In Commemoration of the 1919 Revolution

In remembering Saad Zaghloul and Mustafa al-Nahhas we recall their great effort, self-sacrifice, courage, and that Egyptian nationalism which united and unified us. We recall those priceless days, more beautiful than any myth and sweeter than any dream or song. We remember the 1919 Revolution as one in which the people organised themselves into a strike force which included peasants, intellectuals and women. Women left their domestic domain and set out to join the greater fight in the very field of battle. We must at the same time remember the great success of the 1919 Revolution, for, despite hardship after hardship, no setback succeeded in blocking its path, and its primary aim – independence – gradually, from 1922, to 1936 and 1954, became a reality entailing a dispute between a small defenceless nation and the largest empire known in the history of colonialism.

It was not a revolution with just a single aim, and indeed many other achievements were born from it… such as the positivity of the people, their cohesiveness and perseverance. It is this positivity that drove the people on to rise up without having to be organised, ordered about or incited. It is this positivity that breathed into the people their spirit of innovation, that established their national economy, their literary, artistic and musical sophistication, and liberated the great majority from being victims of the status quo to soaring in the firmament of science and work. It was reflected in the insistence of the people on practising their political rights and obligations, on casting away the shackles of royal patronage and shedding their blood to defend the constitution against tyrants and autocrats. It was reflected in the people's sacred national unity which provided the basis for their nationalism, for their struggle and their inclusiveness with its loud and clear message of: 'It is God who shapes religion and we who shape our country.'

A sense of positivity, democracy and national unity all symbolise the purport of the 1919 Revolution as much as complete independence does. These notions are the revolution's eternal legacy and shining testament which have remained recorded in our hearts and minds through the words of Saad and Mustafa, and through which these notions have become a permanent self-renewing revolution.

I salute our great leaders, those who sacrificed themselves and left behind memories of great and glorious days.

21 August 1986

Good Government

Every party has principles, and these principles vary and conflict as we know. However, the government, inasmuch as it is a government, has firm principles to which all the parties must conform, or to which all the parties should conform and without which no regime would be competent in this region. A government must have a disciplined and responsive administration, it must have intelligence and flexibility, initiative and decisiveness, and impartiality along with keeping a permanent eye on the general welfare.

It must believe in science and accord it every opportunity to perform its task. It must rely on science in drafting, preparation and execution, as no project can come to anything without scientific guidance. It must put all its combined public and private sector strength and resolve into productivity, clearing the path for those who wish to work and allowing them to do so without becoming bogged down with red tape or having to jump through hoops. In the final analysis, productivity is the basis of food production, exports and freedom from debt. It is our only hope of coming out of hard times into more prosperous times. Productivity can only flourish when it is based on the principle of nurturing those who work hard and punishing shirkers, and that should be carried out in an effective way that serves as an example. If we do not do that, people will not put their real faith into work or show a sense of belonging or commitment.

Last but not least, a good government must accord the citizen the respect he deserves as a man to whom God has given dignity. This should be a matter of words and slogans, but should be instituted by deeds and people should be treated respectfully in any situation.

These are the comprehensive principles without which no government deserves its name. The application of the principles of this party or of any other party may be delayed, and party principles may appear to be an unrealisable dream, but when it comes to the principles of democracy then any interference, neglect or deviation from them means simply a deterioration of standards, notwithstanding which party may be in government or what its principles are.

28 August 1986

Our True Wealth

People say that Egypt is the wonder of all wonders, including the fact that the country is collapsing under the weight of its population while at the same time suffering from an insufficient work force. Something similar has happened to its source of income, i.e. the agricultural land, which is being eaten away at and can hardly provide half of the population's food needs, while at the same time millions of feddans[1] have been bulldozed for construction purposes. These are things that do not make sense, and do not arise from any plausible logic. So what do we say here in Egypt?

We should today be talking about surfeit and deficit – the huge size of the population and the scarcity of labour. We are a nation with limited resources, and we will only bring about any radical change to our situation if we launch a preternatural scientific foray into the desert or under the ground. For the moment, our workforce is our real wealth. However, their enormous number does not signify real force or wealth, rather their poverty and backwardness may be also something of a burden. With decent preparation, training, education and culture they can turn into a workforce and national treasure that can be used in our comprehensive development programmes at home. They can be sent to work abroad which will also be to their own benefit. Every person with a trade or a profession will find a better place for himself on this earth, or will be better off than those who have not had the chance of being educated or trained.

We should look after our national treasure with the care it deserves, as it is the only way of creating a dignified life for ourselves. Our primary schools must take in every last child, university intake should be restricted to those willing to specialise and take on leadership positions.[2] From the high schools we will be able to find enough students

1 A feddan is slightly more than an acre.

2 The Nasserite system offered a university place to every student who passed his/her high-school examinations – leading to an unemployable, or underemployed, workforce glut.

to learn the trades and skills needed to work in agriculture, industry or the cultural sector. This training and preparation should be utterly comprehensive and carried out using leading-edge methods so that we can find the best brains and the most efficient hands.

This is our real wealth and our ongoing hope today and tomorrow.

4 September 1986

The National Democratic Party and Our Youth

In my opinion the silent people are in the majority. They are the people who are indifferent and negative. The people who have grown up in the era of totalitarian rule which made them too afraid to participate in politics and turned them into mere spectators. When the going got difficult, they became even more cut off and withdrawn.

Today and tomorrow our hope has been placed in democracy as something that will restore the spirit of that enormous and silent grassroot mass. Democracy, along with the freedom and rule of law that it presages, is the cure for that stultifying disease. It is democracy that calls upon people to offer their opinions and to act. It is the permanent message of every political party and the worth of a party can be measured by its ability to capture hearts and minds, to gather people around its vision, to give meaning to life, and to shape a path for hope and work – particularly among the young who represent the nation's power and future. If you want to know the value of a party, probe its strength and gain some idea of its future, look to the young members and follow their message in this dynamic and renewed political space.

A dynamic party is a party for the youth, a party for the future, since it is our youth who represent our roots, our strength and our future. We depend upon the parties and the state – actually, the parties and then the state – to wrench our youth out of their inertia and to rescue them from their negativity, to spur them into movement and a sense of belonging, to get them to offer up their opinions and their labour, and to stoke their yearning for knowledge, culture, excellence and ambitions to bring about a better world.

The greatest plans and most splendid building projects become threatened by failure if they are carried out in a climate smothered by negativity and indifference. We need a sense of enthusiasm, just as much or even more than we need the experience of older people. We need the people's will, their sincere sense of belonging, their faith in values and their unsullied dedication for we will never find an opportunity to realise our dreams like that offered to us in the shade of freedom and the rule of law.

11 September 1986

Opinion, Experience and Consultation

Our supposed challenges need comprehensive work and a decisive national stance. We need dedicated and serious action to bring into the public arena every penetrating thought and real expertise, without differentiating between the parties or political trends, and without waiting for an official call or governmental organisation. We have some pioneering examples of economic cohesion from the time when we were able to diagnose our economic crisis and suggest a treatment for its ills. We could also mention the debate which took place between the religious and secular groupings within the doctors' union.

Today more than ever we need general intellectual input to enable us to come out of the darkness into the light, from instability to stability. We need this new manner of thinking to take on our most acute problems, such as the terrifying rate of population increase, and issues surrounding education, our youth, democracy, anti-corruption campaigns, the rule of law, convincing leadership, our sense of belonging, agriculture and industry, housing, narcotics, etc. etc.

We must submit our problems to systematic study by specialists and experts. We must make the most of every individual effort that has already been made, in addition to studies made by national councils and the Scientific Research Academy. Then a national conference should be convened to debate these and to ratify the points of agreement. The outcome of all that should be printed up and delivered to the president of the republic and the legal authorities, but the effort should not stop there. The outcome of this research should also be studied by the relative authorities as a first step, followed by their committing themselves to putting the points into action under the supervision of the people and with annual or even daily progress checks. By the grace of God, we have the expertise and qualifications to do this. We are not lacking the enthusiasm or sense of belief in Egypt. What I am calling for is the very least that is necessary for a people who are witnessing their nation pass through a time of trial and who are instinctively committed to extricating it from its woes. In this, there is no difference between rightist, leftist or moderate. History has put them all in the same boat and left them to choose the correct course to steer.

18 September 1986

One Crisis Should Suffice!

We hear nothing other than complaints and we see nothing other than gloomy faces. How much work has been carried out in putting the comprehensive development plan into action, and how much has been realised in the last few years? So why do we hear only complaints and why do we see only gloomy faces? The issue, when laid out at its simplest, is that we are going through a difficult transitional period and we will not be able to reap its fruits in the near future. We need to be patient and forbearing and to work as hard as we can in order to reach the first stage of salvation.

In this delicate transitional period, we actually do have something to offer to our overburdened citizens that can lighten their suffering, make them feel that they are being taken care of and looked after, that can give them greater patience and forbearing, that can dampen down the volume of their complaints and smooth out their wrinkles, without us having to take out a new loan or subsidy to send us looking for cripplingly expensive foreign expertise.

We could improve the way we treat the man in the street, or in the workplace, or wherever he is, so that he will step up to the plate and do his job better. That is his right as a human being and a citizen. If he lacks the character or will, then the law should attempt to remove the cause of this laxity at the same time as according him respect and treating him properly.

We have the capability to create a new type of life for ourselves, to form new, humane and enlightening relationships within an approved budget, if we are resolute in fighting against destructive negligence and lethal apathy, if we look after public cleanliness and our green spaces, if we protect the banks of the Nile, if we cleanse the atmosphere and the street of the dangers to passers-by, and if we apply the scores of laws which have been ignored.

We will be able to take another step towards cleansing our political life of the emergency laws that sully it and shackle our progress, that strip our citizens of the right to form political parties that promote their interests. As we see, much can be offered to the state and its citizens without imposing extra burdens on the budget. When it comes to our daily duty, this should be performed with no need for further reward or thanks. At that point we will be able to vindicate the citizen of his almost infinite suffering by dint of his having shown great patience through this difficult night of transition.

25 September 1986

6 October

As October comes around, the atmosphere is redolent with delightful memories… In fact, we have weighty matters today that call upon us to concentrate on the problems they have engendered, to stand firm in face of rapacious challenges and untiringly to engage all our mental and physical faculties in an effort to confront them. However, there is nothing wrong with remembering happy times, or even sad times occasionally, provided that in doing so we make a constructive connection with the present and the future and that we do not over-exaggerate them. It is correct to say that the October victory will remain a guiding light, akin to the Pole Star in the pitch-black of the night – not because we are enamoured of wars, but because it was, and still is, what rescued the spirit of the Arabs from falling into defeat, from the trough of despond, and from seeing all the values of our life become bogged down in doubt.

It is the day which essentially restored our pride, dignity and hope, and restored them by means of the bravery and sacrifice of our soldiers, by their being trained to perfection and having learnt how to use the most modern weapons and scientific methods of organisation and fighting. That was all carried out in a general positive atmosphere, one brimming with good values, democratic principles and firm faith, vaunting respect for human rights. It then became known as a day of freedom that led to the liberation of our territories, when our efforts were crowned with the most noble of aims, that is peace, while at the same time not being oblivious to the rights of a persecuted and oppressed people whose blood everyone seemed fond of shedding – the people of Palestine.

Every step we take today along the path of peace is a step taken for and inspired by the Palestinians, so let us raise our hands in greeting and honour to our steadfast and patient nation, to our valiant and indefatigable army and to the hero of the day, the late Anwar Sadat, and let us pray for the souls of the great leaders of our war for liberation: Ahmed Urabi,[1] Mustafa Kamil, Mohammad Farid, Saad Zaghloul,

1 (1841–1911), the first political leader in modern Egypt to come from peasant

Mustafa al-Nahhas, Mohammad Naguib and Gamal Abdel Nasser. Let us also send our greetings and best wishes to President Hosni Mubarak, one of the heroes of that day whom fate appointed to shoulder the greatest trust in our modern history. Let us send our thoughts to, and honour, those military leaders who are no longer with us. Let them be an example for us as we continue the fight.

2 October 1986

---

stock. His involvement in politics led to the British bombardment of Alexandria in 1882 and his banishment by the British to Ceylon.

A Day of the People

The people are a force unlike any other, a force that is sometimes so hidden from view under the pressure of daily life that it is almost forgotten. It appears in critical circumstances such as on a scorching day when no one can escape from the sun's heat. These circumstances also include times of elections or referendum, and these are the real festivals of the people, when they demonstrate their positive energy, their influence and their great prestige. People remember this about themselves, and recognise their almighty power and the haughty are laid low. During those tense times, the people emerge in everyone's eyes as the source of authority, the masters of their rulers, in control of their destiny and as a force over which no single person has power, whether their will is respected or falsified, and whether they are given a choice or it is imposed on them.

Campaigning goes on, the media work themselves up into a fury, the first rung of the government and the opposition spread out across the country, launching themselves into the people and delivering fine words and beautiful promises, attempting to win people over with their beaming faces and radiant smiles, offering up their obedience and loyalty along with appearing most concessionary and displaying affection, whereas all they want is for the people to turn out to vote for them and not hide at home, or give any other sort of excuse in those rare times when society is forged into one, when differences fade away, class distinctions are erased, privilege counts for nothing, racism disappears, and the only thing left is the people itself.

If that were the only benefit of democracy it alone would be enough to educate people and improve their behaviour, and it would be a permanent reminder of the inevitability of the day of reckoning even if this escapes people's minds amid the hustle-bustle of work and the thrill of being elected.

9 October 1986

The Responsibility of the Majority

Let us not always be driven into disagreement around the elections for the Consultative Assembly.[1] Let us recognise the results as declared by the authorities and these simply confirm that the National Democratic Party has gained the majority of the votes and that the masses supported it with greater enthusiasm than in the parliamentary elections.[2] The trust of the people is a blessing, a trust and a responsibility as well as an opportunity they should seize in order to make even greater achievements for the benefit of the people and democracy.

Here is a party maintaining its majority in a sort of consensus despite the people's ongoing suffering and hardships and despite the grim situation all around them. The party must deliver its message more forcefully, in a bolder manner. It should issue directives aimed at making inroads towards a future we hope to enjoy, that takes us along a path of progress, freedom and human rights. Anyone who has earned this support, that is, anyone who is elected, should not fear criticism from whatever quarter, neither should apprehensiveness hold him back from making momentous decisions, and the only things he should be taking into account are rational thinking, fairness and the welfare of the public.

And it is our right today to demand that he must rescind all the emergency laws, those which target the press or the judiciary, or which hobble the political will of the people. Moreover, it is our right to demand of him to take a new look at the constitution so that it can develop along with us, or in the best of cases lead the way, as our lives speed on in enlightened progress. It is also our right to ask him to be more open to the opposition in order to create a more fruitful atmosphere of harmony and collaboration between the overwhelming majority and the small minority.

The Revolution had an epochal moment in which it gained the overwhelming support of the whole nation. Unfortunately, however, that did not bear fruit in terms of establishing a democratic government that

1 The Upper Chamber.

2 The Lower Chamber.

could have saved us from many of our difficult moments. And now the opportunity has arisen again in the shade of a democratic system of government, and what we have to do is to smooth out its wrinkles and bumps so that it can get down to business and take momentous steps in political, economic and cultural policy.

16 October 1986

The State and Culture

If the state does have a role in culture, it is first and foremost that of creating the cultured citizen, and moreover if the state is serious about this role it will put resources into promoting culture. If it ignores or overlooks its role, and then spends millions on the promotion of various cultural services, its esteemed efforts may be all in vain or simply vanish into nothingness with no noticeable results. I am not one of those people who are ignorant of, or refuse to acknowledge, services performed in this regard by the state, such as setting up scientific institutions, running theatres, supporting cinematic output, music and the plastic arts, as well as a laudable resurge in book and magazine publishing, both qualitatively and quantitively. This has been the case until today, although there is still a never-ending stream of complaints about the degradation of cultural values and the spread of illiteracy throughout the provinces.

I do not deny that we have emergency conditions, in the economy, society and politics, that have brought us to this low point, and I am absolutely certain that the situation would be much better if we had a solid foundation of culture and stratum of cultured citizens. In a situation like that we might lose a battle but not the whole war, we might lose numbers and equipment but we would still have a solid and strong basis impervious to events and able to fight for survival. Our aim should be that of creating the cultured citizen, or the citizen who loves culture and knowledge and who is unwilling to face life without a sense of what is right, what is good, and what is beautiful.

That individual is formed in the first years of his life, in the home, and if that does not happen, then in the first school years, starting from primary until secondary school. The primary responsibility lies with the ministry of education and teaching, although the ministry of culture has a participatory role in shaping this, just as the media have a role in supporting this and putting it into action. If an individual can be found, nurtured and replicated across a whole generation, he will be bound to create what we dream about but cannot do ourselves. Then, by dint of his existence, his pressure, his demands and his insistence, the newspapers will be full of articles about culture, theatre and cinema will flourish, serious books will be read, and criticism and publishing will experience a heyday. I hope that all of this will be taken into account by those who are planning our culture and teaching programmes.

23 October 1986

Medicine for More than One Disease

In appearance illiteracy and family planning are two problems, but in truth they are one and the same, or are so intricately connected that they are essentially one problem. Illiteracy is the inevitable bitter fruit of ignorance, and producing offspring with no regard to one's situation is likewise the inevitable fruit of ignorance. They are also similar inasmuch as the state declared war on them long ago and spent astronomical amounts in the process, and not only are the results only slightly above zero, but illiteracy has actually increased and housing development has reached alarmingly low proportions. Finally they resemble each other in having the same cure, and even if we do not apply it properly that cure is education and culture – education that takes in all children without exception and makes sure that they finish their schooling, and culture that must form an essential element at every stage of education and that should, at the same time, be intensively promoted across the various organs of the media. I have already ascertained its efficacy in those who have been lucky enough to realise the benefits of education and culture. Illiteracy is eradicated by teaching children to read and think, and by setting a limit on the number of children in a family, and planning for the future can then take place side by side.

Education and culture are the basis upon which we should build the individual, whatever his specialisation in later life. This is a vital duty in an age that is distinct from all others in terms of enlightenment and knowledge, when ignorance is no more than a hiding to nothing. Let us divert what we spend on family planning and the eradication of illiteracy to supporting education and culture. Let the television do more to promote general culture and to gain a greater awareness of those who have missed the education train. We should not let another generation grow up without our having finally rid ourselves of illiteracy and of the medicine we dose ourselves with out of ignorance or blind tradition.

30 October 1986

Africa and Internationalism

An African author has won this year's Nobel Prize in Literature.[1] This recognises and honours, on an international level, African literature that deserves our pride and admiration, particularly since the deliberations for this year's prize have been completely free of the accusations of political interference that sometimes take place. This reminds me of a novel written by an African author that was translated into Arabic in the sixties when there was a peak in translation activities, and although I have forgotten the book's title and the name of the writer, I can still remember the effect it had on me and that I considered it a work of the highest artistic quality.

One of the most wonderful coincidences is that I received a letter from Yahya Abu al-Khayr (of 'al-Mahalla al-Kubra – al-Jabariyya' fame) ten days before the Nobel Prize was announced, censuring us for being mainly interested in the West and its writers, for how our bookshops are missing out on the African literature that is no less magnificent than that of the West, and for overlooking the close geographic and historic ties and connections between us. He went on to praise great writers such as Chinua Achebe, Wole Soyinka, Ezkil Manahlil, Osman Samini, and now the Nobel Prize has confirmed his opinion and vision.

Perhaps in our current translation programme we could turn our attention to this literature so that it can occupy its fitting place in our bookshops and libraries, and perhaps those with an interest in this prize in our Arab East will finally be convinced that it is not being withheld from some ethnicities, that it cannot be achieved by networking or manipulation but by serious hard work, by supporting cultural life with the elements it needs to flourish, by attempting to raise literature onto a higher plane, by taking it from its traditional status to one of innovation and authenticity and by highlighting its special characteristics.

I cannot conclude these words without declaring my sorrow for how the prize has not been awarded to that great man of contemporary Arabic literature, Tawfiq al-Hakim, in the same way it went unawarded

1 Wole Soyinka.

to other literary giants such as Tolstoy, Chekhov, Proust and James Joyce, among others.

6 November 1986

A New Government

We send the new government our wishes for success as it takes on the weighty trust of the nation, and hope that it will direct its ambitions and sense of national duty towards realising the aims it declared in its opening address to parliament, which are old aims that have been taken up again, aims the people long yearned to see realised with patience and forbearance, while at the same time undergoing God knows how much pain and suffering. Even if we do not know the reasons for the departure of the previous government, particularly as it was praised and admired, we can only conjecture that the new prime minister is someone we can rely on in a crisis and who will step forward when necessary to face challenges.[1] For that reason, we are spurred on by our hope that we will experience renewed action, that things will be thoroughly thought out, then carried out expeditiously and followed up with oversight and accountability within the remit of true democracy and complete respect for human rights.

What really gives us hope and fills our hearts with trust is what has been written about the new prime minister's life, which has been one of study and hard work, as well as what has been written about him being an enemy of the parasite of corruption, that he has no tolerance of it and will keep up the fight against it. We have the greatest need of study, hard work and un-corrupt politics while we are being flooded with false statements, promises and pretence. I believe that the new prime minister, having sworn an oath to God that he will truly respect the people, will provide them with unadulterated facts, will not hold back on stating the cure, and will position himself and his supporters to offer a good model for life and un-corrupt politics. I believe that if he does this, he will find that the people offer him not only their patience but their enthusiastic help in confronting challenges. Moreover, I believe the people will make the sacrifices dictated by our circumstances and by our national salvation.

Furthermore, I repeat my wishes for his success and for him to stay in

1 Atef Sedky was elected on 10 November 1986.

power until he has carried out his promises. A rapid change of scenery may keep a theatre audience entertained, but it may cause worry to those concerned, to those who yearn for reform and long for stability.

20 November 1986

Welcome to Parliament

In this noble month, whose name is connected in history with the day when we commemorate Saad Zaghloul's endeavours in gaining Egyptian independence and the establishment of trade union councils, the parliament is sitting again. This is something we welcome after the long recess which has deprived us of its familiar voice, of its intellectual battles, of its alert supervision and its constant striving for more rational governance and a better tomorrow. It is the locus of our pride, the storehouse of our dreams, the home of our peace of mind, our protective shield and the starting point of all our hopes.

This is a good opportunity to renew our call to the majority party to be more magnanimous and insightful and to use its strength and authority and provide freedom to a degree that matches the trust and conviction it has received from the people. We also call upon the opposition to continue their efforts in terms of studying and scrutinising issues, following up on policy decisions and holding people to account, even if this means merely registering alternative opinions in fulfilment of its obligation to the people. I would dearly love to see this parliamentary session pass without dispute or squabbling, but differences of opinion have their own respected traditions and their own rules of engagement which turn them into 'good fights'. On this occasion not only would I like to mention the errors that have been committed, but I would perhaps like us to recall also that there is no political regime beyond error and that democracy is the best system known to mankind despite its flaws. We have lived for years in the shadow of a dictatorship whose positive points are hard to count and whose flaws are uncountable, a time when not a single person dared raise his voice to object to any of those flaws, or to complain about tyranny. We are in no mind today to rush off and censure democracy for its inadvertent or unintentional mistakes.

Let us give a welcome to our venerable parliament. Let us welcome its good side and let us welcome its bad side, for as they say, 'When you water the rose, the weed quenches its thirst.' So ever forwards on the path of freedom, productivity and un-corrupt governance, of confronting our challenges with sound wisdom and a realistic and healthy outlook.

27 November 1986

The Opposition

Due to the great amount that has been, or is being, said about the opposition, this has become one of our most intractable problems and we need to think about what has been, or is being, said, not to defend or oppose it, but because the opposition and democracy are two inseparable parts of one unit. If one is subjected to harm, the other goes down the drain. So what is being levelled against the opposition, and what is being suggested to fix the issue?

It is being accused of going in for mud flinging, settling old scores, and running after sensationalism with no regard for the seriousness of the situation or the risks involved. It is also accused of interfering in serious matters such as defence or party rights with no regard to established political procedures, and of exacerbating the crisis which threatens our very existence and not just our welfare and nation. It has been suggested to the opposition that they should be objective, that they should study the problems and then offer solutions, and furthermore there has been a proposal to establish a government of national unity in which the parties can combine to face our challenges hand in hand.

We declare with full faith that we condemn mud flinging, whoever it is done by, and that the unrestrained settling of old scores adversely affects the public welfare. Just as the opposition has the right to make its opinion heard on any issue, no matter how sensitive, it also has the duty to put the public welfare above any other consideration. When it comes to studying problems and offering solutions, that will take place inasmuch as possible and in more than one way. It will take place in parliamentary committees. It will take place whenever the opposition submits a formal request to participate in dealing with a particular issue that is on the table, and it will take place whenever parliament reviews or debates a project. Furthermore, the party press, their conferences and their publications need to present the various opinions regarding our problems and their solutions.

There are some intellectuals who have been calling for the creation of a government of national unity to confront our challenges. This is a call motivated by the loftiest ideals and we would hope it will fall on receptive ears, but a government of national unity is not assured of success unless hearts and minds agree on an aim that all schools of thought can subscribe to. As our problems are economic, social and cultural, and as every party has its own vision and position, how can we put our hopes in an agreement for a government of national unity when unity does not even break out occasionally in a cabinet whose ministers are all from the same party!

Real collaboration is possible, and could be an alternative to a government of national unity, if the government were to enlarge its circle of participation to include the other parties, if the other parties were to commit themselves to objectivity, sincerity and a sense of nationalism and dedication to the national good, and if they were to hold themselves above exploiting emotions or incitements to rebellion. In conclusion, I cannot say, in spite of everything that has been, or is being, said that the opposition has affirmed its existence, performed its duty to the best of its ability, or exuded a democratic aroma.

4 December 1986

Exam Month

In this month of December every year we face a test of our resolve in confronting our challenges. It is a cyclical test of democracy and of the political parties which the system of rule in our country has relied on for ten years. It is the month when the gates are open for entering new names in the electoral register, and when we are able to count the number of people who set aside their silence and apathy to join the parade of those who participate in public life and take upon themselves the trust of commitment. There are people who consider the silent to be the real majority of the people, and that they are the bitter fruit of autocratic rule that by its very nature places obstacles between the people and politics. Then along came the economic crisis which increased their number and their sense of alienation.

It goes without saying that the current construction process requires every able-bodied person to work and every heart to pulsate with love for his country and with a sincere desire to set it on its feet again.

Among the essential factors for creating the right atmosphere are the activities of political parties, whether in opposition or power, as they try to connect with the people to promote their platform and spur them on to becoming a more viable workforce by endeavouring to set them good examples of how they should think, behave and sacrifice themselves for the country.

Grassroots activity by the political parties not only creates the opportunity for the spread of inspirational words, the promotion of positivity and productive labour, but also creates miracles in terms of highlighting their idealistic struggle, the attraction of their leaderships and the hopes they offer for the shining tomorrow so wished for by everyone.

This is the month when we are given information about the quantity of the workers' achievements, and we come to learn accurately how successful the parties have been in carrying out their promises and in politicising the people. We cannot hope that, within just a few years, we will have been able to make up for decades of lost time, but we can hope that we will have made enough progress to keep everyone happy.

11 December 1986

What We Should Remember

A group of political thinkers claim that it is the irregularities in the practice of Egyptian political parties, such as their violent squabbles, their mud-flinging, and their constant nit-picking, that have led many of our youth to undervalue their worth and behaviour and to lose all faith in each and every party's political activity. Consequently, our youth would appear ready to accept their dissolution and our return to a system based on the application of power, a system that could solve problems without recourse to all the usual shenanigans and hollow sloganeering.

For some reason these political thinkers forget, or pretend to forget, that we have long become used to a system that used its strength to subjugate and tyrannise us and that what is new for us is democracy and a multi-party system, and even if democracy can be found to be responsible for some transgressions, excesses or mismanagement, it is the previous regime that was responsible for leaving us with an almost unbearably heavy legacy of debt, incapacity, run-down finances, neglect in our essential infrastructure, corruption, seething unemployment, the breakdown of the education system, and the sorry events of 5 June in Yemen. Moreover, it is also responsible for terrorism, for the demons of torture it set loose, for making colleagues spy on colleagues as well as on members of their families. It is responsible for having stripped our citizens of their pride and optimism, for corrupting their consciences and morals, for turning them into pessimists and making them apathetic, and for making them set aside their love for Egypt and our God-given values. We are still suffering from that and from the destructive after-effects. We will not be able to drag ourselves out of this situation until we rid ourselves of the remnants of that filth and instil the younger generations with a new spirit in the shelter of freedom and respect for human rights.

Remember that those crimes were committed by people who started out their political lives as devoted revolutionaries but were corrupted by absolute power which by its very nature leads to corruption, which unleashes instincts better left repressed, and changes man from a human being into a destructive beast… Remember this was all not so long ago and it still happens, and then compare all of that with the negative aspects of democracy and party-politics, and you will see the blessings of our present political life which God has bestowed upon us by bringing us back from the edge of the precipice.

18 December 1986

A Conversation in English

Commenting on my opinion piece (25 September 1986) in which I called for people to be treated better in various situations, I received a letter of support from Dr Abd al-Hameed Abu al-Sab', president of the central state administration of rural development in Mariout, in which he expressed his whole-hearted support. By way of analogy, he included his translation of a conversation that took place between him and an English friend who has a close connection to our situation. His English friend was reminiscing about his first day as a civil servant, and how his line-manager called him in to have the following chat:

Manager: 'You are now an employee. Do you know what that means?'

Employee: 'That I am now an employee.'

Manager: 'Well, yes. It means that you are a civil servant, and do you know what that means?'

Employee: 'It means that I'm a civil servant!'

Manager: 'Well, yes. It means that you put yourself at the service of any of the public who make their way to this office.'

That was the first lesson the new employee learnt from his line-manager, and it is a lesson that every employee should be aware of when he starts his job, that he should keep firmly in mind as he starts climbing his career ladder. All civil servants ideally remain in their positions in order to serve the people and it is the people whom they should serve, whose sweat and tears go into paying their salary, and doing anything less is a sign of a corrupt administration and a breakdown of values. There can be no real administration if it is not built upon the true meaning of the concept which is to carry out its real purpose.

25 December 1986

Science in Language Schools

I have received a letter from a Dr Karman Abd al-Wahhab, in which he complained about a directive issued recently regarding the study of science in elementary language schools, starting off with the enormous fees that fathers will have to pay, as well as mentioning that the length of time a pupil is at the elementary languages schools is being increased to eight years, two years longer than at state schools. As for the directive itself, which is the crux of his complaint, it makes the study of science obligatory, starting from year 5, whereas it used to be studied from year 1. This went on for a long while without anyone uttering a complaint about it, and with the children always getting good marks in their examinations. He signed off with his hope that the directive will be revisited before it affects the children badly and before it is too late to stop more children falling victim to it.

In truth, I am not too well-versed in the most important subjects that our youth need to acquire in this era and which they need in the first instance to improve our lives and bring them into keeping with the modern age. Perhaps science is the single activity upon which the secular and ultra-religious can agree. That sensitive directive should have been published with more emphasis upon explaining and justifying it, with more respect for public opinion and more consideration for parents. Had that happened, Dr Abd al-Wahhab would not have sent his letter of complaint expressing so eloquently his rising anxiety and great pain, particularly since he himself is from the scientific elite and his words have particular value both with regard to his own children and to the state itself.

1 January 1987

On the Electoral Law

We welcome the proposal to amend the electoral law as a first step not only towards rescinding all the emergency laws but towards reviewing the constitution itself, even at a later stage, so that it is in conformity with our present conditions, with our state of development and with our legitimate desire for complete democracy. We welcome the sections of the proposal that aim to amend the constitution so that it recognises women's civil rights and dignity. So let's grasp this opportunity to offer up our opinion on the electoral law in general, which we hope will be in keeping with the constitution after it has been reviewed.

Firstly, we would prefer a system of proportional representation so that people vote for a party platform, and not for a personality, or along family or tribal lines. That may be inconvenient for some, but we know in the final analysis that every citizen is instinctively drawn to vote for self-interest and to place his trust in those who support that. In any case, acquiring our political education from the bumps along the route is better than the inertia that comes from a system of government that promotes the cult of personality.

Secondly, we have not decided upon the 8 per cent qualification and we are not convinced that this should just be lowered. In fact, it should be completely removed. Furthermore, it is our belief that no vote cast by the people in freedom and good faith should be wasted. It is our duty to respect the minority, as they represent a different opinion, regardless of their size, and we should go even further than this and promote a method of voting that makes the whole country one constituency and we should apportion the vote across the parties so that it can be translated, in our inimitable manner, into individuals.

Thirdly, in our elections we do not recognise independents. If a man has managed to keep his independence in his private life, should he not also keep it when he decides to participate in practical politics? At which point, he has to choose or declare a new programme, and our past has taught us to think badly of independent politicians or to see those who claim to be independent as opportunists.

Finally, we do not see it as fit and proper that the peasants and workers should have a number of seats set aside for them. On the one hand, they are the majority of the nation and their status should be no less than that of women, as the great legal mind Dr Waheed Ra'fat has stated. And furthermore, we hope that the debate around this plan will bring about the victory of common sense and the public welfare and that further debate will follow.

8 January 1987

Towards a New Ethics and New Traditions

Democracy has form and content. Its form is defined by institutions and laws, by the declaring of human rights, by the freedom of the press and the independence of the judiciary which all combine to provide political life with a healthy climate, a firm foundation, honour, inviolability and health. Its content is what anchors a firm belief in those values both in individuals and in people in general. That is what guarantees that it can be practised freely at home and in public life, such as in the interactions between parents and their children, presidents and those they govern, civil servants and an individual or the public. In other words, only after it becomes the general morality, social traditions, and a complete way of life for people and the whole of existence, does it become content.

There is not much point to democracy if it goes through the motions while at the same time oppressing women, suppressing public opinion whatever it may be, or discriminating. Or if it makes concessions on the grounds of race or religion, or tries to force people into thinking one way, or makes moves towards greater surveillance or throwing its support behind one side of a debate, or spreads false information, or fabricates incidents – which is tantamount to violence, even if the means are different.

It is obvious that oppression, suppression of opinions, injustice, violence, mendacity and misguidance are attributes of a life blighted by authoritarianism, except that they may spill over into a democracy, dressed up as something else and spewing their poison under a false flag.

This could catch us unawares, and well-intentioned as we may be, we might eat away at our values, believing that we are practising our democratic rights as we suffer from the after-effects of the diseases that infected us in the era of injustice and tyranny. The ethics of democracy reject all of that in the strongest way and we will not achieve true democracy until we gird ourselves with true ethics.

15 January 1987

A New World

Perhaps humanity throughout its history has not suffered the anxiety and misgivings suffered by this generation. Their learning and ever-increasing access to information have enabled them to take a broader look at their current and future situation. They know what apparent and latent evils threaten them, what has happened and what will occur after a period of time or even in a century from now. They look at the population of our planet and wonder whether we will be able to feed ourselves, at the quality of the air and how much it has been polluted over the last century, and at what benefits rather than harms the earth.

As we look around this developed world we see suffering due to unemployment, a fear of extermination and a feeling of dread about forces discovered by science which are immensely useful but which do not bring us security. In the under-developed world, backwardness and disease hold sway, along with the spectres of debt, bankruptcy and corruption, their fangs dripping with famine and war. The whole image is bleak, splattered with ugly hues by dint of the side-effects of both progress and of underdevelopment, and this in a time when there has been such mind-boggling progress in communications that the four corners of the world are now so close to each other that you can see the world as a single geographic and temporal unit, operating with uniform economic activity, with a prevailing culture and with a growing conformity of values. The world forever comes across innovations, taking them on before it can digest them, all the while straining to keep balance and worrying about the potential consequences.

In order to work with this new world, we need a new vision, one that considers it as one world with a unity of interests, with a common future, and if the behaviour of one member is found to be lacking, it should be called into line by the others. However, the strong continue to follow their feckless, traditional policies which are based on exploitation and selfishness. The world is in the direst need of rightly-positioned and far-seeing leaderships with a loftiness of intention, who are impelled by great love that pays no heed to boundaries and obsolete values. This is a flood that is threatening everyone anew without distinction, those in the lowlands just like those in the hills or on the mountain tops. The only way to escape is by putting our faith in man and in humanity and through putting an end to poverty and selfishness.

15 January 1987

The Islamic Conference

The Islamic Conference is being held on a peninsula seeping with the blood of Muslims shed copiously in Iran, Iraq, Lebanon and Libya. Perhaps it is being held in these times in response to its tortured conscience on the one hand, and to the awakening taking place throughout some regions on the other hand.

Our first hope is that the Conference will find a way to stop the bloodshed and raise the banners of peace. That is a difficult task, an elusive hope, but no aim is impervious to a strong will if supported by good intentions, and if its path is trodden with determination.

The Conference should then marshal all its fraternal power to recover from the trials which have torn it apart and work out what doctrine and outlook it can agree upon, restate its aim of brotherly cooperation and probity in order to weed out the fake causes of its ongoing altercation and to turn that into a means of freeing the enormous territories it encompasses of dependency and underdevelopment and help them break out of their shackles, thereby reinforcing their cultural unity and reviving inter-country economic activity so that these countries can forcefully confront the current era in an open and uncomplicated way, with a sense of pride in its cohesion, authenticity, freedom, intelligence and effort, and play a noble role which is worthy of the Conference's history – so famous for its give and take, its flexibility and tolerance.

The Conference should then address the world which is bogged down with its many crises with an optimistic message for all, setting loose its pearls of wisdom that are its modus operandi for bringing about a cure, and promote its inclusive human vision which established the Conference up as an act of 'mercy to the worlds'.[1]

The dreadfulness of the current situation may challenge any good intentions, but we believe that simply sitting together in the current circumstances may bring about the much needed urgent reconciliation and delayed victory, and that this will be an expression of the desire of

1 Qur'an, 21:107.

all parties to come together in a brotherly fashion, and of their desire for liberty, progress and hard work.

22 January 1987

Another Path to Glory

Egypt occupies an outstanding strategic position between the continents. It is sometimes impelled by its feeling of strength and by other reasons to extend its reach. And sometimes its weakness makes it the prey of greedy nations. In ancient times, it founded the first empire in history, only to succumb to foreign rule over the course of a long dark night. This unique situation still turns heads in our modern era, tempting people with ideas of greatness and domination despite the fact that conditions have changed. Egypt is no longer one of a small number of great world powers, for new giants have appeared in the world whose strength, compared to Egypt's, is like that of the stars when compared to the planets.

We are apt to overlook this dose of reality sometimes when we are flushed with success. Muhammad Ali overlooked this fact and established an empire ignoring the reality that there were other empires with their eyes set on Egypt, setting himself and his country up for the almost inevitable fate of not only seeing the empire decimated, but he himself saw what he had built up fall apart, sending us back to point zero. Gamal Abdel Nasser also overlooked this when he set the whole country on a collision course with the empires of yesterday and tomorrow. He dragged his country towards an almost ineluctable fate. His constructive work ground to a halt and he too sent us back to zero.

Egypt should base its foreign policy, primarily, on avoiding any challenge with the superpowers, thereby avoiding a sorry outcome. We are like the planets revolving around their stars. If a planet goes too far out of orbit, it freezes to death. If it orbits too close to the star, it burns up. So we have to follow the course charted out for us by time and place.

This is a call for salvation, not for submission. It is not meant to have any bearing on our noble ambition for glory, for there are some very small states, in terms of land mass, population and power, whose political and social cultures put them at the top of the league tables, such as Sweden, Denmark and Switzerland. Superiority is not just a question of power. There is another, more difficult and noble arena in which we can establish ourselves firmly – that of political, social and scientific culture. We must learn the lesson of our history. We must understand where we are in the world, and we must build our plans on the *terra firma* of peace, knowledge and belief.

29 January 1987

It Is People Who Make Civilisation

We need money, and lots of it, in order to improve our situation and to build up our infrastructure. Productivity and services are both in need of funds so they can be established, renewed, revitalised and expanded. However, a quick glance is enough to convince us that we do not just lack funds. We need people to the same degree or more. We need people committed to the general welfare with a sense of trust, devotion and integrity. With people like that our national rebirth could come about with limited funds, but not even unlimited funds will enable us to achieve our aims without this type of person. An arrogant person seizes or squanders money, or loses it due to neglect or sloth, while he is distracted from his duty by thinking only about himself or giving himself over to his base desires.

The crisis is primarily a moral crisis, the bitter fruit of foreign and domestic subjugation, of injustice, privilege, impediments against human rights, of poverty, ignorance and disease. The average citizen has been abused for a long time and now he is paying back neglect with neglect and abuse with abuse in a feckless and quasi-suicidal process. We are just wasting our time coming up with new plans if we do not prioritise looking after the human being, by which I mean educating him, instilling him with culture, providing healthcare, decent treatment and a system of governance. We must cleanse the atmosphere around him of all the miasma so that he can regain his psychological and spiritual well-being, so that he can regain his sense of moral rectitude. At such a time, we will find a firm foundation for our progress and national rebirth, and we will be able to confront our challenges with enough willpower to overcome them or cut them down to manageable proportions. We will be able to make innovations that are both useful and aesthetic in a whole variety of areas, from science and culture to politics and ethics, and the individual will be able to employ his energy and enthusiasm to create a more comfortable life for himself as well as something more important than comfort – glory.

It may be complacent of us to leave this task to the state alone. There is still hope that we may see a diminution of corruption and that the views of intelligent and dedicated party leaders will come to the fore as it is they who are at the top of the list of people who should be revitalising and re-energising our youth. It is they who should be equipping the people with the very idea and the resolve to break out of their manacles, to overcome their pessimism, to save themselves, to save their society, and to turn death itself into new life.

5 February 1987

A New Era

The decree announcing a referendum today has brought with it marked excitement, perhaps because people have now become aware to a great degree of the causes of the suffering they are living through. However, they are still not convinced that there is a similarly powerful decree capable of confronting the challenges posed by these, or of moderating their harshness, even over a reasonable period of time.

In circumstances like these people have great hopes for great change, and the minimum they expect is that the new parliament will tread carefully enough to protect them from precipitous change during its term in power, that it will offer them the same stability that it offers political life in general. In order to achieve this, we must cleanse the political atmosphere of all the impurities that stain it, first and foremost of which are the shackles impeding the people's freedom to form a political party.

It is not enough for parliament to represent the recognised parties, for the unrecognised parties are no less significant. If the new parliament ignores them, I fear it will be forced into holding a new referendum within two years or less and that will be a good opportunity for us to rescind all the emergency laws, to come up with a final draft of our election law and to announce the sort of guarantees that protect free elections from interference. At that point we will have a parliament that deals with the people with truth and sincerity and we will be able to get a move on with taking robust decisions to confront the challenges which are keeping us back. Our hope for all that will have to rely upon the wisdom of the president and his sense of nationalism and democracy.

However, all the fuss over political reform should not make us forgot our most important mission at this time, which is that of development. We should not turn our minds for a second from carrying out the Five Year Plan and for supervising its careful implementation. It is the most important means we have of overcoming our difficulties, of getting out of the straits we are in and of throwing off the burden of hankering for what we do not have. I have often written about the need for us to place a supervisory body in every ministry to focus on the execution of the five-year plan and to follow it up whatever the situation is or however circumstances may change. We must have political reform, and we must brook no delay in our development plan. May God grant us success.

12 February 1987

Electoral Fraud

If fraud is mentioned in conjunction with the elections, we immediately think of the government. However, I believe that a state whose parliament has a ruling majority, in conformity with constitutionalism and democracy, will not accept tampering with free elections. There is notwithstanding a form of fraud practised with all good intention by those who have taken part in the election campaign. This takes place when the candidates try to outdo each other, make promises they have no hope of fulfilling, heap unjustified praise on a segment of the population, attempt to win over people who are not their natural supporters and thereby win a number of seats through manipulation rather than merit. That, in my opinion, is also electoral fraud. It is a corruption of democratic life and a falsification of the will of the voters.

Those who demand integrity and impartiality from the administration should, for their part, commit themselves to their people with honesty and sincerity, and it is only natural for them to take the number of seats in parliament commensurate with their share of the popular vote, and endeavour to see things done with openness and clarity. What we should really like to know during an election campaign are the views of every candidate regarding the many things that concern us, of which I shall mention a few by way of example:

1. Their opinion as to the difficult decisions to be made in order to confront the economic crisis.
2. The stance of the high-ranking Islamic clergy regarding the relationship between religion and the state and the application of Islamic law.
3. Their opinion regarding the positive achievements of the July Revolution, what we should preserve of it, what we should amend, and what we should now ignore.
4. Their stance regarding a peace treaty with Israel and the normalisation of relations.
5. Our relations with the great powers and with the Arab and Islamic states.

We have much trust in our parties' sense of duty towards the nation and its courageousness. It is our right to demand of them to state their positions with absolute clarity so that we can determine on which points they agree or differ, so that there is a level playing field when it comes to us casting our votes. May God furnish us all with wisdom and level-headedness.

19 February 1987

The Festival

We still consider 22 February the Festival of Union[1] and this may be what has led us to our current bloody and distressing, or if you wish, ridiculous, situation. However, insisting on it being celebrated in spite of all that is an acceptable way of reminding us of our age-old longing to bring about our dream of power and glory, of confronting our challenges with a surfeit of good faith supported by a noble lineage and a rich past, and by looking forward to a tomorrow overflowing with a sincere desire for liberation, rebirth and self-realisation.

We have come out of that bitter experience with the sound knowledge that politics is a sea heaving with seduction and dissention, whose waves roar with selfish resentments, and that the Arabs, if they manage to reach a safe harbour for themselves, must set aside their differences, and head as one towards something they can agree upon. If differences are inescapable, then the Arab nations should be free to discuss them on condition that they do not deviate from, hinder, delay or water down what they have agreed upon. There are examples which might make this all a possibility, such as the success of some academic and artistic conferences and offers of economic subsidies, all of which were at some point mired down in political disagreements.

We have no disputes or disagreements when it comes to culture and economics. We have common cultural roots, and a shared zeal for our culture's various embodiments. Our hearts and minds are highly receptive to all innovations that come our way. That is how we have come to have an integrated economy, even though some states have too large a population while others have too much money. We have huge expanses of land which can provide us all with food and clothing,[2] if we can free ourselves from the yoke of greed. If we can restrict our efforts to the fields of culture and the economy, we will be able to bring about a unity of the spiritual and the material and we will become

1 This is a reference to the union between Egypt and Syria 1958–61.

2 The 1952 Revolution endeavoured to provide shoes and basic food for the whole population.

stronger and achieve higher standards of living. Perhaps then the ultimate aim to which the path has diverted us will come to us without effort or obstacles.

It is said that trials are what teach humanity, but I think that we have been through enough to be able to teach the whole world!

26 February 1987

The Constitutionality of the New Parliament

It is inarguable that the electoral law's lack of constitutionality was the prime reason for the call for the dissolution of the parliament. As the court has not yet issued its opinion, and as consequently the claim cannot be corroborated, prudence would dictate giving the benefit of the doubt and a firm decision should then be made. If that does not happen, parliament should still complete its term, not just to ensure stability alone, but because, in spite of everything that has been said, it would not have been a bad thing for parliament to dissolve itself, and what's more it would have been quite a useful democratic experience.

Parliament has made many resolutions and these have been discussed with a great degree of sincerity and courageousness far beyond the normal bounds of debate between the majority and the opposition. Parliament must be a place where the rough and tumble of political life can go on freely, particularly when ferocious party disputes or conflicting visions are concerned.

The unconstitutionality of the law is a failing regarding which we can neither shut our eyes nor remain silent. Therefore, the first thing that we should or must wish for is to be completely reassured regarding the constitutionality of the amended electoral law. I state this on the occasion of a new claim being presented to the constitutional court regarding the amended law. And now we are setting off on our election campaign and all the parties are overtly and covertly competing to win the trust of the electorate. We will see a new parliament, perhaps even before the court issues its opinion on the amended law. So what should we do if the court opinion rules in support of the law's unconstitutionality? Should we then dissolve parliament almost as soon as it has convened? Should we live with it notwithstanding questions as to its legitimacy?

I consider the matter serious enough to warrant the formation of an expert committee, made up not only of judges, to make a ruling on the subject before elections take place. We must be able see the lay of the land before we step forward.

5 March 1987

A Word to the Confused

The government has declared time and time again that no substandard foodstuffs are coming into the country and that it has made the necessary preparations for this in the wake of the meltdown at the Chernobyl nuclear reactor. The opposition for their part have responded that they have received reports about irradiated shipments entering the country and about the inefficiency of inspection procedures, which all leaves us confused and worried, and we are right to be so in view of the risk of the consequences and the threat to the general population being so much greater than any other natural or man-made disaster. Worse than that is the fact that even knowing the truth will not improve matters when it comes to the practical outcomes. Even if we can corroborate the dreadful news reports, we do not have the medical means to lighten the blow – never mind how to respond to it.

The most the government can do in this case is to highlight what is against the law and set out clearly what the public needs to do. This is an absolute necessity. However, the crime is greater than any punishment, and the execution of some criminals or the resignation of a whole government will not compensate for even a small fraction of the expected losses.

In fact, I have recently convinced myself to believe the government, not out of any wish for a sense of security at any price or to absolve myself of useless worry, but also because I cannot imagine that the world knows about the dangers from a nuclear plant's meltdown and that the news calls for us to stop our imports from many countries whose produce may have been affected and yet we still stand there as onlookers doing nothing, or let ourselves be distracted from events which affect our regular life.

I cannot imagine that in any way at all. It is undeniable that the matter is being given the greatest consideration, that all aspects of the situation are being studied and that robust decisions have been taken to protect the lives of millions. As far as that is concerned, the government has done what it absolutely should do. It does not deserve any thanks for taking those measures and they should be strong and watertight. That is why I decided to believe the government and to put my trust in God, the Merciful, the Beneficent.

12 March 1987

What Will Tomorrow Tell Us?

Elections are a national test which takes place across the broadest spectrum. They are a test for the parties and their candidates, for the electorate at all levels, and for the state as represented by its administration. It is a test of the popularity of the National Democratic Party and the other parties, of the fitness of their principles for confronting the problems of our era, of the way they select their candidates, of their ability to hold a debate with the public in order to win them over and earn their support – during an election campaign which shows up how each party is willing to compete and manoeuvre, the extent of its commitment to serious and objective campaigning, the solutions it offers for our many problems at home and abroad, and how this will be translated into action in parliament with each party claiming they will perform better than the other.

It is a test for the voters, those on the electoral register and those who are not. It is a test for how the candidates follow up their election campaign, how they are received in public gatherings and how they take part in the debate and manage to transform this into votes at the polling stations. For all these reasons they give eloquent speeches about how wonderful their party platform is, how much they desire to participate in public life, the extent of their political experience and their sense of nationalism. There can be no democratic life, much less political life, if it does not stand on a broad political base of an informed electorate, if it is not always ready to be influenced and respond, to listen and give answers, to act and react. Without that we are not citizens but subjects, groups of people but not active nations.

I wish the voters every success and I hope that first and foremost this success will restore hope and resolve, and that we will be able to look forward to a better future. This is a test for the state as represented by its administration. A commitment to a free vote is not just a good and moral way to behave – it is proof that it is apposite and appropriate for governance in our modern age, that we have a practical respect for human rights, that the government is a body that looks after our security and peace, and that offers uncorruptibility and progress. I pray to God for success for everyone, candidates, voters and the administration, so that we can start a new life.

22 March 1987

The Hidden Disease

Many true and wise words have been said about the trial, and fingers of accusation have been pointed at absolutist governance, the economic crisis, deviationist tendencies and foreign intrigues. I cannot refute a word of it, or the accusations, and nor do I mean to play down the need for advice and a cure. God has asked us to be upright in everything we say and do but I think that the root of the whole disease lies in something I can characterise with one word: treatment. National unity is a meaningless slogan if not based on full respect for human rights, if it is sullied by unjust and discriminatory treatment, or if it categorises its citizens into first and second class groups. It is a citizen's right to carry out his job and to serve his homeland with all his abilities and sense of ethics in a way no less sanctified than his right to practice his religious feelings. For that reason the finger of blame should be pointed at the state as the institution responsible for establishing the balance of justice and equality among its people.

I would state that treating the people fairly is alone sufficient to contain all the crises and tensions, whereas discrimination causes alienation, worry and instability. Even if all the other causes were to disappear, perhaps the real reason for discrimination is not intolerance, as it would appear, but in fact it is brought about by a corrupt administration which operates on the basis of nepotism, favouritism and patronism, and which does injustice to many, many more Muslims than Copts for whom it appears to be a sectarian issue. National unity is not just a slogan, or fine words or fond memories. First and foremost it means real and serious respect for human rights. May those who follow good guidance be at peace.

12 April 1987

The New Parliament

If we look beyond the discussion about the soundness of the election as claimed by those with vested reasons to say as much, we can state that if the new parliament reflects almost comprehensively the trends prevalent in our time, each trend has its own symbols, and if the number of seats they acquire has changed proportionately to the number of votes received, this has given everyone the opportunity to participate in political activity in parliament, which is a step in our current life towards overcoming obstacles and registering the democratic progress that we welcome with all our hearts. At the same time this also imposes upon the new parliament the trust of the nation which it must assume with enough force to deal with the challenges suffocating us, to find a path for our salvation no matter how long it takes and how much effort it requires.

We demand that the majority should behave with the magnanimity of the strong. They must be open to dealing with the opposition and allow them the space to carry out their duty, just as we demand that the opposition should behave with seriousness and objectivity, apply themselves to the great problems of the day and come up with resolute decisions without going in for horse-trading on the one hand or flattery on the other. We demand that they should continue to track down corruption and its sources, and that everyone, the government and the opposition, should work on building up the country and putting an end to all forms of underdevelopment. I, and perhaps many other people too, hope that alongside this desired work there will be ongoing support for democracy, that firm foundations will be put in place for solving our economic problem in terms of productivity, consumer activity and loans, in putting into action what the constitution stipulates with regard to Islamic law, by placing our national unity on the robust foundations which will enable it to rise above crises and intrigues and make it the ultimate starting point for a complete national rebirth, domestically and internationally.

I hope starting from today that we will devote ourselves to our own preoccupations, that we will only be concerned by our own worries, and that we will not expend our strength on things that do not offer us progress or prosperity in this age which offers no mercy to those who lag behind or those who cannot play their part.

I pray God to grant the new parliament health and well-being, that it may last its term with stability in the shadow of the constitution and with its help. Amen.

16 April 1987

Public Holiday and Remembrance

We are now coming up to a public holiday which invites everyone, friend and foe alike, to a pure feast of joy. The poet, Abu al-Ala' al-Ma'arri 973–1057 noted how sadness stays with us longer than happiness when he wrote: 'Sorrow at the hour of death outweighs all happiness at the hour of birth.'

This is why we do not forget 5 June 1967, and we always remember it tinged with deep pain and latent anger. As for the liberation of Sinai, after long and humiliating years of occupation, we can hardly bring ourselves to mention it at any other time, and some people may recall it with a sense of offence or hostility that detracts from the great feat of the man who brought it about, Anwar Sadat, who in doing so provided an enormous service to his nation that should not be forgotten. Had it not been for the unwelcome deviations in our economic opening-up, as well as liberating our territory he would have brought about our economic liberation and we would have been rescued from falling into the abyss we are in now due to the pressure of inflation, debts, and our shameful dependency on imported food. However, in the same way as justice censures wrongdoing, it rewards good behaviour: 'Whoever does an atom's weight of good will see it, and whoever does an atom's weight of evil will see it.'[1] So, despite disagreements and bad memories, we must recognise the hero of Sinai's liberation for his glorious victory, for liberating the territory of Sinai and his nation, and his sincere endeavours to bring about a comprehensive peace.

Therefore, this day should be an occasion for us to remember our national unity which is the sound foundation of every revolution we have carried out, and every victory we have won in our history. Let us remember the blood shed by the Muslim and Coptic soldiers who fell in battle under the banner of human rights and the duties of a decent citizen. Let it also be an occasion for us to remember our liberation heroes, such as Ahmose I, Umar Makram, Ahmed Urabi, Mustafa Kamil, Mohammed Farid, Saad Zaghloul, Mustafa al-Nahhas,

1 Qur'an, 99:7–8.

Mohammed Naguib and Gamal Abdel Nasser, who live on in our hearts and in the heart of their God. Let us turn Liberation Day into a festival of purity, freedom, social justice, labour and productivity for Egypt which seems to have been created to challenge disaster, crises, intrigues and trials but whose path is always directed towards progress, civilisation, science and faith.

23 April 1987

The Human Resources Conference

An important conference on an educational programme for Egypt has been scheduled for the period of 11th to 13th of April by the New Education League of Cairo's Ain Shams University. Parliament has already prepared briefing papers brimming with pertinent ideas and constructive approaches. Obviously, it is not opinions we are lacking, but we have the greatest need for decisive action to be taken in implementing a reform to a system that has been subjected to a torrent of criticism and complaints.

Education is something that we need to tend to and nurture. It is what guarantees the fate of our primary resource, by which I mean our human capital upon whom depend consequently the future lot of the nation and its creative response to the problems of today and tomorrow. I do not intend to go back to listing all the faults, that would be no more than expressing hostility, and they represent an enormous workload to be dealt with by those responsible and those in authority, and to be stumbled through by those who deal with youth issues at all stages. I think that the whole matter should be handed over to the experts, and I would be satisfied with a statement of general principles that can win over everyone who has a love for his country and hopes for its future.

We always hope to see education establishing a constructive conversation between our inherited values and the modern age with its values, a conversation between enlightened religion and the teaching of culture, aesthetics and sport. We hope that the individual will be able to achieve a working life that offers him success and prominence in whatever academic studies or practical training he engages in. And we hope, and this is most important, that his outlook and behaviour will move on from a reliance on rote learning to a reliance on his intelligence, on his ability to think and innovate, on his ability to face up to problems and solve them. A good education starts off as a response to a simple yet tricky question: 'How do we want the individual to be? And how do we want society to be?' Behind every flourishing nation you will find an outstanding educational system. The most important thing for us is to believe, to come to a decision, and to start.

30 April 1987

The People and the Battle

We are in a civilisational predicament whose outward appearances manifest themselves in a sick economy, declining morals and an alarming political battle, in addition to the bad omens all around us spreading their evil from east and west as the government exerts all its efforts, which to date are represented in its first five-year plan and which are about to be invested in its second five-year plan. But where are the people and what is their role in this battle whose outcome will decide their fate? It would be neither exaggerated nor pessimistic of me to say that the ongoing challenge is still greater than the effort being expended and that we must confront it with all our will and might, armed with patience, strength and perseverance.

We are facing a damnable enemy which must be met face on by an army that is large enough and thoroughly prepared, that is driven by a sense of morality, by nationalist zeal and firm resolve. We must do more than fight it in the arenas of government and party politics. We must prompt a general mobilisation which includes every citizen, calls upon him to offer up his labour, depends upon his self-motivation and his inner conviction, and all the while the essential question is: how can we mobilise such an army? And how can we call upon it to offer up its labour so that our consciences are satisfied that we, in this fateful situation, have done everything we can without complacency, sloth or negligence?

In order to make every individual shoulder his responsibility and set aside his sense of isolation and alienation, we must speak to him in words which affect his very being, just as happened over his deep-rooted history. We must use language other than that of decrees and propaganda, language that embodies ideals, that speaks with true seriousness, that respects human rights and the individual's right to participate actively in decision-making. We must respect the individual in words and deeds. We must also annul the laws which take the edge off his will. We must allow him full freedom to form political parties, support his unfettered freedom of choice, treat him in a manner which complies with his full equality and the rule of law, and we must clear his path by putting an end to government prerequisites, nepotism and favouritism. We must make the individual truly feel that the country is founded on a sense of fair play, that the country belongs to him and that he is responsible for it. We must make him feel that his rulers are no more than hirelings who have been chosen to serve him in exchange for the salary he pays them out of his hard-earned money. At that point, and only then, will the real battle begin.

7 May 1987

The Flood and the Ark

The young man said: 'You are urging me to put my name in the electoral register as both my right and obligation. But what do the elections mean? What do rights mean? And what do obligations mean? They are just hollow words. I am in a state of total despair and utter pessimism. I do not trust anything anyone says, I have no faith in any action, and the present and past mean nothing to me. I was given a substandard education. I was assigned a job that means nothing to me and is of no benefit to mankind – which is actually a form of constructive unemployment, as people say. I am paid such a pittance that I have no independence from my poverty-stricken family. I am deprived of the essential requirements of life, such as love, marriage and housing. I live without hope in a gloomy world, besieged by squalidness, noise, opportunists and thieves on the one hand, and by millions of scoundrels on the other, within an unjust and unreceptive society which calls out mendaciously for the rule of law and fair play but practises discrimination and favouritism. This is the situation for us young people, and the only people who can avoid this are those lucky enough to have a rich father or mother, or who have found a job abroad which can alter the scales. So don't talk to me about elections, rights and obligations, or the tomorrow which is supposed to arrive full of hope and prosperity.'

Actually, had I not heard these raw grumblings time and time again, I would not have come to the point of setting them down in writing and publishing them. It serves no use simply to ignore them and that would not be the mark of a wise person. Perhaps it is the voice of a whole generation and not just of an individual. Perhaps it is the instinctive comment about an era in which our civilisation has been crushed by catastrophes. It could also be the case that this youth, having been overwhelmed by his dire personal situation, has lost the ability to see things as a whole, is doing a great disservice to the idea of constructive work and sincere effort, and can see no glimpse of hope shining on the horizon. But who could not forgive this of a young man who has lost his means of subsistence and subsequently his sense of happiness?

We should ask ourselves seriously how we can provide reassurance to a nation that has within itself such an amount of despair, anger and resentment? How can the nation desist for even a moment from restructuring itself, improving its behaviour and throwing itself wholeheartedly into productivity and reform? We are in a race between the flood and the ark which can only be built with the help of faith, learning and work.

14 May 1987

The Dark Side of the Moon

I read a statistic confirming that the number of those old enough to vote is double that of the people recorded on the electoral register, and that those who performed their electoral duty represent under half of those registered. This suggests that three quarters of the electorate refrained from carrying out their electoral duty so what do we have to say about this phenomenon?

Perhaps those who did not vote include people who refused to vote out of what they see as a sense of conscience over what is taking place. It could be because they reject the regime or believe the elections to be lacking in integrity. Regardless of any discussion as to their opinion, they should not be considered pessimists, and nor should their views be dismissed with the comment that they should just have gone to the polling booths to register their anti-government votes. As for the others – and I fear that they are the overwhelming majority – they are the ones we could accuse of indifference, the people for whom the election campaign makes no difference, for whom events pass by unnoticed, or who simply stand scoffing on the side-lines as if they live in their own world devoid of principles, with no political or moral aims, people ruled by selfishness and immersed in their own issues, people whose stance you might describe as lacking in nationalist education, as having been adversely affected by living under an authoritarian system of government, as having been drained by the economic crisis or as embodying all the foregoing. However, under any circumstances they represent a negative force, a latent force for wrong-doing and hell-bent upon wreaking havoc and bringing destruction down upon us. We have to drag them out of their lairs, whether by raising their awareness, through reform, by setting an example and by ongoing political work. This is the duty of our educated and thoughtful leaders, and of all those who provide general services to the people across the whole spectrum of areas, for they all have the power to bring those scattered forces to the side of constructiveness.

21 May 1987

Hidden Evil

We should not put up with negativity or consider it a minor lapse which can be condoned. It is a latent and dangerous evil against which we must arm ourselves with the same means of resistance we use against aberrant behaviour, pollution and betrayals of faith. Moreover, it is something which exudes unbounded evil and which should be done away with. It is not a solidly rooted characteristic of our nation, rather a symptom of the diseases which infect us in the maelstrom of our political and economic crisis. If it were a particular distinguishing mark of our character, the people would not have been able to come together as one splendid fighting unit, as they did during our consecutive revolutions at the time of the French invasion, the Urabi uprising, the revolutions of 1919 and 1925, or during the military campaigns of 1956 or 6 October 1973.

Let us take a look at how the religious movements have managed to conscript thousands of our young people, and how they have inculcated them with a new spirit of zeal, self-sacrifice, discipline and idealism. Since their activists have succeeded in doing all that, our political campaigners should take a look at what their own message is lacking, for our present situation proves that it is full of positive capabilities and of confused and scattered forces waiting for someone to give the right call, to set about doing the right sort of work, someone who can act as an example and an ideal. It must be mentioned too that we lack neither the zeal nor the commitment, even when it comes to issues of entertainment, such as sport, and we can see this in the way the masses show their support for their sports clubs or in the way all of Cairo erupts following a match.

Hence, our inner core is still good and energetic. We just need to find someone to blow the dust away, to polish it, and to breathe into it the spirit of resolve and hard work. What we really need is to see a comprehensive national rebirth with an energetic and comprehensive basis that is motivated by enthusiasm and that burns with faith and ideals.

We must therefore fight negativity with all the means at our disposal.

It is not the job of the leadership alone. We have to undertake hard work, offer improved services, respect for human rights and unfettered democracy, the rule of law and that sense of fair play which is the very foundation of good governance. We may be able to discern signs of reform in government decrees, but any talk of decrees or reform is in vain if the people are not included.

28 May 1987

Democracy and the Battle

Some people imagine that force is a specific attribute of a dictatorial regime, whereas democracy is distinguished by the element of freedom without coercion. This image is faulty. Democracy is also powerful and able to defend itself most efficiently. Moreover, it is even mightier than other forms of government. It can resort to armed force, just like other forms of government, as well as having some more effective means which other systems do not possess, such as freedom in expressing opinion and debates, and respect for human rights. It can both keep the peace and wage war. In times of peace refined values come to the fore, and even when its opponents force it into war it does not neglect its values. It fights for the law and in the shadow of the law. It meets injustice with fair play and it metes out a deterrent punishment for terrorism without, for its part, sinking into injustice, terrorism or a callous disregard for the law and values.

We may well be going through crises. Some people may well act outside the law, or ignore the rulings of the judiciary. Things may deteriorate to the point where students, parents and teachers all conspire to cheat. Terrorism may take up its operations again and lead to bloodshed. But none of that means that democracy has gone to pieces, is on shaky ground or has lost confidence in itself. Everything we are going through at the moment is the legacy of decades of injustice and tyranny, but democracy demands that it should start by looking at itself, by offering an example and an ideal for chipping away corruption and apathy, for providing the requisite respect for the law and for justice, and for cleansing itself of every last remnant of injustice, violence and terrorism. Then it will be able apply all its capabilities to any battle imposed on it for the sake of freedom and freedom of opinion. Force should only be used against those who only understand force, but democracy is the stronger the freer it is, and the more it conforms with the law and with the ideals of humanity.

4 June 1987

The Greatest Problem

We are indeed facing many challenges, but there is a particularly hard challenge which stands alone like the solid rock of fate. Challenges such as the economic crisis, our loans, low productivity, the negativity rife among the population, the problems facing democracy and foreign policy, are all challenges which can be solved and we will overcome them over time with careful contemplation and hard work. However, behind all that is a problem that appears to be insoluble, or that needs a miracle to be solved, and that is the issue of the population explosion. In our current situation, it is this problem whose roots lie deep within all the other problems, sometimes as the only cause, at other times as the overwhelming cause, or at least as a contributing factor. It is the thing we really should be worrying about night and day. It means that the ship is so overloaded that it is day by day threatened with capsizing even if it manages to stay plague-free and its passengers possess the means of looking after their health and well-being.

Traditional solutions for the problem are no longer valid for our times. In times gone by, invading one's neighbour would have been a means of creating some extra living space and the same can be applied to mass emigration. In our times we can no longer invade neighbours and mass migration can only take place under short-lived emergency conditions. One might add that family planning as we know it has not had any effect. All we have left are the most up-to-date means, such as using scientific knowledge to conquer the desert, or to resort to using sterner measures than we have so far experienced to implement family planning, in order to avoid food shortages, or what is even worse, chaos.

Let us all remain aware that our situation should not allow us to overlook a single one of our population. The least that we have to do is to equip every individual with the knowledge, learning and ethics he needs so that he can manage to eke out a living at home in Egypt or elsewhere if Egypt does not offer him enough opportunity. We have to free ourselves of all other challenges so that we can devote ourselves to the most important one of them all.

4 June 1987

Disease Spreads to the Core

In the flood of gloom, hearts usually turn towards education as a way of beaming ourselves into a better future, and as a workshop for turning out the new models of humans equipped for all branches of modern life and better able to deal with its burdens. Then along comes the phenomenon of general dishonesty, and life comes crashing down around them, mercilessly concealing all hope in a cloud of black dust. To state it more bluntly, it snatches away from us that period of innocence, purity, principles and ideals. It means a demeaning disregard for the achievements of science, knowledge, learning and aptitude for work. It means reaching for the fruit, i.e. the certificate, even if you have to employ devious methods to acquire it, and then you can carry on being in turn corrupt, ignorant and of almost no use to society.

This is an evil that we must marshal our forces to confront and finish off. We must cut it off at the trunk, using our resolve and the weapons provided by the law. We should also take another thorough look at the whole education system and dispense with examinations. We should call experts in to find an alternative system whereby a child's learning ability and achievements can be assessed. Likewise, we should look at teaching methods and do our utmost to root out substandard teachers.

We are now reaping the serious consequences of tyranny and its corruption, of daylight robbery, of having lived with apathy and neglect, of disregard for the law, an era of kleptocrats and of money flooding into the hands of the trusted and privileged few. And now we are reaping the serious consequences of the disregard shown by some powerful figures on the one hand, and of the patience and silence of the people on the other. We are all called upon, and the minister of education more than anyone else, to remedy this disaster at any cost, with any amount of sacrifice, decisively and quickly before we have to croak out our farewell to the world.

11 June 1987

Towards a New Future

Our stance with regard to modern civilisation has two dimensions. On the one hand, we noticed its glimmer after it reached a great peak which made it the object of aspirations requiring almost impossible effort, continuous work and never-ending enthusiasm. On the other hand, our state of underdevelopment enabled us to see its full shape, with all its rudiments and consequences, to see both the positive achievements and negative sides. It has made superlative and startling advances in science, huge strides forward in agriculture, industry and prosperity, created monuments of genius in the arts, literature and culture, and great improvements in governance, administration and politics. However, at the same time it has committed savage crimes, spilt the valuable blood of its children and of other nations' children, mercilessly sanctified materialist market values, exhausted their spiritual sources, and assailed nature, polluting its beauty and reserves. Then it went on to invent forms of power which would enable it to destroy the whole earth and everything on it, both living and inanimate.

It is in this great world of progress and underdevelopment that we make our way towards the future. It is within our power to turn our late arrival on the scene into something good, that is, to turn it into an opportunity to take stock of things and decide on the right direction to take. We have to take on all the new scientific developments and prepare ourselves to innovate with them. We must preserve our lofty spiritual values and rely on ourselves to create a constituent relationship for our society without being bogged down by tradition or blind imitation.

If we do that, we will be able to turn the dishonour imposed on us into something positive. We will be able to prepare ourselves to carry a new message to humanity, containing the very best of our ancient civilisation, and the best that this new civilisation can offer, within an almost perfect human framework with as few flaws as possible.

The hour has come for us to await that thinker who will crystallise this dream into a theory and, more importantly, to wait for the people to come along and turn this into a living reality.

16 June 1987

Terrorism and Stability

Whenever an act of terrorism takes place, we trumpet the claim that it is an attack on our stability. The more this happens, the more we become aware of the effect of terrorism on stability. Consequently, the country's stability is more exposed to the danger of terrorism and all this just plays into the hands of the enemy. However, gentlemen, no matter how rampant terrorism becomes, it cannot undermine stability, for terrorism is just one of the many crimes committed every year but politics assigns it a special place. It may cause a temporary upset or uproar, but it is incapable of undermining the stability of a secure society, and hence we should fight it with all legitimate means without disregarding its effect or overestimating the danger it represents.

Work will not stop for a moment, and nor will development, due to a gun being fired or a bomb going off, and we should not bewail or mourn for our stability. If it can be shaken by a crime, then it cannot be called stability. Stability is civilisation. It is the rule of law. It is respect for human rights. It is labour and productivity. It is a lack of corruption in political life and a never-failing hope. It cannot be shaken by a crime or a series of crimes. The dust of terrorism has spread through one of the most ancient countries in the world and in the most violent and savage ways, but it has not undermined Egypt's stability, damaged its reputation, nor deterred tourists.

Egypt will continue to be Egypt whether it lives in the shadow of security or in the mire of terrorism. Work will not stop, our determination will not give out and nor will our will weaken. People will carry on dying, whether at home, in bed or on the road. It is up to God to do what he wishes, how he wishes and when he wishes.

18 June 1987

A New Five-Year Plan

We have started implementing the new five-year plan which, as you know, is a comprehensive plan aiming to develop all aspects of our economy, society and culture. I am impressed by those who have come up with a national project we can gather around and who have done the research, but what project is more important than progress in a competitive era? And what battle is riskier than that of fighting underdevelopment? The five-year plan is a vital, renewable and available project which only needs sensible and effective publicity in order to be implanted firmly within people's hearts and minds.

This leads me to wonder why, in preparing the new five-year plan, we have not reported on what we have and have not completed in the previous five-year plan? This would be an important thing for us to study and learn from so that we can make clear our determination to get beyond our crisis and embark on our journey forward. The first thing to notice is that the debate on the budget and the five-year plan took place in parliament in an unseemly rush. Actually it is the right of a member of parliament to make whatever useful contributions he wishes to make to a debate, even if this prolongs the discussion by two or three months.

We should just hope that we can make serious and redoubled progress, represented by our commitment to austerity measures in spending, to improving tax collection, and to using the rule of law to instil a sense of order. We should insist upon productivity being increased. We should take another look at state holidays and wasted time and we should draw up sound regulations governing incentives and restrictions based on the assumption that productivity is the very essence of life, of our cultural rebirth and of our hope.

We should also pay more attention to renewing and reforming our teaching methods, and I would say that we almost need to give education in our country a complete overhaul after wasted years of neglect which ended up with students running around with qualifications gained through cheating. Education should also incorporate culture in all of its forms, such as literature, music and the plastic arts. There is no longer any room for complacency in the way we build up the individual or contemplate the future in an age in which progress proceeds at the speed of light.

I do not know how many five-year plans will be implemented until we achieve our equilibrium and until a shining future starts to take shape in front of our eyes. However, I do believe that our only means of achieving this is work, work and more work.

9 July 1987

The Revolution of 23 July

Revolution is the greatest method of testing a people who wish for life. It is a test of their spirit, intellect, will and capacity for innovation and challenging difficulties, of their ability to act wisely in victory and defeat, in hope and despair... The people should not let a huge and significant experiment that took place over the course of time to be of no value or allow it to become as unto nothing due to a flood of mistakes and difficulties.

Revolution does not come about out of the blue, as 'the blue' cannot bring about revolutions. It is not the result of a domestic or foreign plot, for a plot may only exploit existing opportunities or circumstances and cannot create the real ground for a revolution to produce its preordained fruit. Similarly, a revolution does not chant slogans for the fun of it or to mislead people as to its real intent, and, indeed, as various ideas win out over others, the slogans, reacting like the organs of a living body, will immediately start to reflect this.

Not only may a revolution make egregious errors, or sometimes take the wrong path and its downsides may start piling up, but its accomplishments may, through mismanagement, turn into losses or deficits. However, none of that is, or can be, sufficient to call for the revolution to be liquidated and the desire to see it punished cannot slip over into a desire to see people punished or create disorder. All that should spur us on to repair things that have gone wrong, to learn our lessons, to correct the course of the revolution, to snatch its achievements from the clutches of bad luck and miscalculation and then to steer the wheel as forcefully as possible towards creating a just and modern society based on cohesion, national unity, freedom, learning and belief in the luxuriant shade of respect for human rights.

Every Egyptian should see the revolution as a historic enterprise that will remain a symbol of his yearning for liberation from colonialism, oppression and injustice, and a symbol of his visceral desire to live in the modern era with all its enlightenment and miracles.

We should support those charged by history with eradicating the errors of the revolution, promoting its achievements, calming anxieties, and restoring consideration and rights to the eternal people of Egypt.

23 July 1987

Between Suicide and Famine

I read a news item that informed me that twelve million[1] [*sic*] people commit suicide every year in France, but despite that France is a nation that falls in the middle of the suicide table, above West Germany and Britain, and below Denmark, Austria and Switzerland. The number is rather baffling, particularly since it applies to countries which are considered to have the highest levels of civilisation and culture, and some of which are considered to be a paradise on earth.

You may recall the millions of people carried off by death in the Third World, as a result of famine, poverty and underdevelopment. In general, the world is in a bad shape. In the poor South, we find millions of people dying due to poverty and underdevelopment, and in the rich North we find millions of people dying even though they are sheltered by prosperity and progress.

The causes of death in the Third World are well known and have nothing to do with people actually wishing to fall victim to them. However, what leads a person to commit suicide when he is comfortably seated on the throne of civilisation and progress? Is it due to untreatable diseases? Is it due to the burden of work and the weight of responsibility in a world that demands the individual to give ever more and more and to pay an ever higher price? Is it due to the fears and obligations that overwhelm him from all corners of the civilised world and which threaten an individual with annihilation in various ways? Is it because of deprivation of the divine protection people turn to in at times of hardship?

Whatever the case may be, the picture is still an ugly one. This said and done, it does not call for pessimism. The living still not only people the earth, but threaten its stability with a population explosion. Progress is still taking firm steps forward, bulldozing away the mounds of underdevelopment. The North and South are still being summoned to take part in a fruitful discussion that may save humanity from killing itself off, and to bring about enough self-respect to protect it from the destruction wrought by famine and underdevelopment and saving it from defeat and extinction.

30 July 1987

---

1 Mahfouz writes 'million' but he must mean 'thousand'.

The Meaning of Stability

We talk a lot about stability, we yearn for it and call for it to be protected from harm coming from all directions. This is not surprising, since it is the pediment upon which our hopes stand, the starting point for our development journey and the foundation of any wise policy, but just what does stability mean? I imagine that we conflate it with public security, and there is unarguably a close connection between the two, but stability is a distinct element. A stable society is not one devoid of criminality and violence, for if that were the case we would not be able to describe it as stable.

Do we not hear commentators speaking about the lack of security in cities throughout America? Do we not read daily about incidences of rape in London? Do we not follow the news about gruesome terrorist incidents in Germany, France, Italy and England?

However, does anyone dare to criticise the government of those countries for being unstable? If we look for the real meaning of stability in the relationship between the people and the state, we find that it is only stable if based on a foundation of mutual trust – the trust that comes to light when the state performs its obligations and provides services, and when the people respond by supporting the state with their hearts, words and hands. It is within an atmosphere of honesty and openness that this valuable trust can be born, in an atmosphere where people receive fair treatment, which is itself the foundation of rule, in the shadow of the supremacy of, and respect for, the law, and in a space that allows for the respect of human rights.

We may find that within the shadow of stability the people will accept a low income, and a minimum of comforts, patiently put up with many other evils and be able forcefully to withstand acts of criminality, terrorism, temptations, and domestic and external plots. We may find that the people become an invincible body, able to withstand the vicissitudes of the weather, resist epidemics and emerge hale and hearty.

That, without under- or overestimating the issue, is what stability means.

12 August 1987

The Sun Will Rise Again

In order to be able to live, we need to do a bit of underhand dealing. That is not an invitation to do evil, but an evil truth. The powerful, goaded on by power and opportunities, do underhand deals, and the weak, driven on by their powerlessness and provocation, also do underhand deals. The law has almost ground to a standstill, and the workers have given up and gone on strike. People are running around in the wrong direction, and those trying to eke out a living have fallen into the dark web of corruption. In this frenetic atmosphere, it does no good to offer advice, to recount parables or fine memories. This chaotic atmosphere is watched over by greed on the one hand, and by fear and hunger on the other. Nothing should astonish you anymore – such as a trader selling rotten food, importing radioactive foodstuffs, or hawking dodgy pharmaceuticals. And nor should you be astonished at the spread of prostitution and large-scale scams.

Don't expect goodness to proceed from nice words, for the roar of desires has turned us deaf and blind. Don't wait for resoluteness, for those who express it are themselves polluted, and those who carry it out have dirty hands. And work? Does this mean that we should resign ourselves to despair and defeat? Not at all. I have said this because it is what I believe, and not to make light about the situation. Were we not in the same or a somewhat similar boat on 12 November 1919? Or on 22 July 1952? Of course we were. Then overnight it became 13 November and 23 July respectively, so why will the day of democracy, lofty values, and good work not come?

People's nature may lean towards the malign, but their nature will also refuse to surrender or submit to defeat. Their nature also has latent powers of good, of living a decent life and being constructive. They will confront the rot and fight with unsheathed sword as they put out their sincere call for us to take on our values again, to apply science to increasing productivity and the labour force, and, as they do so, they will drive away the clouds of gloom and allow the sun to shine again.

27 August 1987

In Commemoration of the 1919 Revolution – Again

The anniversary of the deaths of Saad Zaghloul and Mustafa al-Nahhas is a vivid and constant memorial to independence, freedom, national unity, democracy and the probity of governance. Those two great men represent a school of thought which is deep rooted in our long history. It is a school we grew up in and graduated from, having found principles which both enrich our hearts and enlighten our intellects, and perhaps it is the right moment to mark that legacy which we love and cherish with the hope that it has gone some way to creating a useful citizen. That school provided us with an education inculcated in us through eloquent words and noble and brave deeds, by setting us a good example of how to be motivated by a love for Egypt. That was what we aimed for and our education could include any new principle as long as it was original, for by that school's very nature we were taught to be open to the new. Over time we became distracted by human tendencies, by socialist tendencies, but Egyptian nationalism remained the be all and end all.

From that love of country grew the concept of national unity. Its roots spread out firmly and our throats warbled its sweet melodies: 'It is God who shapes religion and we who shape our country,' and God supported us and helped us to get beyond our trials and tribulations for we placed our faith in the people as the source of all authority, as the source of power in the state and the pillars of national rebirth. We came together to oppose any form of accursed autocracy, believing in the struggle, in patience and in coping with adversity even if it bore no fruit, or if that fruit was fated to be given to others. We also believed in behaving with uprightness and integrity. We avoided the temptations of life, but we adored what was good, right and beautiful. Influenced by our school we were eventually ready to welcome, and become part of, the July Revolution at the same time as protesting against its monarchical method of governance.

O Saad! How many times did I yell out your name when I was

young! O Mustafa! How many times did I bellow your name when I was a young man! And today as an old man the mention of your names still provides light to a day in need of guidance.

30 August 1987

Unifying the Two Sectors

Poverty-stricken Egypt is going through the bitterest of times. The country can just about snatch a morsel of food from the claws of galloping inflation and it is beset with disputes over its path forward and its values, over everything including housing and medicine. Time passes by and no one seems to care a whit about the country. Fathers walk around in a state of gloom, their children have no future, and Egypt's life is a sad one with no happy memories.

The rich country of yore is floundering as it tries to enjoy the fruit of advanced civilisations. The country's funds have been frozen, smuggled out of the country and dispersed, while some of its citizens are rolling around in luxury. The country's mode of behaviour is provocative. It has completely forgotten that those funds have come from a poor country. It does not return a greeting. It does not speak a language. It has its night-clubs and art, and its home-made dreams.

The government sits on the fence, now speaking the language of the poor, now speaking the language of the rich. It would like to unify the two sectors, bringing them together. In an attempt to do so, five-year plan after five-year plan is carried out, speaking the language of democracy and holding up the banners of the law and calling for increased labour and productivity.

In a climate like this germs breed. Frustrated people take the law into their own hands and the clouds of frightening possibilities gather on the distant horizon.

What should be asked of the government, in addition to the effort it has already made? It needs to clean up its act, get rid of privileges, improve its reputation and devote more resolve and determination to respecting the law and human rights.

What should be asked of the rich in Egypt?

They must wake up from their selfish coma, from their drunken psychosis and their children should pay their dues to the country. They should invest their excess money in the five-year plan – in order to protect themselves as much as to protect the country.

What should be asked of the poor in Egypt?

They have already put up with more than any human being should have to bear. All they have to do is to hone their minds to find the way forward, repeating the wise words they have learnt from their long history: hard times do not mean the end for humanity. They help a person to find his inner strength and to unsheathe his will in order to fight the challenges.

10 September 1987

Cultural Hopes

In our cultural life there are springboards for work and engines for hope which, if we nurture them, will light candles in the stagnant darkness, and this includes following up on the decision which has been made to establish an encyclopaedia. The minister of culture does not need anybody to remind him of cultural affairs, and we should recall his dedication to the service of high culture as represented by the publishing sector and how his ministry has actively contributed to this, whether in terms of productivity, distribution and affordability, as well as what he has personally done recently to remove the red tape from imports and exports of books. Perhaps we will soon receive the good news about work starting on the encyclopaedia project for which we have waited so long.

We should also mention the state television and its cultural services, as well as the role television plays in spreading general culture to the classes deprived of it. This is a historic role for which it should be credited over the decades, but the state television should redouble its efforts with regard to high culture during a difficult time which has little regard for culture and values.

The field is wide open for anyone who wishes to work, whether in showing a selection of cultural works, domestic and international, or in coming up with programmes that deal with intellectual affairs and literature. Public interest in culture could be encouraged, as with sport, although the numbers will perhaps be lower. That is how the television could play a spectacular role in rebuilding our national character which has been so damaged by our national crises.

Then we come to the woes of Egyptian filmmaking, not just its success but its continuity. Should this not require the elite of our cinematographers, creators and producers, to sit down with officials from the Ministry of Culture and research the matter thoroughly and come up with suggestions as to what needs to be done and what legislation needs to be passed to save the film industry from its current ordeal and enable it once again to perform its role in shaping the spirit of society?

I hope that inaction does not turn into despair, but that it spurs us on to action itself.

17 September 1987

Yes

I shall vote for President Hosni Mubarak with a clear conscience, and I call upon every citizen to vote for him and that includes the Wafdists who should be the first to do so out of their sense of nationalism and democracy. I cannot deny that I was surprised by their decision to boycott the elections as a symbol of their constitutional demands and I would go even further than that by stating that I agree with them when it comes to the need for political reform and the need to rescind those laws that are no longer fit for purpose. However, I have to part ways with them when they state that the president is proceeding to the referendum without a programme. We do not need any presidential statement to explain the programme to us. We have actually known what it has been over the six years during which he has publicly declared his attachment to democracy, even in the most difficult of circumstances. We have known him as an example of nationalism, as an ideal of integrity and incorruptibility. We have known him as the defender of independence, the servant of peace, the trustee of Arabism and Africanism, of Islam and of national unity. We have seen him nurture productivity, believing in the power of labour and of the workers, and as the enemy of bureaucracy. God gave him the vision to see inside workplaces and hold discussions with those involved in productivity. As he has done all of this in the recent past, it should not be too difficult for us to see into the near future. Those angered by corruption or the ill repute of some of our laws would not be wrong to pin their hopes on him straightening the crooked, removing the corrupt and steering the country along the path of hope. It would be the best thing for us all if he could continue along his course, helped by the people with the same amount of support that helped him the first time, so that he can draw strength from that support, so that he can derive his sense of responsibility from it and be encouraged to work even harder, buoyed by his overwhelming popularity. It is for that reason that I call upon every citizen to overcome his negativity, which is an evil every bit as great as corruption or laws of ill repute, and to declare his positivity by giving practical support on referendum day, that is, by saying yes to democracy, social justice, clean politics, science and labour.

24 September 1987

Terrorism

We can only understand the phenomenon of religious terrorist extremism by going back into history. The oft-repeated explanations given today that it has arisen as the bitter outcome of torture in prison, or that it stems from the youth's frustration because of the economic crisis, do not hold water. The proof of that is that it existed and went out of control before the crisis, and that torture in prison is a result of terrorism and not its cause. The most those factors did was to exacerbate it. It has existed since Islam first emerged, and I would not be straying from the truth if I state that it is not only an explicable phenomenon but that it was justified during the history of the Islamic state itself. It has existed since the time the Islamic state created a civilisation, absorbing positive and negative elements; since the time the Muslims entered the world scene flush with funds, giving in to their desires. This gave rise to a harsh reaction from two groups of people: a moderate group who promoted piety, abstemiousness and an avoidance of worldly temptations – the very beginnings of the mystical path in Islam; and an extremist group who declared the state and society un-Islamic, unsheathing their swords to effect a complete change in the system of governance. These movements have existed through Islamic history, up to the appearance of the Wahhabis, the Senussis, the Mahdists and more recently the Muslim Brotherhood.

Religious terrorist extremism is the other face of dissolution and corruption and it aims at purifying society and restoring its balance. In times gone by it resorted to violence because there was no other way of expressing opposition. However today there can be no justification at all in an age of freedom and in a multi-party system, particularly now that the voice of Islamism has found its way into parliament. Nevertheless, it would appear that the phenomenon needs new social, political and security solutions.

When it comes to social solutions, that means seriously facing up to the manifestations of corruption within the administration and in our general life. The political solutions must allow people the right to form political parties and to establish newspapers without let or hindrance.

If, at that point, a nation insists on using violence, that means that they are simply a people with a penchant for violence and terrorism who wish to subjugate others by force and through fear. In those circumstances, society can only face up to them with determination and resolve in order to defend their freedom and dignity.

31 September 1987

6 October and the Best of Memories

6 October comes around crowned with good tidings and delight, as an inspiration for renewed energy, application and hope along the road of building up the country and of freedom. It brings with it the best of memories, and the country shares in the happiness as it elects its trusted president. What we particularly need this year is for it to apply balsam to our hearts which are still bleeding from the accusations of betrayal, of working for foreign interests and of savagery raised against the elite of our commanders and the leaders of our national rebirth. Has the October victory managed to save itself from the slings and arrows of outrageous fortune even though some people only consider it a pseudo-victory?

However, the light spreads over us, dispelling the clouds and the dust and the '6th' has become a holiday, a memorial to the glorious, a symbol of our will and courage, and of our political system. By dint of this light, pride has come flooding in through the windows again accompanied by the thrilling chants of victory, paving the way for peace, and calling upon hearts and minds to concentrate on the concerns we have neglected for so long and to set us on the long path towards rebirth in these modern times that move at record speed.

6 October represents the fruit of a people's determination and their insistence upon a noble life, of the sacrifice of intrepid soldiers who offered up their souls unstintingly for their homeland, of planning carried out by people who lived up magnificently to the trust we placed in them. This is an opportunity for us to congratulate the leaders, and to apologise not only to them for the verbal abuse they have been subjected to but also to the Egyptian people who have been accused of fecklessness and stupidity, for having been duped and for having honoured vicious traitors and agents of foreign powers. It is a day of victory, a day for learning our lesson, a day of solace, a day of reflection and a day of hope.

1 October 1987

And Nothing Is Being Said about Culture

Fine words were spoken about every type of activity but not a word about culture. This is what came up in a long discussion about the achievements made in the first five-year plan that I followed with interest and satisfaction, impressed by the numbers and details. However, what caught my attention is that there was not a single word about culture. Not a question was asked, and of course no response had to be given on the matter. How could that be, when the field of culture has seen memorable and laudable achievements?

The issue, to put it bluntly, is not one that occurs to us or over which we lose any sleep. We do not begrudge it any amount of fine praise and eloquent words when required, but left to our own devices we do not notice culture. That shows most clearly our disregard for its state of decline which is not only evident in our failing cinema, theatre and popular music, or in the enormous drop in the number of serious books produced and in the readership, but it is also just as evident in the place culture occupies in our minds.

Do we still look at culture superficially, seeing it as a luxury, a nice extra touch, or just light entertainment? Is everything that is being said about its role in building up an individual's character, of polishing his intellect and spirit, of developing his ambition – is all of that no more than constructivist rhetoric and prosaic fragments from the past? How can we persuade the unconvinced that the deterioration of culture is one of the foremost causes of much that we suffer from and complain about, such as people's lack of a sense of belonging, their reclusiveness and their falling victim to dark thoughts? Culture, gentlemen, is the key to the personality we are trying to construct. It is the firm foundation of our national rebirth. May God keep the way ahead smooth.

8 October 1987

Axioms of the Revolution

'Everything is open to discussion.' That is an oft-repeated statement that is supported by the spirit of democracy and that accords with the challenges of the crisis. We accept that conditional upon the benefit of the discussion for the general good, and the general good means, first of all, the welfare of broad masses of the people. With that in mind, anyone who wishes can discuss the survival or privatisation of the public sector, whether free education should be subject to a more rational system or abolished, the problem of housing and employment, as well as other intractable subjects which require just solutions.

These problems were originally great achievements made by the July Revolution. At the time they were rightly considered to be great feats, positive accomplishments of the Revolution, which brought about change to the traditional social make-up of our society, which moved us degrees closer to a more just society, and which enabled the poor to enjoy some sense of fairness not experienced since the time the pyramids were built. However, haste and the desire to achieve satisfaction led to mistakes being made, with so much rotten working its way into the country's infrastructure that it went off-target and hastened it towards precocious old age.

It might be right for us to take a new look, to straighten what became crooked and rein in aberrant behaviour, so that we can work on in the spirit of the Revolution which came about for the sake of the people and for the betterment of the broad grassroots. Our thinking should not be affected by self-interest, or class interests, otherwise we will have stripped the legacy of its positive elements while the negative aspects that we have inherited, such as the state of emergency, the discredited laws and the latent desires for authoritarianism – an ever renewing list – are things whose ugly face may never disappear.

We must beware lest we end up ridding ourselves of the positive elements and keeping the negative, lest we fall into a suicidal abyss while deluding ourselves that we have found the heaven of reform.

10 October 1987

MPs' Opinions and Their Wishes

Following any question posed in parliament, and during any debate, particularly one on the budget and the five-year plan, many members speak up, either for or against. Opinions and comments are stated and ministers give their responses, either defending or clarifying. Sometimes they make serious commitments and the debate then moves on to the parliamentary schedule. I would say that any opinion uttered by a member of parliament actually comes from the people and is occasioned by the harsh reality experienced by the masses who are attempting to alleviate their issues and bring about some reform. No issue debated in parliament should be allowed to vanish as if it had never been raised.

Formerly, every ministry used to collate the relevant opinions and wishes of members of parliament by means of their parliamentary secretaries, and during the parliamentary recess they would go over them with their sub-committees and interested parties in Cairo and the provinces. They used to provide an appropriate response to every issue, whether it had to do with expediting or deferring a matter, providing the reasons why something could not be carried out, or answering questions raised by the Committee for Financial Affairs before its annual report. Members of parliament would discuss all these with the relevant minister and the result would be reported to parliament.

I have no idea how the system operates today. Even so, we must preserve the essence of the subject no matter how much the form may have changed. If there is no parliamentary secretary to carry out this task, then the speaker of parliament should form a parliamentary follow-up committee to collate the opinions and wishes of the members and communicate them to the relevant ministries, demanding that they must provide unequivocal answers to be communicated, in turn, to the members of parliament, so that the parliament, at the appropriate time, is provided with good information. As I have stated, the opinion of a member of parliament is actually the opinion of the people, and the opinion of the people must be crowned with resolution. If this principal is upheld, no good word will be spoken in vain.

23 October 1987

The Desired Awareness

Our challenging issues are such that we might compare them to labour pains. The laws which impede our democratic progress, our inability to provide enough food and housing, the deficiencies in teaching and education that threaten our youth, providing enough useful and decently-paid employment, the pollution of our environment, the filthy state of our cities, the corruption in our administration and finances, the absence of the rule of law and our diminished sense of national belonging – all these things and more are symptoms of an unhealthy birth, our birth from nothingness or quasi-nothingness into existence and nothing more.

Our essential problem is a civilisational one. It is that we are lagging behind in all modern economic, social and cultural areas, and this has condemned us to fall behind the developed nations in everything from A to Z. We live in fear of coercion and hunger, overcome by humiliation and alienation. Perhaps we should really have a deep emotional response to our state of catastrophe, a feeling that should pain our consciences, plunge us into wretchedness and pierce the nation to its very marrow. That feeling should spread and its effects should be felt to such an extent by the mighty and the weak, by men and women, that we end up hoping for reality to be overturned and rush forward to change it with all our will and intelligence, and our desire for a better life. It does not matter how long it takes for us to achieve what we want, or how long the road we must cover. The important thing is that we carry on working and struggling hour after hour, day after day. A man who lives fighting for a better life is preferable to a man who gives up in despair, and a man with a job is better than someone who has lost all awareness.

We must fill ourselves with awareness. We must imbibe energy from work. We must free ourselves from everything that hampers our minds and spirits. We must live up to the challenge of having fallen into the pit of apathy and idleness. If we do not drag ourselves up by our bootstraps, there will no one to hold a hand to us. If we do nothing to stave off death, no one is going to sit there mourning us, and in the final analysis this will serve us right. One might say that fate, in all its guises, is only what we create for ourselves.

29 October 1987

Anticipated Hopes

If I were to ask my soul what it is hoping for in the near future, it would not be able to come up with the term 'comprehensive development' from the broad-ranging question. On the one hand the subject includes all activities – from agriculture, industry, teaching, science, health, culture, administration, and general security to defence, scientific research, communications, public hygiene, foreign policy, and so on. On the other hand, it is a reality that mobilises forces to implement it in accordance with scientific planning, vigilant monitoring and executive follow-through – not just a dream and fine hopes. Last but not least, it is a necessity dictated to us by our lives, and required by our existence in this era in which we lag so far behind.

However some activities take up more of my thinking time, not because they are more important, for they are all equally as crucial as any other activity, but because they play a direct role in building up the individual, and it is the individual who is the pivot, the driving force, the aim. That is why I am so obsessed with supporting democracy, with making sure that it has sufficient checks and balances, and that it remains free from impediments. It may be that revising the constitution is something that can be postponed in order to maintain stability in these critical times, but there would be no harm in rescinding many of the discredited laws, by way of example, and what brings me to have an interest in doing this is that it would be the best possible guarantee of our having a decent labour force as well as being an open invitation to the people to head towards the positive and to participate in building up the country from a position of responsibility, and with a sense of nationalism and dignity.

I am also interested in the concept of teaching as something which deals with the most valuable thing we have, which is our manpower, and no one can be unaware of its role in inculcating the citizen with a sense of his nation and its place in this era, with a sense of culture, religious and nationalist education, and in preparing him for a suitable job in these difficult times. I am also minded to see that our administration should become efficient, achievement-orientated, and in the service of the people, and not remain some opaque and backward apparatus that is expert at torturing them with ignorance and inaction, if not with malintent also. Every day that passes without productive work holds us back a thousand years.

5 November 1987

Author, Thinker, Fighter

The death of our great writer, 'Abd al-Rahman al-Sharqawi,[1] was an unwelcome shock that greatly unsettled me during this year in which we have also mourned the passing of Tawfiq al-Hakim and more recently of Kamal el-Mallakh.[2]

In fact, my friendship with al-Sharqawi started up in the Opera Club at the start of the 1940s, before he embarked on his literary life. It was my great fortune to follow his birth as a writer, and then his development and the great success he achieved.

I first knew him as a pioneer of the new poetry when we published his wonderful poem 'From an Egyptian father to President Truman'. Then he amazed us with his great novel 'The Earth' which turned him into a pioneer of Arabic contemporary socialist literature. Following his *succès d'estime,* he turned his attention to the theatre and became one of the pillars of poetic theatre. At this juncture I recall 'Young Mehran', which created an uproar in government and popular circles when it was performed, and before that 'A Beautiful Disaster', which was the first play to be written in modern Arabic poetry and made an enormous contribution to the struggle of the Algerian people for freedom and independence. He followed up his dramas with many more works such as 'Acre, My Homeland' and 'The Peasant Leader' about Ahmad Urabi and his revolution.

The late al-Sharqawi also occupied himself with biographies of the great figures of Islam, including the Prophet, the Caliph Abu Bakr, Ali, the Caliph Umar ('the one who distinguishes between right and wrong') and the great leaders of Islamic jurisprudence. He presented the biographies in a unique and new contemporary manner by means of his enlightening and modern vision.

However al-Sharqawi was not just a writer and his rich life extended into the battle-field as one of the leaders of an enlightened and humanistic national rebirth. He kept his finger on the pulse of thought and

1 (1920–1987), a writer instrumental in the creation of the modern Arabic novel.

2 (1918–1987), archaeologist.

intellectual output up to the last moments of his life. His last days witnessed him making a working trip to the Soviet Union within the framework of his role as Secretary of the Soviet Afro-Asian Solidarity Committee. It was his fate to be struck down just as he was working with that enthusiasm which finally sapped the life from him.

He lived his life as an intellectual and a fighter and died a martyr to the cause.

When it comes to al-Sharqawi as a friend, he freely gave us the loyalty, affection and goodness which make us feel his loss even more intensely. May God grant him mercy upon mercy.

11 November 1987

Democracy Is a National Programme

There has been much talk of a 'national programme' around which everyone can flock. Perhaps a more appropriate title is 'renaissance' to send the right work message for the coming period. I do not think that there is an individual in any party, or a single sane citizen among the whole nation, who does not aspire for a real and comprehensive renaissance for all aspects of productivity and services in our country, a renaissance upon which everyone can incontestably agree despite differences in terms of the means and the aims, unless they think along party lines or quibble over the time-scales or programmes involved. The only alternative to this notion in peace time would be a call for a one-party system fashioned from a sense of nostalgia.

A renaissance means the renewal of the nation, the rationalisation of productivity and services. It means confronting the challenges posed by debt and negativity. It means challenging political aberration, dissolution and terrorism, and charting a secure route through the foreign political storms. All those items need serious and ongoing work on the part of the government, just as it needs trustworthy and alert opposition parties. We must set to work, we must have an opposition, we must carry things out and we must have oversight and criticism. These are the blessings of democracy and the real guarantee of firm action.

In order for that to come about in the best way possible, the opposition must commit itself to its principles without hesitation or platitudes, while taking care to remain serious and objective. The government must heed criticism and take it on board. It must include the opposition in its committees and conferences. It must accord it unhindered freedom of expression in parliament. The opposition is a bitter restorative, and we must rid ourselves of the bad habits we acquired during the era of absolute rule. The correct path for us to follow must be that of opinion and counter-opinion within the framework of freedom, oversight by the people, and human dignity.

13 November 1987

The Fight

The achievements of the current five-year plan are evidence of the enormous effort that has been expended and of our having confronted our deteriorating situation with the resolve to move beyond the crisis. However, why is it that not a single person among the oppressed masses feels the fruit of that effort? Why does he view the numbers with confusion and suspicion? The issue is that the individual only recognises the value of work if he gains something from it, if he has a palpable sense that his livelihood, his life and his freedom are assured. That is still far beyond most people's grasp and will only come about when we have completed two or more five-year plans, not as the result of undeniable neglect and laxity but essentially because the gravity of our deteriorating situation is the starting point from which we are working.

New work on the issue has started from the point of the total breakdown of everything, from essential infrastructure to industry and agriculture, and even the formation of a new type of Egyptian. All effort is being expended with the purpose of lightening the yoke around our necks, of putting things right and this has been neglected and delayed by mistakes we have made. At the same time, life moves forward, the population increases, demands multiply and people's feelings of bitterness are exacerbated. The situation must be laid out for people with honesty and sincerity. We must redouble the amount of work we do, negativity must be fought relentlessly, self-discipline must be total and good examples must be clear and apparent.

The government must do everything within its power to convince people of its seriousness, dedication and fitness for purpose. It must create opportunities for them to participate in work, while requesting their patience and forbearance and while spurring them on to change the current situation and triumph. We should not forget that there are many people lying in wait for us, following our convulsions with a greedy and exploitative eye, hoping to see the suffering people polarised or led astray for their own aims. We are fighting backwardness, hard times and the malintent directed at us and we must sweep them all away.

19 November 1987

The Modern Age

While doing their research on me, the press have asked me more than once: 'What period would you like to have lived in?' At first the question is both alluring and confusing and makes me search the recesses of my memory for the glimmer of eras which have left an indelible mark in terms of lofty values, startling achievements and personalities whom we might wish to emulate. However, the moment I overcome my astonishment at being asked this question, I realise that our modern age has no competition and that it is the greatest age of all despite everything said about it and despite our reservations. I would really like to see its negative aspects disappear, and among these aspects it should be enough for me to mention the power of total destruction that this age possesses or the damage it continues to do to the natural environment. But what age is free from negative aspects? Or should we just forget all about the deadly seasonal epidemics, slavery, total ignorance and superstition, among other things?

The least that we can say about our age is that it is the living epitome of all the ages that have gone before, and that the only ancient values which deserve to survive, such as belief systems, ethics, arts and literature, are those that people have not stopped practising or to which they still have a strong attachment. We can add to this what our age excels in, which is scientific progress on two levels: the theoretical and the technological. These are what have left their stamp on our age, they are its miracles, and they are what have produced things we could never have imagined previously, entailing enormous changes in our vision, in culture, in the way we act, as well as in the other traditions and rituals of life.

Our age is one which has realised the dreams of yore. It has created dreams people could not even have dreamt about. It is an age of the past, present and future. We should not prefer any other age to this one, or dismiss its wondrous influence on our intellect, on science and on technology. As much as we get out of our era, learn to live with it and add to it, we also live in it and learn how to live in it, and we thank God for allowing us to live in it.

26 November 1987

Unity Is Our Cornerstone

Relations have long been established between Egypt and many Arab states, and these have been officially recognised as cordial relations that have in actuality never been cut off for a day. When it comes to their significance, these relations have a clear effect and resonate in the souls of the millions who consider all the Arab states to be one nation. It is up to us to turn these relations into an objective reality and a starting point for a good, new life. But before we leap we must draft a map showing borders and capabilities so that we can read clearly what lies within the realm of the possible or the impossible, what is permissible and what is not, so that we can see where we are treading in light of the current situation and world politics, and be guided by lessons from our recent and distant history.

The first thing we have to do is to confront our current problems and imminent dangers in a way that will finally produce a lasting and just peace for the whole region. Our Arab nation is today in the strongest need of peace and stability so that it can use its forces to build up its economic and cultural unity, and it is this unity which will provide all parties with benefits and progress, which will give it a unified stance vis-à-vis our ever-present challenges, such as raising the standard of living, becoming part of the scientific age, and being protected by a defence force which provides the Arab nation with some gravitas and dignity. Any success we achieve in this field of activity should be able to call upon those who are still hesitant to overcome their differences to change their outlook on the present and the future.

Success in establishing a cultural and economic union will pave the way for something even more important and risky – without interfering with domestic or external problems – as opposed to starting off with the political aspirations that, as the past has taught us, usually falter in the midst of domestic and external plots. We should not forget that those aspirations have proved abortive, and we have learnt many lessons about the risk factors. However, thank God that our guiding principle in this fourth era of the July Revolution can be characterised by wisdom and alertness and has gone beyond sensational or impulsive actions. So let us hope for the best. Let us work unflaggingly. And let us put our trust in God.

3 December 1987

The Rule of Law

It is all too easy for us to call for the rule of law, and it is all too difficult for us to bring it about. I state in all sincerity that we may well overcome all of our problems in the short or the long term, and we may well conquer the desert and make it bloom, but equality remains a lofty hope, a distant dream, a cliché – as we are still cowed by the powers that be. That attitude is as deeply enmeshed in us as the blood in our veins. It is one of the chivalrous virtues in our value system, so how can we come to see it as just one more of our faults and overcome it with the necessary resolve?

No activity takes place in our country that does not sidestep the law and regulations, whether out on the street, in a hospital, or at school, and elsewhere. Once a project starts we quickly see nepotism come into play and those with vested interests come to the fore. The *dramatis personae* may change from era to era, but there is no era devoid of them, and equality will not prevail until the very last person among them has grabbed his share. Down the line from them are the people who are forced to spend their lives queueing, those who have spent an eternity waiting for a telephone to be installed, confused fathers, and tortured sons who can do no more than bewail their lot and call silently to God for help.

This is no great secret. It is an outright scandal that every citizen knows, and they also know that the law only has supremacy over those who do not know the right people. They know that the exception proves the rule and they believe that their lives pivot around injustice. They are ground down by resentment, their sense of belonging is challenged, they retreat into their own selfish sphere of activity, lamenting the world around them. Don't look for a medicine or sermon to cure this disease. Don't think that education will provide a quick fix. Just make respect for the law a legal obligation. Make sure that wrongdoing is followed up and subjected to the full force of the law. This particular aspect of democratic life must be cleansed of all blemishes.

10 December 1987

A War on Two Fronts

All around Egypt wars flare up, threatening to go on and on and to drag others in. Fleets are assembled, hatred flares up, relations break down relentlessly, and billions disappear into Satan's hell – all of which serve to dash the hopes of those patiently looking forward to seeing their lot improved.

Inside the country a battle of a different type has broken out between destruction and urbanisation and the efforts being expended to improve our listless lives, centred on education, productivity and administration, whose ultimate aim is to reshape the average citizen and to save him from despair and dejection. People are leading this domestic battle as they plunge headlong, at the same time, into raging waves of corruption and dissolution which are so numerous and frequent that they have become normal, with the criminal managing to stay out of the limelight, and crime inciting our youth to reject all the normal values of life. However, we have not lost hope. We still hope that the workers will overcome the scourge of the elements of nihilism and defeat. Do we need someone to come along and remind us how we love our country to the point of despair? Do we need someone to come along and remind us of the consequences of importing so much, of the rampant and greedy crooks, of the folly of useless adventurism, of the risk of sticking to national plans when we do not possess the means to carry them out?

I do not think that anyone needs to be reminded of all this. So how have we come to this when we are not only still paying an almost impossible price for our fecklessness and mistakes?

What we need today with regard to foreign affairs is a policy that protects the ship of state from the raging storms, a policy rooted in our actual interests, which tends to our circumstances and situation and which is evidence-based. What we need domestically is to work, to insist upon work, to continue to work, to invite the people to participate actively in sound thinking, to carry out useful work, and to see the rule of law imposed so that we actually deserve to be saved and so that we merit a more noble life.

17 December 1987

The Era of Truth and Reality

We recognise all the negative aspects of our lives as easily as we recognise ourselves when we look in the mirror. Moreover we have studied their dimensions, causes and consequences in a great number of conferences, for, after all, specialised national assemblies are no more than permanent conferences that have analysed the disease and prescribed medicine and, had we taken all their recommendations seriously, we would not be in the situation we are in today. However, what we lack is the boldness to implement those recommendations.

Implementation has not been held back just by financial issues, as evidenced by our enormous debts, but it has been obstructed by obsolete traditions, self-interest and blind bureaucracy. Even so, I have noticed recently that the conferences have now set themselves a different course, new aims, and a different attitude. Their recommendations have aroused a new and unprecedented level of interest. The best example of this is the teaching conference which was not just a talking shop or platform for people to prattle on about their difficulties or problems.

Just as new life has managed to percolate our teaching lives, we hope, after the conference on productivity, that new blood will start to course through us and extricate us from a state of failure and bring us into a new civilisational rebirth. There is no longer any room for slothfulness. Our problems have weighed down upon us grievously and we must now have a mass mobilisation in order to find decisive solutions for our challenges no matter how unconventional this may seem, no matter how harsh this may seem. We should have started this long ago, and we have no excuse for having neglected our duties and rights. Today we must face up to the truths and the results of our long slumber and neglect, of having been led off track by our dreams and hopes. Today we live in an era of truth and reality, of pain and glory.

24 December 1987

Society and the Youth

What is society's duty towards our youth? It is important for us to know what this duty is so that, should we be unable to perform it in full due to difficult circumstances, we will at least be aware of the reasons, not go overboard with blame or accusation, and be able to patch things up. What is society's duty towards our youth? Society must provide them with a general education which eradicates illiteracy. It must also provide them with a religious and national education as well as giving them sports lessons. Society must breathe into them the spirit of life and the world, and must highlight the uplifting aims of life.

They must turn to forms of labour for which they are equipped, from manual labour to international scientific specialisations, and the jobs must be offered according to natural selection alone without any nepotism or horse-trading. They must be given the opportunity to work both at home and abroad with wages that keep up with the cost of living. The housing crisis must also be resolved as this is no less important than education, work and wages. We must make our youth feel that they are living in a country that operates under the rule of law and that only under the rule of law can they achieve their full potential. They must also feel that no family, class or party privileges block their route and leave them with a sense of national alienation.

We must respect their political and fundamental ambitions for personal growth free from impediments, and we must provide them with free sources of culture by opening new libraries, cultural centres, youth clubs, and radio and television programmes.

Last but not least, our leaders should set the best example by showing how they work hard, how they are incorruptible and people of integrity. Our leaders should be their guiding light.

Society should take a long look at itself and ask what it has offered our youth and whether it has fallen short. This will allow us to clarify the actual situation and enable us to see that society should demand perfection of itself before demanding it from our youth.

31 December 1987

A New Year

There are good signs that point to progress and call for a sense of optimism. The export fair with all its fine and beautiful goods, and the defence fair along with the challenges and innovations it revealed, not to mention all the good news we have heard about the construction of new industrial cities – all these mean that we are actually taking steps forward, that we are making progress even if not with the requisite speed. However, we note all this progress at the same time as we are going through the worst wave of corruption, dissolution and loss. Just imagine what we could achieve if we could rid ourselves of all these plagues, if we could overcome our weakness, our negligence and sloth, if we could remove the obstacles that impede the path of our youth.

Imagine what our strength and resolve could be. Imagine how much we could improve our lot. Imagine how we could set forth to a higher state of cultural rebirth. Teaching methods are being revised and tomorrow the wholesome fruit will be enjoyed by a new generation that brings the promise of good things. Productivity will be the central focus of our interest and I expect to see serious work being carried out along with real innovation. The day will come, perhaps sooner than we imagine, when we revise our constitution, when we cleanse our democracy of its blemishes and then a miracle will take place with the law having de facto supremacy, when our populace will no longer have to suffer through their dealings with government institutions and prisons, when every citizen will enjoy his rights and will offer up his duty without distinctions of class, family or religion. We may not live long enough to witness that halcyon time, but we can satisfy ourselves by seeing the signposts that point to it and the steps that will bring us closer to it.

The country is not devoid of sincere, unblemished true believers with a sense of belonging who are working night and day. They may be only a small number, and it may even be difficult to make them out with the naked eye, but they do indeed exist, the proof of that being that we have not yet disappeared from the face of the earth. They are the minority who found refuge on Noah's ark and who were saved from the flood of dissolution, corruption, reaction and opportunism. They are the salt of the earth. It is through them that life will be renewed, that the sun will rise and light up our tomorrow. Don't tell me that I am dreaming, for what divides dream from reality is just a slight thread along with that human energy which is called the will to survive.

7 January 1988

Thoughts on the Smuggled Billions

Some experts and media personalities have spoken so frequently of the billions smuggled out of the country that we have been inclined to believe them. Astronomical amounts are considered lost to the country, while those in possession of those funds live a life apart from ours. Their hearts and hopes float around outside the country and at the first sign of danger, they simply drop out of sight, as if they never existed.

Just a fraction of all that money could bring about miracles in dragging the country out of its predicament, in moving our comprehensive development plan to its desired horizons. Naturally there is no point here in calling upon their conscience or sense of nationalism, as they appear to be beyond the law, but would it not be possible to try to speak with them in the language of mutual interests? By this I mean, by way of example, that we could suggest that they finance the import of our basic necessities and items needed for our development. They would make some profit out of this, which they could then invest in our development plan, at the same time as being offered all the usual facilities and privileges allowable, in addition to their services being acknowledged. That means we would have clawed back some of the lost money and repurposed it for the common good. It also means that we would have regained for the nation some people who would otherwise be lost to us and who can now hold their heads high.

Those people speaking about the smuggled money speak about it with the confidence of those who know every last individual involved. We should open up negotiations with them. Should we not call upon them to take part in the nation, especially since this will entail no sacrifice for them, but rather the opposite since we will be giving them a chance to increase their profits and to have a sense of national belonging? These are just the thoughts of a man exhausted by thinking about the state of the country and its fate. I hope they may be something more than just thoughts.

14 January 1988

The Blood of the Revolutionaries

The Palestinians under occupation have risen in revolt. They are revolting against the forces of annihilation which threaten them ever more with eviction from their homeland and with wiping them out of existence. The Palestinians are presenting an ongoing challenge to armed tyranny with their noble and unarmed wrath. They have an example in other people who have fought for their liberation without the use of weapons, who achieved victory through patience, suffering and perseverance, and with the insuperable power that comes from fighting for what is right. The Israelis could also learn a lesson about tyranny from the colonialists who deluded themselves that their power could not be defeated by justice and right. We really did hope that the establishment of peace with Israel would mark a distinctive change of era and of ways of thinking, that it would be the foundation stone of a comprehensive and just peace that would change the face and the future of the region. It did not take long until we were brought back down to earth by a series of hostile provocations, starting from the bombing of the Iraqi nuclear site, moving on to attacks on Lebanon, and most recently by the way the Israelis have beaten, arrested, shot and deported unarmed demonstrators.

The conscience of the whole world has been shaken at the oppressive measures you Israelis have taken to using, and which you used to a great degree in creating a homeland for yourselves at the expense of its inhabitants who are now dispersed across the world. You have pained the world's conscience by your actions but have turned a deaf ear to its call for you to show some restraint. You should have done this without needing to be called upon to do so, if not at the call of your own conscience, having suffered so much oppression and injustice at the hands of tyrants. How can you think of being imperialists when that time has passed? Why can you not be what you promised, which is to be a nation of freedom, ethics and justice?

It is a catastrophe in the full meaning of the word both with regard to the present bloody events, and also with regard to those who allowed themselves to dream about a just and comprehensive peace. In spite of everything, we do not wish to lose hope as we wait, hour by hour, for the voice of right to rise up and for the path of goodness to be victorious.

21 January 1988

On Productivity

Productivity is our life, so it should be no great surprise that a national conference on the topic is being held. It should also be no surprise that the conference will concentrate on studying the most important centres of productivity, how we relate to productivity and how it can be improved, how products can be better marketed at home and abroad, along with other issues related to the topic. However, the basic question is still how to create a productive person – a person who considers productivity the mainstay of his life, of his dignity, of his values and of his sense of satisfaction.

The first thing we have to accept is that productivity is a religious obligation. It is the primary lesson in religious education and a child should grow up with the same respect for it as he has for prayer, fasting, giving charity and studying. Second comes what we mean by good educational and vocational preparation for the individual, both hypothetically and in practice, for the crafts, professions and the higher specialisations are no more than degrees of the same integrated pyramid where every citizen can take the rightful place his studies and inclinations lead him to without having to decide whether those are to the advantage of the individual or society.

Then we come to the great role played by fairness. That is the basis of labour, just as it is the basis of governance, and is generally followed by the concepts of reward and punishment – 'From each according to his ability, to each according to his needs.' Then comes the attention that should be paid to a person's livelihood, to his health, culture and education. And let us not forget that we have to deal with the issue of over-employment as an impediment and inhibitor of work. This should be treated by a redistribution of jobs, by retraining workers for new jobs or by easing the red tape on working abroad. As for any subsequent glut of workers, they should be reassigned jobs by the Ministry of Labour which can reserve the right to use them as a reserve labour force to be used according to demand or for special requirements.

We must also take a new look at the weekly and seasonal holidays. We suffer all the problems of a poor people but we like to live like aristocrats... Consequently, we can see that productivity is not just a specialist area or the special preserve of economists, but that its leading role, over the long term, should be played by people with a specialisation in religion, media or culture.

27 January 1988

The Age of Science and Scientists

When I read, in the *Al-Ahram* newspaper, about the achievements made by the Egyptian scientist Ahmed Zewail, and when I learnt about the worldwide success of the architect Hassan Fathy, I experienced one of those very rare moments of satisfaction. This is due to the fact that I consider scientific achievement to be the foremost driver of a nation's progress, power and prosperity. In fact, nations cannot live by science alone, and science itself, moreover, can only flourish and bear fruit within an integrated society that stands on the firm foundations of political systems, ethical principles, robust beliefs and the highest standards. However, science remains a singular jewel in this crown, and scientists are still being accorded leading positions.

Today we have various scientific cadres, institutions of research and study, but they are not allowed to perform their role as they should be, or they remain in the shadows, and they do not make any memorable mark on the public. It is our duty towards civilisation – as we ourselves are part of this world in which underdevelopment is tantamount to a death-wish – to empower the populace with labour, supervision and guidance, to accord scientists the status they fully deserve, and to highlight them as part of the scientific educational establishment so crucial for our further development. We should do this in order to disseminate the truth and to win over the hearts of the people.

We should implant science within our religious and nationalist education as well as within the stories we tell our children. We should also publish accessible works on scientific culture, and the television should broadcast a series about research institutions, promoting discussions with scientists as enthusiastically as it promotes our sporting and musical celebrities.

Greetings to every Egyptian scientist who has achieved recognition for his work abroad.

Greetings to the Egyptian researchers who are overlooked because they have chosen to carry on working in Egypt.

4 February 1988

The Map of Our Youth

Our youth, the harbingers of a nation reborn, are characterised by some basic and intrinsic attributes. They believe that the age they live in has a grand purpose and consequently they wish to play a personal role that matches this, acting out of a real sense of belonging, with an alert social conscience, and employing their determination, hope and perseverance as they follow their route through the various levels of education and work. In the light of these attributes, what does the map of our youth look like?

It is unarguable that there are some young people who have set personal aims for themselves, focusing on finding good jobs or working in the professions, and there is no reason why they should not do so for they are the children of the privileged elite. If they have any setbacks in their lives, these are to do with money and free time and only rarely do their concerns go beyond the personal or things which affect them personally. They just get on with their lives, free from social hindrance or frustration.

There are others, and perhaps they are the majority, whose paths are strewn with thorns, whose education has been substandard, who have enormous problems finding work, and if they do have a job their salaries are insufficient for their essential needs which are housing, being able to afford to get married, and a sense of self-satisfaction. They live dull lives, with a sense of mistrust, and without any feeling of belonging or participation in general life. They reject everything around them, dream of emigrating, are at permanent risk of falling into a life of uselessness.

Then there are young people who have set a purpose for themselves in life, who enjoy a sense of belonging, of optimism and faith. These are the people in whom the essential attributes of a reemergent youth are evident. Unfortunately, their thinking can lead them off towards extremism, and some may go as far as breaking the law or shedding blood.

Therefore our general interest should do all it can to bring this group back into the fold of the law, to make them heed good advice, to redirect them, along with all their faith, optimism and sense of belonging, towards a higher aim, to making them the foundation stone of our rebirth, to making them the bulwark of the nation against deterioration and corruption.

We have a faith-oriented system that sanctifies learning, hard work, human rights and the nation. Our success in those matters means that we need to save the first group from their own self-absorption and to lead the second group out of their sense of confusion. For God guides those whom he wills to the soundness of the way.

11 February 1988

The Concerns of Today and Tomorrow

Our foreign policy is full of dynamism, energy and hope. It has taken the correct steps and deserves to be crowned with success. However, that should not make us forget our critical problems at home, and, what is more, we should concentrate on the two most serious issues which have us in an iron grip.

They are in fact two difficult issues which should be keeping us awake at night. The first issue is that of run-away inflation. The second one is the threat of drought. People are always complaining about inflation. There is a permanent sense of anger, and whenever people sit down to eat that is what they talk about. Productivity may be the decisive cure, but that will only take place over the long term, with slow steps forward, and I fear that we do not have enough patience to wait for it as the scales have already tipped too far. There must be some urgent steps that can be taken to pull inflation back down or the senior official responsible should declare his inability to do anything and face the music. When it comes to the issue of drought, we are not in any confusion as to the cause, but the experts all have different opinions regarding what we need to do and how to prepare ourselves for it. However, it is unarguable that the people will be called upon to take on new forms of behaviour and to give up many old habits, no matter how hard that may be.

Parliament must decide not only to submit these two issues to study and debate and come up with proposals, but also to hold a conference of experts at the national level.

The drone of complaints fills our ears, and the letters we receive from committed citizens are missives of pain and fear, bringing us to recall the dire situations we have lived through in the past. I will refrain from talking about those in order not to sow further confusion and to avoid exacerbating people's fears, but at the same time we must be wary of, and reject, a false sense of security and demand the same level of openness as we have thankfully seen from the minister of electricity.

We must gain a proper awareness of our current situation. We must recognise the dimensions of our worries so that we can step forward guided by knowledge and realism. We must all, the people and the government, shoulder our responsibilities.

18 February 1988

Political Reform

There are great signs of positivity in our life which we should recall so that we can draw some resolve and hope from them, such as the palpable progress in our relations with the Arab states, our ongoing quest for peace, the freedom of the press, and the opposition's movement in parliament towards objectivity, a sense of equilibrium, constructive participation, the particular attention that the opposition is paying to the deterioration in educational standards, their attempts to speed up reform and renewal, their serious endeavours to remove corruption and to clamp down on drug use, and their campaign to hold discussions with Islamist associations as well as their outstanding activity in conservation in Cairo.

These and other items deserve our praise and encouragement. However, all this has still not achieved our hopes with regard to an emerging nation when compared to the suffocating economic crisis we are is going through, or the grind of daily life at the hands of a deficient administration. For these reasons, I allow myself to take up once again the call for political reform as the foundation stone of any real national rebirth. Some people may think that we should attend first to our most urgent issues, but I am daily more convinced that the real solution for our stubborn problems has to be preceded by comprehensive political reform. Political reform is not some sort of side issue. At its barest level, it means turning attention to who governs and how he governs, as well as to the aim of governance. This topic should take in all views regarding reform to the economy, to productivity and distribution, to education, health and culture, *inter alia*.

With all due respect to the president's view about the need to put off revising the constitution, we should start by rescinding all the emergency laws which do not require constitutional amendments for this purpose, so that the forthcoming elections can be carried out in a greater climate of democracy, with a cleaner bill of health, and in an inclusive manner. That will be the first chapter in the way we handle problems and the way we choose the best vision and most appropriate methods to confront challenges, with as much participation from the people as possible.

3 March 1988

War

The dreams of our young people generally revolve around independence, democracy and national rebirth. The question of war is neither on our mind nor in our subconscious. So how surprising it has been for me to witness our country plunging into successive wars the multitude of which no one of any generation thought they would witness. I have witnessed the wars of 1948, 1956, 1967 and 1983, as well as the war in Yemen. I and millions of other people have lived through the dire consequences of those wars in terms of the damage inflicted upon the people and the country's coffers, the destruction wrought on our essential infrastructure, on agriculture and industry, the corruption, apathy and dissolution that have affected the citizen, and the degradation of our age-old traditions and ways of behaviour. Moreover, we are still living in an atmosphere of war, with some Egyptians volunteering to go and fight in our brotherly country of Iraq, or being tempted to go and take part in the Gulf War – almost as if those Egyptian volunteers find some comfort the thought of war!

War is a hateful thing, but it may be imposed on us as a matter of self-defence, in which case it would be a holy war, to be waged by people even if they are not ready for it or a match for an aggressor. There may also be difficult and impelling circumstances that make us launch a war even if it is not in direct defence of our homeland, but in that case there are certain prerequisites:

Firstly: the aim of such a war must be clear and convincing to the soldier and the citizen alike so that they are willing to make sacrifices no matter how great.

Secondly: we must have a strong army that is capable of achieving victory and of coping with the horrors of war even if it drags on longer than the planners could foresee.

Thirdly: the country should be prepared for war, economically, psychologically and socially.

War is not a question of gallantry or emotion. It is a historic responsibility that decides our fate for hundreds of years or even forever.

10 March 1988

Identity and Aim

People often wonder: 'Who are we?' They also maintain that we must know our identity in order to define our aim. However, the current reality is what defines our purpose – which at all times should be based on our current reality and not on our identity. Hence, war may break out between two states with the same identity, or a close friendship may arise between states with different identities. Moreover, an objective, when made clear and when in receipt of people's support, can have resort to the relevant identity as a supporting factor in asserting itself and in anchoring itself in people's minds. We have many identities, all of which have merit. We are Egyptian, we are Arab, we are Mediterranean, and last but not least, we are all offspring of Adam and Eve.

In 1919, we announced our campaign for independence, and Saad Zaghloul called upon our Egyptian identity as a symbol that should unite us in our struggle. In the 1930s, we started trying to be more western and Taha Hussein declared that we were people of the Mediterranean basin.

In 1952, dangers to the Arab nation sprang up on every side, and Gamal Abdel Nasser appealed to Arab nationalism. In the 1970s, Sadat found that we were drowning in a dreadful situation from which only our Egyptian-ness could extract us and he brought us back to it, setting it alive again in our hearts, with the result being the crossing of the Suez Canal, the liberation of Sinai, and peace. Our aim today may be comprehensive development, or making an effort to catch up with the modern age – and that is a vital objective the only alternative to which is disintegration and extinction, but we will only be able to bring this about in the best way within the framework of Arab cultural and economic integration. Consequently we Arabs need to come together in a robust, physical and spiritual union that can help us to bring about a just peace in this bloody and divided region and then we will be able to make use of our Egyptian-Arab-Mediterranean identity to move forward securely into the modern age.

17 March 1988

Culture and the State

Under an authoritarian regime, the state has draconian powers to oversee and control the direction, output and distribution of culture. It sees that as both its right and duty. When it comes to a democracy, its edifice stands on a basis of freedom and in its shade all flowers blossom and political currents flow freely, for governance is shaped by people's intellects, conscience, criticism and natural development. The role of the state in a democracy should be restricted to creating the right climate for thought and creativity and directing culture inasmuch as possible to everyone. I shall take a further step here in translating my opinion on the cultural role of the state into the following points:

1. Enact legislation to guarantee freedom of thought and creativity, to accord copyright protection to cultural output and to guarantee the rights of authors and creators.
2. More attention to be given to cultural education at all stages of education and across all the media
3. Enable free access to books in branches of Dar al-Kutub, cultural centres and youth clubs.
4. Establish encyclopaedia and dictionary projects, and information centres; institute a comprehensive plan for re-publishing the Arabic classics and for translating non-fiction and art books.
5. Award general prizes to encourage good writing and discover new talent; organise trade fairs and exhibitions.

Art is a social phenomenon and a cell in the body of any society. If a society is sick, the cell will be too. If a society flourishes, the cell does too. Artistic activity should be a matter of free competition, without any state interference that may harm its development. It just needs to be nurtured by responsible criticism, well-planned education and public opinion – all within the shelter of the law.

It may not have escaped your notice that I do not aim to see art hived off from the state, but to see it freed from the state's grip inasmuch as possible. My suggestions are based on ideals of socialist democracy and not unfettered democracy.

24 March 1988

Towards National Solidarity

Our proud and ancient nation is going through hard times – that goes without saying. Despite the effort being expended and the first signs of progress glimmering here and there, the suffocating crisis has an ever-tight grip on the basic essentials of our lives, such as foodstuffs, medicine, housing and labour, not to mention the dangerous storm clouds on the horizon.

All these circumstances call for us to show national solidarity in the shade of our democratic system and within the rule of law and order. Solidarity may well be a duty in times of war, but what we go through every day, and what tomorrow may bring for us, already feel like a state of war or worse. It should be clear to everyone what the advantages of solidarity are. It broadens the circle of choice when it comes to electing the right man to the right job. It allows every constructive opinion to reach the ears and hearts of people without hindrance or resentment. It turns debate into a thing of sincerity and frankness, rather than a bout of self-aggrandisement and self-serving argumentation. Finally, it encourages difficult decisions to be made without fear of artificial repercussions due to the fact that the right positions are held by the right people at a crucial time.

As a preliminary step towards that, we should start by rescinding the Parties Law, which is the one which seems the most irreformable, out of respect for human rights, thereby allowing our citizens free rein in forming whatever parties they wish. Refusing to legalise a party that actually exists is simply a social farce. The law may object to the intrusion of reality, or attempt to hold it back, but it cannot abolish it.

In the same way, it would be sheer vanity to think about national solidarity when we choose to overlook fellow citizens whose opinions and presence matter to the nation, such as the Islamist associations, the Nasserists, the Marxists and others. To put it bluntly, if we want national solidarity, we have to think along national lines too.

31 March 1988

The Long-Awaited Mahdi[1]

Is it possible to hope for a real national rebirth if we do not have all-round good citizens?

The citizen is the foundation, the means, the objective… Yes, we go on about forms of government, for we cannot overestimate or overlook the types of regime in charge, and we cannot deny the disparity in their efficiency or their relative positive or negative impacts, but for all their differences they would be nothing without the good citizen.

This is a truth which our modern history at the very least will have taught us. When it comes to the history of other nations, let us look at Japan. It prospered under two diametrically different forms of government. It prospered under a fascist regime before the war, and it has prospered under a liberal form of government after the war – because it had the merit, in both situations, of having good, trustworthy and dependable citizens. However, we have failed under two diametrically different forms of government. During the liberal era, the constitution was promulgated and governance turned into an ongoing argument which in the main distracted its supporters and others from reform until that era ended with the burning of Cairo.[2] There then followed a period of socialism whose principles were grounded in fairness and reform, but then turned into challenges with the state's coffers being raided, and defeats, inflation, degeneration, all leading up to the assassination of Sadat… But why?

Are nations not reborn in the shade of liberalism? Are nations not reborn in the shade of socialism? Of course they are, but during those two eras we did not possess those good, fitting, trustworthy and dependable citizens – and here I do not differentiate between the rulers and the ruled… In fact, the two are both chips from the same block and both groups were found to be up to the eyeballs in corruption. Hence, we need to find the right medicine, concentrate on building up the character of the individual. Education should pay heed to

---

1 Messiah.

2 A reference to Black Saturday 26 January 1952.

the important message it conveys, and so should the media, as should those who are leading our development, the delays to which have caused our principles and values to be swept away.

If we could build up this new type of person, it would guarantee our success. If such a person existed, it would make it impossible for our lives to be riven with corruption, oppression or infringements of human rights, with apathy or neglect. We just need to ask this new type of citizen: 'When are you going to arrive?'

7 April 1988

The Confessional

The good citizen is absent to a large degree, and in saying this I do not differentiate between the people and those who govern them. Everyone is part of the very same society at the very same time and they all share the same culture to a great degree, but it is absolutely apparent to everyone that our major flaws today are negativity, a weak sense of belonging, hypocrisy and an ever increasing lack of integrity.

The public look on but pay no attention. They can hardly make it to the voting stations, and even then they vote out of self- or family interest. They see hypocrisy as a virtue, a way of achieving what they want. They seem to have forgotten what it means to work hard. Simple deception has become their daily way of life. They do not hesitate to use compound deception, attempt to import foodstuffs tainted by radioactivity, distribute substandard food items or rent out an apartment block that is not destined to stay standing for very long.

Those in the government also have their negative side. They only act together in times of crisis. They double deal with those above them as well as those below them. They take bribes or pocket commission. They trade in the foodstuffs of the people. They behave like the masters of the people, not their servants or hirelings. They act above the law at the same time as singing its praises. They act as if the land and their jobs have been set aside as a religious endowment for them, their children and relatives.

It is a gloomy picture, but it is true in its broader strokes and no small hard-working group of people can change that. If it is our very nature that has brought us to this point, we should just vanish into nothingness or commit suicide, but it might just be possible to snatch victory from the jaws of defeat. I have painted a rather miserable picture, but I do not think we should despair. We should remember what has brought us down into this abyss and we should be asking what can extricate us.

14 April 1988

Political AIDS

How have despicable morals spread? I shall just concentrate on the two key causes which have come together to take over our good and decent nation like an AIDS epidemic and destroyed its immune system. These are a system of government based on authoritarianism and oppression, and a suffocating economic crisis which is rattling our sense of stability and social security. I shall not go on about their pernicious effects as we have already listed them off the way a sick person reels off the symptoms of his illness, such as a high temperature, nausea, headaches and shooting pains.

This is a condition which strips the citizen of his dynamism and satisfaction in life. It surrounds him with fear and paranoia. It drives him to attack the ruler, by showing up the victims of hypocrisy, mendaciousness, fraud and schizophrenia. Then it plunges him into silence, negativity and a lack of a sense of belonging as he can do no more than eke out a simple living, ever ready to break the law and break away from our noble traditions. He may become so agitated that he goes out and kills or rapes, and with no other outlet left to him he may become addicted to drugs or commit suicide.

When it comes to those who practise tyranny, over time they start behaving in a high and mighty manner. Their hearts harden and they do not hesitate to further torture the victims and scoff at all our values starting from human rights and a sense of national brotherhood. They become blinded by their love of spoil and aggressive behaviour, and they transgress every form of traditional behaviour and any law they wish.

This is what tyranny and crisis have done to us. They have caused some people to rule over others, and then they have also managed to control us.

We cannot deny that that we have embarked on the cure recently with our change of direction towards democracy, with the ongoing campaign for labour and productivity and the ongoing attempt to gain control of the crisis.

However, we cannot get away from the fact that we need to take a new and decisive step so that this night is not followed by another night.

21 April 1988

The Road to Peace

Will this night be followed by another? Of course, it will. That is beyond all doubt. If we have not applied ourselves devotedly to changing our current situation with far-sighted watchfulness and enlightened wisdom, the process of change will be taken over by the exigencies of our time and random other phenomena. However, rushing off to take the medicine is better than succumbing to the disease.

We have to complete building up our democracy and abolishing the emergency laws. We must accord people the freedom to form political parties. We must adhere in word and deed to the rule of law and respect human rights. The elections must be held in complete freedom so that we can have a popular form of government in which the efforts made by the state work together with the response and enthusiasm of the people, and so that the people support the state in its effort to confront danger and crisis under the banner of fairness and in a state of total national unity. I have expressed my hope on this matter many times, but unfortunately I have to restate it at a time when the emergency laws have been extended. I also have to restate my belief that the popular rule we hope to see will be capable of bringing everyone back to the straight and narrow, back to a sense of belonging and nationalism, that it will dress our wounds and restore our dignity and self-respect. At that point, people's strengths will be completely unleashed and they will be able to work towards greater productivity in a constructive manner. Even if people end up having to put up with the pain for a long time, their pride, sense of solidary and optimism will help them to cope with all the trials and tribulations.

The time has come for us to be a nation of liberals, a nation of law and order which fights poverty and expresses its presence in terms of innovation. Freedom is not some magic wand that can produce miracles, but it does provide an ideal climate for any reform to the economy or productivity, to education and health, and everything. Indeed, 'God will not change the condition of a people until they change what is in themselves.'[1]

28 April 1988

---

1 Qur'an, 13:11.

On Religious Education

As children we received a complete religious education. We learnt the commandments and ethics. We studied the easier verses of the Qur'an, the outline of the Prophet's life and some Islamic history.

It is an accepted fact that religious education should cover all of those subjects, but it should also make a conscious effort to impose on them some new objectives which, on the one hand, incorporate something of the spirit of our age in itself drawn from religion. And there is no 'on the other hand'. In that way, we will be able to educate our children with a love of science and knowledge, with a sense of reverence towards science and scientists. To help us do that, we will find ideological underpinning in the Qur'an and in the reported statements of the Prophet that we can use to inculcate a sense of veneration towards work and a sense of devotion to it. We will be able to teach children that dedication to work means a better life for the individual and for the population in general. Our religion can provide us with enough verses, statements by the Prophet and convincing narratives to enable us to fill our children's hearts with a love of freedom and democracy. We can teach all these to our children and then set their minds to thinking about them, as we underscore the concept of decisions being made by consultation, and various other incidents that history reports about the Prophet and the rightly-guided caliphs. We can fill children's hearts with a love of social fairness, starting with the principle of human solidarity, equality and the value of charity. We can instil in children a permanent sense of respect for human rights and their significance in Islamic history, turning that into a solid foundation for national unity and cohesion.

The individual who grows up with a sense of reverence for these principles, that is the oneness of God, prayer, fasting, charity, making the pilgrimage – that individual is worthy of life in our world. He will have been equipped for it with the best spiritual and material values.

5 May 1988

The Key to Reform

In the president's May Day address, he mentioned some very important matters. Most of them deserve praise and appreciation while offering points for further discussion. But the question I would choose to discuss is that of workers' wages. I choose this topic even though it means that due to lack of space, or because some important issues have already been dealt with, I have to set aside issues such as productivity – for you already know all about that – and the enormous achievements which have provided us with a sense of revitalisation and hope. There is no space here to talk about faith in democracy or what the people have to do in the face of a shortage in the waters of the Nile. Despite all those issues, I have chosen the problem of wages, as, in my opinion, it lies behind so much of the negativity we are suffering from in our lives and has cast its shadow over productivity, public services, political life, ethics and our sense of belonging, to mention but a few things.

One of the unfortunate disparities is that revolutionary policies, through subsequent stages of the Revolution, have raised the living standards of many groups in our society – farmers, labourers, craftsmen – but in a haphazard way. It is as if the Revolution has chained its workforce[1] to low wages which have long since been too low to cover the bare necessities of life.

Giving fair treatment to this group of people, who represent the backbone of the nation, is no longer simply some noble or human act, it also means giving them back their life balance, providing some psychological stability to all those who work with their brains or their brawn to bring about our comprehensive development and forthcoming national rebirth, whose frustration is reflected in the way they treat ordinary people in our various institutions and offices. Giving them fair treatment does not mean just giving fair treatment to one group of people, rather it means reviving the dynamism of work and our public services. Giving them fair treatment would be the first decisive step

1 It is clear from the context that Mahfouz is speaking about civil servants here.

towards removing all known tinges of corruption from our lives, such as apathy, neglect, bribery, exploitation and cultural degeneration.

I would think very seriously before marginalising the question of wages, or considering it to be some emotional side issue. It is both of those, as well as being essential for labour. It is the driving force, the throttle and the hope of our labour force.

12 May 1988

Praying for Rain

In 1986 an important and comprehensive study was carried out in various national councils on the shortage of water in the Nile and the expected consequences for agriculture and energy. They issued recommendations to be followed in the management of the waters of the Nile, and for energy and agricultural policy.

The national councils have worked, since their inception, persistently and with dedication, and in accordance with the expertise and zeal of the council members. During the period when my personal circumstances allowed me to be present at their meetings, I would listen happily to what Dr Mohammed Abdel Qader Hatem, the General Secretary of the councils, had to say about the councils' recommendations and whether they should be put into action, proving that their efforts had not simply died a death.

I would like to believe that the special recommendations regarding the Nile received due attention from the experts, if they had not already headed them off by being on top of the issues.

From the minister of irrigation's words in *Al-Ahram* we know that he has been trying to address the issue for a long time, and this should give us a feeling of relief, but it was also noted that this was carried out in secret, with no public invitation to the masses to participate, even though the project was completely under his control. The matter does not end there. He went on to accuse the great writer, Ahmad Baha al-Din, of rabble-rousing when he published the first data on the subject.

It goes without saying that this type of approach is something we have inherited from the authoritarian era. It is something we need to free ourselves from, now that our era has become democratic. The coming days will confirm the truth of the effort that has already been made. When it comes to what we, as a people, can do, we must shoulder some responsibility and show solidarity. We must actively line up to confront the challenge, and we must show our best side when called upon to do so.

19 May 1988

Between the Ebb and Flow

It has been decreed that the local council elections will be held on a party-list proportional representation basis... That has been decided while we are still calling for the rescinding of the emergency laws as a first step in political reform, followed by a reform to the law governing parliamentary elections. We had heard fine words in that regard, so how has this setback come about?

You can ignore what has been said about the new law being constitutional. It most certainly does not accord with the spirit of democracy, and only serves to give more power to the majority party which does not need it. It will also increase pressure on the opposition and make it further isolated. It absolves the government's performance from the popular oversight that circumstances demand. It will also generally mean that the government's new programme will not be the fruit of calm and comprehensive thinking as much as it is the fruit of a pause in the anger engendered by the sharp tension between the government and the opposition with regard to the emergency laws being extended.

What is the state today of the hopes that revitalised us when discussions started up between the National Democratic Party and the opposition parties? On that day we hoped that the discussions would continue, that they would cleanse the air, that they would subject our most important problems to study and research, and that they would bring us to some form of draft agreement regarding the essential elements needed for our national rebirth. We hoped for all that, and we said: the sensitivity of the situation, the risks involved and the gloom on the horizon should make us surmount the many difficulties and convince all sides to make concessions. We also said: we are going to see a better form of government, a wiser opposition and more sincere collaboration. Otherwise we will sink back down into aimless chaos or simply carry on in enmity and obstinacy. Does this mean that we should resort to despair? Personally, I refuse to countenance it.

26 May 1988

A Naïve Question

I have observed with surprise what goes on with investment companies, and I have noted the steps taken on their behalf with wonder and astonishment. Were I an expert in the matter, or if I even worked in the field, I would be able to offer my opinion, but as it is I shall make do with some musing. If the investment companies are actually as they describe themselves, then they are operating without a safety net for the investors or any control over their adventurism, so how is it that some people have enough faith in them to hand over their life savings on a plate? If they are as they describe themselves, how did they manage to set up their operations in broad daylight and how did they manage to turn into giants with branches all across the country? Where has the state been? Why has the state suddenly woken up and why is it trying to apply principles that it should not have delayed implementing for a second? Why this constant darting from draconian to gentle, from brawn to brains?

We do not need to discuss the government's right to protect public or private funds. That is in fact one of its most important duties towards individuals, communities and the national economy, and the government should always be beyond reproach in that regard, steering a sharp course away from anything that looks like impropriety. It should practise its economic guardianship in a fair and prudent manner without infringing upon the interests of the depositors and without too much heed given to the sensitivity of investors whom we invite to work in our country within the parameters of stability and the rule of law. It is surprising that the subject has been brought up in the cabinet and the Party has decided to study it, but that no one in a position of authority has thought to contact either those who set up these companies or a small group of depositors so that their opinions can be heard and discussed.

I would hope that we can manage to come up with the right fix for any problem without being forced to step over a trail of mistakes to get there.

2 June 1988

Religion in the Modern Age

There is a clerical elite. We simply cannot ignore that fact. These clerics are not just to be found within the religious associations, they are dispersed throughout the body of the nation to varying degrees. Our reformers and policymakers should bear this in mind. They should consider these clerics as a sort of network just waiting for someone knowledgeable and prudent enough to work with them, to head them in the right direction for rousing the nation from its slumber and taking it on up to the highpoint of its firmly established national rebirth.

It is one of the blessings of God upon us that our religion is one of both this world and the next world. It calls upon us to build up the earth, to venerate learning, to consider work as a form of worship, at the same time as showing mercy to both worlds by its attitude towards human rights and by recognising the equality of religious beliefs. Our age is nothing but the age of science, work and human rights, and it would be a prudent thing for us to make religion the starting point of our culture and national rebirth. That would guarantee the creation of the type of good human being who can make the particular things he needs in order to live a noble and enlightened existence, a person with a developed sense of belonging and optimism, one who lives an upright life through hard work, who has a love of science and knowledge, and a love for humanity.

You should most certainly not be put off by the fact that we sometimes come across a young person who thinks or behaves badly – even if he has received the type of good education which teaches him to respect truth, to have no fear of anyone and not to feel that he has to kow-tow to authority – he is still going to be part of the solid basis of our comprehensive rebirth by dint of his faith, his optimism, his enthusiasm, and his ability to take on challenges. We have in our youth an incredible resource and we should invest this wisely. Let us not be like those corrupt trust fund kids who fritter their fortune away.

9 June 1988

Between the Sacred and the Profane

Every government is a religious government to some extent. By that I do not mean that power lies in the hands of clerics, or in the hands of a person who claims to be infallible or that he is God's shadow on earth or any of the other guises behind which a dictatorship tries to hide. By that I mean that a government commits itself to be bound by certain ethics in its various dealings and the laws it passes. This is because religion, from a historical perspective, is the principal teacher of ethics to mankind, and every single government commits itself, in its constitution and laws, to act predominantly with reference to ethics, traditions and values. Hence we might term it a religious government in terms of its ethical content, even if it dismisses or completely disavows this suggestion.

Hence, in the Soviet constitution we can find values of religious origin, such as equality and justice, and similarly we find punishments that are akin to, or even harsher than the most severe punishments stipulated by the Qur'an. In fact, in practice there is a gap between what should be and what is, and when corruption takes hold of the system, this gap widens and renders any trace of religious content invisible, particularly to those looking for higher ideals. Their anger then leads them to see everyone as infidels – the state and the people – and to reject the law and everything around them as they call for the establishment of a religious government as a means of cleansing society and moving forward.

The desired government actually does exist, and even if its essence has been covered in layers of dust, it can still be brought back to itself by means of a comprehensive and deep-reaching reform that would also end up narrowing or even plugging the gap, by revising or re-categorising some issues. If that brings with it some wisdom, sound perception and understanding of the spirit of religion, and some response to the requirements of the age, we will deservedly be able to hope for a new life in which there is boundless good for all. Some experts and opinion-makers, who are far from being radicals, have stated as much, and their views on the matter have been repeatedly broadcast. They say that the difference between existing laws, and the laws the people are calling for them to be replaced with is, in fact, slight, and that with some amount of work it will be possible to reconcile all the constants and variables. If that is the case, then why are we talking about it and not just getting on with it? Why don't we take ourselves out of the gloom and pessimism and into the glimmering light of day that promises all this good for everyone, as well as the prospect of human rights and national unity?

12 June 1988

Between Extinction and Survival

We are at a level of underdevelopment that no noble people should have to accept. This fact is as clear as the searing sunlight on a scorching summer day if we compare Egypt to the developed world. If the gap keeps increasing at its current rate, it will not be long until we are doomed to extinction or end up working like pack animals for those in the advanced world. They have already conquered space and split the atom. They are attempting to be able to control genetics while we are having great trouble establishing our essential infrastructure, working our fingers to the bone as we fight for our human rights, while all the time trying not to throw in the towel and just say sod it all! When set against the First World, our most treasured dreams seem like no more than faint legends from dark ages long gone.

Peoples may slumber and be cowed, they may be appeased and forced to be patient, but life is unforgiving. Time is not kind. The fossils of creatures that have become extinct bear witness to that. As a matter of self-defence, and in order for us to retain a shred of dignity and pride, I call upon the parties to continue their meetings and include parties which have not been legally recognised, as well as expert academics, opinion-makers and union leaders. I call upon them to examine the state of their homeland, to subject the current state of affairs to criticism, and to look to the future in the light of their past and of their future so that they can extricate us by coming up with some proposals and recommendations to light our way through all these issues of governance and life. As an example of that, I am reminded of the Wafd conference that took place on consecutive days just after Ismail Sidky's prime ministership and which formed internal committees for policy, economy, education and culture, etc., revealing a reform faction reflecting the modest aspirations of the time.

We must do something, for this time we are threatened with extinction or worse, and in this life justice will be realised, either by us or against our interests. We need to join the march of progress before we become just one more catastrophic example from history.

23 June 1988

Egypt's Role

A magazine published something of significance, which is that we are a small state with limited resources, but we play the role of a large state in the region. Is that something for which we should be praised or castigated? Shouldn't a state's role accord with its size and capabilities?

This might be due to Muhammad Ali, who breathed new power into the state and increased its capabilities to the point where it became the strongest unit of the Ottoman Empire eclipsing the empire itself. He was right to dream of Egypt occupying that position, but he forgot that he was playing on a stage much wider than the Ottoman Empire – on the world stage where the great powers and their interests lay in wait to smash his plan into smithereens.

Gamal Abdel Nasser had no excuse. He had a mission which was even more important and laudable for Egypt, and he was so taken with the notion of Egypt being a great state that he believed it, and made us believe it, until we woke up from that dream on 5 June 1967.

We should not aspire to a role greater than our capabilities. We should remember the famous proverb, 'Don't bite off more than you can chew.' Moreover if we are striving for peace within the framework of wisdom and the interests of Egypt, then that is most welcome, but we should do so without reckless ambition, or feckless provocation, without overestimating our capabilities or underestimating those of others. I must state that our foreign policy is characterised by prudence, composure and common sense, and that it has learnt useful lessons and rational advice from the trials we have been through. One might say that all this praiseworthy activity accords us a modicum of dignity and may help us to solve our domestic problems, but that it is also necessary in a world whose borders are disappearing and upon whose horizons there shimmer the signs of some sort of world unity. In this world we should neither set ourselves apart nor withdraw into isolation, rather we must take a positive part which is commensurate with our capabilities, and we must do that with prudence and armed with good intentions.

30 June 1988

The Man of the Hour

What should we think and how should be behave?

We do not think about our free time, nor about a life of luxury, but about the flood of economic, political, intellectual and existential challenges which have put our lives into an ongoing state of tension and lurking danger, and which have caused us to use up all our wisdom and expertise in order to reset our path towards a future brimming with possibilities. We the people, the parties and the state, must all bear in mind the prevailing atmosphere when we think about, or resolve to issue, a decree. We have to concentrate on the general interest, and follow a methodical route towards the country's welfare. We have to overcome whatever the familiar struggles of life throw at us, the issues raised by legitimate rivalries under normal circumstances and the manoeuvrings of the political parties. At a time of danger our thinking and decision-making need to change and our intentions should all be directed towards one objective, which is that of national salvation with all the sacrifice and self-denial that demands. The last thing we should be seeing is someone crowing over the downfall of his adversary or some sort of *schadenfreudefest*.

The government may find itself in a position of strength and try to control everything and keep old conflicts alive out of arrogance.

The opposition may find itself in a difficult position, with no freedom of movement, with its efforts bearing no fruit and with it having no role to play in governance as it cries out in the wilderness and floats up a certain creek without a paddle.

Do you counter stubbornness with extremism, or arrogance with outright hostility? Under normal circumstances you should, or even must. However, speaking of today, the situation is greater and starker than that. We are in a situation that calls for prudence and sacrifice and the winner will not be the person who mistreats his opponent or tries to sully his reputation. The clever, shifty or sly person will not win either. The country and our history are both waiting for a prudent person to save them, someone who does not act out of self-interest, someone who progresses through the ranks with one aim in mind – the welfare of the country.

7 July 1988

The Revolution of 23 July – Again

You find me here reminiscing about the days when the July Revolution was born and about its dazzling growth, for they were days sweeter, more delightful and happier than any I have since witnessed with their wonderful treasure of beautiful hopes and wishes. We found our lives up against a crude barrier behind which chaos, corruption, tyrannical rule, and a disregard for values or laws were piled up. After one great push, that barrier came crumbling down and the corrupt disappeared into thin air like motes of dust. Tyrants and autocrats were reduced to nought just as superstition crumbles in the face of hard science. Class divisions and the system of privileges were shaken, and the sun of justice rose on the horizon.

Victory followed victory, like one long sweet dream. The republic rose up on the debris of the monarchy, and through agricultural reform set about immediately handing the land back to its owners. The British evacuated Egypt and the nation was liberated. We were promised a constitution the like of which had never been seen. The sons of Egypt were swept into positions of authority and everyone was resolved to bring about a comprehensive national rebirth based on increased productivity and just distribution for a small nation which had been through so much strife and deprivation. At that time, full of optimism, I stated: 'Egypt is now being guided along her path, is dealing with its citizens' concerns and is sketching out the lines of progress unhindered. There is no such thing as a throne that cannot be toppled, or an occupation that cannot be removed. May God grant that I live long enough to see the fruit ripen and my dear homeland strong and stable, enlightened by science and illuminated by culture, a country with no disease or poverty, no hunger or cares, no corruption or hypocrisy, no injustice or oppression, a nation of freedom and love, taking pride in its glorious history, looking forward to a glowing future and enjoying a lofty status among the nations.'

At that time, I was already over forty, but my sheer enthusiasm took me back to the prime of my life and I went about repeating its battle cry and singing its anthems.

31 July 1988

A Call to Life

We have lost the ability to be amazed, to be worried or to be interested. In our endeavour to eke out a living and beset as we are by fear and anxiety many of our noble characteristics have disappeared. We live in an age where we all run around trying to keep ourselves going, an age where some people live in fear of being unable to earn a living and others fear they will never be able to so, in an age where the rich huddle together in fear, and where everyone feels alienated from the world of humanity, from its sublime values and its gentle rhythm.

All around us great achievements and essential reforms are taking place and a devoted and sincere minority carry on working night and day, but good work is just like bad work – the two go on and people also go on being obsessed by their own interests. Events pull us along, or we pull events along, without any reaction or echo in our consciousness or effect on our way of thinking. Existential catastrophes and social plagues threaten us, and we take a quick look at them and then choose to ignore them. We neither think about them seriously nor do we task other people with thinking about them – as if they are part of some drama or form of entertainment, or as if they are faint glimpses from ancient history.

When are we going to wake up? When are the well-springs of life going to issue forth? When are we going to weed out the roots of inaction and negativity? When are the embers going to flare up again? This is a call to life, directed first and foremost to ourselves. This call does not need the support of any force outside ourselves. What the state does is by nature for the long term. I am calling on support from yourselves. You have the will to say, 'Let it be', and it will be. We can only get over our current situation with our own free will. Challenges may well kill the weak, but they create those who are immortal.

4 August 1988

The Trust Borne by People

How can wakefulness take the place of luxuriating in bed? How can a people stir, change their world and determine its destiny? The humanities speak to us about the role of the economy and politics, about the role of the parties and capable leadership, about the influence of upbringing, education, the arts and literature, and indeed these are all indispensable and vital factors, but does the individual not have a role to play in this risky and innovative arena? He actually does. He does have a role, that is unless it has been decreed that he should just sit down like a hungry man waiting for the skies to rain gold and silver down upon him.

The individual is capable of weeding negativity out of himself, and of making himself self-sufficient. In spite of appearances, this is possible. If a free man opts for this and opens up a new path in life for himself, but he must first ask himself, 'What should I do?', before resorting to the traditional question: 'What will the government do for me?' I do not mean that he is capable of solving problems on his own, but that he should start thinking about finding solutions for them. If he has not been able to find that in most situations, he should move on to thinking more generally, to taking a greater part in society and developing a sense of belonging.

The individual should learn that he possesses enormous strength which can be weakened by laziness and dissipated by apathy. That strength is his free will. It is the source of hidden strengths which he can amass himself without even noticing and then use wisely to bring about deeds which less driven people may think of as miracles, and in the twinkling of an eye circumstances will start to change, the darkness will lift and delusions will disappear, but there is no use in any of that if we do not take life seriously or see it as a struggle.

The brevity of our lives, the shadow of death, our preference for good times and our hankering after worldly delights, lead many people to see life as such a form of entertainment, game, or opportunism that they have made it a refuge for cowards and shirkers. But it would not be a life worthy of its blessed name if we do not take it seriously or see it as a struggle. Let us then set in progress those elements that drive the economy, politics and history, and let us not sit patiently waiting on the sidelines.

11 August 1988

Remembering the Dead

23 August is the day when we commemorate the dead with tears and grief, when we commemorate that generation of glorious leaders, Saad Zaghloul and Mustafa al-Nahhas, who are symbols of the greatest popular revolution in our history. We must remember our revolution and its two leaders, particularly during these days as we fight against negativity, using all our resolve so that the people remember that it was they who were once our strike force, our steadfast will, our firm resolve and a fount of talented creativity.

The people had finally woken up, desirous of their dignity, and they boldly challenged the English and the king and placed their faith in national unity, throwing off with their own blood the patronage that had been imposed upon them. They prudently created the kernel of a new economy, expressed themselves in the various forms of art, and rescued one half of their number – women – from the lowly position of subservience and pushed them on towards the fields of science and a completely emancipated choice of jobs. Then they cast their light on the universities and can be credited for supporting the theatre, intellectual activity and music.

It was an age of the people, of leaders, and of learned individuals, artists and intellectuals. It was the age of Egypt's revolutionary, confrontational creativity. It was an age of independence, civilisation and democracy.

Let us remember that exquisite life in all its wondrous beauty and let us remember its two leaders as symbols of sacrifice and self-sacrifice, of loyalty to the people and as our greatest role models. Let us remember how they kept on with their struggle, both in exile and at home in Egypt, in government or in prison, always offering love to people and expressing their outrage at colonialism and dictatorship. They both lived noble lives and died poor, leaving behind them a people fired up to better their lot and ever yearning to be part of the modern world.

25 August 1988

Behaviour in Hard Times

If the problems have piled up and are out of reach of solutions, if it is too difficult to remove the gloom of frustration by means of sincere hard work alone, then people must take a new look at their situation. This is not a call for a coalition which would touch the very essence of democracy, but it is a call for an exchange of opinions to take place away from party political or legitimate disputes in the nationalist, scientific and objective climate required by the harshness of our times and determined by our desire to attain some relief.

It is my right at this juncture to ask about the Productivity Conference which we hoped would bring about some positive points, but what happened to our hope? Productivity is not something that we can just forget about or put off for another day. It is perhaps our first hope in confronting the challenges and crises which have burdened our lives with permanent tension. If we have not been able to set up an inclusive nationalist front, then perhaps a conference that brings together experts and scientists can do the job, particularly if it examines the valuable research carried out by both chambers of our government. Then all we will have to do is to repeat the experiment with all our other problems, such as the population explosion, debts, unemployment, and inflation.

Let every problem have its own conference. Let every conference come up with recommendations. Let the recommendations have their own timetables, and even if the government is not convinced by all the recommendations, it might be convinced by some of them and take note of the sincere intentions which may have slipped its attention due to the pressure of parliamentary work. How wonderful it would be if every conference represented science, expertise and all other disciplines, as well as representing successive generations, for in the final analysis it is their present and their future.

1 September 1988

Forgotten Honours

Following the prize announcement, I received an international telephone call from an Arab brother who asked me what my feelings were about being honoured by the world while my homeland has not honoured me!

I was greatly surprised by that. Whatever it was like at the start, and no writer's path can be devoid of difficulties or obstacles, I later received enough recognition to satisfy anyone, to revitalise my ambition and help me get through the hard times. I was awarded all the literary prizes, such as the Qut al-Qulub al-Damardashiyya prize, the Arab Language Academy prize, the Ministry of Education prize, the previous State Prize, the Honorary State prize, and a number of cinema and television awards. I have been conferred the Legion of Merit, First Class, and the Order of the Republic, First Class. Many of my works have been adapted for the radio, television and cinema, and on each occasion they have invited me to talk, although I have sometimes turned that down on the excuse of my weak eyesight and my natural aversion to public life. More important than all that has been my reception by the masses, even when a boycott of my works was announced, as well as the attention of critics and intellectuals who have worked on and analysed my writings. The award of an honour by the president of the republic has crowned all previous, and if God so wills it, all future acts of recognition – an honour which exceeded all dreams and imagination.

Having said all that, how can it be said that my homeland has not honoured me? It is surprising that my credits might be overlooked by someone who has deserted his country, and the world is not devoid of deserters, but this time the omission came from those who grant the awards, so how did that happen?

Thus I would state that I have been completely honoured by my country and this should always be mentioned alongside my praise and gratitude.

1 September 1988

How Do We Face the Enemy?

We are facing a grinding economic crisis, and rampant and savage inflation which portends further disastrous consequences if we stand here doing absolutely nothing. It may yet be a while until we can see any results of the effort expended in carrying out the five-year plan or until this has any effect upon the average citizen who is ground down during his daily life. In circumstances like these, the brand of social cohesion should burst into flame within people, and everyone should know his duty according to his ability, and by that I mean every individual, every group and every institution at all popular and official levels.

The first thing that must disappear from our lives is ostentation and profligacy, as they are the last things we need in a grinding crisis. We must take on rational new ways of living which under normal circumstances would be considered a virtue, but which are an absolute necessity in these extraordinary circumstances.

We have an ongoing need to rationalise our birth rate, energy, water management, food supply, and particularly everything to do with amenities, and tired old pomp and traditions.

It is not really fair for us to direct this call to everyone equally, however to each according to his ability. It should first be directed to the state, calling upon it to serve as an example in not spending a single penny that is not for public benefit. It should be directed to those who have the ability to spend money like water with no thought given to the conditions and feelings of poor Egyptians and without considering that their behaviour is paving the way for the monster of inflation to decimate the ranks of their fellow Egyptians who live on a fixed income. It should then be directed to everyone who has the opportunity to show self-restraint rather than spending amounts he cannot afford. Every single person should take another look at his life, question his conscience, draw strength from within and remember that he is a member of a group whose existence is derived from harmony, cohesion and humanity.

8 September 1988

Between Confrontation and Flight

Thinking is free. It can range around any subject when it wishes. However it must first experience its age and face its challenges. That is when we see the difference between those who face up to life and those who take refuge in flight as they hope to find some comfort. The history of civilisation is simply a record of the questions thrown up by humanity's reality so that he can enrich his life and find a sense of self-fulfillment. He may one day wonder about the source of his food, his behaviour in the world, about the time he will spend in the afterlife in the shadow of the divinity, how he can cross the deserts and oceans, about evil and the wisdom of his existence, about obligation and choice, about governance, security and fairness, and so on.

The passing of an era along with its questions and answers does not mean that it no longer has any relevance, for humanity may acquire expertise that helps it to survive its whole life, and these pieces of expertise may increase, but in any age the prime focus remains those questions which humanity's reality and stage of development inspire. What then are the questions which lie before us today as a developing nation living in this period of time? Perhaps they should revolve around the one aim that can be summed up in the phrase 'comprehensive development'. A small phrase with wide repercussions, it includes budgetary balance, agricultural and industrial rebirth, a scientific revolution, reclaiming the desert, protecting the environment, reforming education and culture, religious education, health, defence, the population explosion, the firm anchoring of democracy, national unity and human rights. If we want to be certain of living in our time and working for our todays and tomorrows, we should take a look at the issues which worry us and at the questions which occupy us. Are we actually living a life or are we seeking refuge, for understandable reasons, in fleeing to an era of questions that have long been answered? Or should we be thinking about an age whose questions have not yet been posed? I do not wish to place any impediment in the way of thinking, and nor do I wish to dismiss anyone's vision of the future, but I would call upon us firstly to face up to matters as they are.

15 September 1988

The Explosion

In the aftermath of the population explosion things were said that do not bear repeating, but how can we confront it? Let us ask a different question: why are people intent on having so many children? And the response is that they are intent on doing so as a natural means of overcoming the fact that they are threatened by diseases, by infant mortality and other factors, out of respect for historical and environmental traditions, or to create the labour that they need to earn a living, or because their career horizons are limited and all they can do is take comfort in sex.

There are many ways of dealing with this, including calling upon people directly, and perhaps this is the most ineffective way, and even if we see no harm in doing this or even urging people to have fewer children, the real way of dealing can perhaps be made clear in what I am about to say.

Firstly: we should focus on raising the standard of living and expanding general services, particularly health, as well as trying to increase employment rates at home by any method. That is what hopes were pinned on during the execution of the comprehensive five-year plan.

Secondly: education and culture should be disseminated as widely as possible. What should be noted here is that educated and cultured people accepted the idea of family planning long ago, even before the problem of over-population became a consistent issue in our lives.

Thirdly: we should prepare those of our youth who cannot find a job for working abroad by teaching them a trade or a craft in accordance with the needs of foreign countries, and an effective policy should be drawn up between Egypt and foreign countries to organise this operation.

Some countries have resorted to draconian measures, but we hope that we will be able to treat our problem without being forced to resort to those, even though self-defence may entail people making some costly sacrifices.

22 September 1988

Dream and Reality

My beautiful and persistent dream is that I see our people waking up, that our people wake up and regain their conscience and will, that they take possession of their power and sovereignty, that they become the source of authority, that they become the ruler of the rulers and the driver of events, that the rule of law prevails, that human rights are sanctified, that sleaze disappears from public life, that productivity and creativity have free rein, that the era of clientelism goes to hell and is replaced by one of democracy and freedom. In any case the States have offered false patronage and have themselves been in great need of direction and patrons.

Both before and after the Revolution we tried being a client state, being a revolutionary nationalist patron state, and a wise political patron. Our intentions differed and our aims were many and various, but defeat and mistakes came down upon us all, as the only type of rightly-guided patronage can come from the people. During successive eras of clientelism, both before and after the Revolution, colonialism became even more rampant. We lost our independence. We were afflicted with defeats and corruption. We drowned in a sea of debt and inflation and terrorism played havoc with our dignity and security. Had faint glimmerings of the people's awakening not pierced the sky's darkness over periods of our history, we would not have re-emerged from our tombs or addressed any of the issues.

O dear people! Wake up and arise! Throw off your bad habit of ascribing your bad luck to a particular regime or man. Do not deny your share of the responsibility no matter how invincible or strong your adversary may seem. You are responsible for the failure of the last democratic experiment. You are responsible for the failure of the socialist experiment. Were it not for your forbearance, no autocrat or tyrant would have remained in power. Face the truth! Face the truth, confess, regret and expiate. Regain your legitimate rights no matter what method you use, and may God be with you.

29 September 1988

A Word Amid All the Hubbub

Here's a general image of our life today: a people stand patiently in front of the monster of inflation, exhausted by the crisis of their youth, as the state carries out a long-term plan with undeniable zeal, but without sufficient resources when compared to the enormity of the problems and in an environment encumbered by apathy and indifference, where outbursts of anger occasionally reveal the victims among the people and the police undermine our independence and launch feckless attacks on the sacred unity of our nation.

And now a word must be addressed to the Islamist associations, and a word must be addressed to the state.

To the associations I would say that no era of Islamic history has been devoid of opposing groups, some of whom managed to live together in the shadow of legitimate differences, and some of whom killed others in civil wars which tore apart the Muslim comity and undermined its unity and strength. In our era, intellectual differences are dealt with in a democratic atmosphere by debate and discourse, and only the feeble, the tyrant or the terrorist resorts to brute force. After all, what are you but an Islamic group with your own type of thinking and vision? You are not the only people in the arena. There are other Muslims who have their own way of thinking and vision.

Every group has the right to live, as true believers, in the shade of their own way of thinking, to lead their own lives in a way which satisfies their conscience and meets their obligations. However, going beyond that and using force to impose views on other people goes against the law. It threatens public security and is a bad omen for the independence and essential unity of society. It is inevitable that society will counter that by unceasingly defending itself and its supremacy unless it has lost its worth and content. Your effort should be within the law and should not lead to either your, or the security force's blood being shed.

To the state I would say that it must redouble its efforts to build up the country, to remove corruption, to bring about what is right and just, to guarantee the supremacy of the law. Our ultimate safety lies in perfecting our democracy and in respect for human rights, so let any and all parties be formed, grant freedom to the existing parties in order to bring the masses on side and educate them. Inculcate their hearts with enlightened awareness and let the people move on and regain their health and well-being so that their voice can be heard above the tumult.

The omens are flying all around us carrying messages of gloom, and staying silent simply means submitting to an unknown future which is not in our best interest.

13 October 1988

The Day of Victory and Peace

This is a day of significance, and of what significance in our spiritual history! It is not simply the commemoration of a triumphant battle, even if our army astonished the world by manifesting courage unimagined by our adversaries, by performing so efficiently that it set itself up as a modern-day wonder – it is because we did so in the manner of a startling and humane revolution, and that we learnt a valuable lesson whose purport is that no matter how dreadful people's situation is, they are still capable by means of their belief, conviction and knowledge, of rousing themselves from the slough of despair, fragmentation and disintegration, and springing back to a peak of hope and self-confidence to face anew the challenges of life. In that lies the division between two eras, the era of despair, darkness and frustration, and the era of rapture, of aspiring for justice, peace and civilisation, and during that era of extended rapture they announced new and firm principles for peace, calling any and every person to accept them. However, the only thing we managed to produce was the bitter fruit of anger, mistrust and boycott.

And now the whole Arab world is taking another look at itself and returning to those principles although this is only happening after it has wasted billions acquiring arms which have only been used for fighting among ourselves.

Peace be upon those valiant fallen soldiers, peace be upon the singular hero of the day Anwar Sadat, and peace be upon Gamal Abdel Nasser who made such an effort to rebuild the army on the morrow of its catastrophic defeat.[1]

That day, having achieved its objective, which was to bring peace, should have been the beginning of our reconstruction, of forging the difficult path towards progress and prosperity, had it not been exploited by the basest opportunists for their own pressing interests. It was the reckless consumerist liberalisation of the economy which thwarted both our day of victory and peace and which threw us into a suffocating predicament leading us then to use everything we have and do not

1 In reference to June 1967.

have in order to extricate ourselves under the banner of our wise and democratic leadership. Our hope remains anchored in our strength of will which brought about the miracle of victory and which should also bring about the miracle of salvation.

16 October 1988

Respectable but Criminal

No society is free of crime, but I am not speaking of the usual rogues, such as recidivists who get involved in crime for a multitude of reasons, the criminally insane, or terrorists.

There is another type entirely. In appearances he looks like the man in the street. He practises a legitimate profession. He may be a man of standing and influence. And yet he may be deceitful and corrupt and use devious, harmful and destructive methods in his work as he is driven by greed or self-centredness. His lack of a sense of conscience proves that he is like a sick worm in society and not a working member of it.

When it comes to those crimes, in our time we have seen enough varieties to be able to call this a phenomenon and I shall provide a few examples just to jog your memory. There was the case of the rotten food which had been marked for distribution with the wholesaler's full knowledge of its being unfit for human consumption. Then there was the food which wholesalers had taken great care to import into Egypt with the full knowledge that it had been irradiated. Then there were the reports of frayed electricity cables still being used long after they should have been replaced. And the hundreds of cases of arson, and the victims, as well as other things we come across all the time.

What does it all mean? It means that there are criminals hiding behind the guise of respectable people and that their devious methods have taken normal corruption to new levels of violence. The average citizen, for whose human rights we have been calling, in their eyes has fewer rights than an animal or a vegetable.

The matter cannot rest patiently until we come up with ideas for cleansing society, and until education and civilisation bear fruit for all humanity. We must investigate and pursue. We must take draconian measures to put an end to crime and to those criminals who hide behind respectability. They are the worst type of criminals.

10 November 1988

Climbing Out of the Animal's Jaws

The gap between our income and our expenses is responsible for the disruption in our economic life, and consequently it is responsible for our daily sufferings and our repeated crises. It is evident that as a primary policy we depend on loans and aid to plug that gap and to be able to continue with our development. Hence our persistence in holding talks after talks with the international financial institutions and with friendly states. It seems like our only route out of these grindingly hard times is to depend upon others with all the knocking on doors that involves, begging to be treated nicely and ending up worn down by embarrassment and obligations.

We have not yet got accustomed to dealing with our affairs by ourselves alone and without loans or aid. That type of thinking is alien to us, and nor can it be noticed in our forward planning, even though things can suddenly descend upon us due to some existential or political crisis that does not wait for a convenient moment. I cannot at the moment call for us to repudiate our loans or foreign aid, but I would demand that we institute some thinking based on new foundations – the loans and aid cannot go on forever. So let us think about our problems as if we had to confront our fate without any reliance on loans or aid. In a situation like that would it not be possible for us to steer people's minds towards a new type of thinking and new modalities, towards changing our attitude and creating ourselves anew?

Have we held back our spending as a country in crisis should? Have we managed to collect all our tax revenues as a country burdened with oppressive loans should? Have we pushed productivity to the limit? Have we got our life/work balance right?

This is a call for new thinking within the framework of our current system. It is also a call for us truly to free ourselves.

17 November 1988

Culture and Life

Culture is the most important means we can rely upon to bring about our, and our lives', full potential. By culture, I mean the customs, traditions, thoughts, beliefs and tastes that a man acquires in his struggle with his environment. Culture moves forward and develops, just as life does, not remaining in one condition unless it has frozen and turned into some sort of burden for man to carry rather than being a driving force and an inspiring spirit. Accordingly, a culture's influence on other cultures is a necessity dictated by the fact that people live in close proximity and mix with each other, not just so that they can get along with each other but also because they draw on what cultures can offer in terms of advantages and expertise which offer greater opportunities for people to choose what is best for their survival, and, in the final analysis, because this leads towards the unity of all mankind.

We often speak about cultural encroachments in the context of preserving our identity, but although these encroachments should not be an end in themselves, identity should also not be the highest ideal in all circumstances. The question that should be asked before all others is what should our lives be like in this modern era? What elements of existence do we need in order to survive, to make progress, to overcome our problems, and to bring about this high ideal for ourselves? The essence of choice is life itself and all the spiritual and material progress it should have in order to bring about as much happiness as possible in this life. If we cannot do that, our root identity has no value, and other people's culture will also have no value.

Our aim is that better life we all hope for, and all paths leading to that are valid as long as they are all authentic, pertinent to this age, a combination of those factors, or can produce something completely new to the world. This is an ongoing struggle, whose starting point by its very nature is our ancient heritage to which we should apply our intellect, our will and a knowledge of our current state of affairs.

24 November 1988

A Wise and Just Decision[1]

The attempt to plug the gap between salaries and prices is a wise and just decision, and officials are to be praised for drafting the new budget. The decree appears to fall under the category of services, but its effectiveness will not be on labour and productivity alone, but on the spirit of justice, self-discipline and ethics. As much as I have raised this point, I can still not overemphasise how relevant it is – not just from the point of view of caring for the poor and treating them correctly, but because this has previously been ignored for the sake of other important and pressing aims and this almost brought an end to the whole five-year plan by disregarding the value of the people who carry it out, leaving them to face the ghouls of inflation and spiralling prices with no help or support.

Leaving people on fixed incomes to suffer has been responsible for the government's loss of prestige, for the ineffectiveness of the law, for the suffering of the masses at the hands of petty bureaucracy and neglect, of apathy, aberration, corruption and a diminishing sense of belonging. This is what has led to our stumbling about in general confusion, and even if it is not the only thing responsible for it, it is one of the main causes. If workers are treated fairly, they can be asked to apply themselves seriously to work, productivity and self-discipline, they can be held to account for poor work ethics, neglect and apathy, management can be made fair and effective again, and it can regain its prestige and play an active role in development and security, in rolling out fair treatment and justice, in bringing about real stability for the individual and for society so that they can resist negative trends no matter how dire their situation, and fight against underdevelopment no matter how deep-rooted it may be – but more importantly so that labour can deserve the trust of the people who, in turn, will respond to that ideal by offering their support, devotion, and hard work. It is indeed a risky decree, but the potential results are great.

25 June 1977

---

1 This essay, missing from a previous volume, included here.